The Trials of
Isabella Mary Kelly

Her legend and the truth

Maurie Garland

Published by Brolga Publishing Pty Ltd
ABN 46 063 962 443
PO Box 12544
A'Beckett St
Melbourne, VIC, 8006
Australia
email: markzocchi@brolgapublishing.com.au

All rights reserved. No part of this publication may be reproduced, stored in a retrieval system or transmitted in any form or by any means electronic, mechanical, photocopying, recording or otherwise without prior permission from the publisher.

Copyright © 2005 Maurice John Garland

National Library of Australia
Cataloguing-in-Publication data
Garland, Maurie.
The trials of Isabella Mary Kelly : her legend and the truth.

ISBN 1 920785 69 8.

1. Kelly, Isabella Mary, 1809–1897.
2. Women pioneers – New South Wales – Manning River Valley.
3. Frontier and pioneer life – New South Wales – Manning River Valley.
4. Women – New South Wales – Social conditions – 19th century.
5. Manning River Valley (N.S.W.) – History.
I. Title.

994.402092

Author Maurie Garland would like to note that correct dates for Isabella Mary Kelly should be: 1802?-1872.

Printed in Singapore
Cover Design by Trish Hart – http://www.trishhart.com
Typeset by Diana Evans

To the memory of "Unk"
John Nance Truscott (1892–1965)
on whose knee I snuggled as a young boy
enthralled as I listened to sea stories
… and so much more.

Acknowledgements

Having retired as teacher in 2001, I was able to work every Tuesday as a volunteer in the Archives of the Manning Valley Historical Society, and follow my historical interests more fully.

I established a rudimentary website for the Society, which operates a Museum in Wingham open to the public seven days a week. It was not long before the website began to receive emails covering questions on all aspects of the Society.

Among the first of these was a request from a lady in West Virginia, USA, who had noticed we had an article in one of our Journals (advertised on the website) on Isabella Mary Kelly. She was related to a man named Charles Skerrett, who had been gaoled as a result of charges brought against him by Isabella Kelly. Could I send her the Journal? Was there any other information I could send her?

The Journal article was sent, and my interest aroused. Little did I realise I had started a journey that would take more than three years to complete.

There are so many who have made a contribution to this book in their own way.

I would like to thank my fellow volunteers at the Manning Valley Historical Society for their enthusiasm and support of this project, particularly our Tuesday archives group: Mal, Rosemary, Jack, Glenda, Pam, Judith, John, Carol, Frank, Lyn and Dallas.

I started digging for more information on Isabella Mary Kelly, first of all in the archives of the Society, and then making many trips to the NSW State Archives, the State Library, the Mitchell Library and Land Records. Thanks go to the staffs at these institutions for their valuable and willing assistance.

I must mention the legacy of Gordon Dennes (1892-1975) to the Manning Valley Historical Society's archives. Although at times hard to read, much valuable information was obtained from his records. He had read through a number of the Dungog Bench Books and Letter Books recording information concerning

Manning residents. Some of these books could not be found in State Archives, but those that were available confirmed the industry and accuracy of Gordon Dennes.

Sue Edwards, friend and teaching colleague of many years, read some early chapters of the book for me, and amongst other things, gave me that very valuable word "context".

Rob Oakeshott, NSW State member for Port Macquarie, and Robert Lawrie, NSW Parliamentary Archivist, facilitated the recovery from State Archives of the original handwritten 1860 Select Committee records, which never reached the floor of Parliament let alone public scrutiny (partly because of their sensational allegations against the Attorney-General), and have remained buried until now. An invaluable resource, it took me quite some time to transcribe them. (On the back of the bundled papers was the note "to be destroyed".)

Dr Bill Birrell, Wilf Connors and Jim Revitt were gracious enough to give me their time to discuss characters and background information on the Manning Valley. All have published their own books on the Manning Valley. Similarly, Harry Boyle and Cynthia Hunter provided me with information about the Dungog district.

Therese Archinal, author of The Andrews on the Manning, has been unstinting in her reading of the manuscript, and giving me feed-back, particularly with her expertise on the Andrews family. She provided many small bits of information, which I was able to follow up with research. For example, Therese found a printed pamphlet issued by Isabella Mary Kelly in 1862, of which I can find no other record or reference – it was inside one of the books belonging to Joseph Andrews' library, housed at the Museum in Wingham.

Di Morrissey, the internationally recognised Australian author, asked to read the manuscript as she had finally decided to write one of her fictional books set in the Manning Valley, the place of her birth. Her support and enthusiasm have been greatly appreciated.

John Ramsland, Emeritus Professor of History at the University of Newcastle, and author of two books on the Manning Valley, gave his valuable time to read through the manuscript, and offered me so much constructive advice for its improvement and publication. There were also the many conversations on background material to the story, as well as providing an introduction to the book.

Eric Richardson, President of the Manning Valley Historical Society and a walking encyclopaedia of Manning Valley history, has been both a friend and mentor throughout the researching and writing of this book. He has given so generously of his time, knowledge and sage advice. I have deeply appreciated the phone calls with sudden thoughts about the book; his reading the manuscript; his sustained encouragement; the contacts of people who might offer information or assistance; and his general camaraderie with his own particular brand of humour.

If, despite the assistance of all these wonderful people, the reader should find any errors, then (mea culpa) the fault is all mine.

Maurie Garland
Manning River, 2005.

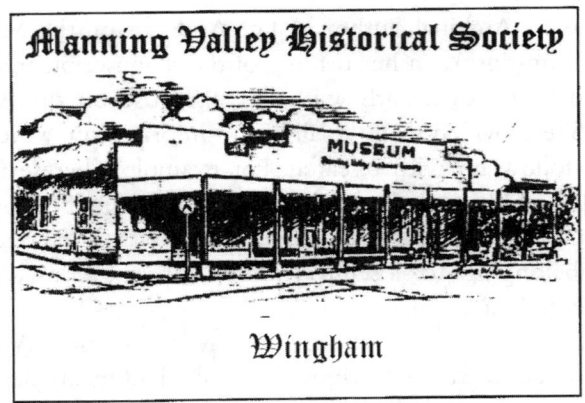

Introduction
A Woman Alone, A Woman Excluded
By John Ramsland

From her obscure birth in Dublin to her equally obscure death in Sydney, Isabella Mary Kelly, the pioneer settler of Mt George on the Upper Manning, provided all the ingredients of a myth — one that has grown and been made more colourful with each passing generation. She has been as much the victim of the embellishment of half-truths and falsehoods and the uncritical fabrication of gossip, as she was the real victim in many of her experiences on the Manning River of New South Wales, of local sectarian vindictiveness, rivalry and jealous in early colonial times. The myth of Isabella Mary Kelly has survived even into the twenty-first century, but not much of the historical truth.

In this ably researched study based on an insightful exploration and re-examination of forgotten, neglected or overlooked official colonial documents, Maurie Garland has succeeded in piecing together her life and times in real historical terms. In doing so he has exposed, for what they are, the distortions and misconceptions of popular myth-making. The real person of Isabella Mary Kelly has been located from beneath her public persona so long encrusted in the mythology created in press articles, frequently under the title of "Peeps into the Past". The "peeps" were somewhat misleading to say the least. The distorting curtain has at last been drawn back and the character of Kelly has been revealed in this well-constructed biographical narrative.

But what were these popular myths about the redoubtable, the early colonial Manning settler and property owner, Isabella Mary Kelly?

At certain times and by certain writers of popular history she has been totally confused with her namesake Kate Kelly, the sister of the iconic bushranger Ned Kelly. Kate married and produced three children but suffered an abrupt and tragic death at the early age of thirty-six. A colourful life, but not that of Isabella Mary Kelly, who in the same year of Kate's birth, was about sixty years of age, a confirmed spinster and definitely had had no children. Kate Kelly, at no time, lived on the Manning, but such mythological confusion is persistent even to the present day.

Akin to this totally false association with the notorious Ned Kelly, it was frequently claimed that Isabella was a member of the so-labelled "Black Kelly Clan" of Ireland who, it was stated were noted for their 'fierce unrestrained tempers and pig-headed pride'. Such an idea became the basis of the way that Isabella was portrayed in the press. She was thought to have been a brutally sadistic flogger of assigned convicts and a cold-hearted murderess of local tribal Aborigines.

Undoubtedly Isabella Mary Kelly was an unusual woman for her time as a property owner and a cattle baroness, but she was also an intelligent and capable one. Maurie Garland's incisive narrative, based on significant sources that have not previously been addressed by historians will unfold her real story for the first time for the discerning reader. He gives us a fresh chance to see how she lived, thought and acted in the context of a difficult pioneering environment. The layers have been skilfully scraped away to reveal a fresh and lively portrait of both her life and her times. The frontier-settler world and its rugged landscape of the Upper Manning has been accurately evoked, together with the rigid divisions on the sectarian and gender lines that clearly existed very strongly. Maurie Garland has recognised that to reach for the truth in colonial history, the rose-coloured glasses have to be thrown off for an unflinching gaze at Australian's pioneering past through the prism of the life of a solitary but passionate, able and determined woman.

And what are the lessons that we can learn about the life experiences of such a woman?

We have to recognise that relationships on the Upper Manning and other places in the valley in early colonial period were frequently split by religious prejudice – there was much anti-Catholic and anti-Irish feeling amongst Protestant settlers that manifested itself at times in a great deal of vindictiveness and

Introduction

ill-feeling toward others of the Catholic faith. As well, the idea of a woman being a sole property owner was not popular – only men, it was claimed, should play that role, only men could buy or sell cattle. The pioneering worldview was intensely patriarchal and male dominated. Isabella Kelly presented a threat and challenge to this axis of power by her very presence. Her status in the Manning Valley disrupted the established order of things.

Colonial society in early New South Wales was noted for its litigious nature. People went to law courts over the slightest of issues. Isabella Kelly was tried on a trumped-up charge and as a result spent the darkest time of her life in a damp sandstone cell in the women's block of "C" wing at Darlinghurst Gaol.

Henry Lawson, the celebrated writer, later described Darlinghurst Gaol, where he had been a frequent short-term inmate, as

Staircase and doors of iron – no sign of plank or brick –
ceiling and floors of sandstone, and cell walls two feet thick;
Cell like a large stone coffin, or like a small tomb, and white,
And it strikes a chill to the backbone on the warmest summer night.

(Henry Lawson, 'The Song of a Prison', October 1909).

In a mid-nineteenth century official inquiry, scathing comments were made about conditions in the women's wing at Darlinghurst:

> The whole of the cells in the upper portion of the women's wards [where Isabella Kelly had been placed] were swarming with bugs; about the ceilings, walls, the hinges of the doors, they were in masses of an inch or more in diameter.

The living conditions inside the cells were thus deplorable and soul destroying, especially to a woman of Isabella Kelly's accomplishments. Is it any wonder that her health was seriously and permanently impaired by the time she left the cell that was 'like a large stone coffin' and was released into Forbes Street, Darlinghurst through the prison's heavy gates?

Maurie Garland's story of her life makes compelling reading from its very beginning to its sad end.

John Ramsland
Emeritus Professor of History
The University of Newcastle, NSW

Contents

Prologue: The Manning Valley 1

Part 1. A Woman Alone
1. The Settler was a Woman 11
2. The Marriage Proposal 21
3. A Woman in Charge of Convicts 33
4. Before the Bench 49
5. Trouble with Neighbours 57
6. Bushranger Stories .71
7. Fire 81

Part 2. Convictions
8. Stolen Cattle 89
9. Forged Documents 101
10. Trial 114
11. Fallout 122
12. A Window of Doubt 131
13. A Hidden History 140
14. The Laird of Taree 152
15. Waterview 162
16. The Chief Justice 168
17. Committed 176
18. Perjury 184

Part 3. The Lie of the Land
19. Aftermath 199
20. The Disputed Lease 213
21. The Smear 219
22. A Worried Man 240
23. Slander 247
24. What is a Forgery? 258
25. Back in the Valley 267
26. The Rich Insolvent 272
27. Confession 286

28.	The Trust of the Trustees	293
29.	Assault and Battery	298
30.	Judgement	306

Part 4. Where the Truth Lies

31.	Petitions	319
32.	The Select Committee	324
33.	Question 843	347
34.	A Final Decision	375
35.	Slipping Away	391

Appendix

1.	Completing the lives of some characters	401
2.	From Smith's Weekly of August 9, 1924 – "The Discomfiture of a Termagant"	406

Notes and Bibliography 413

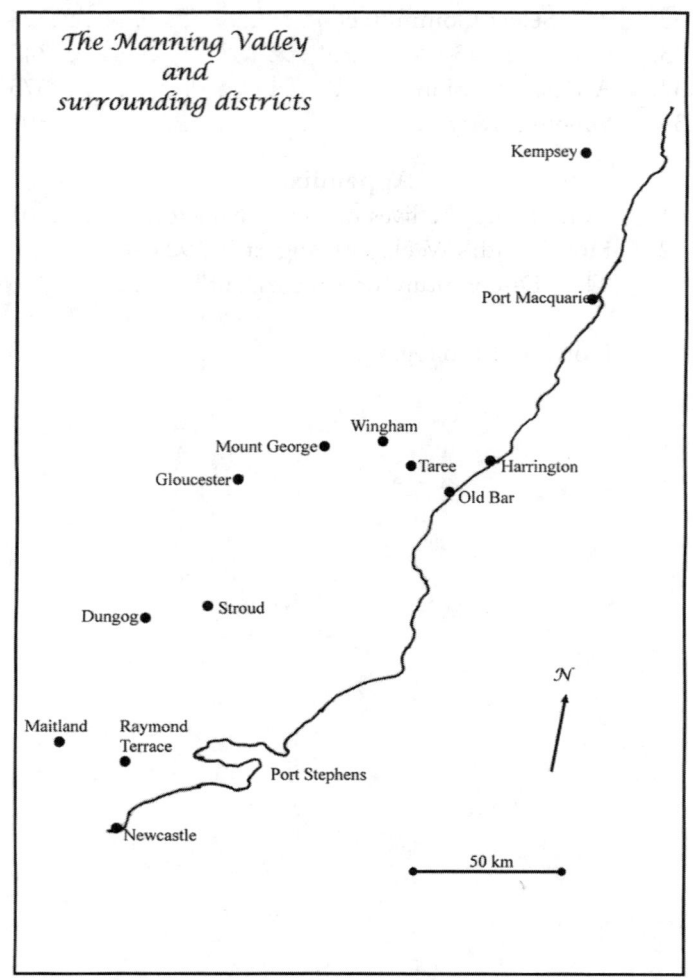

Prologue
The Manning Valley

Today, driving north on the dual carriageway of the Pacific Highway, about 160 kilometres along the coast of New South Wales from Newcastle, the highway comes to the crest of a mountain near a driver rest-stop just before the Taree turn-off, from where travellers get their first glimpse of the beautiful Manning Valley. Taree nestles in the middle with breath-taking mountains rising sharply behind. Further up the valley is the town of Wingham, with its many historic buildings, some dating back to the nineteenth century.

Coastal shipping travelled as far upstream as Wingham, but beyond that point the Manning River is impassable. Taree and Wingham were both established in the 1850s, but grew very slowly over their first few decades, before becoming the dominant towns and river ports of the Manning Valley. At the time of this story, the current villages of Tinonee and Cundletown, both situated on the banks of the Manning River, were the main centres of population.

Further upstream again from Wingham, the small rural area of Mount George still shows its rustic charms. On the southern side of the river, towering mountains dominate the landscape. The highest, called Mt. Gangat, is sometimes with clouds clinging round its peak, sometimes brooding. Mount George, on the northern bank of the Manning, was once the property of Isabella Mary Kelly, bought by her in 1838. Originally, Mount George had been on the main land route from Maitland to Port Macquarie via Gloucester, but has long since been by-passed. In the nineteenth century, this area was referred to as the Manning Flats.

Many articles have been written about this pioneering

woman at Mount George. An historical article called "The Men Who Dared Miss Kelly" was written in 1927 for the well-known Sydney magazine *Smith's Weekly*. The subheading of "Pioneer in Skirts" became a common sobriquet for Kelly, although the most commonly used word in connection with her was "notorious".[1]

This particular story starts by stating that Miss Kelly was someone to be feared, as she "had influential friends in high places", and hence Magistrate Cook was powerless to stop her from doing as she pleased. Two men named Coe and Snape buy the adjoining property to Kelly, on her southern boundary (the author not realising that the river was the southern boundary) and build a hut there, assisted by two aborigines and a convict. Miss Kelly, mounted on a horse with a pistol in her hand, orders them off, as she believes they are there to rob her of her cattle, with the result that over the coming months a war breaks out between the two parties.

One night Kelly hamstrings two of their horses, poisons the dogs and lures the aborigines into the bush, never to be seen again (suggesting their murder without explicitly stating it). Coe and Snape admit defeat and decide to leave, stealing Kelly's cattle as they depart. Six days later Kelly, with two helpers, catches up to the party, re-captures the cattle and returns to Mount George. The bodies of Coe and Snape are found the next day and taken to Dungog. Magistrate Cook finds out they are escaped convicts, and knowing Miss Kelly has influential friends, decides not to proceed against her in the matter.

Such was the fame of Isabella Mary Kelly.

The Pacific Highway no longer passes through the main street of Taree's central business district, much to the relief of travellers and residents alike. Driving into Taree, following the old Pacific Highway, the Manning River is crossed via the Martin Bridge. Following this former highway north through Victoria Street (until recent times the main street of Taree), through Chatham and toward Cundletown, the Dawson River is crossed, just a short distance from its confluence with the Manning River.

Following the Dawson River upstream, the property of Brimbin is reached. Originally owned by Major Archibald Innes, it was sold to James Atkinson, who then leased it to Miss Isabella Mary Kelly for seven years in the 1850s as her second property

Prologue

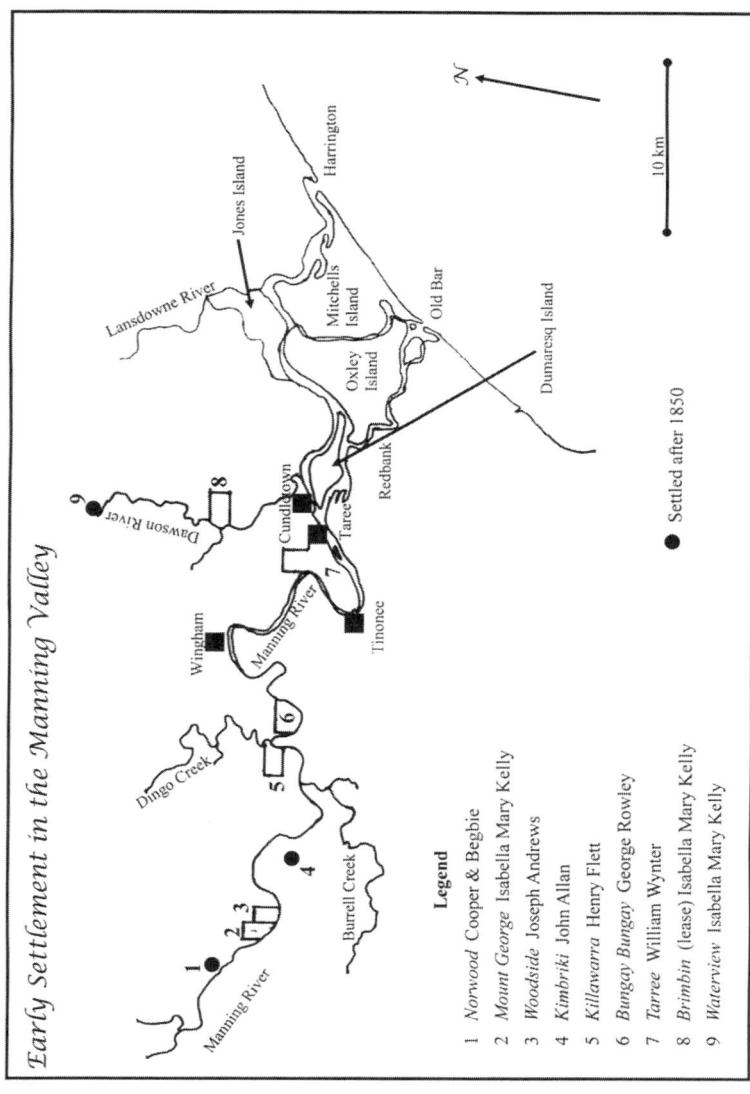

in the Manning Valley. There is still a clearing in the thick bush where the original Brimbin homestead stood. Here many more allegations of unsavoury events were connected to Isabella Mary Kelly.

Below are the opening paragraphs from the story on Isabella Mary Kelly set at Brimbin in the book *Australia's Wicked Women* by James Holledge, published in 1963:[2]

> The sizzling summer sun beat down mercilessly on the courtyard of a large rambling station homestead at Brimbin in the Manning River District of New South Wales. It was a January morning in the 1830s in the peaceful Australian bush – but the scene might well have been conjured from the depths of hell.
>
> A man was fixed to a whipping post. His two arms extended round it, and his wrists were bound tightly with cords. Two armed servants stood guard over other convicts forced to watch the grim scene as one of their comrades was flogged for a trifling misdemeanour.
>
> Such scenes were common in Australia's convict days, but this one was probably unique because of the identity of the station owner who was methodically cutting the tortured victim's back to ribbons.
>
> Wielding the whip like a maniac was a short, stocky, square-jawed woman. Flaming red hair cascaded to her shoulders and she laughed cruelly when the previously silent man began to moan as each stroke thudded home.
>
> She was young, still in her twenties, and wore breeches and riding boots like a man. A white blouse, stained and tattered, was her only concession to femininity and strong, muscled arms bulged in its sleeves as she swung the whip with vicious strokes.
>
> Suddenly the woman stopped for a moment and tore off the impeding garment. Bare to the waist, sweat glistening on plump curves, she then continued the flogging until she could hardly raise her arms from exhaustion.
>
> Her name was Isabella Kelly, and she remains one of the most sinister mystery women in Australian history. No one knows for certain who she was or whence she came – but she set herself up as the despotic queen of the whole Manning River district.
>
> She grabbed land and lorded it over convicts and aborigines who came under her control. A mad sadist, she hated

Prologue

men and gloried in her power over them.

Today, the crossing of the Dawson River at Brimbin is still in a bushland setting, and bears the name "Kate Kelly's Crossing" rather than "Isabella Mary Kelly Crossing", with Kate Kelly being the sister of bushranger Ned Kelly.

In the 1920s, Isabella's reputation was such that a Taree newspaper noted that mothers in the district had used the name of Isabella Kelly to frighten their children – "the bogie man will get you" became "Isabella Kelly will get you"[3]. With the rise to fame of Ned Kelly in the late nineteenth century (and such as Isabella's reputation became), Isabella Kelly became confused with Kate Kelly, even though Kate was born fifty or more years after Isabella.

In the 1980s, Jim Revitt (ABC Broadcaster and Manning Valley historian), was one of a number to complain publicly of the misnaming of the crossing, but to no avail.[4]

A little further upstream from Brimbin was the 42-acre property called "Waterview", which was Crown land until Kelly bought it in 1858 at the expiry of her Brimbin lease. Here Isabella Kelly built a small cottage and stockyards. It too became the scene of great rumour and innuendo when a girl, employed as a servant by Isabella Kelly, mysteriously disappeared. Some supposed that Isabella Kelly had murdered the girl in a fit of rage.

The Manning River and its many tributaries begin their journey to the sea on the eastern side of the Great Dividing Range, many kilometres from the coast. It is only at Taree that the river becomes a delta – the only true delta in all Australia's river systems. This delta contains a number of islands, the main ones being Dumaresq, Oxley, Mitchell and Jones.

In a parliamentary report on the Manning River in 1889, Sir John Coode described the main entrance of the Manning River at Harrington as "one of the most, if not the most, dangerous bars on the coast of the Colony, as shown by the number of wrecks and loss of life upon it."[5] Strong winds and shifting sand banks often caused ships to spend days waiting for the right conditions to cross the bar.

The lesser entrance to the Manning River is to the south, at Old Bar, but is only navigable by small boats. Despite the occasional great flood, and lesser flooding in between, the flow of the river is not sufficient to keep both outlets open at all times, and the Old Bar entrance has closed up a number of times in the last 170 years.[6]

John Oxley was the first European explorer to pass through the Manning Valley in 1818, followed by Henry Dangar in 1825 and 1826, Robert Dawson also in 1826 and Thomas Florance in 1827. The Australian Agricultural Company (commonly known as the A. A. Company) gained a grant of a million acres of land, extending from Port Stephens to the south bank of the Manning River. Robert Dawson, the A. A. Company's manager of estates, named the river "Manning's River" after the Deputy-Governor of the A. A. Company, but it was not long before it became the "Manning River."

When settlement began, it was on the northern bank of the Manning. John Guilding, a West Indian, received a grant of 2560 acres at "Mooto", in 1827, and a year later had 40 acres under cultivation. Despite 400 grazing cattle and the cutting of cedar, Guilding eventually ran into financial difficulty and left "Mooto" and the colony in October 1829.

In 1828 Arthur Onslow took up 1920 acres on nearby Jones Island, but the next year the grant was withdrawn when he failed to sign a bond, and Onslow returned to India. Although Hart Davis gained a grant of 15000 acres in 1829, the property remained unoccupied.[7]

The first permanent settler in the Manning Valley was William Wynter, who arrived in the Manning Valley in September 1829, about ten years before Isabella Mary Kelly. Aged about 43, Wynter was accompanied by his wife, Elizabeth, and three children, Thomas, Mary and William. The eldest son Delamore, aged about 12, had been left in England to complete his education, but joined the rest of the family some eight years later.[8]

The family arrived in Sydney on May 9, 1829, after a six months voyage via Cape Horn. Wynter applied for a grant of land in recognition of his naval service and, as he had assets of just over £2000 which could be used to develop the site, Governor Darling wrote, "Let him select four square miles (2560 acres)"[9] on a Land Board report dated July 2, 1829. How Wynter came to choose the Manning River and the particular site of his grant is not clear, but it was an excellent choice involving first quality

Prologue

alluvial land.

In a letter to Thomas Mitchell, the Surveyor General, addressed from the "North Bank of the Manning" and dated "29th October, 1829", Wynter wrote, "I understand that the Selection I have made is known to the natives in the neighbourhood by the name of Taree or Tarlie."[10] He called his property "Tarree" – the aboriginal word "tarrebit" was the fruit of the fig tree.

Writing in 1866, John Blunt said William Wynter's "operations were on rather a large scale. He planted a vineyard; prepared for the manufacture of wine; cultivated a portion of the soil; had his flocks of sheep and herds of cattle."[11]

The adjoining forests were rich in cedar and Wynter established some cedar-cutting camps. The Wynters were isolated at first because they were the only permanent settlers in the Manning Valley. But there was a growing number of other people moving about in the district, especially as cedar was cut out of other areas. The isolation was emphasised by the absence of boats visiting the Manning, so that it was difficult to receive mail and supplies as well as get produce or timber out of the Valley.

Wynter decided to build his own boat in order to fight this isolation. William Bird, a shipwright and one of Wynter's assigned servants, completed the construction of the boat at Wynter's shipyard on the Manning River. The boat, a two-masted brigantine-rigged schooner, 16 metres long and weighing 48 tons, was named *Tarree*.[12] This began the long tradition of ship-building on the Manning River, which carries through to the present day.

The "assigned servants" were convicts, who were assigned to settlers by the Government to work as labourers. They had to be provided with food, clothing and accommodation, but otherwise cost nothing. If they failed to follow instructions they could be taken before a magistrate and punished.

At Mount George eight convicts were assigned to Miss Kelly. In 1841 two of these men absconded from Miss Kelly's service, with the result that each man received fifty lashes as punishment in the penal settlement of Port Macquarie, to the north of the Manning Valley. Later, settlers wishing to have their convicts punished were permitted to take them south, to the more convenient Dungog Bench.

The Trials of Isabella Mary Kelly

Aborigines had lived in harmony with their environment in the Manning Valley for centuries. With the coming of Europeans, the aboriginal eco-system began to be destroyed. The settlers would clear their land, put up fences and keep the aborigines out. Animals, hunted by the aborigines for their meat as food and for their skins as warmth in winter, were pests to the settlers, and consequently killed. Within twenty five years of the arrival of the first settlers, the Government was requested to send blankets to be given to the aborigines.

William Wynter seems to have had harmonious relations with the native inhabitants, treating them with respect. The youngest Wynter boy, William Junior, had no other children to associate with and often went hunting with the aborigines, learning to speak their language fluently.[13]

Wynter had been the only permanent settler in the Manning Valley for most of the 1830s. Although some land had been bought by speculators, it was only towards the end of this decade that four other genuine settlers came to the Manning Valley – Thomas Steele, Henry Flett, George Rowley and … Isabella Mary Kelly.

Part 1
A Woman Alone

―◼◆◼―

"Miss Kelly was a most extraordinary woman."

— John Allan

Isabella Mary Kelly circa 1863

1. The Settler was a Woman

Miss Isabella Mary Kelly sailed into Sydney Harbour on November 17, 1834, on board the barque *James* carrying 109 passengers, having left London on June 29, and sailing via the Cape of Good Hope. Isabella Kelly and the Rev John Dunmore Lang (famous in the colony of New South Wales as an outspoken and controversial Presbyterian minister) were two of the fourteen first-class cabin passengers.

Much of Isabella Kelly's life before her arrival in New South Wales remains a mystery. The only known fact about her birth is she was born in Dublin, probably between 1802 and 1806. When she was eight years old she became an orphan. Her brother took her to London and there, Sir William Crowder, a Justice of the High Court, became her guardian.[1] His family relationship to Isabella, or why he became her guardian, is not clear. Sir William and his wife, Ann, had six children born in the period 1789 to 1799 – Thomas, Ann, William, Richard (later Sir Richard), Frederick and George. The Crowders were Protestant but the Kellys were Catholic.

Isabella Mary Kelly said she came to the colony of New South Wales for health reasons. She brought with her letters of introduction to men like Mr Macarthur, Arthur a'Beckett and his brother Sir William a'Beckett, indicating her elite connections within the colony.

Before leaving for New South Wales, Kelly had been staying in Paris, where she met a lady, who, when told Kelly was going to New South Wales, replied that her daughter was married to the Attorney General there. His name was John Plunkett, and co-incidentally he would later prosecute a number of court cases on her behalf. Isabella agreed to take a parcel and a letter out to the daughter, which was duly delivered on her arrival.

The Trials of Isabella Mary Kelly

Isabella Kelly brought goods to the value of £2000 to Sydney, which she then proceeded to sell. Among these were cases of French plate glass, French and English goods, plated mirrors, a piano (sold for £210) and 900 sovereigns. She was obviously a woman of capital and substance, but it is not apparent from where this personal wealth came.[2]

Isabella Mary Kelly stayed in the colony for nine months. She had not initially intended to stay in the colony permanently, but at some point during this time, Isabella Kelly essentially made a commitment to a life in the colony.

Kelly was lending her money out on mortgages, and sometimes, when liquidity problems arose, she borrowed money. On one such occasion, she borrowed from Arthur a'Beckett, who then refused to charge her any interest. She purchased land, including a number of blocks for speculation at Maitland.[3]

But first she would have to return home and put her affairs in order – and home was always London. Although Irish, she said, she did not know any families in Ireland.[4] Kelly sailed out of Port Jackson on August 21, 1835, on board the *Resource*, and returned to Sydney on January 30, 1837, on the *Columbia*, bringing with her the sum of £1900.

This modern aerial photo of the area originally known as the Manning Flats shows the river (lower loop) with the railway line (built in 1913) above it.
1. This is Mt George on the northern boundary of Isabella Kelly's property.
2. This is Woodside House (Joseph Andrews).

The Settler was a Woman

During the next nineteen months, her movements are difficult to trace, but she did apply for land in the Bathurst district without success.

On August 8, 1838, Kelly attended a Crown Land Sale held at The Treasury in Sydney, purchasing 895 acres of land "near Mt. Kangat" (which evolved into Gangat) on the northern bank of the Manning River.[5] The property, the Survey Plan of which was lodged at Port Macquarie in December 1836, cost her £223.[6]

Kelly called her property "Mount George." There has been speculation over the source of the name "George", with some claiming it was named after George IV, although he had been dead for nearly ten years. Others claimed it was named after the newly appointed Governor of New South Wales, Sir George Gipps, in which case Kelly, being respectful of the Governor, would more likely have called it Mount Gipps.

The most likely nominee for the honour is George Crowder, the youngest of the Crowder family, who may well have treated Isabella Kelly as a younger sister.

Isabella Mary Kelly is unique in the history of New South Wales – she was the only single female who was a settler in her own right.

Isabella Mary Kelly was a *single* woman in every sense of the word. She was entirely without any bond of marriage – either currently or in the past – nor was there a male companion in her life.

This single woman *chose* life as a settler in a remote district of the colony.

John Allan, whose property at Kimbriki[7] was not far from Mount George, wrote his memoirs and included reference to Isabella Mary Kelly with whom his family socialised. He cogently pointed out that "Miss Kelly was a most extraordinary woman", and by way of explanation, "she had a number of Government men [convicts] under her – and was her own overseer."[8]

This was the amazing part for a woman of her era. While other women may have owned stations, and remained in Sydney, content to relay orders to a male superintendent, Isabella Kelly ran the station herself. She was an excellent horsewoman and not afraid to get her hands dirty.

The Allan family was one of a few families to remain on good terms with Isabella Kelly. As a female settler, though,

The Trials of Isabella Mary Kelly

Isabella generally did not receive much sympathy from other settlers – rather the reverse. Kelly was in contrast to widowed women who continued on as settlers after the death of their husbands, always receiving the greatest of sympathy from the surrounding community.

As soon as Isabella Mary Kelly bought her land in August 1838 (and before she took up residence there), she applied to Police Magistrate Gray, at Port Macquarie, for assigned servants (convict labour). Because a female was asking for convicts to be assigned to her, Magistrate Gray hesitated and wrote to the Governor, in a letter dated November 1, 1838, asking for guidance, stating that, "She is of age and we understand is possessed of considerable property."[9]

In reply, in the margin of the above letter, Governor Gipps asked Gray for more details about Miss Kelly, "Has she friends in the colony? When did she arrive? Is she a bona fide settler on her own account – or has the land been assigned to her, only for the purpose of getting servants? Was it purchased of Government in her name, and if so when?"

Gray did not appear to pursue the answers to these questions and Kelly complained directly to the Governor that her request appeared to be ignored. The Governor replied to Gray, on the back of a letter, "It rests with Miss Kelly to show that she is entitled to be considered a new settler."[10] This clearly proved to be the case and Kelly eventually received her assigned servants.

In 1839, she was able to take up residence on the Mount George property. At that time it was on the main route north from Maitland or Port Stephens to Gloucester and through to Port Macquarie. She said she initially bought 200 head of cattle – 100 cows and 100 calves – at an auction in Maitland, and then hired four men to drive them up to Mount George. The cows were £6 each. Later on she bought more cattle. With horses in short supply at the time, Kelly paid £100 each for some horses, and £110 for a mare.[11] Afterwards she also acquired sheep.

Theodor Müller, a Swiss national, spent six months visiting the Manning Valley in 1859, three of which were spent working for Isabella Kelly as a shepherd. Although it was twenty years after Isabella Kelly settled in the valley, and long after the practice of assigning convicts to settlers by the Government had ceased, his journal gave some useful insights of Miss Kelly and the way of life for settlers in the Valley.

Müller arrived in Sydney in 1857, aged about thirty, and began a nineteen-year odyssey, travelling from Sydney to Brisbane indirectly – always on foot – and working in the various districts along the way. He returned to his hometown of Aarau, and wrote a book in German called *Neunzehn Jahre am Australien* (Nineteen Years in Australia), which was published in Switzerland in 1877.[12]

In March 1859, after spending eighteen months in the Maitland district, Müller walked north through Gloucester, and on to an area near Mount Gangat:[13]

> I heard dogs barking in the distance, a sign that a settlement was close by. Happily I stepped up my speed, and walking from the thinning bush into a wild mountain valley I saw two large log houses in front of which a well-dressed man and an elderly lady were engaged in an animated conversation. They were standing by a small fire with their backs turned on me.
>
> My approaching alarmed two large dogs, which were lying there, and their loud barking immediately betrayed me to the two people, who very friendly beckoned me to come closer and ordered the dogs to be quiet. I was offered a seat on a long log lying beside the fire, and after the usual questions of where I came from and where I was going to, the conversation turned to the possibilities of my obtaining work in the country, upon which the lady suddenly asked me if I would be prepared to watch a flock of sheep.
>
> I hesitated a moment to accept the offer, as I had never before tended sheep, but as this was as good a way as any to come to something again, I consented to take up the shepherd's staff, so poetically referred to in the books. A contract, in duplicate, was drawn up immediately, by which I undertook to tend a flock of approximately 2000 sheep at an annual wage of 28 pounds Sterling, plus board and free accommodation. The gentleman, who was a friend of this lady, whose name was Miss Kelly, signed the contract as a witness. He left that same day, as he was planning to make a trip to New Zealand [Overseer Corcoran, who was leaving Kelly's employ.]
>
> Miss Kelly, who had to go to Sydney on business the following day, left me with two boys; the older one, who was approximately 14 years of age, had to look after the house and do the cooking while I was absent. The other boy, two years

younger, had to help me tend the flock, as I did not yet know my way in this wild country …

Miss Kelly was at least sixty years old, small but stocky, and solidly built. She was an excellent horsewoman and, as I heard later from other people, had in the earlier days on her own tamed wild horses, which she caught in the bush and trained them until they were excellent saddle horses. Even now, at her age, she still sat on a horse straight and firmly and rode at great speed on the narrow zigzag mountain roads.

Very often, when searching for horses and cattle, she spent the night under a tree all by herself. She would have some food with her, a small bottle of gin and, to safeguard herself against attacks by men, she always carried a loaded pistol hidden under her dress.

The most famous of her horses was called Calendar. The Australian Stud Book records Calendar as foaled in Great Britain in 1834, and the sire of Camden, who won the AJC Homebush St Leger Stakes in 1855.[14]

Theodor Müller, well educated and from a family of some means, seemed to enjoy the menial jobs he took, particularly gardening. He described his working conditions:

I started my job on a Monday and that same day my "boss" left for Sydney, where she was involved in a Court case,[15] which might keep her there for at least two months. We, the three people who stayed behind, would for many weeks be the kings of the castle. Of the two houses mentioned before, we, the station hands, used one as our residence. The other one was Miss Kelly's private residence, and remained locked until her return. …

The furniture in the [workers'] house consists of rough wobbling tables and chairs, which often are already half wrecked when a new occupant moves into the cabin. The bed consists of a straw mattress resting on a piece of bark attached to four poles, which are hammered into the ground. Everybody provides his own blanket. The cooking utensils, which are provided by the employer, consist of an iron cooking pot in which the meat is cooked, one or two water kettles, and sometimes a frying pan, and a tin to bake the bread. Each week the workers receive ten pounds of salted meat, ten pounds of flour, two pounds of sugar, and one quarter-pound of tea, which does not exactly enable anybody to live in abundance …

Even with your pockets filled with money you cannot buy a thing here, because the next township, at least in those days, would be more than thirty English miles[16] away and the communications were still very poor. The owners of the sheep stations, therefore, usually kept a supply of clothing and other articles, which their employees could buy on credit. At Miss Kelly's I used these facilities myself.

The younger boy was Andrew Mort, an orphan. Isabella Kelly had visited the Benevolent Asylum (more colloquially known as a "Poor House") in Sydney[17] and brought him to the Manning two years previously. Andrew was employed on a seven-year indenture to Miss Kelly, which would release him when he was sixteen. In previous years, Richard Smith and Frank McDonough were two other such orphans, who had been indentured to Miss Kelly.

Not only did Andrew Mort work as a shepherd, but also as a personal servant, often accompanying Miss Kelly as she moved around the district. She provided his food and clothing, in exchange for his work.[18] Andrew could not read or write, and Kelly did not regard it as her responsibility to educate him.

There was another function, which Andrew (as well as Frank and Richard) served, probably without realising it: that of chaperone. Socially, it was awkward and sometimes even inappropriate for Isabella Kelly to be alone with men. At her house there were usually female servants, but away from the house, a boy like Andrew could be a third party insulating her from what would be considered compromising situations for a female in nineteenth century society. Further, if anything untoward were to occur, the boy would be a witness.

After only three months of working for Miss Kelly, Theodor Müller decided to resign his job as shepherd:

> Gradually the weather improved somewhat, and early in June Miss Kelly returned unexpectedly. She brought another shepherd,[19] as in the meantime our flock had increased by some hundreds of lambs, which made it necessary to split the flock. Immediately at our first encounter I was unfavourably impressed by the rough and arrogant attitude of the newcomer. He was married, and brought his wife and an approximately twelve years old girl with him. In a short time I dis-

covered that he was also a bigot, and that he had little inclination to befriend me.

I became tired of being a shepherd, and one day I asked Miss Kelly, who was still staying on the property, to release me from my duties. However, she insisted on my sticking to my contract, as otherwise I would not be entitled to any wages. As I had received some clothes from her on credit, I waived the money owing to me and made myself free.

She was reluctant to let me go, as she realised that, on the whole, I was much more modest and reliable than the other shepherd, who was often very rude to her and demanded a lot. As a parting gift she presented me with a beautiful blanket and a draft for twenty shillings on a farmer near the Barrington River, who owed her money.

In the afternoon of the 21st June, the shortest day in Australia, I left Miss Kelly's sheep station, where I had learned so many new things and set out for the Barrington River.

Much of the legend of Isabella Kelly has made her out be mean-spirited and spiteful to all men, yet here in these last paragraphs was an example of a much warmer heart.

With Isabella Kelly's property in the foreground, this crossing of the Manning River was on the main route north in 1840.

The Settler was a Woman

Isabella Mary Kelly had very ambitious plans for Mount George. At the eastern end of the Mount George estate, on rather hilly ground, a new township was surveyed, which she called Georgetown. On March 3, 1842, an auction was held for blocks of land in Georgetown. An advertisement, in the *Australian* newspaper, read:[20]

> A most splendid portion of that Lady's [Miss Kelly] Estate, situated at the crossing place of the Route from Maitland, Port Stephens, New England, to Port Macquarie, having a portion cleared on the River, and now subdivided into allotments of half-acre each, more or less, comprising 1000 acres of fine land on the banks of the Manning and Creeks thereof, all described, staked out, and charted as Georgetown.
>
> Very little has been made known yet as to the importance of the Manning River, its splendid waters, alluvial flats, agricultural qualities, and pastoral command of country, whether as to sheep, cattle, or stock of any kind …
>
> The Timber is stated as the finest growth and description as cedar, flooded and other gums, oaks, barks, corkwood, fig, hickory black, variegated satin, and other woods … The Water is abundant and pure … The Situation is, of all others, the most important resting place for the traveller on his route to or from Port Macquarie … The soil here will produce any grain or vegetable …

Streets had been laid out named Isabella, Gipps and Church. Also mentioned in the advertisement was the George Inn, actually Kelly's house, which would have upstairs rooms added once a licence was granted.

The town land auction was a dismal failure – not one block sold.

Probably the main reason for the failure was its isolation. Kelly believed in Georgetowns's future on the basis that Mount George would continue to be on the main route north. The A. A. Company owned a huge tract of land on the southern bank of the Manning River, which they would not allow travellers to pass through. There was a shallow crossing of the Manning River at Kelly's Mount George property, which was popularly used by people travelling up the western boundaries of the A. A. Company's land. Even travellers between the two coastal towns of

Port Macquarie and Port Stephens would pass through Mount George at this time.

As the A. A. Company reduced its land holding there, and consequently its control, it was not too long before other routes to Port Macquarie were found, further down stream.

Ironically, a steamship, *Sovereign*, had steamed into the Manning River in March 1842, the first to do so. Shipping, carrying produce and passengers to and from the Manning, would prove to be the major force of development in the Manning Valley during the nineteenth century. As shipping could travel no further up river than Wingham, the upper valley communities were left behind in growth and development.

2. The Marriage Proposal

Of course, a single woman operating in such a male-dominated environment became the subject of much rumour and gossip.

The main story rumoured in the district about Isabella Mary Kelly was the reason behind her arrival in the colony. In the most popular version, Isabella Kelly had been born in Dublin, and her father, being a wealthy doctor there with a good practice, was able to send her to France to finish her education.

The story went on to claim that Miss Kelly met and fell in love with a British Army officer, and they decided to get married. All the wedding arrangements were made and on the day of the wedding in London, she turned up on time at the church only to find the groom was late. She waited and waited, but he never arrived. Finally she went home, unmarried and humiliated.

According to this account, when Isabella checked up on her reluctant groom, she found that he had gone to Sydney on Army service, having already sailed. She decided to follow him to Sydney, but after her arrival in Sydney, she found that he had swapped duty with another officer and left for India. This was the end of the matter for her.

One source[1] even gave the man a name – Major Wilford. Supposedly, this experience made her determined never to marry, and began a hatred of all men.

Tellingly, neighbour John Allan made no mention of this story in writing his recollections of her.

About eighteen months after her arrival at Mount George, a man did propose marriage to Isabella Mary Kelly. His name was Henry Flett.

Henry Flett was born on April 1, 1810 in Pulteney, a suburb of Wick, in the county of Caithness, Scotland. Pulteney is not far

⊰ The Trials of Isabella Mary Kelly ⊱

⊰ Henry Flett ⊱

The Marriage Proposal

from John O'Groats at the northern tip of the Scottish mainland. In general, it was an impoverished part of Scotland.

He was named Harry Flett at birth, the same as his father, but was always called Henry and always wrote his name as Henry Flett.[2] He was the eldest of eleven children. His brother George, a year younger, later joined him in the Manning Valley.

Henry Flett arrived in Sydney on October 21, 1833 on the *Mary Catherine*,[3] having sailed from Liverpool on June 15. His occupation was listed as a cooper (barrel maker). He went to Bathurst, with a letter of introduction, and worked there for several years, before moving to the Williams River. There Flett became Superintendent of the Underbank estate owned by John Lord, which was situated about sixteen miles out of Dungog.

In December 1837, the Police Magistrate at Dungog, Thomas Cook, received a deputation from five aborigines, headed by a man called Derby, who appeared to be the tribal leader, and who Cook described as most intelligent and speaking English quite well. Derby told Cook that Superintendent Flett was detaining a number of aboriginal women against their will at houses on the Underbank estate.

On receiving the deputation from Derby, Cook wrote a note to Flett requesting him to release the women immediately, as the Governor had given him strict instructions about native women being detained on properties. Magistrate Cook asked Derby to deliver the note to Flett personally. When Derby returned to Cook, he said Flett read the letter, ripped it up and threw the pieces into the fireplace, saying, "There – go and bring another."[4] Flett had threatened to shoot him if he did not leave the estate immediately – without the women.

Magistrate Cook immediately wrote a letter to the Colonial Secretary, outlining the case and giving his concerns about the detention of the aboriginal women. The Colonial Secretary referred Cook's letter to Attorney General, John Plunkett. In a letter to Cook eight days later, Plunkett wrote that unless the women were returned to their tribe, other tribal members could be roused to acts of aggression and revenge against settlers. He reminded Cook that his district had previously been the scene of bloodshed, but he was not sure that adequate laws existed to handle the situation.[5]

Plunkett suggested that if Cook thought the women were

being detained for the purpose of prostitution, then he should charge Flett with running a disorderly house. Also, Henry Flett could be severely punished by the Government withdrawing all assigned servants from Flett personally or his employers.

To this end, Plunkett personally interviewed John Lord and threatened removal of all assigned servants from Lord's property. When Lord told the Attorney General, that Flett was leaving his employ in March, and would be leasing a property from Chief Justice Dowling, Plunkett replied he would advise the Chief Justice not to allow Flett to take the lease.

On January 4, 1838, Henry Flett appeared before the Dungog Bench, charged with keeping a disorderly house (brothel) in the district. Two witnesses, who were Flett's assigned servants, made depositions claiming to have seen Flett, on another occasion, refuse to let an aborigine take his wife home. The Bench committed Flett to take his trial in Sydney. When Plunkett received the depositions from Flett's committal, he declined to prosecute, evidently believing there was insufficient evidence to gain a conviction.

On February 15, 1838, Henry Flett wrote to the Colonial Secretary to complain of the way he had been treated, concerned mainly with the possible loss of assigned servants from his workforce:[6]

> The complaint mainly rested on the evidence of two of my own assigned servants, a motive for whose malignity I could well have established satisfactorily. That evidence I do not hesitate to characterise as a tissue of falsehood coupled, I will admit, with facts sufficient to give their tale an air of truth.
>
> The charge appeared to be founded on the circumstance of allowing and in fact encouraging the aborigines about the establishment, a practice which the settlers in all the districts of the colony find abundantly to their advantage to follow, and I do not hesitate to assert that on no farm in the Country have they continued to live with more friendly dispositions than at the establishment with which I am connected.

This case of aboriginal women being detained by white settlers for sexual purposes was so widespread in so many districts that on May 21, 1839, Governor Gipps issued the decree that,

The Marriage Proposal

"All persons reported in such abominable unchristian proceeding, will immediately lose their licence and may be prosecuted as illegal occupiers of Crown Land or otherwise as the law directs."[7]

Flett's lease with Chief Justice Dowling did not eventuate, perhaps because of the Attorney General's intervention. Instead Flett took a five year lease of 1600 sheep and 130 head of cattle from a man named Grayson Hartley at a rent of £400 per annum.[8] At the end of five years, Flett would have to return the same number of sheep and cattle but of an equivalent sex and age. The lease also included Hartley's remaining eighteen months tenure of a farm called Caringulla.

Henry Flett left the Dungog district and moved to the Manning Valley.

On October 14, 1840, Henry Flett paid a 10% deposit on 820 acres of land at the confluence of Dingo Creek and the Manning River, with the balance of the money paid a month later. It cost thirteen shillings an acre for an all-up price of £533, and was given the aboriginal name of Killawarra by Flett.[9]

In 1841 (an exact date cannot be traced) Henry Flett, aged thirty-one, married Mary Wynter, the twenty-year-old daughter of William Wynter of Tarree.

Sometime between his purchase of land in October 1840 and his marriage to Mary Wynter, Flett proposed marriage to Isabella Mary Kelly, who was probably about five years older than him.

She refused him.

Flett told Isabella Kelly that if she ever revealed his offer of marriage to anyone, he would become her most bitter enemy.

Why was he so concerned to keep the proposal from public knowledge? There can only be one answer: it would be seen for what it was – a money-grab and a land-grab. Kelly was a wealthy woman, who not only owned her own property but owned many other valuable assets. In a nineteenth century marriage, all these assets would become his – and Flett was heavily in debt at the time.

Henry Flett dominated the men around him, and while he would have naturally expected to dominate his wife, it is hard to imagine Isabella Mary Kelly married to a domineering husband. Kelly was Catholic (although a Catholic raised by a Protestant), and Flett was a Protestant. This obstacle itself would have proven difficult to solve, with Kelly expected to convert to Protestantism.

For Isabella Mary Kelly, marriage would be disastrous. Not only would she lose control of her wealth, she would lose the thing she valued most – her *independence*.

Did she tell anyone? She did not say whether she did or did not, but it is hard to believe that she did not indicate when socialising, that she was single because she *wanted* to be single, not because no one would marry her. No one ever recorded in their memoirs that they had been told the secret. Even after Isabella Kelly publicly revealed the proposal in Flett's presence, it was never mentioned – either in newspapers or in memoirs.[10]

Over the next twenty five years, Henry Flett would oppose Isabella Mary Kelly on any available occasion. And as his power increased so, too, did his opportunities.

Henry Flett's marriage to Mary Wynter would prove lasting and successful. A total of eleven children were born to the couple, the last being born twenty-five years after their wedding.[11]

But Henry Flett was in extreme financial difficulty. He owed £800 to Grayson Hartley, as he had not paid rent for the last two years of his five-year lease of the sheep and cattle. On February 14, 1841, Flett borrowed £1000 from his solicitors, Carr & Rogers at the astonishing interest rate of 20%. £500 was an unsecured cash loan, and the other £500 was by mortgage with Killawarra as security, payable on February 14, 1843.[12]

Flett needed to earn £200 per year just to pay the interest, on top of the £400 p.a. for the hire of the stock.

When this debt was coupled with the economic depression of 1841–43, it was not surprising that Flett did not make any repayments of the mortgage agreement. Consequently in February 1843, Killawarra was lost on mortgage to Carr & Rogers, although the Fletts continued living there.

On May 31, 1843, Henry Flett filed for insolvency. His debts amounted to £1973 and his listed assets were £677, leaving a net deficiency of £1295.[13]

An "official assignee" was appointed, similar to the role of a "receiver" in bankruptcy, whose job it was to try and make sure *all* the assets were collected and all aspects of the insolvency were correct. When the insolvency process was completed, the insolvent applied for a clearance certificate, which, on receipt, left him free to resume any business activities he wanted to or was able to. This contrasted with bankruptcy, where restrictions were placed on post-bankruptcy activities.

During the process the official assignee would hold meetings of creditors, and the insolvent would undergo examination, making sworn depositions as to his financial situation in response to questions from the Official Assignee or any of the creditors.

Basically, Flett said he had very little in the way of assets. The insolvency was advertised so that creditors could come forward and "prove" their debts by making a statutory declaration of the amount Flett owed them, with a failure to do so meaning no future claim could be made on that debt. The whole process could take twelve months or more.

The numerous meetings held during the insolvency worked towards a plan of distribution of assets to creditors, and a final acceptance of this plan by those creditors. All costs of the insolvency were deducted from the assets before their distribution, as well as a 5% commission (usually) for the Official Assignee on the gross value of the assets raised.

On June 5, 1844, in the Supreme Court (Insolvency), Flett's plan of distribution was confirmed. The sheep and cattle had been mustered and sold for £162, but by the time the costs of the official assignee, as well as his commission, had been taken out, there was only £37 left. The plan yielded a dividend of 7d in the pound – creditors would get just 3% of their money.

Next, Flett applied for his clearance certificate, clearing him of all debt and obligation. This was granted eight days later on June 13, 1844. By paying £15, he was allowed to keep the furniture in his house.

During the insolvency Flett said he was renting a property at Charity Creek and another near Cundletown, suggesting there may have been a lot more cattle and sheep than he indicated during the insolvency – it would not be too hard to hide assets in the Manning Valley of the 1840s from an Official Assignee operating in Sydney.

Carr & Rogers found a buyer for Killawarra, but he withdrew from the sale shortly after. After the insolvency, Henry Flett remained living on Killawarra, with most settlers in the Valley unaware that he no longer owned the property.

Flett's father-in-law, William Wynter, was also caught up in the economic downturn of the 1840s. After receiving the title papers to his grant of land on June 29, 1839, he mortgaged Tarree for the amount of £700 to Elizabeth Bell, an English woman, who operated in Australia through a solicitor with power of attorney. In the following year he took out a second mortgage.

On May 28, 1843, when full repayment of the Bell mortgage was due, William Wynter was unable to make the repayments and Elizabeth Bell foreclosed on him. At a hearing on February 7, 1844, the Supreme Court ruled that William Wynter owed Bell £1043. Wynter did not defend Bell's suit in the Supreme Court – obviously, he did not have the money.

On November 28, 1844, the Supreme Court order became final and Elizabeth Bell became the owner of Tarree.[14]

Living in England, Bell retained Tarree for fourteen months before selling to Owen MacGreal on February 14, 1846. Not much is known about MacGreal, other than he came to the colony as a convict on the *Forth* in 1835, after being convicted in Leitrim, Ireland, of forgery and sentenced to transportation for life.[15]

MacGreal, who had sheep and cattle running in the district, signed an agreement with Elizabeth Bell to buy Tarree for £1000. Bell was generous in her terms – perhaps a sign, in keeping with the economic climate, that few buyers were coming forward. MacGreal did not make a deposit, and there was an escape clause – MacGreal could withdraw from the deal anytime within the first eighteen months, and the sale would not be registered until then.

Owen MacGreal was just six months into his contract to buy Tarree, when Henry Flett offered him £250 to withdraw from the contract. MacGreal accepted.[16]

On June 30, 1846, only two years after his insolvency, Henry Flett bought Tarree from Elizabeth Bell for £1100.[17] Flett paid a deposit of £200[18], and took out a mortgage with Bell to pay the balance with interest at 6% p.a.

The Marriage Proposal

What money was this, and where did it come from? How was Flett able to accumulate £450 within two years of being declared insolvent and apparently left with no property, stock or money? It undoubtedly placed Flett under the suspicion of hiding assets during his insolvency.

With the agreement signed, Flett and his family moved onto Tarree. The Wynters had never left Tarree, and continued living there under the ownership of Bell and MacGreal. Now in the hands of their son-in-law, the Wynters were allowed to retain use of "The Gardens", their cottage and the surrounding gardens, a little west of the present-day bridge across the river.

Henry Flett now settled down to the task of developing Tarree. He took in tenant farmers and gave out clearing leases to clear the dense semi-tropical bush, which covered most of the property. Roads were built to gain access, particularly one down the peninsula to the river at Tinonee. Flett drained much of rich alluvial soil land, prone to minor flooding. His main crops were maize, wheat and tobacco.[19] Flett now showed his capabilities, coupled with hard work and a single-minded drive. He needed to earn a lot of money, in a short time, so that he did not lose this property also.

On April 4, 1851, Flett paid all money owing to Elizabeth Bell, more than twelve months ahead of schedule.[20] For some unclear reason, Flett found it necessary, only six months later, to take a mortgage on Tarree for £862 from solicitor George Rogers.[21] This mortgage was due on October 23, 1853, and was at the rate of 10% interest, rather than the 6% he was paying with the Bell mortgage.

When this mortgage became due, Henry Flett was unable to pay and once again faced the prospect of foreclosure. Flett decided to solve his financial problems by taking one hundred acres out of his 2560 acre Tarree property, and creating a township, to be called Taree – his own property was spelled "Tarree" with a double "r", but the name of the township always had a single "r".[22]

This investment was quite risky. When Chatham, in between Taree and Cundletown, went on sale in 1841, many allotments sold initially, but the township did not develop. Georgetown had been a flop in 1842. So Flett was taking quite an entrepreneurial risk, but faced with the loss of Tarree, there was no viable alternative.

There were two things in Flett's favour. Firstly, there had been a great influx of settlers into the Manning from 1850, mainly because of the cheapness of land compared to the Hunter Valley. Secondly, Flett's choice of site was inspired. The town was close to the river and running parallel to it, on a section of the river where large ships could tie up to load and unload their cargo from wharves on the riverbank. When the big flood of 1866 came, the township of Taree was surrounded by floodwaters, but was not flooded itself.

The auction for the Taree allotments, held on December 19, 1854, resulted in forty allotments sold – a resounding success for Flett. On January 12, 1855, Henry Flett paid off his mortgage of £862 and all the accrued interest.

Flett continued to increase the number of tenants on the rich alluvial farmland of the Tarree peninsula until, eventually, he had about a hundred tenants on the books, with Taree providing a service centre for this growing population.

In the space of just over ten years, Henry Flett had gone from insolvency to become the richest and most powerful man in the Manning Valley.

William Wynter did not live to see the birth of Taree. He died, aged 67, at Port Macquarie, on October 13, 1853, and was buried there. He had spent much of his time working with the Lands Commission, and had travelled to Port Macquarie for that purpose, suffering a heart attack as he arrived. It is thought by many that it would have been much more appropriate, if this much-loved settler could have been buried on Tarree, the property he pioneered and spent so much of his labour establishing.

After his death, his widow, Elizabeth Wynter made a dower claim against her son-in-law Henry Flett. In an age when the man, as the head of the house, owned all the family assets, the dower laws were there to protect the wife after her husband's death, as all the family assets would often pass from father to son, bypassing the wife completely.

In this particular case, it is hard to see how the dower law would apply as the property had passed from William Wynter to his son-in-law rather than his son, and in doing so it passed through the hands of a third party, Elizabeth Bell, and a fourth party, Owen MacGreal. So legally, it was probably a deal that Flett did not have to make with his mother-in-law.

On August 14, 1855, Elizabeth Wynter and Henry Flett came to an agreement, which they registered with the Lands Commission. In return for his mother-in-law releasing him from all dower claims, Flett granted her an annuity of £30 per annum, and use of The Gardens and its immediate surrounds, for the rest of her life.[23]

Elizabeth Wynter lived for another sixteen years.

George Rowley

3. A Woman in Charge of Convicts

On September 9, 1840, George Rowley was one of a partnership of four who bought a 640-acre property at a convenient crossing of the Manning River, about ten miles downstream from Mount George. Rowley's partner, Thomas New, paid 34 shillings per acre at auction in Sydney, for a total cost of £1088.[1]

Rowley named the property Bungay Bungay, and it was situated at the junction of Dingo Creek with the Manning River, opposite Henry Flett's property of Killawarra, not far from the present-day township of Wingham. Rowley and Flett would form a close friendship that would last long after Rowley's departure from the district in 1854.

George Rowley, the son of the Colonial Secretary in Grenada, was born in 1811, and was originally a sugar planter in the West Indies. He married there in 1838, shortly before migrating to Australia. The first of his fourteen children was born in 1839 on the Paterson River in New South Wales and the last in 1865 at Berrima.[2]

On August 15, 1842, George Rowley became a Justice of the Peace, an honorary position in which he could witness the signing of legal documents.[3] With the absence of Police Magistrates, who were paid for their services and had legal training, the Justice of the Peace role was extended into that of a Community Magistrate, arbitrating in contractual disputes.[4] Settlers contracted workers for their farms, and either party could take the other before a Magistrate to settle a dispute.

If a settler met a difficulty with an assigned servant, the settler could take the convict before the Community Magistrate, who would examine the case and impose an appropriate sentence. Occasionally, the assigned servant would take his master before the

Magistrate for breaching the conditions of his indenture.

For a criminal offence, individuals could go to the Magistrate and make a charge against any individual. The Magistrate would then take depositions from witnesses and decide whether or not a *prima facie* case had been established. If the Community Magistrate decided the *prima facie* case had not been established, he dismissed the case. Otherwise the defendant would be bailed to appear for trial at a major centre such as Maitland or Sydney.

The depositions taken by the Magistrate would then be sent to the Attorney General, who, after reading through them and taking into consideration the probability of a successful prosecution, decided whether to proceed with the prosecution or to dismiss it.

If more than one Magistrate was in attendance at a hearing, they all sat at a bench in front of the appellants. In civil cases between two parties, the majority decision ruled. In criminal cases, if at least one magistrate was convinced that a *prima facie* case had been established, then a committal usually followed.

There was a downside to Community Magistrates in that they had no legal training and could make errors in law, innocently or deliberately.

Added to this, the decisions of the Community Magistrates were not open to public scrutiny as there were no qualified lawyers attending these courts and there were no newspapers to report on proceedings – they were a law unto themselves. While most Community Magistrates were honest in their Court dealings, the position was open to abuse without consequence.

Rowley was virtually the only Community Magistrate in the Manning Valley throughout the 1840s, although his partner, Thomas New, became a magistrate for a short period before his sudden death in 1845. During this period, George Rowley was the only means of justice for settlers in the Manning, unless they took the matter south to Dungog or Stroud, or north to Port Macquarie. As a result Bungay Bungay became the centre of the Manning Valley, often known in later years as the "cradle of the Manning".

The census[5] of 1841 revealed that there were 76 assigned

servants out of a population of 300 in the Manning Valley. At Tarree, owned by William Wynter, there were 25 people (of whom 14 were convicts); Bungay Bungay owned by George Rowley and partners – 30 people (8 convicts); Mount George owned by Isabella Mary Kelly – 13 people (8 convicts); Killawarra owned by Henry Flett – 21 people (13 convicts). Of the 300 people in the Manning Valley, there were 237 men and 63 women, but only 23 houses.

With eight convicts assigned to her, Isabella Kelly's expectations of useful cheap labour were not fulfilled. Some assigned servants did not like working for male supervisors, let alone a female boss. Some were content to work out their time. Some were openly defiant or, at best, passive resisters. Some were murderous.

In 1843 John Chapman, a convict assigned to Miss Kelly, was charged with the murder of an aborigine by the name of Mickey Ugly, belonging to the Gangat tribe. It appears that John Chapman had been cohabiting with Maria, an aborigine who, although she belonged to Mickey Ugly, had borne a child to Chapman.

When Mickey Ugly went missing, his tribe began searching for him, believing from the start that Chapman might have murdered him. On January 8, the remains of Mickey Ugly were found in the ashes of a fire, which had been deliberately lit for the purpose of disposing of the body. George Watson and another man, from the Yankangat property (adjacent to Mount George and later known as Woodside), had heard the screams of the aborigines who discovered the body. They went looking for Chapman and captured him. Maria was found hiding in the kitchen of Miss Kelly's house – Kelly was away at the time.

The matter was taken before Community Magistrate George Rowley at Bungay Bungay. Maria told Magistrate Rowley that Chapman asked Mickey Ugly and herself to cross the river and hunt paddymelons (a small kangaroo type animal, rather easily caught). As they moved into the bush, four men – Chapman, a shepherd and two bullock-drivers – appeared from behind a tree. One of the bullock-drivers wounded Mickey Ugly with a shotgun, and the shepherd then killed him with a musket. His throat was cut and the body burnt. Chapman had returned over the next two days, to re-light the fire and continue burning the body.

He had warned Maria that the white men would kill her if she told them about it.

Magistrate Rowley committed Chapman for trial and sent the depositions to the Attorney General, as required. No communication was ever received back from the Attorney General. Chapman was eventually released from prison without a trial.[6]

Whatever happened to Chapman after his release, he was not returned to Isabella Mary Kelly at Mount George, as was the normal practice.

George Rowley went to the Stroud Bench on May 20, 1843, to gain its support in disciplining two of his own assigned servants. Elizhu Smith, who had been transported for life in 1836, appeared before Magistrate Philip Gidley King charged with neglect of duty. George Rowley stated under oath:[7]

> On the 24th February the prisoner left out a considerable number of sheep that had been entrusted to his care. The original number was 506 – of these 26 were unaccounted for – some having been found on the run dead, and others were never found at all. Previous to this he had lost several sheep at different times, and I am sure that this loss was occasioned by the sheer carelessness of the prisoner.

After admonishing Smith for his neglect, Magistrate King discharged him. Rowley immediately brought a second charge of neglect of duty against Smith. Enumerating the losses of sheep made by Smith during April and May, Rowley finished his deposition with, "All these losses must have arisen from the carelessness of the prisoner. The prisoner is old and a good shepherd when he is inclined."

Magistrate King sentenced Elizhu Smith to *fifty lashes*.

On the same day, Rowley charged John Talley with disobedience of orders. Rowley stated that he ordered the prisoner to work but had only been met with refusal. After warning him he could be charged, Talley had again refused. Magistrate King sentenced Talley to *fourteen days* in the cells.

In the same period, Robert Easton, an overseer from the Manning Valley working for the A. A. Company, charged his assigned servant George Blunden with losing sheep. Easton informed the Stroud Bench that Blunden was "a great sleeper and lets the flock wander".

Blunden was sentenced to receive *thirty-six lashes*.[8]

These sentences were re-enforcements of discipline of the servants assigned to Rowley and Easton. Isabella Mary Kelly needed the power of the Magistrates to support her control over the convicts assigned to her. She found she did not always get that support.

George Grist, John Jobson, Benjamin Tedsall and Joseph Brindley were four convicts assigned to Miss Kelly, who had all arrived in the colony on board the *Earl Grey* in 1838.

Both Grist and Tedsall absconded from Kelly's service. There is little resource material on this incident giving no details on how they were recaptured, but it is recorded that both runaways received *fifty lashes* at Port Macquarie on April 24, 1841. Benjamin Tedsall was also convicted of robbery, and in addition to the lashing, served the following twelve months in irons. After completing their punishments, the convicts were returned to Kelly's service, as was the usual practice.[9]

Joseph Brindley received a mention in the Dungog Letter Book in May 1842, when the Chief Constable stopped him as he passed through Dungog. Brindley was taking a horse to the Rev Mahony at Maitland for Miss Kelly. His pass was not in order, but nothing further eventuated, indicating that it was genuine.[10] Brindley died in the hospital at Port Macquarie in January 1843 and was buried in the cemetery at Port Macquarie – the cause of death was not recorded.[11]

On August 30, 1844, Kelly charged George Grist with neglect of duty at the Police Office in Dungog before Magistrates Thomas Cook and Vincent Dowling. In her sworn deposition Isabella Kelly said:[12]

> About 12 months ago through the carelessness of the prisoner [George Grist] I have lost 13 head of cattle, which were then in his charge. I gave him 12 months time to find them, telling him that if at the end of this time he did not find them, I would have him brought to court. He has not found them. I have suffered such losses owing to this man's carelessness or worse. That although reluctant to come to a Court, I

cannot allow his conduct to pass.

In May last I desired him to take a quantity of Pigs to the [A. A.] Company's place at Ganget, and take a boy with him as an assistant. He would not take the boy, and on his return I found that he had lost one of the pigs, which was the best of the lot. This man has been insolent to me on several occasions.

The decision of the Bench was, "To be worked for two Calendar Months on the Tread Mill Sydney and then returned to his employer."[13]

Some time later, Isabella Kelly discovered that Grist was residing in the district, and had been paroled with a ticket-of-leave, which was only granted to prisoners with no convictions over the previous *four* years. This was all rather irregular, as the ticket-of-leave also required an endorsement by the person to whom the convict had been assigned, and no one had approached Kelly. Further, Grist had been released from prison after serving *only one month* of his two-month sentence. Kelly let the matter rest for the time being.

While in Maitland in the next month, Isabella Kelly engaged John Fox on a twelve-month contract as a shepherd, to replace George Grist. As a former convict with a ticket-of-leave, Kelly told Fox to report to the authorities and update his ticket so they knew of his whereabouts and current employment. The "ticket", an abbreviation of "ticket-of-leave", was the documentation needed by every convict on parole.

Kelly had not travelled far from Maitland when Fox caught up with her and said he had been unable to get the ticket altered. Kelly gave him one pound as an advance on his wages, telling him to go and get his ticket altered, and not to return until it had been done. Fox never arrived at Mount George.

Isabella Kelly took out a warrant for Fox's arrest, charging him with obtaining money from her under false pretences. At his trial in December, John Fox said in his defence that he had obeyed his mistress *literally* – when he could not get his ticket altered, he did not return. Fox was convicted and returned to prison with the cancellation of his ticket.[14]

A Woman in Charge of Convicts

In his memoirs, settler John Allan wrote two rather cryptic lines about John Jobson: "Miss Kelly had a man named Jobson to look after the cattle, but she allowed him no horse. He had to do it all on foot."[15] As it was well known that Miss Kelly had horses available (although expensive), many of Allan's readers have misinterpreted this as cruelty on Kelly's part to one of her assigned servants, or that she did not trust him enough to let him have a horse.

In the phasing out of assigning convicts to settlers, convicts were not generally re-assigned from one master to another after 1841. John Jobson, who was re-assigned from Isabella Kelly to her overseer Thomas Turner, seems to have been an exception, and perhaps it was allowed to pass through because Jobson had remained on the same estate. Allan, who did not arrive in the Valley until 1851, was obviously unaware of this re-assignment.

This transfer was unfortunate for Jobson, as there came a time when Turner could not *afford* to clothe Jobson or provide a horse for him to carry out his duties as a stockman, with horses being in short supply in the colony, and relatively expensive to buy.

On April 28, 1845, John Jobson travelled to Port Macquarie and went to Police Magistrate Gray to complain about his master. Jobson made a sworn deposition, signed with an "X" and the usual notation of "his mark" written under it:[16]

> John Jobson ... states no slops [cheap clothing] of any kind were issued to me by my master or any one on his behalf at the November issue of slop clothing and at the previous issue of clothing in May 1844, I received only one shirt, one pair of trousers and a pair of boots.
>
> I was minding the cattle (between 200 and 300 head) by myself and on foot, and sometime between May and November I received one pair of boots, being then barefooted. I have been under the orders of no person but Mr Turner. About two months after the last issue ought to have taken place, I asked Miss Kelly for my slops – she told me she had nothing to do with me, to ask my master. He was present at the time, and I accordingly asked him for my slops, when he told me he had no means of getting me any clothing ...
>
> Before coming to the Bench to complain about not receiving my slops, I again asked Mr Turner for them, telling

him I had nothing to wear. He said he had no means of getting them for me. I then asked him for a pass to go to Port Macquarie to the Police Magistrate, which he refused to give me, and I left the farm the following day and proceeded to Port Macquarie.

Settlers were required to provide food and clothing for their assigned servants. Each convict should have received per annum: 2 jackets; 2 shirts; 2 pairs of trousers; 3 pairs of shoes; 1 hat. Often these were part-issued on a six monthly basis.

The Chief Constable stated that a summons had been served on Turner but he failed to appear when called. Magistrate Gray ruled that John Jobson was to be withdrawn from Turner's service and returned to the Government. He was then assigned to the Royal Engineer Department in Port Macquarie to make bricks. On receiving his ticket-of-leave the next year, Jobson returned to the Manning Valley, married and raised a family on Mitchell's Island.

On May 14, 1845, Miss Kelly took Benjamin Tedsall before Magistrates George Rowley and Thomas New, at the Bungay Bungay Bench. Kelly charged Tedsall with theft and gross language. The Bench found him guilty and sentenced him to fourteen days imprisonment. Miss Kelly asked that he be returned to Government when he had finished his sentence, as she no longer wanted him.

It was not too long before Kelly discovered that Tedsall had not served any of his prison sentence, and was working for Rowley on his Bungay Bungay property.

Isabella Mary Kelly wrote a letter of complaint to Governor George Gipps. Dated October 13, 1845, and written from Kent House in Kent Street, Sydney, Isabella Kelly wrote:[17]

> Miss Kelly of the Manning River begs to lay before His Excellency the Governor the following representation that George Grist per "Earl Grey" her assigned servant was brought before the Dungog Bench of Magistrates on the 30th August 1844 and sentenced to Two Calendar Months; that within One Month of the date of his sentence (unusual it is believed according to regulations) applied for his Ticket-of-

leave without her signature and obtained it and has been living in her neighbourhood and has used threats against her, so much so, that she fears serious consequence from him and thinks he is an improper person to be allowed in her District and she has no confidence in any appeal.

Also that another Assigned Servant to her, by name of Benjamin Tedsall[18] per "Earl Grey" was brought before the Manning Bench on the 13th May 1845 on a charge of Theft & Gross Language, was sentenced to 14 days confinement and ordered to be returned to Government with her approval; that this man was at large immediately after his committal and was then employed by one of the committing Magistrates Mr Rowley and as this man like the former was kept most improperly in her neighbourhood, she trusts His Excellency will be pleased to order him to be removed, as she considers she has sufficient proof of their malignity to do her further injury and as she believes the former punishments have not been properly registered or are unnoticed that would entitle them to such early indulgencies; she trusts His Excellency will call for these particulars from their District whereby he will see that these men are not deserving persons and are unprecedented, with the cases of other men.

Governor Gipps ordered a report from the Principal Superintendent of Convicts, Captain McLean of Hyde Park Barracks, who was in charge of all assigned servants in New South Wales. McLean demanded a report from the Police Magistrate Gray at Port Macquarie, as well as Magistrates George Rowley, of Bungay Bungay, and Thomas Cook, of Dungog – and they all resented it.

The Report from Capt McLean divided each page into two columns with a heading of "Miss Kelly stated" on one side, repeating the main points of her letter, and a heading of "The Facts are these" on the other.[19]

Under this heading of "The Facts are these", McLean reported that Magistrate Thomas Cook said Grist had been sentenced to two months on the treadmill in Sydney but the sentence had not been carried out. Further, he had not notified Gray of the sentence (as he was required to do). He included the depositions taken by Cook in the case.

Police Magistrate Gray said that as a result of not being noti-

The Trials of Isabella Mary Kelly

fied by Cook, he had no offences recorded against Grist for the last four years when he received Grist's application for a ticket-of-leave, and hence he had recommended to Capt McLean that Grist's ticket-of-leave be issued.

The application for the ticket-of-leave, which had been written in January 1845 and granted in June 1845, was included in the report. McLean continued:

> In April 1845 a complaint was made by the Police Magistrate of Port Macquarie against Miss Kelly (paper marked C) in consequence of which Tedsall and another man were, in June of that year, directed by His Excellency the Governor to be withdrawn from her service, and the men (in order to save expense) were allowed to remain at Port Macquarie as it was stated that they were required for the Royal Engineer Department – it now appears that Tedsall had already been returned to Government by Miss Kelly, which was not known in my office.

This was not completely true. There was *no* complaint against Kelly, as the attached report showed. It referred to John Jobson, who had complained about his master Thomas Turner. Further, Kelly had *requested* that Tedsall be returned to Government. McLean continued his report to the Governor with:

> … that the sentence passed on him [Tedsall] was not carried into effect, in consequence of his extreme orderly and good conduct, his services being urgently required, the want of a constable to take him to Port Macquarie, and the generally alleged ill treatment by Miss Kelly of her assigned servants, as well as the want of veracity, which is said to characterize her in most of her transactions;
>
> His Excellency will, however, observe by the enclosed letter from Mr Rowley (marked E.) that Tedsall is now returned to Port Macquarie with a recommendation that the sentence before-alluded to, may be remitted.

There it was – in black and white – an official report by Captain McLean to Governor Gipps, that Miss Isabella Mary Kelly ill treated her convicts and regularly told lies.

Where did it come from?

It came directly from George Rowley, whose report to

A Woman in Charge of Convicts

Police Magistrate Gray, dated January 13, 1846, read:[20]

> On the 14th May last, Benjamin Tedsall[21] was brought before my partner Capt New (since deceased) and myself on a charge of generally disorderly conduct – after a patient hearing of the matter, we adjudged him to suffer imprisonment for 14 days – his mistress desiring him at the same time to be returned to Government.
>
> The Govt. Constable stationed here under my control at this particular moment being engaged on public duty – and no convenient escort occurring to forward the Prisoner to Port Macquarie – it occurred to us to employ him in the interior of a few days to assist the man Lewis (a prisoner of the Crown) whom the Police Magistrate had recently sent to erect a lock-up at the Manning, in such duty. Within a day or two after this, the said Lewis and the Govt. Constable himself both absconded – for which offence they were duly brought before the Police Bench at Port Macquarie and punished.
>
> Finding the man Tedsall suitable to the work [which] I had the superintendence of, I continued him at it, immediately acquainting the Police Magistrate, Mr Gray of my having done so, and seeking his permission to retain the man as a substitute for Lewis

Rowley then went on to criticise the lack of facilities provided by the Government and that he used Tedsall to construct a combined lock-up and room for court hearings as well as a constable's hut. Rowley continued:

> With regard to the sentence of punishment, which I had passed on Tedsall, it has not yet been carried into effect – the extremely orderly and good conduct of the man from the moment he came under my notice and throughout has been so marked, in opposition to the charges and character produced against him by Miss Kelly that I felt happy he has not suffered, what might possibly, I now think, have been an undeserved sentence, and it was my intention on my being finished with his services, to have enquired as to what would be my regular process in the matter, to have obtained for him a remission of his sentence ...
>
> It was a matter on the mind of my brother magistrate and myself at the time of the trial, of some doubt as to the man's culpability – his subsequent conduct has led me to suppose those doubts were rightly founded – and this coupled with

the generally alleged uniform ill treatment by Miss Kelly of the persons in her establishment for which she has rendered herself notorious I believe throughout this district – and the departure from veracity which characterizes that individual in most of her transactions – are the reasons which operated upon me in not having as yet pressed the punishment upon the man.

On January 25, Rowley wrote a personal letter to Capt McLean asking that the sentence on Tedsall be remitted, adding that, "I have known him in my neighbourhood for some years as a well conducted person."[22] While Rowley claimed the offence was light, the original sentence of fourteen days was also extremely light for the period – especially for theft. Rowley's letter was also attached to the report.

Governor Gipps wrote in the margin of the report, "I perceive that some irregularities certainly have been committed, but that they are scarcely of a nature to require further notice than that which they have already received."

And there the matter ended.

Both George Rowley and Thomas Cook gave prison sentences to assigned servants of Isabella Mary Kelly, and then proceeded to ignore their implementation.

Why? There can only be one reason – they did not take her seriously; she was a joke; she was trying to be a man; it was ridiculous putting a woman in charge of convicts. Should anyone have to take orders from this silly woman?

To his credit, Police Magistrate Cook admitted his mistake, and in his subsequent relations with Isabella Kelly, treated her fairly and supported her when necessary.

Magistrate George Rowley did not.

For Rowley, it had not been about Benjamin Tedsall, it was about George Rowley coming under scrutiny for his actions as a magistrate – he was not accustomed to it, and he did not like it.

In his reply to the Governor, Rowley took the offensive and accused Kelly of ill-treating her convicts. Rowley gave no other evidence of this ill treatment other than Tedsall was so well behaved in his own custody Kelly *must have* ill-treated him. At no stage did Tedsall make any allegations against Kelly – if he had done so, Rowley would have been quick to report it.

In fact there is *no record* of any convict assigned to Isabella Kelly making any allegations of cruelty or ill treatment against her.

Rowley ignored the fact that in his position as a magistrate, any infringement by Tedsall could result in a serious punishment, using the full force of the law, but *imposed by Rowley* – of course Tedsall would be on his best behaviour around Rowley.

In his report, Rowley downgraded the charges against Tedsall from "theft and gross language" to "generally disorderly conduct". Rowley lied when he said, "immediately acquainting the Police Magistrate, Mr Gray of my having done so": in his report, Gray said he knew nothing about the matter when the request for a report arrived from Capt McLean. Having received Rowley's report, Gray did give a *posthumous* approval to the way in which Rowley had used Tedsall.

The depositions taken by Rowley were not provided, so we do not know what was said at the hearing or the nature of the theft committed by Tedsall. The depositions provided by Cook corroborated all of Kelly's statements in her letter of complaint – there is no reason to believe the Bungay Bungay depositions would not have done the same.

On the other hand, Kelly's evidence against George Grist at Dungog is far from that of a convict suffering ill treatment – and Grist did not deny the evidence Kelly gave. Grist refused to take the boy with him, and Kelly did nothing but accept it. Yet Rowley would have us believe she victimised her assigned servants.

In dealing with her assigned servants, Kelly relied on the magistrates to *support her authority* – and she did not get that support.

John Allan wrote that Isabella Kelly used to take her convicts to Port Macquarie to be flogged.[23] Whether he received his information from Kelly personally or from others in the Valley, he does not say, but these events were before his arrival in the Valley.

Similarly, George Hill, who settled at Bungay Bungay in the late 1850s, said: "Stories are told how Miss Kelly once marched two convicts before her to Port Macquarie to be flogged",[24] with the indication that it only occurred once.

Certainly there were two convicts assigned to Isabella Kelly – George Grist and Benjamin Tedsall – who had each received fifty lashes at Port Macquarie in 1841 for absconding from her service. But if they *absconded*, then Kelly would not have marched them to Port Macquarie.

Kelly may have taken others convicts to Port Macquarie, but with many of the Port Macquarie records lost, there is no record of it. By the early 1840s, settlers in the Manning Valley were permitted to take their convicts to the more expedient Dungog. (In 1846 Port Macquarie closed as a convict establishment, with inmates removed to Sydney and elsewhere.)

The Dungog Bench books did not record *any* convict flogged because Kelly brought them to the Bench, as it did for Rowley and Easton. No one considered these two men to be cruel to their convicts in any respect. There was one difference: this settler was a *woman*. And the subtext was: Any woman, who could cause a man to be whipped, *must* be cruel.

Over the next thirty years of her life, while her contemporaries would make many allegations against Isabella Mary Kelly, George Rowley was the only person who ever claimed she ill-treated her assigned servants.

Throughout the twentieth century long after her death, and contrary to the evidence, the legend of Isabella Mary Kelly's cruelty to her convicts grew and grew.

Shortly after the second *Smith's Weekly* story on Isabella Kelly ("The Man Who Dared Miss Kelly") was published in 1927, an article in the Taree newspaper *Northern Champion* related the many rumours circulating in the district about Isabella Kelly, without confirming or denying them.

The author recorded one rumour as she "even drove chained convicts fifty miles on foot to Port Macquarie to be flogged after they had saved her own life in a swollen river". [25]

This printed rumour, which had come from settlers Allan and Hill, grew into one of the two core stories of her legend.

In an article entitled "Amazon of the Manning", which appeared in the magazine "Famous Detective Stories" of 1947, embellished the story:[26]

> She aroused the antagonism of Captain [Thomas] Cook and his fellow magistrate, Dr E. McKinley, by her stark brutality, and in the end they refused point blank to convict and flog the unfortunate convicts. This did not perturb Isabella unduly. She took her custom elsewhere – north to Port Macquarie. ...
>
> Two of her assigned servants committed some small misdemeanour so Isabella saddled up her horse and with pistols handy, marched the men to Port Macquarie. Attempting to cross a flooded stream during her trip, her horse was swept from under her by the current.
>
> One of the convicts, at the risk of his own life, leaped into the turbulent stream and pulled her out. Overflowing with "gratitude", Miss Kelly forced the man and his companion to continue the trip to Port Macquarie, where they were both soundly flogged as per schedule.

Most articles on Isabella Kelly after "Amazon of the Manning" contained this story. There were a number of variations, including one where Kelly "rewards" the convicts with sex before taking them on to Port Macquarie to be flogged. [27]

"Amazon of the Manning" also compared Isabella Kelly with Major Mudie: "Isabella Kelly was often labelled a female Major Mudie; she was, but there is a difference. Mudie got what was coming to him, but Isabella didn't."

Three convicts assigned to Major Mudie of Castle Forbes (near Singleton in the Hunter Valley) were hanged in 1833 as the ringleaders of a group who rampaged throughout the district as part of a revolt against their repressive master, Major Mudie, who was accused of inhuman mistreatment of them. The Governor ordered an enquiry which confirmed Mudie's brutal behaviour.

In no way can Isabella Kelly ever be linked to Mudie, as this event occurred two years *before* her arrival in the colony, and six years before she settled in the Manning Valley.

Nevertheless, James Holledge wrote in "Australia's Wicked Women":[28]

> Isabella Kelly was a crony of the infamous Major Mudie ...
> An inhuman monster who gloried in the flogging the prison wretches assigned to him, Mudie had tutored the Irish

girl in his methods. He also sold her the cattle that formed the nucleus of her stock and lent her the services of several overseers to keep order amongst her convicts.

James Holledge also had a bare-breasted Isabella Kelly tying convicts to a post and personally whipping them until she was overtaken by exhaustion (as related in the prologue).

These stories were repeated and embroidered in "historical" articles printed in the Sydney newspapers *The Sun*, *Daily Telegraph* and *Sunday Telegraph*. None of the authors appears to have ever researched or sourced their stories; they simply reproduced the previous articles and enriched them with their own creative writing.

Why did such outlandish tales grow? A *woman* was in charge of convicts.

4. Before the Bench

There were a number of occasions in the 1840s when Isabella Mary Kelly summonsed men to appear before a Bench of Magistrates for various reasons, but on one occasion she herself received a summons. But then, at the same time, several of the Valley's leading citizens were similarly summonsed.

Surveyor John Gorman was the Commissioner of Crown Lands in the vast and largely virgin area of the Manning Valley and Port Macquarie district. In November 1844, Gorman had received a letter from Henry Wynter (son of William Wynter of Tarree) complaining about George Rowley[1]. While it was quite common for settlers to illegally run their cattle and sheep on Crown lands, George Rowley had arrogantly gone one step further.

Wynter had obtained a lease of Crown land, which adjoined Rowley's Bungay Bungay property, and which Rowley had been using as a run for his sheep. Henry Wynter advised Rowley that he had taken a lease of this Crown land, and requested him to remove the sheep. Rowley arrogantly replied with a letter to say he had been using this land as his "back run", that everybody considered it always as his run (despite only four years in the district), and that he intended to keep using the run as his own.[2]

Unsure of his legal position, Gorman wrote to Governor Gipps asking permission to take legal proceedings against Rowley, as well as a general authority to prosecute anyone else illegally using Crown lands. The Governor wrote extensive notes on Gorman's letter expressing his deep concern about "unauthorised intruders".[3] Gorman subsequently prosecuted Rowley, resulting in Rowley being fined for trespass.

Gorman went on to discover another two stations illegally used by Rowley and New on the upper Manning River, but withdrew his prosecutions against them when he realised the stations came within the New England district, out of his jurisdiction.[4]

Gorman then travelled throughout the Valley seeking trespassers. On September 29, 1845, at Port Macquarie, John Gorman charged the Flett brothers, Mary Cann and Isabella Kelly with illegally occupying crown lands.[5]

Although Henry Flett pleaded not guilty before Magistrate George Jobling, he offered no defence. Gorman stated to the Bench he had visited the Crown land in question, which had about 680 sheep running on it, as well as a hut and a yard. A shepherd there told him he worked for Henry Flett, and Flett owned the sheep running there. The Magistrate fined Flett one pound, with Flett stating he would immediately remove himself from the Crown land completely.

Perhaps mindful of the inconsequence of his brother's not guilty plea, George Flett pleaded guilty. Despite Gorman giving mitigating evidence to the Magistrate by suggesting that, as the Crown Land in question was adjacent to Killawarra and George Flett might not have realised he was trespassing, Magistrate Jobling fined him one pound also.

Mrs. Mary Cann, a settler in her own right, was represented by Robert Searle. Mary Cann had come to the Manning Valley after her second husband had committed suicide by hanging himself in their barn. Robert Searle was a convict assigned to her husband, and Mary was permitted to bring him with her and the children, when they moved to the Valley. Searle later became her third husband.[6]

Pleading guilty, Searle stated Mrs. Cann intended applying to lease the land. Magistrate Jobling declared this to be a more serious offence than the previous two cases, as Mrs. Cann admitted being in occupation of the land for seven years, and Commissioner Gorman had advised her to obtain a lease in February. He fined Mary Cann five pounds.

Miss Isabella Kelly did not appear when called, and her case was tried in absentia. The Constable stated he had visited her Mount George property on September 18 (eleven days previously) to deliver the summons, only to find her absent. Her overseer said she was either in Sydney or Maitland, and he sent the summons on to her.

Before the Bench

John Gorman stated he had visited Crown Land adjacent to A. A. Company land and found cattle running there, with huts, a stockyard and milking yards. He was sure Miss Kelly had been in occupation of this land since February, and he told the man encamped there how to get a lease. He had also written to Miss Kelly advising her how to go about leasing Crown Land five months ago. The Magistrate found Kelly guilty, and fined her five pounds.

Isabella Kelly was most upset to receive notification of the fine, and wrote a letter of complaint to the Colonial Secretary.[7] She enclosed a letter from Thomas Mitchell, the Surveyor General, dated two months *before* the date of her fine, apologising for the delay in her application to buy land at Burrell Creek, because it was "awaiting measurement by Mr Gorman of 40 acres … which may interfere with your application". So, although Kelly was illegally camped on the land, she had, in fact, applied to purchase it.

Unfortunately for Kelly, Governor Gipps wrote on her letter, "I regret I can not see cause to remit this fine." To further rub salt into her wounds, the Lands Commission received a better offer for this Burrell Creek land, with the result Kelly did not gain ownership of it.[8]

Isabella Kelly then successfully applied to lease 650 acres at the junction of Burrell Creek with the Manning River. On November 4, she wrote to Surveyor Gorman complaining of a man illegally encamped there. The man was subsequently fined at Port Macquarie for his trespass.[9]

Life never seemed easy for Isabella Mary Kelly.

In the late 1840s there were two unrelated occasions when Isabella Kelly took her contracted servants (as opposed to assigned servants) before the Bench at Dungog. This was done under the Masters and Servant Act, which sought to protect the rights of both parties.

On February 24, 1847, Isabella Kelly summonsed Thomas Grier with absconding from her service, meaning that Grier had broken his contract (usually twelve months) with her.

On Friday, October 22, the Clerk of Petty Sessions from

Dungog wrote to Miss Kelly informing her Grier had surrendered himself to the Dungog Bench, and had been released under his own recognisance of £5 bail. Miss Kelly was required to either attend on the following Friday to prosecute him, or if she did not intend prosecuting him, she was to let the Bench know by letter.[10]

The Dungog Deposition Book records that on October 29, with the sanction of the Bench, the two parties reached agreement on the dispute outside the Court, but did not record the agreement itself.[11]

On April 8, 1848, Isabella Kelly summonsed a second servant at Dungog. He was named Davis.[12] The case had previously been before a number of different Benches, so that two days later, Police Magistrate Thomas Cook wrote a letter to the Port Macquarie Bench seeking information:[13]

> ... The Plaintiff and Defendant have been working at cross-purposes to the annoyance of the different Benches and the obstruction of justice. In the absence of the prosecutrix [Kelly], who did not appear when the case was called, we thought it best to dismiss the Defendant until we could communicate with you on the subject, to learn the truth or falsehood of his statements. The more so, as he said you had cancelled his agreement with Miss Kelly, and otherwise given judgement against her.
>
> It should not be forgotten that the Plaintiff in this case is a Female, and the Defendant a plausible fellow, enough to talk down any woman. Miss Kelly may have her peculiar temper, but ... she has craved the protection of this Bench and it is our wish to afford it so that it does not interfere with your jurisdiction.

Magistrate Cook's use of the phrase "peculiar temper" suggests that he is well aware by now that Isabella Kelly will stand up and defend herself vigorously when she believes she has not been treated fairly. This was three years after Isabella Kelly had written to the Governor complaining that Cook and Rowley had not enforced sentences on convicts assigned to her, with Cook's attitude to Isabella Kelly in marked contrast to that of George Rowley.

Cook added a postscript to the letter, to the effect that since writing the above letter, Miss Kelly had arrived at Dungog, and swore to him that she had been delayed by floodwaters. She said the river and creeks had risen so quickly that an eighteen-year-old youth had been swept from his horse by the current and drowned. Cook said that Kelly still wanted the charges against Davis to be heard, and added that he thought she would be hard done by if the case was not enquired into.

On June 9, 1848, Davis was brought before the Dungog Bench charged by Miss Isabella Mary Kelly with generally stealing and slaughtering her cattle since the previous October, but in particular, "feloniously killing a bullock in the end of December or beginning of January last, for his own use, and without her knowledge or consent". Davis was given £50 bail to appear at a committal hearing.

The outcome of this affair is not recorded. It may be that it was transferred to Port Macquarie, for which there are no extant records.

Later in the same year, two men were charged before the Dungog Bench with slaughtering an ox belonging to Isabella Kelly, but the action was not initiated by her.

During March 1848, four valuable oxen belonging to Isabella Kelly got away at Cooly Camp on the Paterson River. Three had been recaptured, but the remaining ox remained on the loose and was often seen roaming around in the area. This ox was easily recognisable because of its distinctive horns: one turned up while the other formed a loop and turned down.

On August 22, 1848, at Clyde's View, on the Williams River, nine-year-old Thomas Logan, together with his younger brother, was on his way home from school, when he saw the bullock with very distinctive horns. He also noted the ox had an MK brand on its side, and together with another bullock branded differently, was being driven along the road by two men. When he got home, Thomas told his father, Thomas Logan Senior.

In the morning Logan Senior heard the report of a gun, and on investigation found George Stokes and Thomas Hughes with a slaughtered beast, which may have been a bullock or a cow. Hughes took the hide to a tanner, and although the brand missing, it was generally believed that the hide belonged to the bullock with unusual horns.

On December 1, Isabella Mary Kelly gave evidence before the Dungog Bench at the committal hearing of Hughes and Stokes:[14]

> [eleven bullocks] were again brought down by two of my own people named [Thomas] Turner and [Frank] McDonough, and left in charge of Mr McKay near this place. At this time I came down myself and went on with the cattle as far as Mr Holmes, and sold a number on the road, and drove four of them to Cooly Camp, to which place I accompanied them myself and had them placed in Cooly Camp paddock.
>
> They remained there for some time and I frequently saw them from the door. A black girl used to take them to water outside the paddock, and they broke away from her. I saw three of the bullocks near Clarencetown … I immediately informed Mr Holmes, who picked up two of them, and Mr McKay picked up the third. The fourth I have never seen since. …
>
> It was altogether a remarkable bullock, so quiet that the boy called it "sobersides" … I reared it myself and it was branded MK on the off side [by] my own hand alone. …
>
> I remember speaking to Mrs. Bugden … and told her if her boy would bring it in I would give him 5 shillings. …
>
> I have not heard anything of the missing beast till written to on the subject by Mr Abbott, Chief Constable, about a fortnight ago. I had given the bullock up as lost.

Here, in her own words, was another example of the way in which Isabella Kelly involved herself completely in the running of her property by herding and branding cattle.

In these committal hearings, the defendants were permitted to cross-examine the witnesses. In reply to a question by defendant Hughes, Isabella Kelly stated that it was not possible for the missing beast to be back on the Manning with the rest of her cattle, as she had recently mustered her cattle, and the bullock with the distinctive horns was definitely not there. The defendants were committed to stand their trial.

On February 17, 1849, Stokes and Hughes appeared before Mr Justice Dickinson, at the Maitland Circuit Court. While the Logan family initiated the prosecution, it appears that Isabella

Kelly took no part in the trial itself, as she was not called as a witness.[15]

On the evidence of nine-year-old Thomas Logan, Hughes and Stokes were found guilty of cattle stealing. The prisoners were sentenced to three years hard labour at Maitland gaol.

It hardly seems possible, that the evidence supplied at this trial could justify a gaol sentence: the stolen beast could not be identified as a bullock or a cow; the hide had the brand missing; and with no mention of the distinguishing horns. On the other hand, only *four* jurors needed to be convinced of the prisoners' guilt, rather than twelve.

Such was the seriousness of the charge of cattle stealing.

Joseph Andrews

5. Trouble with Neighbours

In 1845, six years after the arrival of Isabella Kelly, Joseph Andrews arrived in the Manning Valley, and took up residence on the property next door and down-river to Isabella Mary Kelly. Over the next twenty years Joseph Andrews would exert a major influence, both good and bad, on the affairs of Isabella Kelly.

Andrews was born at Ballycairn, Londonderry, Northern Ireland, on January 10, 1814, the fourth of eight children.[1] Although born in Ireland, the Andrews family were of Scottish descent, and always regarded themselves as Scottish.

Joseph's intellect must have been recognised at an early age, as the family was not wealthy, and despite having two elder brothers, Joseph was the only son to attend a University. He studied theology for four years at Glasgow University, with the intention of becoming a Presbyterian minister, but this did not eventuate.

Aged 21, Joseph married Ann Dickson, aged 16, in Glasgow, and decided to migrate to the colony of New South Wales under the leadership of the Rev John Dunmore Lang. Coincidently, Dr Lang had been a fellow passenger with Isabella Mary Kelly, on the *James* in 1834. Born in 1799, Lang[2] made the first of nine voyages to Australia in 1823, and Lang's first group of Presbyterian emigrants sailed to Australia in 1831.

Joseph Andrews was in a group of fifteen teachers, who travelled to Sydney on board the *Portland*, arriving on December 3, 1837. Dr Lang had selected the teachers, and in return for their passage money of £60, they had to sign a teaching contract.

During the voyage, Joseph and Ann's eighteen-month old baby, Samuel, died and was consigned to the deep. Joseph's brother Robert, younger by two years, accompanied him to Sydney on the *Portland*, setting up business as a saddler and harness-maker in Hunter Street, Sydney, where he became quite wealthy.

In Sydney Joseph was appointed Schoolmaster in the Parish

of St. Philip, and in June 1839, Ann Andrews gave birth to their second child, Agnes. Over the next twenty-two years, Ann bore fourteen more children, all but one becoming adults. Joseph transferred to Dunmore, on the Paterson River near Maitland, in 1840, where Andrew Lang, the brother of Rev Lang, had built a Presbyterian School on the property he owned there.

At the end of 1844, Joseph resigned from teaching and settled on a 705-acre property adjoining Isabella Mary Kelly's Mount George land, and renamed it Woodside, after his mother. Robert Andrews had bought the property for £129 several months previously, and in January 1847 sold it to brother Joseph for £500 – a fine example of fraternal enterprise.[3]

As the main road north from Maitland and Port Stephens passed through the Mount George and Woodside properties, Joseph Andrews soon discovered a constant stream of visitors was knocking on his door. Country hospitality of the time made it almost impossible to turn anyone away, so Joseph Andrews opened a hotel in July 1848, with travellers paying to stay there and drink there. A number of years later, as other hotels opened, Joseph closed his.[4]

Holding a liquor licence proved to be quite profitable, as well as making Joseph well known in the district, with the side benefit of knowing most of what was happening there.

In his first few years in the district, Joseph Andrews had a very cordial relationship with Isabella Kelly, and supported her as a witness in a court case involving cattle stealing. The evidence given by the various witnesses at this trial gives some insights into their lives as settlers.

Isabella Mary Kelly travelled to Stroud, to take out the warrant (evidently not trusting either the Bungay Bungay or Dungog Bench). The *Maitland Mercury* reported there had been an increase of cattle stealing in the district and that Miss Kelly had taken out a warrant for the arrest of "three notorious parties", adding that Miss Kelly "declared that instead of six hundred head of cattle, she can only muster one half of that number".[5]

Three weeks later, the *Maitland Mercury* reported the arrest of three men on charges of cattle stealing. It noted that, "The prisoners have long been suspected of being extensively engaged in cattle stealing, though proof, until the present instance, has not been procured against them." When their hut was searched, a large number of hides had been found with the brands cut out.

The two charged were William Branston, a shoemaker, and John Walker, both of whom had been previously questioned on similar offences but never charged. The third was released under bail but not charged.[6]

The trial took place in the Maitland Circuit Court on Monday February 15, 1847.[7] Circuit Courts, where judges and prosecutors travelled around the countryside, were necessary because of the difficulty of getting witnesses to appear at trials. It was very costly for witnesses both in the earnings they lost while away from their farms, and the expenditure on travel and accommodation.

The prisoners appeared before Mr Justice Dickinson, from the Supreme Court, and a jury of four men. The prosecutor was John Hubert Plunkett, Attorney General of New South Wales, with barrister William Purefoy appearing for the defence. After an opening address, outlining his case, the Attorney General called his prime witness, Kelly's servant boy, Francis (Frank) McDonough.

Frank told the court he was not sure how old he was – he thought he was twelve, because Miss Kelly had told him so. Miss Kelly took him from an Orphan School about three or four years ago, and he had lived with her since then. His job was to milk the cows – there were twelve of them – and to mind the cattle and horses. Miss Kelly had four working bullocks, and their names were Bluey, Rodney, Gilbert and Merryman.

One Wednesday about twelve o'clock, Frank said, he had been watching the cattle grazing near the Manning River, when he saw two horsemen driving off the four bullocks. He recognized the two men as being Walker and Branston, who lived on a property about a mile from Miss Kelly. He followed them, without them seeing him, and watched as they drove the bullocks across the river. Merryman broke away, but Walker rode after him and steered him across the river, assisted by his dog and some of his own bullocks in the lead. [Walker had some of his own bullocks grazing on Miss Kelly's pasture with her permission.] The cattle would not normally cross the river unless driven, and they never crossed at that section of the river. Once across the river the men and bullocks disappeared into the scrub.

Defence Attorney Purefoy could not elicit much from Frank under cross-examination. He did not know what month it occurred. None of the paddocks around there were fenced. The river was wide but not deep at the crossing. Miss Kelly had not quarrelled previously with either of the prisoners.

The prosecution called Miss Kelly, who deposed that on Wednesday, September 16, Frank had come running back about three o'clock and told her what had happened. She thought at first that the bullocks might have been taken across the river to Mr Edward's place, to be used for ploughing, but when she sent a man to check, she found that Mr Edwards had not borrowed them.

Under cross-examination, Kelly stated she had not told Frank what to say, she had told him to tell the truth. She had not offered him a reward if the prisoners were convicted.

Defence Attorney Purefoy spent quite some time re-examining Frank and then Miss Kelly again, trying to establish that there had been collusion on the story, hence making Frank's evidence tainted. It was not successful, but he did pick up some minor discrepancies in their stories.

The third prosecution witness, William Lamthier, deposed he was a shoemaker, who had been working for William Branston for twelve months. Walker had come to Branston's place in delicate health, about four months before the theft. Walker had some young bullocks and cows of his own. He particularly remembered the morning of September 16, when Branston and Walker had ridden off at eight o'clock in the morning, taking shoes with them to drop off to customers.

Branston's hut was high on the riverbank, Lamthier continued, and from his workshop, he could see all over the Flats. Later in the day he saw Walker and Branston return, driving bullocks across the river, but not at the usual crossing place. A couple of the bullocks belonged to Walker and Branston, but the others were not. On their return to the hut, Lamthier said to Branston, "You have been a long time away". Branston replied, "Yes, we have done for her bullocks now". On the following Sunday, Lamthier went to see Joseph Andrews and told him what he saw.

Joseph Andrews deposed that after William Lamthier came to

see him on the Sunday, he had then gone and told Miss Kelly. Branston and Walker went away for a short period. On their return, Branston told him they had taken some bullocks down to Redbank [half way between present-day Taree and Old Bar] and sold them to Mr Denny, a timber cutter. He told Branston that little Frank had seen him take the bullocks, and that Miss Kelly was blaming him for their theft. Branston denied it and was dismissive of Frank's story, but he did not say anything to Branston about what Lamthier told him.

Under cross-examination, Joseph Andrews described Branston's land as good and his hut as tolerably comfortable. Some of Branston's cattle were grazing on Miss Kelly's run. Cattle would occasionally stray and, especially in winter, they would head for the scrub. Since then Branston had borrowed four of Andrews' bullocks, and they were still with Branston.

That completed a strong case for the prosecution. Purefoy then outlined the case for the defence. The first defence witness was Robert Searle, the former convict servant of Mary Cann, and now her husband.

Searle deposed that he lived on a farm on the Manning, about 15 or 16 miles away from Branston's farm. Both Branston and Walker had called at his farm on the evening of Tuesday, September 15, staying that night and all of the next day. They departed on the Thursday morning. He was absolutely sure of the day and the date because his step-son, William Chapman, had left his place on the Wednesday.

Under cross-examination by the Attorney General, Searle stated he came to the colony as a convict, fifteen years ago. He had been assigned to work for James Cann, on the Paterson River. After Mr Cann committed suicide, Mrs Cann and the family moved to the Manning River. As an assigned servant he had been permitted to move with the family. He had received his conditional pardon about two years ago, and six months ago he married Mrs Cann.

The prosecution could not budge Searle on his alibi for Branston and Walker. At this point Mr Justice Dickinson asked Searle if he "fully understood the nature of an oath". He warned him of the penalties "in this world and the next" for falsely swearing on oath.

The Trials of Isabella Mary Kelly

Mr Purefoy called William Chapman as his next defence witness who corroborated Searle's alibi for Walker and Branston. Under cross-examination the nineteen-year old stated that he occasionally went to church, when in Sydney, but not in the Manning Valley as there were no churches there. He had known Walker, who had been a stockman for his mother, for about three years. He could swear that Walker and Branston had no cattle or stock whips with them.

As the third defence witness had not turned up, the defence was complete. When the Attorney General summed up, he made the point that, even if the jury believed the evidence of Searle and Chapman, this did not necessarily jeopardise the evidence of Frank and Lamthier. Their recollections of which day the offence occurred might have been inaccurate – it was possible for *both* the prosecution and the defence witnesses to be telling the truth.

Being able to say *precisely* which day events happened was always a problem with country people giving evidence in trials. In their day-to-day lives they could never recall the day of the week, the day and, often, not even the month. Usually they relied on a comparison with some other important event occurring. Mr Justice Dickinson, in his summing up, stated that he agreed with this point made by the prosecutor.

The jury did not retire very long before returning with a verdict of guilty. The Judge sentenced the prisoners to *ten years transportation.*

The sentence was well received by the community. Several weeks later the *Maitland Mercury* recorded that after Branston and Walker were imprisoned, many cattle had been retrieved from their possession, and gave high recommendation to Miss Kelly: "Considerable praise is due to that lady for the firmness she displayed from first to last in bringing the misguided and wretched men to justice."[8]

By 1851 Isabella Mary Kelly was generally at war with many of her neighbours. The cordial relationship she had initially held with Joseph Andrews had deteriorated completely, so that they were no longer on speaking terms.[9] Much of the problem was caused by stock animals – horses, cattle, sheep, pigs – straying onto

Trouble with Neighbours

the other's property, often causing damage to crops or gardens or fencing, or just grazing.

Andrews' pigs caused more trouble than any of the other animals as they could be extremely damaging to stockyards and gardens. There were upwards of two hundred[10] of them and were much harder to control as they were not confined. Kelly had some pigs, but only a small number.

Another problem for Isabella Kelly was the occasional disappearance of a horse, apparently stolen. According to Joseph Andrews, she would become suspicious that a particular person had taken the horse or knew something about its disappearance, and accuse them of taking the horse, often getting it wrong and accusing people who were completely innocent.[11]

All these problems were accentuated by the fact that the track north from Gloucester, passed through the Mount George property itself, as well as the Woodside property. Not-so-close neighbours taking stock south, or bringing stock into the district, of necessity had to pass through Kelly's property because of the river crossing adjacent to Mount George.

Isabella Kelly was concerned that stock passing through her property often spread out over the property, eating the grass, which her own stock needed. It was not unusual for farmers to pay a property owner to let their cattle or sheep graze on his property. Kelly had taken to the practice of impounding stock

This late nineteeth century photo looks across the Manning Flats. The Manning River is unseen at the foot of Mount Gangat. Part of Woodside is in the foreground.

that strayed from the track, over her property, and charging a release fee – a practice that, although perfectly legal, caused much ill feeling.

On January 2, 1851, at about midday, Isabella Kelly thought she heard the bleating of sheep, in the distance.[12] Kelly and Mary Canning went out to check, and discovered over a thousand sheep spreading out over her property. (Recently Isabella Kelly had employed Mary Canning for four weeks to look after the place, while she was away on business. When Kelly returned, she was very displeased with Mary Canning's performance, and dismissed her. Canning had now been re-employed by Kelly for a few days work, probably on a trial basis.)

With the help of Mary Canning, she herded about six hundred of the sheep into her stockyard. Kelly rounded up a second lot with the assistance of Edward Reece, one of her workers, and Robert Whitehead, the shepherd accompanying the sheep. As they were putting these sheep in the stockyard, some of those already captured escaped.

At this point John Brislane, a man she had never seen before, rode up, and clearly, he was very angry. Mary Canning screamed as she thought Brislane was going ride over the top of Miss Kelly, but as he pulled up with his horse's head over Kelly, she gave the horse a hit on the nose with the switch in her hand.

"What are you about?" Brislane demanded. Brislane had been overseer on the Bungay Bungay Property for George Rowley for the last six years. Kelly told him she was impounding the sheep and charging 2d per head for their release. This was not the first time she had encountered problems with Rowley's sheep.

John Brislane went over to the stockyard and started removing rails in order to release the sheep. Charles Mathers, an employee of James Atkinson of Brimbin, was at Mount George buying some cattle for his master. Kelly asked him to put the rails back again, and as he did so, Brislane knocked the rails down again. Kelly went to the house and got a chain and lock, asking the men to fasten the rails with it. A struggle then ensued between Brislane and Edward Reece for the chain.

While the struggle continued, Patrick "Paddy" Connolly rode up. He was a settler, who had moved into the neighbourhood with his wife and family in the last twelve months.

Connolly had been a visitor to Mount George only the week before, when Kelly gave him a drink of Porters (a brewed beer). Kelly told Connolly to go away and mind his own business, but Connolly grabbed her by the neck and kicked her in the back, knocking her down. Brislane and Connolly turned on Reece, who departed the scene on foot, at some speed, with rocks thrown after him.

Brislane and Connolly then turned on Mathers, who was standing by the fence. Brislane knocked him down. As Mathers got up and tried to run away, Kelly also decided to make a run for it, but Brislane knocked her down by a blow to the head with the handle of his stock whip. He then hit her with the whip on the arm and shoulder – she thought it was about eight or nine times. Brislane and Connolly drove the sheep out of the stockyard, and departed.

Isabella Kelly went to Stroud to swear out a warrant for the arrest of Brislane and Connolly. With George Rowley as the only Magistrate on the Manning, and being the owner of the sheep, there was no point going to Bungay Bungay. A committal hearing was held at Stroud on February 13, 1851.[13]

In her deposition, Kelly said she heard the sheep and went looking for the shepherd, John Whitehead. She found him lying on the side of a log, and told him she intended to charge Rowley 2d. per head, as Rowley's sheep had passed through property before in shearing time and eaten all her grass. The shepherd said he could not control the sheep as his dogs would not work, but when she called the shepherd's dog Lassy, the dog helped her and Mary Canning pen the sheep. She impounded the sheep because they had not kept to the proper road that passed through her property.

Next, Mary Canning gave her deposition, which contradicted Isabella Kelly on a number of points. John Brislane had only touched Miss Kelly lightly on the shoulder with his finger, which resulted in Miss Kelly calling him a scoundrel. She did not see any lumps on Miss Kelly's head after the fracas, but had seen bruising on her arm.

Under questioning from the Bench, Mary Canning stated that Kelly had struck Brislane when he touched her on the shoulder. She had not told anyone that Brislane had offered her marriage, Canning said, and before this hearing Brislane had told her to tell the truth no matter what he should suffer. Mr Andrews had pointed out the boundary line between his place and Miss Kelly's to her, and she remarked that the sheep were on his land when Miss Kelly impounded them.

Edward Reece deposed that Brislane said he would get the sheep out if it cost him his last drop of blood. He punched Brislane in the mouth after Brislane had struck his hand with a rail, skinning his knuckles. He saw Connolly kick Miss Kelly twice. After Brislane left with sheep, he felt the lumps on the top of Miss Kelly's head. The next day, when he was driving some cattle along a public road, Connolly invited him to his house, but he declined. Brislane and Connolly then set their dogs onto him and dispersed the cattle.

Charles Mathers gave evidence similar to that of Reece.

John Brislane voluntarily offered his defence. He called at Woodside and spoke to Mrs. Andrews, who told him the shepherd had the sheep there for about two hours, but had left half an hour previously. He found Miss Kelly impounding the sheep, and offered to pay her for any damage the sheep had done, as the sheep "had been harassed at Bungay and suffered much, owing to the scarcity of grass during shearing". Miss Kelly became abusive and struck him with a stick.

Shepherd Robert Whitehead had little to say. He showed Mr Andrews where the sheep were impounded; Andrews said it was on his land. He did say before Court opened that his wages and job with Mr Rowley depended on the testimony he gave today.

Joseph Andrews deposed that both Canning and Whitehead had shown him where the sheep were impounded and it was his land. Patrick Connolly declined to make any statement in his defence.

The Magistrate committed both Brislane and Connolly for trial on two charges each of assault and rescuing impounded sheep.

On Thursday March 6th, the Circuit Court arrived in Maitland on one of its bi-annual sittings. Like the Branston/Walker trial, Brislane and Connolly appeared before Mr Justice Dickinson and a jury of four. Once again the Attorney General John Plunkett prosecuted the case on Isabella Kelly's behalf, and William Purefoy appeared for the defendants.[14]

Isabella Mary Kelly deposed that she thought Connolly was intoxicated at the time, but Brislane was not. After Brislane had beaten her, she had dragged herself about a hundred yards over to the house, and sat on the steps. The men had used bad language and kicked her bonnet around the yard.

Under cross-examination from Mr Purefoy, Kelly stated that she knew they were Rowley's sheep before she seized them. Mr Rowley's sheep had been annoying her and had destroyed her property for the last eight years. She knew her boundary line, and the sheep were definitely trespassing when she seized them.

She never struck Brislane, Isabella Kelly declared, and after Brislane struck Reece with a chain, she said to her men, "Surely two of you are enough for one man. If he beats you, beat him." Brislane refused to pay the 2d per head. Brislane swore at her and she replied, "You scoundrel, I'll make you pay for this."

After Brislane had departed, Kelly said, Mary Canning had refused to go with her to the place where the sheep had been impounded [to identify where the sheep were impounded, preparing for a court case]. Canning said she would rather give evidence for Mr Rowley.

Edward Reece corroborated Kelly's evidence up to the point where he ran away. After that he heard Miss Kelly screaming, but could not see exactly what Brislane and Connolly were doing. Charles Mathers gave similar evidence.

Mr Purefoy opened the defence by claiming Miss Kelly was not a creditable witness, and her evidence should not be believed. Secondly, the place where the sheep had been seized was not on her land, and hence, she had seized them illegally. Thirdly, he could not justify the behaviour of the defendants, but the illegal seizure gave them extenuating circumstances. Perhaps the defendants used more force than was required, but they had been greatly provoked. Connolly was only trying to protect Brislane from what Connolly thought was unfair violence on him.

As the first defence witness, Mary Canning, deposed she and Miss Kelly had initially seized the sheep about a quarter of a mile [400 metres] from Miss Kelly's stockyard. She knew the spot where they were seized, and afterwards pointed it out to Mr Andrews.

Canning's account of Brislane's behaviour was similar to Miss Kelly's, but less violent on his part. Brislane asked for the sheep to be let out of the stockyard, but Miss Kelly said she wanted to count the sheep and have 2d. per head. Brislane put his hand gently on Kelly's shoulder and begged her to let them go, but Miss Kelly struck him with whatever she had in her hand, saying how dare a scoundrel like him lay hands on her.

That evening, Canning said, Miss Kelly called her into the bedroom and showed the black bruising on her arm. Miss Kelly said to her, "Look, Mary, where Brislane and Connolly beat me. Will it not be a horrid thing, Mary, for those men to go into court after beating me in such a way as this. But, Mary, I will have sport in court, bringing this charge against them. The judge and jury will think it very wrong of them for such doings, and they will be hooted out of court." Miss Kelly laughed as she said this.

Under cross-examination Canning denied she said to Miss Kelly that if Kelly had been nicer to her, she would have been her witness. She did not know Miss Kelly's land generally, but she knew the spot, where the sheep were seized.

The next defence witness was Joseph Andrews. He produced a sketch of the locality, claiming it to be more accurate than the Government one shown to the Court earlier. He had no doubt the sheep were seized on his land and not Kelly's. He always heard of Brislane as a quiet, sober and careful man. Connolly was a quiet, industrious man.

Andrews then betrayed the ill-feeling he felt for Isabella Kelly. He had known Miss Kelly for some years, and would believe her oath, only if it was corroborated by other evidence. He would hesitate otherwise. Cross-examined, Andrews deposed that Miss Kelly had frequently impounded his cattle, but he had never impounded her cattle.

George Rowley, the owner of the sheep, deposed he was a magistrate. He had been driving cattle and sheep along this road, which passed through Mr Andrews' land and Miss Kelly's land, for years, as there was often no other passable road. Brislane, his employee for six years; was a quiet, careful man, and respectful in his manner. Miss Kelly had appeared several times before him as a magistrate. He would not now believe her on her oath, although he had done so before.

Cross-examined by Mr Plunkett, Rowley said he did not believe Miss Kelly on her oath, because she had come before him,

Trouble with Neighbours

in his role as a magistrate. On one occasion she had faithfully promised the Bench that she would pay an award at a later date, but when the constable went to collect the money on that date, Miss Kelly said she would not pay and never intended to pay. No, he could not swear that she had not paid him since then.

The Attorney General addressed the jury and the Judge summed up. The jury retired to consider their verdict, taking only a few minutes before returning with a verdict of guilty. Justice Dickinson sentenced both Brislane and Connolly to *twelve months* prison.

Rowley's testimony that Kelly reneged on paying a debt is hard to believe, but there is no other source material to either confirm or deny it.

Joseph Andrews, in his enmity of Isabella Kelly, had joined Magistrate George Rowley in declaring his belief that Kelly regularly lied under oath. For Isabella Mary Kelly, who always regarded herself as a Lady, this was a monstrous allegation. It struck at the very heart of her honour.

George Rowley would take every opportunity he could get to repeat this testimony that Kelly had lied under oath on many occasions.

Joseph Andrews would come to regret his testimony.

John Brislane was born in Tipperary, Ireland, and came to the colony as a convict. He had been charged and convicted of grievous assault, and transported on the *Forth* in 1835.[15] Receiving his ticket-of-leave in 1839, he may have worked for the A. A. Company before becoming an employee of George Rowley.

Whatever the relationship between John Brislane and Mary Canning may have been, no marriage took place. Brislane appears normally to have been a good citizen. Perhaps it was simply the sight of this diminutive female preventing his progress that caused him to so violently lose his temper. Why not just ask Kelly to count the sheep and let her sort it out with Rowley?

Patrick Connolly, an Irish Catholic born in County Monaghan in 1812, arrived in the colony as a convict in 1836. He was convicted on February 29, 1836 of abduction and received a sentence of seven years transportation.[16] He could not read or write, signing his name with an "X".[17]

Connolly married Sarah O'Neill in East Maitland, in 1843. He may have met Brislane in his eight years as an employee of the A. A. Company. Connolly and his family settled at Khatumbuhl in the Manning Valley, not far from Mount George.

In April 1851, Sarah Connolly petitioned Governor Fitzroy for mitigation of her husband's sentence. She wrote that she was "left with three infant children in an unprotected state in the bush".[18] She said that her husband's attack on Miss Kelly had been wholly unpremeditated and had been caused by him being under the influence of liquor. Attached to the letter were a number of testimonials from Phillip Gidley King, the Prison Chaplain and others.

When asked for his recommendation, Justice Dickinson wrote that Connolly and Brislane had been convicted on very clear evidence, and while they had been very unmanly, they probably thought they had good reason to free the sheep from Miss Kelly. He had read the references to Connolly's good character, and had decided to recommend that both Connolly and Brislane be released from prison after they had served six months of their twelve-month sentence.[19]

As a result of Sarah Connolly's petition, both Connolly and Brislane were released in September and returned to the Manning Valley. They both lived long lives, reaching the next century, and became reputable citizens and family men.

In 1911, a *Wingham Chronicle* article described Isabella Kelly as "an undersized woman of a decidedly masculine cast of character". The article discussed the incident involving John Brislane and Patrick Connolly, saying that the two Irishmen "laid hands on" Kelly and even though "the assault was not serious", they were each given a gaol sentence, which "was at variance with public sympathy".[20]

Paddy Connolly grew in popularity as he aged despite being gaoled on another occasion for cattle stealing. He had the image of an Irish rogue who liked his drink. Connolly's Creek is named after him.

The crossing of the Dawson River at Brimbin is the only place in the Manning Valley currently named in memory of Isabella Mary Kelly – and it is incorrectly named.

6. Bushranger Stories

The most commonly used words used in connection with Isabella Mary Kelly were "eccentric" and "masculine" (because she was doing "men's" work). There were rumours, though, that she dressed like a man and mounted a horse like a man, a practice greatly despised in that era. It was the start of the mythology of the "Notorious Miss Kelly".

Twentieth century drawings of Kelly for articles in the magazines or books usually depicted her astride a horse in the male fashion, and with two large pistols in holsters strapped to her hips.

Nothing could have been further from the truth. While Isabella was expert on a horse, chasing horses or cattle down gullies and zigzagging through wooded areas, she always rode *side-saddle*, in the female manner, and never straddled a horse like a man.[1]

Isabella Kelly was always a *lady*.

But it was the pistols that really intrigued people – so unusual was it for a woman to possess one, let alone be able to use it. And it was the pistols that gave rise to the stories of her entanglements with bushrangers.

Those contemporaries who wrote about Miss Kelly always mentioned the pistol (or pistols) hidden beneath her dress – yet no one said they actually *saw* Miss Kelly with a pistol. Joseph Andrews, living next door to her for so many years, said he heard she had pistols but he had never *seen* her with a pistol.[2]

Isabella Kelly's own security must have been a great concern to her, as she was a woman, single and alone in such a remote area. Robbery and rape, even murder, must have been a constant worry. Kelly certainly did not carry a pistol on her hip, as many tabloid newspaper articles have suggested. At the same time, it may have been the one story about herself she was keen to promote – in the interests of her own safety.

The Trials of Isabella Mary Kelly

A story, which appeared in the *Wingham Chronicle* during the 1930s, told of a visit by Miss Kelly to the McLeod family, and of her sleeping in the room of their young daughter, Catherine:[3]

> On several occasions this lady arrived late in the evening, and asked to be furnished with a bed. Of course hospitality was the order of those days, and no one was ever turned away. But as the family at this time was large, the only bed that could be spared for a lady was in a room where Catherine and her sister slept.
>
> There were two beds in this room, and the two girls slept in one, and Miss Kelly in the other. It is well-known that Miss Kelly always carried pistols, supposed to have been loaded. These she would lay beside her bed, or under her pillow while she slept.
>
> She was accompanied by a large watch dog. On retiring she would say to the dog, "Lie there" – pointing to a spot beside the bed. There the dog would take up his position, and not stir away all night. Naturally the girls were terrified, and if they were restless and happened to stir during the night, an ominous growl would be heard from the dog. She was asked to leave the dog outside but plainly refused.

Any settler needed to use guns in the operation of their station or for their own protection, and Isabella Kelly was certainly armed. Charles Langley of the firm Rich, Langley and Butchart, who were stock agents in selling her cattle for many years, recalled visiting her Mount George property in the early days:[4]

> Yes, I knew her for years. She is an eccentric woman. She was going to shoot me one night, the first time I ever met her. I went to her home one night, coming down the Manning, when it was raining very hard, and she thought I was a bushranger, I suppose. It was a long time before she would let me in.

One of the first anecdotal stories to be printed about Isabella Kelly and firearms came from Henry Edwards, a Cundletown bootmaker, who became very popular as a writer of verse and a columnist for the *Manning River Times* and other local newspapers, always writing under the pseudonym of "Hawkeye".

In 1913 Hawkeye wrote:[5]

> Miss Kelly became, and continued for some time,

monarch of all she surveyed. There is no doubt she was a martinet [strict disciplinarian] and certainly only a remarkable woman could keep up the lonely independent life she led.

She always carried arms. Many travellers passed through. One night three drovers camped near her house.

In the morning, the younger member of the party went up to ask for some milk, and passed a large dead turkey lying by the track, about 30 yards from the house. He mentioned the fact when he was at the house.

"Yes", said Miss Kelly, "I shot it during the night. I saw it in the moonlight and thought it was one of you fellows sneaking up to the house. So I shot it!"

The drovers moved on immediately after breakfast.

Often, as in this case, there was an obvious flaw in the story: in the morning the drovers seemed unaware a shot had been fired during the night, yet any such shot fired at night would have echoed over a great distance.

One can see in this article the seeds of many of the nonsense stories that would continue to grow about Isabella Mary Kelly throughout the twentieth century – her use of a gun; her callousness to the man she thought she shot; the use of the word "monarch".

In guaranteeing the accuracy of his story, Hawkeye prefaced the article by stating that his "authorities" for the stories in the article were "among the most unimpeachable on the Manning River, and vouched for on reliable data".

Edward Hunt highlighted the use of guns by Isabella Kelly in a novel he wrote, which was serialised in the *Wingham Chronicle* over twenty-five weeks beginning in February 1958, but was not published elsewhere.[6] At least the Church of England minister warned his readers that "where research fails, imagination may succeed" – and not much research was done.

Beginning with the false premise that the main street of Wingham, Isabella Street, was named after Isabella Kelly, Hunt wrote eight chapters on the life of Isabella Kelly as the sixteen-year-old leader of the Black Kelly Gang of outlaws in County Clare, Ireland. The jilting of Isabella Kelly follows this, as the aptly-named Capt Coldair leaves her standing at the altar.

And so it went.

The Trials of Isabella Mary Kelly

There were two core myths on Isabella Kelly: one was her cruelty to convicts; the other was the story of Edward Davis and his gang of bushrangers bailing her up.

In 1840, Edward Denny Day, a Police Magistrate, had been in charge of the posse which captured bushranger Edward Davis and his gang in a shoot-out, leading to their hanging in the following year. The Davis Gang (known contemporarily as the 'Jewboy Gang' because Davis was Jewish) had roamed the Hunter Valley and surrounds, with a hideout claimed to be at Pilcher's Mountain near Dungog.

The story involving Isabella Kelly with bushrangers originated in *Smith's Weekly*, a tabloid magazine printed in Sydney between 1919 and 1953. Throughout the 1920s, each weekly edition contained an article about convicts or bushrangers, bearing the imprimatur of fact. Most of the articles were written by the "Man in the Mask"[7] with readers presuming the secret identity of the author enabled him to write the *truth* in his historical articles, without fear of retribution from anyone. At the same time it ignored the fact that the publisher was still legally responsible for the material the magazine published, and for this reason, there was never any mention of people like George Rowley, Henry Flett or Joseph Andrews.

The understanding that the story would attract a greater readership if thought to be true rather than fictional has a parallel with the modern-day "based on a true story" phrase which characterises so many movies. As a result, the articles took a true event or some real characters, usually convicts or bushrangers, and freely embellished them, adding dialogue and a drawing, often by Stan Cross, the noted illustrator.

Gordon Bennett, a resident of Dungog and owner of the *Dungog Chronicle*, was the "Man in the Mask",[8] with the result that his articles included number of stories from around the Dungog district about Captain Thomas Cook the Police Magistrate and bushrangers led by Edward Davis. Many of these articles appeared in Bennett's *Dungog Chronicle* after their appearance in *Smith's Weekly* but not under Bennett's name.

Bennett may have drawn some inspiration from the novel

"Castle Vane" by J. H. M. Abbott,[9] published in 1920, which contained fictionalised episodes of the Edward Davis bushranging gang, reaching a climax with their capture by Edward Denny Day. In a *Dungog Chronicle* article written under his own name, Gordon Bennett reminded readers that the novel "Castle Vane" was "fiction with a certain basis of historical fact",[10] but gave no such warning about the articles he wrote under his nom-de-plume of the "Man in the Mask".

In 1924, the seminal article on Isabella Mary Kelly and bushrangers appeared. Although not attributed to the Man in the Mask, its detailed knowledge of the Dungog district makes it obvious that it was written by Bennett. Entitled "The Discomfiture of a Termagant"[11] (a nagging, scolding woman or shrew), there were subheadings of "Scorn for Bushrangers", "The She-Devil Fights" and "Helpless, But Biting".

In this story, Isabella Kelly is in the Dungog district in September 1840 with two of her convicts, named Charles Mathers and Edward Reece. After telling Magistrate Cook she is not afraid of any bushrangers, she is captured when a gang of bushrangers, led by Thomas Buckingham, throw a sack over her. Assisting Buckingham are three members of the Davis Gang, but not Edward Davis himself.

The spurs on Kelly's heels injure one bushranger as they rob her of £125. One of the assailants, named Alban, is a former convict assigned to Kelly and he tries to whip Kelly in retaliation for the cruelty he has suffered at her hands, but Buckingham physically prevents him. After the bushrangers ride off, she is freed by Mathers and Reece. Taking a pistol which was hidden under the flap of her saddle, Kelly then rides after the bushrangers. Catching up to the five bushrangers, she charges at them. As they flee and escape, Alban drops £25 when shot in the arm by Kelly. Later Kelly tells Magistrate Cook it was worth losing £100 to see the look on the faces of the bushrangers as she charged at them. (The complete story appears in the appendix.)

Mathers and Reece were the two men who defended Kelly when she was attacked by Brislane and Connolly in 1851, but they were not convicts, and may not have been in the district in 1840. One can see a number of similarities to that case in this story: Kelly was actually whipped by Brislane; Mathers and Reece were unable to protect her; Kelly had the gumption to resist her attackers. And the committal hearing of the case was in the Dungog record books, where one suspects Bennett gained much of his inspiration for his stories.

In 1928 came the story "Gun-woman of the Manning",[12] printed in *Smith's Weekly* and the *Dungog Chronicle*, with a sub-heading of "When a bushranger crossed swords with Miss Kelly – and lost". In this story a convict named Thring arrives in Sydney in 1838 and gets himself assigned to the A. A. Company in Gloucester, as he has known Miss Kelly from before his arrival in the colony, and has a debt to settle with her. He turns bushranger and, with another man named Fenning, invades her property.

Thring wants her to sign documents, after which he tells her he will rob the place and burn her house down. Kelly turns the tables on him and, snatching a pistol out of a draw, shoots him without seriously wounding him. She then captures Fenning, and takes both men to Magistrate Cook in Dungog, warning the Magistrate not to let them loose or she will come back and flog the Magistrate personally.

The opening sentence stated that Lambert Thring, Convict No. 11652, arrived on the *Elizabeth* in 1838, convicted of forgery and was transported for seven years. This had all the semblance of fact, and may well have been true, but with no disclaimer, most readers would assume the rest of the story to be factual rather than fictional.

An article entitled "Amazon of the Manning" by C. K. Thompson, which appeared in a magazine named "Famous Detective Stories"[13] in 1947, included a drawing of Kelly carrying a pistol in a holster on her hip, and kicking an apparently unconscious man in the ribs.

> One day at the end of 1840, Miss Kelly set off from Brimbin with a dray load of hides and tallow to be sold at Maitland. Two convicts were in charge of the dray and she accompanied them on horseback.
>
> On the return trip, as she was crossing the range at Wallarobba, she was bailed up by the Jewboy gang of bushrangers …
>
> They tied her to the wheel of the dray, took a pistol from

her, stole the £60 she had got for the hides and tallow, and departed.

As soon as they had gone, Isabella ordered the convicts to set her free, got another pistol which she had hidden in her saddlebag, mounted her horse and set out after the gang.

She caught them up after a five miles' chase and opened fire. One bullet struck Marshall in the shoulder, dropping him to the ground. He had a fair amount of money on him, and Miss Kelly took the lot. Then, having kicked him soundly in the ribs, she set off again after the rest of the gang, which had scattered in the bush.

… the story is that they [the bushrangers] kept away from their lair at Pilcher's Mountain for some time, in case this fiend in woman's form should seek them out and liquidate them.

MANNING RIVER AMAZON
BY C. K. THOMPSON

The title page of the article on Isabella Mary Kelly in "True Detective Stories" of July 1947.

The story is an anachronism and forgets that in 1840 pistols were of the single-shot percussion type, which took about two minutes to reload, with the consequence that most bushrangers tended to carry at least six pistols. That one person, with one single-shot pistol, could rout five armed bushrangers is an impossible story, whose only inspiration came from the fact that Isabella Kelly was a *woman* who could use a pistol.

The Trials of Isabella Mary Kelly

Thompson's story is basically the same as the 1924 article by the Man in the Mask in *Smith's Weekly* entitled "The Discomfiture of a Termagant" except bushranger Edward Davis has been *substituted* for Thomas Buckingham.

Reading through the rest of Thompson's article in conjunction with the Man in the Mask articles of the 1920s, the reader can see the many influences originating there. The author says he heard many of these stories about Isabella Mary Kelly on a recent visit to the Manning Valley.

This version of the bushranger story was repeated in *A Treasury of Australian Folk Tales and Traditions* by Bill Beatty in 1960 with one small addition: after retrieving her stolen £60 from the bushrangers, Kelly in turn robs the bushrangers of their own money.[14]

In 1963, James Holledge printed a similar version in *Australia's Wicked Women*.[15]

Also in 1963 came a brief reference to Isabella Kelly in the book the *The Bushrangers* by William Joy and Tom Prior:[16]

> 'The Jewboy' and his gang caught a tartar, however, when they held up Isabella Kelly, a red-headed termagant of the Manning River area, who thought nothing of giving her assigned servants a sound flogging herself.
>
> Isabella, the story goes, not only chased the gang and recovered the money they stole from her, but conceived a tender passion for the dark-haired handsome Jewboy.
>
> She became a regular visitor to their hideout with food and ammunition and is said to have become so amorously exacting that 'The Jewboy' fled to another district to avoid her.

This was a nice spicy twist – Edward Davis was unable to satisfy the lust of Isabella Kelly. The use of the word "termagant" is reminiscent of the *Smith's Weekly* article involving bushranger Thomas Buckingham.

An "historical" article about Isabella Mary Kelly appeared in Sydney's afternoon daily newspaper, *The Sun*, in 1975 under the heading "Jilted Girl Became Queen of the Manning". After being robbed and then released by her convicts, Kelly chases the gang on her horse Calendar, catches them, and wounds Marshall:[17]

> ... She reloaded as she stood over the wounded man and kicked him viciously in the ribs until he agreed to lead her to

the gang's hideout.

After returning to the dray and ordering the convicts to proceed to Brimbin, Isabella Kelly set out with Marshall for the Jewboy's lair on Pilcher Mountain.

There the amorous-minded woman got her money back from the admiring Davis and proceeded to charm the whole bushranger brood. For weeks thereafter she rode secretly to the bushrangers' camp. She took the men food and ammunition and according to local gossip distributed her favours generously among them.

Indeed the hot-blooded woman's ardour was such that the romantic bushland trysts were finally ended when the outlaws became sated with love. Without informing Isabella Kelly they quit the hideout and rode south ...

Soured anew by this experience, Isabella Kelly returned to the seclusion of her properties.

Now the *whole gang* were unable to satisfy the lust of Isabella Kelly.

In 1985, James Holledge, repeated his version of the story as an "historical" article in the Sydney newspaper, the *Sunday Telegraph*, using a heading of "Isabella Kelly – a bitter, sadistic hellcat of a woman" and with subheadings of "Sex-hungry tyrant lived by law of the lash" and "Treated her convicts as a male harem". Accompanying the story were photographs of Isabella Kelly and a scene of old Dungog, reinforcing the authenticity of the article.[18]

The most recently published article on Isabella Mary Kelly was printed in 1996 by the *Daily Telegraph* under the title of "Isabella Kelly, tyrant of the Manning River" with a subheading of "Gun-toting sadist forced convicts to join her harem", beneath the only known photo of Isabella Mary Kelly.[19]

This article was a cumulation of all the allegedly historical articles on Isabella Kelly that had preceded it. All of these writers of the tabloid press owed a debt to Gordon Bennett, the Man in the Mask.

In 1985, Wilf Connors published his book *Pioneering Days Around Taree*, in which two chapters were devoted to the story of Isabella Mary Kelly.[20] Here was one of the rare occasions when a creditable account of her story was published.

The Trials of Isabella Mary Kelly

But Connors included the story of Kelly being held up by the Davis bushranging gang. He says this story came down to him in his family from his ancestors, Ben and Mary Saville, who he claims were on friendly terms with Isabella Kelly. Connors says that Kelly wrote down her story and gave it to them, but it was later swept away in a flood.

Despite this, Wilf Connors was a lone voice trying to set the record straight.[21]

Les Murray, the internationally acclaimed poet, was just one of many residents of the Manning Valley to be taken in by the scuttlebutt about Isabella Mary Kelly. The poem "On the North Coast Train", which appeared in the literary magazine *Quadrant* in 2003, has Isabella Mary Kelly sleeping with bushrangers, poisoning aborigines and flogging convicts.[22]

Murray has been as much a victim of the tabloid press as the rest of the Manning Valley. Perhaps someday a different poem will be written.

The story of Isabella Kelly being bailed up by the Davis Gang was never mentioned by *any* of her contemporaries. At least *one* of a number of settlers, who wrote about the pistols, would definitely have written about any brush Kelly had with bushrangers, if it ever occurred. Nor has any newspaper report or official document from the nineteenth century been found to cite it.

It beggars belief that Kelly could have recovered money stolen from her by bushrangers at the point of a pistol in 1840, and the first reference to it, *from any source*, is in the 1920s.

There is another reason why this bushranger story (and all the other stories) was able to grow. Isabella Mary Kelly was always a woman alone, even more so after her death. She had no descendants and, so far as is known, no close relatives living in New South Wales.

There was *no one* to defend her reputation.

7. Fire

There is no detailed description of Isabella Kelly given by her contemporaries. Even when Isabella entered Darlinghurst Gaol, there was no detailed description of her as there was for other prisoners. The few descriptions usually commented only on her shortness, suggesting she was about five foot (152 cm) or a little more.

The only photograph of Isabella Mary Kelly that has survived to the present day (and possibly the only one taken) is full-length and depicts her leaning on a high-backed chair with a riding crop in her hand. The photo is rather poorly focused and does not give a sharp picture of her face, which has the generally hard appearance of most pioneering women. Even though it is a black and white photograph, her hair does look decidedly black.

Many of the tabloids wrote that Isabella Kelly was a fiery redhead, presumably because she was Irish. While she may not have had red hair, she certainly had the fire. All who met her seemed to agree she was hot tempered, cantankerous or just generally feisty, while she herself admitted to a "hasty"[1] temper. Moreover, she would not be stood over and told what to do, especially by those men who expected her gentle compliance with anything they said. But worse than that, she was a woman who spoke her mind.

Men were threatened by her behaviour. She did not adopt the role expected of a woman – obedient to a man – a wife to a husband, a daughter to a father. In a sense Isabella Kelly was a direct challenge to male supremacy in colonial society – and her challenge would be answered.

Women were scandalised by her conduct. Although she had female servants working for her in her house, she was often a woman *alone* among men (usually with a young boy servant), and doing men's work. Sometimes she needed to camp out on a track overnight and, by necessity, men accompanied her. At no time was there any suggestion of impropriety on her part, but eyebrows were nevertheless raised.

Isabella Mary Kelly remained single her whole life and no one, who actually knew her, ever suggested she had a sexual encounter with anyone. While this may sound rather odd to the ears of the modern reader, she was a *lady* from the nineteenth century English upper class, who was *single* and *respectable* – sex was out of the question.

Despite the fact that many people of her era thought it rather improper for a woman to be involved in horse breeding, Isabella Kelly was a breeder of quality horses, especially in her earlier days at Mount George. Her most famous horse was called "Calendar", and most of the early settlers who wrote their memoirs, remembered this horse.

The people in the Manning Valley always called her "Miss Kelly", partly because of genteel formality and partly because she had few close personal friends in the district.

In her business operations, she could deal with all comers, but when it came to socialising, Kelly would only "visit" those she regarded as Ladies and Gentlemen. John Allan's father had been a chemist, his brother William was a veterinary doctor and John himself had been to a boarding school and had private tutors – so she could certainly visit the Allans.

While many today would call her a snob, she was what she was – a product of the English class system. There were a number of people in the Valley, like the Allans, who got along very well with Miss Kelly.

John Allan was aged about seventeen when his family arrived in the Manning Valley in 1851, twelve years after Isabella Kelly settled in the district. His father George had paid £120 to the A. A. Company for the right to select 200 acres of their vast estate. While his father and brother, William, went on ahead to the Manning to select their two hundred acres, John stayed in Sydney with his mother.

On the Manning, George and William met Joseph Andrews, who suggested a particular site to them, across the river but not far from Woodside, named Kimbriki. They liked it so much that,

Fire

as soon as they saw it, they decided to make it their selection.[2]

George Allan returned to Sydney for the family. They took a boat to the Manning, but it was wrecked as it crossed the bar into the Manning River at Harrington. Some of their possessions and furniture, which they had brought with them from England, were rescued. Joseph Andrews sent his dray and bullocks down river, and their remaining possessions were brought up to Kimbriki.

After they moved onto Kimbriki, Miss Kelly very graciously offered Mr and Mrs Allan accommodation in her house until their own was built. The Allans accepted, and stayed at Mount George for several months. The sons, John and William, camped on Kimbiki building the homestead.

Kelly had built a very grand house at Mount George shortly after her arrival there. When advertising the sale of land at Georgetown in 1842, she wrote:[3]

> The House has swallowed up the immense quantity of 25,000 feet of sawn timber alone; independent of the corresponding outlay expended on the well built premises.
>
> The Verandah is eight feet wide [2.4 metres] and all rooms are eleven feet high [3.3 metres].
>
> The ceiling is lined with rosewood, cedar and a wood called beech.
>
> Six Rooms On The Ground Floor ...
>
> The Kitchen is detached, also the stalled stable, Stockyard, Piggery, etc.

The house was magnificent, considering the remote nature of the region. Most settler families had a first house consisting of one or two room and a dirt floor. Kelly did not stint on furnishing the house, which over the years grew to eight rooms.[4]

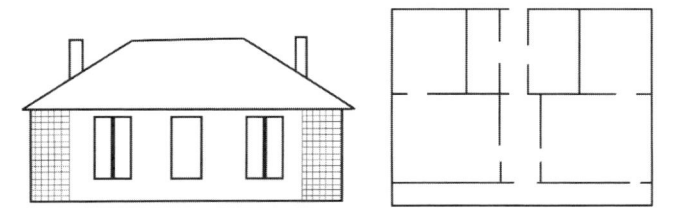

This drawing of Isabella Kelly's house and its floor plan have been copied from the advertisement for Georgetown, 1842.

The Trials of Isabella Mary Kelly

Robert Cox, who died in 1932 aged one hundred and three, recalled arriving on the Manning in 1849 and working for Joseph Andrews. He knew Miss Kelly and helped her (together with an aboriginal stockman) to brand cattle and horses. He said that in the early days there were only three settlers in the district with shingle roofs – George Rowley, Joseph Andrews and Isabella Mary Kelly – the others used bark.[5]

By this time, Isabella Kelly had made the decision to move away from Mount George, further down the valley, while still retaining possession of Mount George – perhaps the constant battling with neighbours, Joseph Andrews in particular, was getting the better of her. She decided to take a seven-year lease on the property called Brimbin, on the Dawson River, north of present day Taree and over twenty miles (32 km) from Mount George.

Later in the year, Isabella Kelly went away for a period on business, leaving her Mount George house locked and unoccupied. When she returned she found her house had burned down – there was nothing but ashes.

Worse still, Isabella Kelly believed the burning had been caused by human hands, as there was no sign of any bushfire and it would have been impossible for it to just catch fire. It was heart breaking for her, "all my out buildings, and the finest house in the whole district" burned to ashes.[6]

John Allan wrote:[7]

> She was quite a celebrity when we came here. I always got on well with Miss Kelly. She often came and stopped the night with us after we got our house built.
>
> Father had not left her house over a month before it was burned to the ground, and it was such a nice finished house, lined with cedar. She had applied for a carpenter to be such as one of her assigned servants, and she got a really good workman. It was always thought the house was "set on fire". Amongst a certain lot, Miss Kelly was disliked very much and many of the old hands had a "down" on her.

It was the most prestigious house in the district. All the expensive furniture, all her clothes, and many personal items were gone.

Isabella Kelly went to see George Rowley, as one of the two Community Magistrates in the district. Although James Hawthorne had become a Justice of the Peace earlier the same

Fire

year, all magisterial and police actions originated from Bungay Bungay, as the courtroom, lock-up and police residence were there. Rowley had control of the constable, and was the only person in the district, who could launch an investigation.

But Rowley declined to take any action at all.[8]

As it was later in the day, Kelly asked to stay the night, but Rowley refused – a considerable insult for any woman at that time.

Rowley could have sent the constable to make some investigation, but did not. At the same time, no one seemed to have any idea who the arsonist might be, if, in fact, it had been deliberately set on fire.

Frustrated, Kelly decided to travel to Port Macquarie, to see Edward Denny Day (popularly known as Denny Day), the Police Magistrate stationed there.

Captain Day was born in Kerry, Ireland, in 1801. After resigning from an army career, he migrated to the colony mainly for health reasons. He soon established himself as a Police Magistrate of high repute.[9] In 1838 Governor Gipps despatched him to the Myall Creek after the massacre of aborigines there, where Day was responsible for the capture of eleven of the perpetrators. Seven of these men were later executed.

In 1840, Day had been in charge of the posse which captured bushranger Edward Davis and his gang in a shoot-out, leading to their hanging. Denny Day was a hard man and ran a tight court. At the same time, he was highly respected for the fairness and justice of his decisions on the Bench.

Still, Isabella Kelly managed to lose her temper with him. Kelly recalled:[10]

> I complained of his [Rowley's] treatment to Mr Day, and Mr Day made some remark, which made me angry, and as I am very hasty, I said, "Thank God I was never turned out of any assembly for being in a state of intoxication – no man can tax me with that."
>
> With that Mr Day was in a great rage and the veins in his flesh rose in indignation, and Major Innes said to me, "I would not like to be in your shoes Miss Kelly, for he is a most vindictive man."
>
> I said I could not help it after the way he spoke to me … I was myself angry about my house being burned down and I spoke in haste.

The Trials of Isabella Mary Kelly

Kelly's reference to Day being drunk came from an incident in the previous year. The *Sydney Morning Herald* reported that Day (the Superintendent of Police in Sydney) had been intoxicated on the night of the Mayor's Fancy Ball, and a subsequent meeting of the Executive Council dismissed Day as a result.[11] It was an issue that Day was obviously sensitive about.

Kelly said she generally had no complaint to make about Magistrate Day, as she did with most other magistrates.

The burning of her house had been confronting for Isabella Kelly in many ways. Apart from the loss of the house itself and the valuable assets it contained, there was her belief it had been burned down deliberately with no indication who would do such a thing. A neighbour? Someone passing through? Someone out for revenge?

On top of this was the indifference of the Magistrates, who did not seem to care and who made no attempt to investigate the fire (apart from the fact they had a very limited ability to investigate).

The following paragraphs appeared in the Wingham Chronicle in the 1930s:[12]

> The late Miss Kelly was regarded one time as a very wealthy woman, and built a fine house at Mount George. ... One of her assigned servants was an architect. He designed the house, and superintended its construction, no reasonable expense being spared - workmen being procured from Sydney.
>
> She promised to give this man his freedom when it was completed. After waiting some time, he found she had conveniently forgotten all about her promise. So when, one day, the fine building went up in smoke, the neighbours, who knew of her promise, said "Serve her right!"

There were always rumoured stories circulating about Isabella Mary Kelly.

Towards the end of 1851, Isabella Kelly moved to Brimbin, while retaining Mount George. For Kelly the move was fateful in many ways, with the main difficulty being that it split her operations. The distance between the two properties made it difficult to supervise both. At the same time, she seemed to have cordial relations with her neighbours at Brimbin.

Then she met Charles Skerrett.

Part 2
Convictions

"I don't know how I came to do such things for a mere stranger."

— William Turner.

Charles Skerrett

8. Stolen Cattle

On April 29, 1854, Charles Skerrett, accompanied by two men, rode onto the Brimbin property to see Isabella Kelly.[1] Brimbin was on the main "road" from Maitland to Port Macquarie, where travellers could cross the Dawson River just above the highest point navigable by boat. The eight-room house, stockyards and stockmen's huts were in a clearing of the dense bush, near to the river but on ground that was flat, and high enough to be above the general flood level.

Skerrett had met Miss Kelly a few months before, when he had ridden past her near Brimbin, introducing himself and asking if he could get a drink of water.[2]

Isabella Mary Kelly was raised in the upper echelons of society. Her judgement of the men she met always began with whether they were "Gentlemen" or not. A good indication of a Gentleman was the way he dressed, his manners, and particularly his manner of speech – it showed education, and education was mainly attained by the upper class with money.

Charles Skerrett impressed her. He was aged in his late thirties and married with nine children, one boy and eight girls. He told Kelly he had cattle and horses on the MacLeay River, and had recently been living in Port Macquarie.

After only three years at Brimbin, Isabella Kelly decided to move her headquarters back to Mount George – she would build another house at Mount George, but it would be a slab cottage on a much lesser scale than her original house. Four years still remained on her Brimbin lease, but she had taken a lease from the A. A. Company at Ganget, across the river about five miles from Mount George.

Skerrett indicated he would like to take over the lease of Brimbin, if Miss Kelly was leaving. Isabella Kelly said he could have the remainder of her lease at Brimbin for a rental of £10 a year, but she wanted four rooms of the house – a bedroom, a parlour and two small scullion rooms – for her own use, until the cottage she was building at Mount George was completed.

The other two men with Skerrett, Mr Millar and Mr Anderson, were both shipwrights and had accompanied Skerrett to Brimbin for the specific purpose of witnessing an agreement, if one was reached. When Skerrett offered to write out the agreement, Isabella Kelly declined, saying that she always liked a disinterested third party to write out the two copies (one for each party) of an important agreement.

The documents were duly written by Anderson, signed by both Kelly and Skerrett and then witnessed by Miller and Anderson. Not part of the written agreement, were one hundred milking cows, which she owned at Brimbin and were up for sale. She told Skerrett he could have their milk until they were sold.

Before leaving, Charles Skerrett told her that he would soon be in a position to buy her cattle as he had recently come into an inheritance of £1500. He was going to Sydney that afternoon to pick up the power of attorney from the firm of Brierly, Dean & Co. Kelly told him he would be quite welcome to buy her cattle, but she could not personally sell them to him, as she had placed them in the hands of the firm of Rich, Langley and Butchart, and any cattle he wanted to purchase, would have to be bought through them.

There was a legal reason why she could not personally sell her cattle, although she did not tell him this. She had taken out a lien with Rich, Langley and Butchart, meaning she had borrowed money from the firm and used her cattle as surety – hence she could not legally sell any of the cattle without the firm's permission. She had given the firm the minimum price she wanted for the cattle, and they were to deduct the loan from the proceeds of any sales.

Skerrett told her that when he was living at Port Phillip, he had been a magistrate for nine years; he was a Roman Catholic. Isabella Mary Kelly was impressed.

If Charles Skerrett had been a magistrate in Melbourne for nine years then perhaps, she thought, he could be a magistrate in the Manning Valley – it might solve some of the problems she had with the Manning Valley magistracy. Without telling Skerrett or anyone else, Isabella Kelly wrote to Peter Faucett in Sydney, and asked him to use his influence to have Charles Skerrett made a Justice of the Peace.[3]

Peter Faucett said he was rather bemused at receiving Miss Kelly's letter, as she must have thought he had more influence than he did. They had met shortly after his arrival in the colony. He had passed the letter on to the Attorney General, John Plunkett, who had prosecuted several cases involving Miss Kelly. The Attorney General asked him to make further investigations as to Skerrett's suitability to be a magistrate.

One thing particularly amused Faucett. One of the reasons given by Miss Kelly for making Skerrett a Justice of the Peace was he belonged to the Roman Catholic faith – hardly a good reason, Faucett thought, in this country.

Isabella Kelly was a Roman Catholic, receiving visits from itinerant priests, in a predominantly Protestant valley, at a time of much religious intolerance.[4] There is an inference here that Isabella Kelly believed many of her problems with magistrates derived from the fact they were Protestant (generally Presbyterian) while she was Catholic.

On May 22, Skerrett returned from Sydney, and visited Kelly again, in the company of Mr Miller and Mr Nichols. Isabella Kelly was getting lunch at the time and Charles Skerrett followed her into the kitchen, leaving Miller and Nichols in the other room.[5]

Recalling the conversation, Isabella Kelly said:[6]

> He told me that he had purchased all my cattle. I remarked to him that I had never authorized them [Rich, Langley and Butchart] to sell more than 250 head. What could I do for beef and milch [milking] cows for my station?
>
> He said, "How many fat cattle do you require? I will let you have them at the rate I paid for them."
>
> I said, "What was the rate?"
>
> He said, "£800."
>
> I thought it was well to let them go at that price.
>
> He then said, "Whatever you may want, you may have. How many do you think you require?"
>
> I said, "Seventeen or eighteen bullocks, and about half a dozen milch cows."

The Trials of Isabella Mary Kelly

He said, "I will let you have these at what I gave for them."

Kelly was astounded. She had only authorised the firm to sell two hundred and fifty head of cattle, yet they had sold him all five hundred head. Not only that, £800 was much more than she expected to get for them – perhaps she was not so unhappy all her cattle had been sold.

When Kelly asked Skerrett for the documentation of the sale, he told her that he did not have any with him but she could expect to receive a letter in a day or two from Rich, Langley and Butchart.[7]

On the following Monday, Thomas Findley, accompanied by Angus Cameron, went to Brimbin and asked Miss Kelly if he could buy a fat bullock from her. She told him she could not sell him one as Charles Skerrett had bought all her cattle.[8]

On June 4, Charles and Maria Skerrett, with the nine children, took up residence at Brimbin. They arrived on horseback with their furniture, mainly bedding, on a sled drawn by bullocks.[9] They were now all living in the same house at Brimbin – Miss Kelly in her two rooms (and two small storage rooms) and the Skerretts in the remaining rooms.

It did not take Isabella Kelly too long to realise that Charles Skerrett would not live up to her initial impression of him. The Skerretts were in dire straits financially, and she gave them at various times, a bag of flour weighing two hundredweight (about 100 kg), seventy pounds of salt (about 30 kg), forty pounds of tallow (animal fat from which candles and soap could be made), tea and sugar, as well as "clothes for his naked children".[10]

On June 14, Skerrett asked if he could muster the horses for her. Kelly said he could and she would give him a pony and a horse for his trouble, but he was not to break them in or do anything else with them until everything connected with the sale had been finalised. The agreement for the mustering was drawn up and signed by Kelly and Skerrett, with Mr Miller and Mr Nichols as witnesses.

When Skerrett returned several days later, he said that as she would not let him break-in the horses, he did not want to muster them anymore. The usual practice in these situations was to write another agreement, which voided the original, and it too would need to be witnessed. Charles Skerrett suggested that, rather than write out a new agreement, they tear up their own copies of the original muster document in front of each other. Kelly watched as Skerrett tore up his agreement, and threw the pieces into the fire.[11] She too tore up her agreement, and disposed of the pieces in the fire.

Isabella Kelly did not realise that Charles Skerrett had not torn up his agreement at all – he had torn up some other paper.

The Bungay Bungay police district was formally created in 1853, a year before the towns of Taree and Wingham were established. This was about the same time that George Rowley left the district, moving to Sydney. That left James Hawthorne, who had become a Justice of the Peace two years previously, as the only Community Magistrate in the Manning Valley.

Police Magistrate Denny Day, began visiting the Manning on a regular basis to conduct hearings on the Bungay Bungay Bench, usually the more serious cases. Hawthorne joined Day on the Bench on these occasions, while conducting his own sittings in Day's absence. Unfortunately the records of these sittings have not survived.

On June 21, just over a fortnight since the arrival of the Skerrett family at Brimbin, Isabella Mary Kelly was served with a warrant for her arrest on a charge of cattle stealing.[12] Because of the seriousness of the charge a constable went to Brimbin to arrest her. As she was escorted away, Kelly sent her young employee, Richard Smith, to tell Charles Skerrett of her arrest and to ask him to meet her at the Bungay Bungay Police Office.

Skerrett arrived at the Police Office with Mr Bates, a nearby farmer and gentleman on friendly terms with Miss Kelly, and they bailed her out.[13] She was given bail of £40 with two sureties of £20 each. Skerrett signed one of the £20 sureties – he did not have to pay any money, just guarantee to pay if Kelly failed to appear in court.

On July 19, 1854,[14] Isabella Mary Kelly appeared before Magistrates Denny Day and James Hawthorne for the committal hearing.

The Trials of Isabella Mary Kelly

George McPherson, a settler from Dingo Creek, and Charles Turner, a butcher from Wingham, had taken out the initial warrant against her on May 17. The cattle stealing involved branding two of McPherson's calves[15] and one of Turner's[16] on Kelly's Mount Ganget cattle run.

In her defence, Kelly told the Bench that she was not actually present at the branding of the calves, as she was on the Mount George estate near the ashes of her burned-down house, about to leave for Sydney; she was waiting for her young servant, Richard Smith, who wanted to do some branding; it was her stockmen who did the branding down in the stockyard, not her.

Further, Kelly said, she gave written notice of the branding to both George McPherson and Paddy Connolly, as well as giving a verbal notice to Ann Andrews, the wife of Joseph Andrews. Kelly told the Bench that if they thought someone did have to be prosecuted for this offence, then it should be her stockmen, not her, as she had not instructed them to brand other people's calves.

Magistrate Day told her that she had to take responsibility for her servants' actions, and hence, he was committing her to stand trial in Sydney for cattle stealing.[17]

There can be little doubt this prosecution of Kelly was nothing more than a conspiracy aimed at embarrassing Isabella Kelly.

It was not unusual for neighbours to be in dispute, particularly when it came to branding calves. With no fences between cattle runs, cattle would mix, often resulting in arguments over trespass one way or the other. As the newborn calves grew, arguments could develop over who owned which calf. Most times the injured party would demand the calves back or take two equivalent, unbranded calves, so their own brand could be placed on them.

By giving the neighbouring settlers notice of the branding, Kelly had given them (or their stockmen) the opportunity to be present at the branding, and to protect their interests. Many settlers did not give this warning.

McPherson and Turner did not approach Kelly on the matter, they simply took out the warrants against her. Neither man appeared to have been in direct conflict with Kelly at the time. Although there was a link between McPherson and Joseph

Andrews (McPherson was married to Joseph's sister Jane, suggesting Andrews could have had some influence), and there was a link between Turner and Skerrett in the sale of cattle, nothing definite can be established.

When the depositions taken at the committal hearing were sent to the Attorney General, he declined to proceed with the prosecution on the ground Miss Kelly had notified her neighbours of the branding – *there was no case to answer.*

Kelly found these events very disturbing. Not only had her character been smeared, but she could see absolutely no grounds for the Magistrates to *commit her* for trial. She believed Magistrate Day was getting revenge for the way in which she had insulted him three years ago in Port Macquarie, after her house burned down – and Major Innes did say Day was known to bear a grudge.

Isabella Kelly wrote letters to both Magistrate Day and Magistrate Hawthorne, threatening to sue both of them for misuse of their magisterial power.

Isabella Kelly received word that Skerrett may have stolen one of her horses, and could not believe it – a *gentleman* would not do such a thing. Joseph Andrews had met Charles Skerrett riding his horse and towing a horse bearing Kelly's MK brand. Questioned about the horse, Skerrett told Andrews he had taken a servant of Miss Kelly's from Gloucester to Brimbin, and was returning the horse to Gloucester. When Kelly approached Skerrett about the horse, he said, "Don't you believe it, I never touched a horse belonging to you."[18]

On July 17 Isabella Kelly ran into Major Innes on the road near Brimbin, and fell into conversation with him. Innes had been the original owner of the 930-acre cattle station, naming it with the Scottish "Braynbyn", which later evolved into "Brimbin".[19] Innes had originally been Commander of the convict settlement of Port Macquarie, but had resigned his commission to pursue his substantial and widespread commercial interests. He was based at Port Macquarie and was at one time a Police Magistrate.[20]

When Kelly mentioned Charles Skerrett to him, Innes replied that Skerrett had leased a property from him in Port

Macquarie in the previous year, and as a result of trouble caused by Skerrett, he had terminated Skerrett's lease. Major Innes asked her how she came to meet Skerrett because he was "the biggest scoundrel unhung".[21]

If warning bells had not been ringing before, they were now. And Isabella Kelly had still not received a letter from her agents Rich, Langley and Butchart about the sale of the cattle to Skerrett more than a month ago.

Later, the same day, Skerrett approached her and asked her if he could kill a fat bullock. She said to him, "Mr Skerrett, I have not received a letter from my agents, and I will not allow you to deal with the cattle until I hear from them. But if you want to purchase one, I will sell you one for cash, and return you the money when I find that you have purchased my cattle. But I would not give it to you without the cash."[22]

Skerrett agreed. When the bullock was brought into the yard for slaughtering, Kelly asked for the £4. He told her he did not have the money, but would go to Cundletown to cash a cheque and pay her when he returned. Kelly let the bullock be slaughtered.

Skerrett left, but he did not pay her that day, nor on any other day.

A week later, Isabella Kelly finally received a letter from her stock agents, Rich, Langley and Butchart. There was no mention of Charles Skerrett having bought any cattle – indeed there was *no mention* of Skerrett at all.

The firm had written the letter to tell Miss Kelly that they had sold *none* of her cattle, and further, they no longer wanted to deal with her cattle as they thought her asking price was too high, making them too difficult to sell. They suggested she place the sale of the cattle in the hands of Dodds & Co in East Maitland. Finally, could she settle her account with them?

Isabella Mary Kelly took the letter and rode out looking for Skerrett, accompanied by young Richard Smith. Kelly recalled confronting Skerrett:[23]

> Skerrett was in the garden, chipping.
> I took the letter and said: "Mr Skerrett, I am surprised! You call yourself a *gentleman*, and to tell me an untruth! To

have told me you bought my cattle from Rich, Langley and Butchart!"

He said, very smoothly and quietly, "Well, Miss Kelly, I have been disappointed in money matters, but", he said, "if you now tell people I have not purchased your cattle, I shall never be able to muster them."

I said, "I am surprised!"

He said, "Be off from here, you damn bitch!"

I told the boy to go and get my horse, and started [to leave.] When about 200 yards from the house, he [Skerrett] came running without his hat, and said, "Come here and take away your murdering Chinaman."

Skerrett wanted her to get rid of the Chinese stockman staying in one of the huts. Kelly had employed this unnamed stockman for about three years, to look after some of her mares.[24] Kelly said, "Allow him to remain here until I return – I will pay you for the hut he occupies – you can deduct it from the price of the bullock."[25]

Skerrett said he wanted her to sign an agreement that he could still rent Brimbin. He was probably frightened she would terminate his sub-lease of Brimbin (written on May 29) as Major Innes had done in Port Macquarie. Having signed a legal agreement, Kelly felt obliged to stick by it and replied, "Oh, the place is yours by the agreement already written."

She returned with Skerrett to the house. She was flustered. She now did what she would normally never do – she allowed Skerrett, rather than an independent third party, to write out the agreement for the hut of the stockman. To compound this error, she signed the document without reading it properly. Her reading glasses, which she had been using for two years, were in the baggage on her horse, but she did not get them out.

Kelly recalled that Skerrett "brought me back. I got off my horse, and took the document in my hand, and without glasses tried to read it. I read as far as 'sixpence a week.' Seeing neither horse nor cattle named in the document, but 'sixpence a week,' I signed it without notice. I do not know the date even."[26] When Skerrett asked one of his daughters to witness the agreement, Kelly refused to allow it. Skerrett then called Ann Richards, Kelly's housemaid, and she witnessed the document.

The Trials of Isabella Mary Kelly

Isabella Kelly could not believe that Skerrett had lied to her. He was a gentleman and she had put so much trust in him. She immediately left for Sydney and went to Rich, Langley and Butchart, to find out for herself. When she asked the firm about Charles Skerrett, they told her that they did not know of such a person, and had never met such a person.

Complying with the firm's request, Kelly placed the sale of the cattle in the hands of Dodds & Co of Maitland. She spent about five or six weeks away from the Manning River, leaving in the last week of July and returning in the first week of September by the steamer.

She was in no hurry to return to the Manning. She had established that Charles Skerrett had lied to her, but what else could he do?

When the steamer stopped over at Raymond Terrace, a man told her that Skerrett had taken some of her horses – he had seen her MK brand on them. Kelly soon confirmed it. One of the horses had been shipped on board the *Collaroy* from Morpeth, and she recognized it – a chestnut horse with a star on the forehead.

On her return to the Manning she immediately went to see Charles Skerrett. He was absent, but his wife, Maria, was there. She asked Mrs. Skerrett why her husband had sold her horses. Maria Skerrett told her "they were in great distress and that really and truly it was a case of necessity".[27]

Kelly said she would make further enquiries.

Some time later, Isabella Kelly received a letter telling her Skerrett had sold some of her cattle to Charles Turner, one of the men who charged her with cattle stealing. She went to Turner's property. He was absent, but there in his slaughter yards, she found five hides with her MK brand on them. There was a sixth hide that may have been hers, but she could not be sure. Charles Turner had bought seven cattle from Skerrett for £24,[28] in what he claimed was a *bona fide* sale between himself and Charles Skerrett, although Turner would know that Skerrett was a doubtful owner of any cattle bearing Kelly's brand. She asked the stockman to cut out the brands and left, taking them with her.

Skerrett made a public claim to *all* of Kelly's cattle by placing a notice in the *Maitland Mercury*, appearing on Saturday, September 23, 1854, with a repeat on the following Wednesday. The notice cautioned "any person or persons from buying or selling any of my cattle, formerly Miss Isabella Mary Kelly's, and branded as follows …"

Isabella Mary Kelly decided to charge Skerrett with cattle stealing, but she would not go to the Bungay Bungay Bench – Magistrate Day[29] would be there – and went to the Dungog Bench instead, about seventy miles away.

Kelly reached Dungog, accompanied by young Richard Smith, and went to the Police Office on Monday, September 25.[30] She made a sworn deposition before the Police Magistrate, that Charles Skerrett had stolen seven of her cattle and sold them to Charles Turner. The Magistrate granted the warrant, and ordered the arrest of Charles Skerrett. This necessitated a constable travelling to the Manning and arresting Skerrett sometime in the near future.

While at Dungog, Isabella Kelly began legal proceedings against Charles Turner, charging him with malicious prosecution (concerning the warrant taken out by Turner over the branding of the calf).[31] As McPherson was not similarly charged, it can only be seen as retaliation for Charles Turner slaughtering the cattle Skerrett claimed to have sold to him. Kelly pursued this matter through the civil courts but without success.

It may have been here at Dungog, that Isabella Kelly placed her own notice in the *Maitland Mercury* to appear on the following Saturday, September 30:

> I hereby give public notice that no person is authorised to sell cattle, my property, and bearing my brands, except [my stock agent] Mr Alex Dodds of East Maitland. And further, that any person or persons found trespassing on my cattle runs on the Manning River, or removing either horses or cattle without my written order, will be prosecuted with the utmost rigour of the law.

Isabella Kelly and Richard Smith began their return journey to the Manning, most of which was through thick bush on land which was very sparsely inhabited. When they had gone some of the way, she saw Charles Skerrett standing behind a large gum tree – he had followed them all the way to Dungog. He tagged after them as they rode on. Greatly concerned, Isabella said to twelve-year-old Richard, "Stand back, do not keep to the road, or you will see your mistress murdered."[32]

She stopped at a blacksmith's shop to replace a shoe cast by her horse, telling the blacksmith that a man named Skerrett was following her. When they were about to leave, the blacksmith asked Richard to take their horses behind the scrub where they would not be seen, and asked Kelly to go out through his wife's bedroom. There they mounted their horses and rode off.

Kelly later recalled: "I rode seventy miles that day, and when I got off my horse, my head was so dizzy, I could hardly stand"[33] (keeping in mind that riding side-saddle accentuated her head movement).

Isabella Kelly did not see Charles Skerrett again that day.

9. Forged Documents

All of this was becoming too much for Isabella Mary Kelly. She had been in constant battle with her neighbours for years, and had moved to Brimbin only to run foul of Charles Skerrett there. She made a momentous decision – she would sell up and leave the district – but first she would like to leave on friendly terms with everyone.

Her first action would be to drop the threatened lawsuits against Day, Hawthorne and Andrews.[1] She asked her friends, Robert Easton of Burrell Creek and James Cosgrove of Sydney, to go and see Andrews with a view to making her peace with him.

Easton and Cosgrove went to Woodside and waited all day before Andrews returned home. He agreed to meet with Kelly. The two men and Isabella Kelly returned to Woodside on another day for the reconciliation. Andrews told Kelly he had no animosity towards her and had never done her an injury, but she had done a great deal of injury to him.[2]

Kelly reiterated to Joseph Andrews her intention of selling all her cattle and horses, and her property, and leaving the district. Andrews recalled: [3]

> I said, 'Miss Kelly, sell your cattle! Mr Skerrett has shown me a document wherein is contained a Bill of Sale of all your cattle, and twenty head of your horses, for £600, £400 of which is paid down in cash, and the remainder by bill.'
>
> 'My God!' she replied, 'I never sold a beast to him!" …
>
> She said, 'He will never claim a beast.'
>
> I said, 'I believe he is making preparation to sell some of the cattle.'

If she had not sold her cattle to Charles Skerrett, and if he had not paid her £400 in cash with another £200 by promissory note, *how could Skerrett have a Bill of Sale?*

Further, Andrews wanted to know why she had been telling everyone that Skerrett had bought her cattle. He said quite a number of people were coming to him at the Inn and telling him that *Miss Kelly told them* she had sold her cattle to Skerrett.

Kelly replied that she had only ever told *two* people that Skerrett had bought her cattle – Thomas Findley and Angus Cameron – and that was only because they asked to buy a fat bullock from her, and at that time Skerrett had led her to *believe* he had bought her cattle.

The meeting ended with Kelly agreeing to cease all legal action against Andrews.

William Turner was nineteen years old, and appeared to be no relation to Charles Turner.[4] He and his father, Samuel, were rough carpenters contracted by Miss Kelly to erect the cottage for her at Mount George. Like most labourers of the time, William could not read or write. His father said that just the two of them would work all week and on Saturday night, William would disappear, sometimes returning on Monday, sometimes on Tuesday.

Late in May 1854, William was on his way to see Miss Kelly, when he met Charles Skerrett, who had just been visiting Miss Kelly. They introduced themselves and became friendly. William and Samuel finished their work for Miss Kelly in June and moved to a property about six miles from Brimbin.

On June 19, one of those events happened which caught the interest of the whole valley. The river was in flood, and one of Miss Kelly's stockmen drowned while trying to cross the river on his horse. It took over a week for the water to subside. The dead horse was found strung up in a tree not far from the crossing, but what aroused so much community interest was the curiosity of the drowned stockman being found in a standing position, arms clasped round a tree, seemingly trying to cling to life.[5]

The inquest at Bungay Bungay held a large attendance. Country people in particular always had trouble remembering precisely when events occurred, for apart from church on Sunday, the days of the week held little meaning. In this case, people could later give exact dates of events at this time, relative to the drowning, the finding of the body and the inquest.

Sam Turner had been there when the drowned stockman had been found. That same afternoon he recalled going to Andrews' Inn, where he met Charles Skerrett for the first time. Sam and his son William then accompanied Skerrett on a social visit to Brimbin, the first time he had been there.[6]

In the evening of July 12, barely five weeks after Skerrett had moved to Brimbin, Sam Turner, William Turner and Charles Skerrett rode over to Joseph Andrews' Inn. In between a few drinks, Skerrett asked Andrews to tell him *who* had been saying that he had not purchased Miss Kelly's cattle. Andrews told Skerrett that no one in particular had said he did not buy Kelly's cattle – it was the general opinion of *everyone* (no one knew him to have that much money).

Skerrett said, "Will you look at my documents and be convinced?"[7]

He gave Andrews a Bill of Sale:[8]

Brimbon[9], Manning River
6 June, 1854

Sold this day to Charles Skerrett, all my cattle and brand, with my interest of Brimbon Station, and twenty unbroken horses, for the sum of £600 – £400 paid cash, and £200 by a bill of twelve months; the horses to be selected by Mr Charles Skerrett, either off the Manning Flats or Brimbon Station; the above £400 I now receive in cash, and possession of the above named cattle I this day give to the said Mr Charles Skerrett.

Isabella Mary Kelly

Witnesses:
    Jane Skerrett
    Margaret Skerrett

This Bill of Sale was in Skerrett's writing, and the signature of Isabella Mary Kelly appeared on it. So too were the signatures of Jane Skerrett and Margaret Skerrett, the daughters Charles Skerrett, aged fourteen and sixteen respectively, acting as witnesses to the document.

When Skerrett had been at the Inn two months previously, on or about May 20, he told Andrews he had bought all Miss

Kelly's cattle for £800 with Andrews replying that he had made a bad deal on them – they were not worth that much. Andrews commented that it was a much better bargain than Skerrett had stated to him in May. Miss Kelly had at least 300 horses. If, in addition to the cattle, Skerrett could pick any twenty horses he wanted, Andrews claimed they alone would have to be worth at least £300 or £400.

Skerrett wanted to know if this proved to Andrews that he had indeed bought the cattle. Andrews replied that it did, but he did not like to see Skerrett's children signing such an important document. Also, he did not like Miss Kelly's signature – it did not look like her usual signature.

Joseph had received quite a lot correspondence from Kelly during their on-going dispute, and he asked his wife Ann to go and get some of the letters, which contained Miss Kelly's signature. The signature on the Bill of Sale was similar to this signature: [10]

Isabella Mary Kelly

When they compared the signatures they found that, in the Bill of Sale, the bottom of the letter "y" at the end of "Mary" and "Kelly" were straight lines. In the correspondence produced by Andrews, the letter "y" had loops, similar to this signature: [11]

Isabella Mary Kelly

Charles Skerrett must have been concerned. He told Andrews he would go and get a receipt for the £400 from Miss Kelly. Andrews told him it was not necessary, as it stated in the Bill of Sale that £400 had been paid in cash – that was a sufficient receipt.

A week or two later, William Turner said he received a message that Charles Skerrett wanted to see him.[12] He said he went to see Skerrett, stopping at a friend's place along the way to have a few drinks.

Skerrett told him Miss Kelly had given him a receipt for the cattle and had signed it, but he needed a witness. He really had bought her cattle. It was definitely Miss Kelly's signature. Would

William witness it for him?

Turner said he objected at first (acknowledging he knew it to be illegal to sign such a document without being *present* when the money changed hands), but being under the influence and being hard pressed by Skerrett, he eventually signed his name as a witness to the receipt. As he could not read, Skerrett read him the receipt (or some portion of it) or Skerrett told him what was in it – William could not remember.

Two weeks after Isabella Kelly's journey to Dungog to charge Skerrett, Constable Tippin rode to the Manning from Dungog and arrested Charles Skerrett. As the constable and his prisoner began the journey back to Dungog, Skerrett sent his twelve year old son, James, to ride over to William Turner and tell him his father had been arrested.

Turner mounted his horse and soon found Skerrett and Constable Tippin a short way along the road. Skerrett told William that Miss Kelly had taken a warrant out against him for cattle stealing, and the receipt, which Turner had signed, was for the cattle she accused him of stealing – *so Turner was in this as deeply as he was.*

Constable Tippin allowed Turner to ride down the road with Skerrett and himself. They could talk, but only a little without Tippin hearing. It was late in the afternoon, so they stopped at Andrews' Inn for the night.

That night Turner and Skerrett slept in the same bed. This was not unusual for men of that era – it was cheaper – and certainly no sexual connotation would ever be placed upon it. In this case, the Police Office probably paid for the accommodation.

According to Turner, during the night Skerrett said to him, "You will have to swear to that paper you signed your signature, or else I will get into trouble, and you deeper than me. You know your signature when you see it."

Turner replied, "This is a pretty mess you have brought me into, I did not expect it from you."[13]

Skerrett said if Turner had not signed the Receipt, Miss Kelly would have robbed him of all his money (meaning Kelly could repudiate the sale and keep the money as no one had witnessed the exchanging of money or the writing of the receipt). Kelly told him he could pick out any twenty horses he wanted except one particular chestnut horse. *Turner would have to swear to that.*

William Turner would now have to swear at a Police Office, before a magistrate, that he had seen Miss Kelly receive the money, and he had signed the receipt after he had seen this. The alternative was to admit he had borne false witness to the Receipt, which would then lead to a charge of perjury against him.

The next morning quite a few people stopped at Andrews' Inn before travelling on to Dungog to attend the committal hearing. Miss Kelly was there, but kept to herself over one side of the room. Skerrett and his daughters were there talking to other guests about the charges. Joseph Andrews noted that the girls were critical of Miss Kelly for denying their father had bought the cattle, stating that she had been paid £400 in £100 notes. Both William and his father were also there.[14]

Charles Skerrett asked William Turner to ride to Maitland and get Mr Chambers, a solicitor. Skerrett wanted Chambers to go straight to the Police Office at Dungog and represent him at the committal hearing. Turner rode off immediately, and on his arrival at Maitland, delivered the message to Chambers, who immediately set off for Dungog. When William Turner arrived in Dungog, expecting to be examined by the magistrate, he found that the hearing was over.

Isabella Kelly reiterated her charges against Charles Skerrett before Magistrates Brown and Forster on the Dungog Bench.[15] The Magistrates asked her why she charged him in Dungog rather than on the Manning. Kelly replied she could not get justice there.[16] In somewhat of an anti-climax, the Dungog Bench decided to transfer the case to the Manning Bench, without taking any depositions.

William Turner said that he and his father returned to the Manning with Skerrett and his daughter, calling in to the Andrews Inn on the way home. Joseph and Ann Andrews had also travelled down to Dungog.

At the hotel, Skerrett showed the Receipt to anybody who wanted to read it:[17]

Brimbon, Manning River
6 June, 1854
Received from Mr Charles Skerrett the sum of £400, full amount due to me for all my cattle and twenty unbroken

horses, which I have sold to him this day.

Isabella Mary Kelly

Witness – William Turner

Joseph Andrews read it and noted three things.

Firstly, the receipt had the same date as the Bill of Sale – June 6, 1854. He was under the distinct impression that on July 12, Skerrett said he was *going* to get a receipt, not that he already had one.

Secondly, the signature of the witness did look like the rather rough signature of William Turner he had seen at the hotel.

Thirdly, when he looked at the signature of Isabella Mary Kelly, the letter "y" in "Mary" and Kelly" *had loops*. So, according to this, Kelly had signed the Bill of Sale and the receipt on the same day, but had signed them with two different styles of signature.

Ann Andrews, Joseph's wife, also recalled speaking to Charles Skerrett at the Inn after their return from Dungog. She asked him if he remembered telling her in *May* that he had bought Miss Kelly's cattle (at the same time he told Kelly had bought the cattle from her agents). Skerrett did not answer at first, but when she repeated the question, he said, "Don't you tell Miss Kelly that".[18]

On October 18, 1854, the case came before Police Magistrate Denny Day, assisted by two Community Magistrates, James Hawthorne and John Croker, at the Bungay Bungay Bench. Kelly's depositions, accusing Skerrett of cattle stealing, were read out.

Skerrett's defence was simple – he *owned* the cattle – Kelly had sold him her cattle and twenty horses. He had the *proof*, and produced three documents – the Bill of Sale, the Receipt and an agreement signed by Kelly for Skerrett to muster her horses.

For Isabella Kelly, sitting in court, this must have come as a shock. She had heard of the Bill of Sale from Joseph Andrews; she may have heard about the receipt; but the agreement to muster the horses – it was *genuine*, it was the one where she had torn up her copy and thought Skerrett had done the same.

If Kelly did not realise it before, it must have become very clear to her now – Charles Skerrett had set out to deceive her right from his first arrival at Brimbin.

The defence called William Turner to make his sworn deposition: He had been at Brimbin on June 6; he had seen Charles Skerrett give Miss Kelly £400 in four £100 notes; he had seen Charles Skerrett write out the receipt; he had seen Miss Kelly read the receipt and then sign it; he had then signed the receipt as witness.

The defence called Joseph Andrews and handed him the Bill of Sale. Andrews deposed, "I believe the document now handed to me, marked No. 2, is the document Skerrett showed to me, and I still believe this signature to be the signature of Miss Kelly."[19]

Andrews was then handed the Receipt. He deposed, "I have looked at the paper now handed to me marked No. 4 and I believe that signature to be that of Isabella Mary Kelly."[20]

This was the same Joseph Andrews who had raised doubts about the signatures, and had those doubts personally confirmed by Isabella Mary Kelly. Andrews had told Kelly he held no animosity towards her, but this was obviously not the case.

Ann Richards had served twelve months as Miss Kelly's housemaid, and at the completion of her contract, had entered the service of Charles Skerrett, necessitating a move from one part of the Brimbin residence to the other.

Ann deposed she witnessed the signing of the lease of a cottage on Brimbin. Part of this lease stated that Charles Skerrett had recently bought all her cattle.

Isabella Kelly must have been shocked by this evidence. This was the lease concerning the Chinese stockman witnessed by Ann Richards, which Kelly admitted she had not read properly because she was upset after confronting Skerrett. Kelly was certain there was no mention of cattle in it – these lines must have been added *after* she signed it, and this could only have been done with Ann's compliance.

Magistrate Denny Day adjourned proceedings to November 22. Charles Skerrett was given bail of £200 with two sureties of £100 each. Day cautioned the public against buying cattle from Charles Skerrett, which contained the brands of Miss Kelly.[21]

Who paid the bail? Skerrett? Had his sale of cattle and horses exceeded £200? At least with the sureties, money did not have to change hands.

After the hearing, Isabella Kelly was shaken. She now realized the full extent of Skerrett's designs on her. And since her journey to Dungog, she was scared of Charles Skerrett.

She decided she would not go back to the Brimbin house that night, where she lived in one part of the house and the Skerretts lived in the other. Instead she went to Andrews' Inn, and took accommodation there, at her own expense, while she awaited the completion of her cottage at Mount George, only a short distance away.[22]

On his way home from the hearing at Bungay Bungay, William Turner met Charles Skerrett as they were crossing the Manning River. Once again, Skerrett reminded Turner he would have to stick to his story come what may.

William Turner went home to where he was then working at Dingo Creek, about four miles from Bungay Bungay. He was very worried. He had falsely witnessed the receipt. He had now sworn a false deposition at Bungay Bungay. Charles Skerrett kept pulling him deeper and deeper into his web of deceit, and he saw no way out. Next he would have to bear false witness at Skerrett's trial.

Working on this Dingo Creek property with William Turner, were John Lewis and Joseph Giles. Turner told them he had perjured himself at Skerrett's committal hearing. He told them he had been unable to sign his name until Charles Skerrett, with some difficulty, taught him. They told him to run away and leave the district. William Turner stayed no longer than a week on the Manning before he left, telling no one else that he was leaving. First he went harvesting at Dungog, and then on to Maitland. He spent two and half years in Sydney, before moving to Queensland.[23]

The hearing on November 22 was held over until December 20, 1854, because of Miss Kelly's ill health. On that day, the Bungay Bungay Bench again consisted of Police Magistrate Denny Day, with Hawthorne and Croker assisting.

Margaret Skerrett gave her deposition with her father, Charles Skerrett, acting as her solicitor. Skerrett handed Margaret the Bill of Sale and began questioning her. She saw Miss Kelly sign the Bill of Sale. She heard her father say he wanted someone other than his daughter to witness the payment of the money. She did not see the money change hands.

Under cross-examination from solicitor William Mullen, acting for Miss Kelly, Margaret stated:[24]

> The document was written in Miss Kelly's front room. The signatures of the parties signing were all done at the same time, and with the same ink. Miss Kelly, my father, my sister and myself, were the only parties in the room. My father and another man, named Turner, were about the place; also Ann Richards ...
>
> I was not present when Miss Kelly cautioned my father not to remove any of the cattle. I was present in the room when Miss Kelly signed the paper; she was sitting down when she signed it. When she got up I sat down, and used the same pen and ink – it was immediately after she signed it. I saw my sister sign it also; she signed before I did.

Here in the last two sentences was an obvious contradiction – Margaret sat down and signed straight after Miss Kelly but her sister signed before she did.

The committal hearing was now complete. Magistrate Day committed Skerrett to take his trial in Sydney and sent the sworn depositions to the Attorney General.

Joseph Giles, although working at Dingo Creek with William Turner, had previously been working at Cundletown, not far from Brimbin. He had first met Charles Skerrett in June 1854. Skerrett would pass his place of work once or twice a week and they would occasionally fall into conversation. Like many people, he attended the hearing at Bungay Bungay as an interested bystander.

One day Joseph Giles met Charles Skerrett on horseback. Skerrett said he was on his way to Dingo Creek, so Giles fell in with him and, as they rode along, they talked about the court case. Giles recalled:[25]

> [Skerrett] asked me what I thought of Miss Kelly's case.
>
> I said, "I don't know anything about the law – I know nothing about it."

Forged Documents

He said he was no man for the law – he was a man for business.

I said, "If you paid Miss Kelly for those cattle you bought, she must be a very bad woman to deny it. You have William Turner and your own daughter as evidence."

He said then that William Turner was good evidence – that he was afraid of his daughter's, and that he would give me or any other person £20 to back William Turner's evidence up.

Joseph Giles declined the offer of this bribe. Of course, it did not matter that he too, like William Turner, could not read or write. Some months later Giles left the district, moving to Maitland, and taking with him the testimony of this offer of a bribe.

While waiting for the trial of Charles Skerrett to commence, Isabella Kelly heard he had taken a trip to Sydney, and decided to visit Brimbin in his absence. She needed to get some of her papers and belongings, and stayed there overnight. In the morning while still in bed, Kelly was startled by a commotion outside. Maria Skerrett came running up to the house and knocked on her window, calling out to Kelly that her daughter Jane had broken her leg.[26]

Isabella Kelly went out on the veranda half dressed, and saw one of Jane's sisters carrying her on her back. Kelly immediately sent James Skerrett off on a horse to fetch Dr Stevenson, while she sat down at Jane's bedside and bathed her with vinegar and water. Kelly's servants told her that Jane had mounted a horse bareback, and it had bucked her off, breaking a bone in her thigh. When Mr Bates arrived, Maria Skerrett told him the story of how Jane had broken her leg.

On reaching Dr Stevenson, James Skerrett found that the doctor had recently suffered injuries in a fall from his horse, and was unable to ride to Brimbin. The doctor told James what should be done for his sister. When James returned to Brimbin, Kelly had set Jane's leg as well as she could, "with strappings and a piece of band box".[27] Isabella Kelly stayed several days, caring for Jane, before leaving Brimbin.

It was notable that in an emergency of this kind Isabella Kelly was immediately sought.

Charles Skerrett was educated, intelligent and extremely charming, even charismatic. He had an instinct for what impressed his victims, and told them what they wanted to hear.

He said he had been a magistrate for nine years – this was an unequivocal lie, he was never a magistrate. He told Kelly he was Catholic, and though he was probably born a Catholic, his children were baptised as protestants in the Church of England,[28] and he was buried in the Church of England section of Rookwood cemetery. But what had impressed Kelly more than anything else was the way he presented himself as a *gentleman* – albeit a gentleman with no money.

He seemed able to talk people into doing things they would not normally do. When William Turner was later asked why he signed the receipt, he said, "I don't know how I came to do such things for a mere stranger",[29] as he and Skerrett had met on no more than a dozen occasions.

Skerrett would run his story past people and get their reactions. Then he would try and plug any holes he found, sometimes creating more problems. He told Andrews in May that he bought Kelly's cattle for £800, and received the reaction that he paid too much for them. In June, the Bill of Sale was for £600 but twenty selected horses had been added to the cattle, making it much more than a bargain for him, as he did not realise that he had over-compensated.

Skerrett had problems with The Bill of Sale right from the start. Anyone who had done business with Miss Kelly, like Joseph Andrews, knew she would not allow a signatory to also write the document. Further, she would certainly not allow any children, let alone the children of the signatory, to sign such an important document as this.

Both Skerrett and Kelly were living in different parts of the *same* house – there would have been many opportunities to arrange witnesses. Ann Richards was an adult, employed by Miss Kelly as a full-time servant. She could have been one witness of the document at any time, as she did on the lease of the Chinese stockman's hut. Skerrett did not recognise the full implications of the problem until he ran it past Andrews. The receipt then became necessary, before it too developed its own set of problems.

Charles Skerrett was an excellent "spin doctor", to use a modern media term. He was very good at re-assigning people's motives for events. It was *he*, Charles Skerrett, who did not want his children to witness something as important as the exchange of the money, so it was *he* who insisted that William Turner witness the receipt. Later on it would become *Miss Kelly*, who insisted on Skerrett's daughters witnessing the Bill of Sale, because, in his story, she was desperate to sell the cattle.

This was only the tip of Charles Skerrett's iceberg of deceit.

10. Trial

On April 5, 1855, Charles Blake Skerrett stood trial at Central Criminal Court in Darlinghurst, Sydney, for cattle stealing, namely the seven cattle he sold to butcher Charles Turner.[1] There was a complication in the indictment: the verdict rested on whether the jury of twelve[2] believed the Bill of Sale and Receipt were forged documents – but the charge was cattle stealing not forgery.

The judge was the Chief Justice of the Supreme Court of New South Wales, Sir Alfred Stephen. John Hubert Plunkett,[3] the long-serving Attorney General, prosecuted the case as he did in two other cases involving Isabella Kelly, and was briefed by John Ryan Brenan, Kelly's attorney. Arthur Holroyd, the defence barrister, was briefed by John Dawson, Skerrett's solicitor.

The prosecution began by calling Miss Kelly, who recounted her side of the story, from the arrival of Skerrett at Brimbin. At his committal hearing, Skerrett produced a Bill of Sale, signed by two of his daughters, and a Receipt signed by William Turner. She swore that both these documents were forgeries.

Joseph Andrews testified he told Skerrett it was imprudent to have his daughters witnessing their father's signature. Skerrett replied that he would get a receipt, indicating he did not currently have one, yet both the Receipt and the Bill of Sale bore the same date of 6th June, 1854. He informed Skerrett the Bill of Sale did not have Kelly's usual signature as there were no loops on the "y" in "Mary" or "Kelly". When Skerrett later produced the Receipt, the signature had loops. Accordingly, if it was a *bona fide* sale, then Miss Kelly had signed her name two different ways on the same day. He believed these signatures to be "mere imitations" of Miss Kelly's signature.

Skerrett told him that he had paid Kelly £400 in four £100

Trial

pound notes, Andrews said, two of which came from the Commercial Bank and the other two from a Melbourne bank.

Attorney General Plunkett called a man from the Commercial Bank as his next witness, who deposed that the Commercial Bank had never printed any notes with a value higher than £50. When the stock-agents Butchart and Rich were called, neither was in attendance despite subpoenas issued to them.

Fourteen-year-old Richard Smith was a less than impressive witness, who seemed quite out of his depth in the courtroom. The *Sydney Morning Herald* reported: "the religious training of the boy had been very imperfect, and although he had an apparent knowledge of a future state of rewards and punishments, his evidence was admitted, a question as to its admissibility was reserved."[4]

Richard Smith stated he had come to live with Miss Kelly when he was eleven years old. He was employed watching Miss Kelly's horses and cows. He was present in the room when Mr Skerrett told Miss Kelly he had bought all her cattle from her agents in Sydney. Mr Skerrett told Miss Kelly he had paid £800 for them.

Recalling Miss Kelly for cross-examination, Defence Attorney Holroyd put it to her that she had been responsible for two defence witnesses not appearing at the trial.

Holroyd said Jane Skerrett was unable to appear to testify on behalf of her father as she had broken her leg. This had been as a direct result of Miss Kelly firing a pistol near the head of the horse, which Jane was riding. The horse had taken fright and thrown her off.

Kelly emphatically denied this, declaring she did not fire a pistol. After Skerrett's committal hearing, Kelly said, she had returned to Brimbin to pack some of her things. When she heard that Jane had been injured, she was concerned for Jane and had assisted her.

Secondly, Holroyd accused Kelly of hounding William Turner with threats of prosecution – so much so, Turner had left the district in fear of her. Kelly strongly denied this, saying she had never made any threats to him.

Despite William Turner's non-appearance for the trial, his deposition, made at Skerrett's committal hearing, was read to the

Court: Turner had seen Charles Skerrett pay the money to Isabella Kelly, and he then signed the Receipt as a witness.

Having called all his witnesses, Plunkett rested the case for the prosecution.

Arthur Holroyd began the defence with a long speech, reviewing the evidence. He claimed that the sale of cattle from Kelly to Skerrett had been a *bona fide* sale.

His first witness was a man who worked in the Bank of Australasia, where cheques signed by Miss Kelly regularly passed through his hands. Judge Stephen disallowed the evidence on the ground that the man's opinion was based on cheques which Miss Kelly had not acknowledged to contain her signature.

Next, Margaret Skerrett was called. It was after Christmas when she saw Jane's accident. Jane was riding a horse out of the paddock, bare-back, when Miss Kelly standing at the gate fourteen yards away, fired a pistol. This resulted in Jane breaking her thigh when the horse threw her. Jane was taken to a neighbour's place, and Miss Kelly visited Jane in the bedroom. Now Jane was only able to just crawl about.

On June 6th, Margaret continued, Miss Kelly called her sister and herself into her front room. After Miss Kelly read out the Bill of Sale and signed it, both she and her sister signed the document as witnesses. Her father said that he would not have a member of his family sign the Receipt. As William Turner had come to get some nails from Miss Kelly, her father asked him to sign the Receipt. She had seen a few bank notes in her father's hand.[5]

Under cross-examination by Mr Plunkett, Margaret sobbed and wept as she gave answers to his questions, which were sometimes conflicting and sometimes confused. She could swear she signed the document on the June 6th – no, it was not the 5th or the 7th or the 8th – she did not know any other day that William Turner was there. She did not speak to Miss Kelly much, and did not like her.

Miss Kelly rented two rooms from her father, Margaret said, in an agreement witnessed by Ann Richards. At this response, Justice Stephen interrupted to point out this was impossible as Ann Richards' signature was on one document only, and it was dated 24th July.

Ann Richards told her that she had witnessed an agreement, Margaret said, and Father told her that Miss Kelly rented two rooms from him. She saw her father holding the notes (the cash paid to Miss Kelly) carelessly in his hands. He had brought the money from Port Phillip, but she did not know the amount or the bank of issue.

Margaret stated Mr Pearce set Jane's leg. She had not seen Miss Kelly with a pistol before, and she did not notice what kind it was. She did not know if anyone spoke to Miss Kelly about firing the pistol, as she was not listening.

When the documents were signed, Margaret continued, her elder sister Catherine was about the farm, but she did not know where. Sometime after the sixth of June, a box of her father's papers had burned, but her mother kept the Bill of Sale and Receipt elsewhere.

Finally Margaret's ordeal was over.

While the latter part of Margaret's testimony about the fire seemed rather obscure, there was a point to it. Charles Skerrett needed a story to cover the question of why Miss Kelly would deny the sale of the cattle and horses to him, when she knew that Skerrett could produce the Bill of Sale and the Receipt. According to Skerrett, the small fire in the Skerrett household explained this. Kelly heard about the fire, and thought both the Bill of Sale and Receipt had both been burned – hence she felt free to deny the sale of the cattle. But as Skerrett was able to subsequently produce the documents, Kelly declared them to be forgeries.

The next defence witness was thirteen-year old James Skerrett, who, in contrast to Richard Smith, was described by the *Sydney Morning Herald* as "bright and intelligent".[6] James deposed he heard his father ask his mother for money to pay Miss Kelly, and saw him get some notes but he did not know how much. His father had received a large amount of money by selling two drays and two horse teams at the Port Phillip diggings.

The next defence witness, Phillip Dew, deposed that Miss Kelly had told him Skerrett bought her cattle. He then bought cattle from Skerrett for £70, but Miss Kelly reclaimed the cattle from his wife, while he was away. As a result he lost the £70 he paid Skerrett.

The Trials of Isabella Mary Kelly

Samuel Turner stated Miss Kelly told him that Skerrett had bought her cattle. His son, William Turner, had been hounded out of the district because of Miss Kelly's threats. On one occasion, Samuel said, he had gone to Miss Kelly's house seeking payment of £36, but Miss Kelly said her "notes were too heavy" [indicating the notes were large denominations, and inferring that Kelly had £100 notes].

John Davis deposed that Miss Kelly told him Skerrett had bought her cattle. Earlier in the trial, Holroyd had put it to Miss Kelly that she made an offer of employment to a man in Sydney, and she had told this man that Skerrett had bought her cattle. Kelly had denied making the statement and denied ever meeting such a man.[7]

Catherine Skerrett, the eldest daughter, corroborated some of the evidence of her brother and sister.

The defence rested.

Attorney General Plunkett replied at considerable length to the defence.

Justice Stephen summed up, saying there had been a great amount of perjury given to the Court by one side or the other throughout the trial. If the prisoner was guilty then he was guilty of infamous fraud and deceit. If he were innocent then the prosecutrix was equally perjured in receiving £400 and depriving the prisoner of his *bona fide* property. The jury could not escape from coming to one of these conclusions.

The jury retired and returned twenty minutes later with a verdict of *guilty*.

In reaching their verdict, the jury stated, they believed the Bill of Sale and the Receipt were both forgeries.

Passing sentence on Charles Skerrett, Sir Alfred Stephen stated he agreed completely with the verdict of the jury. He was horrified at the conduct of the prisoner, who had induced his own children to commit perjury for his own fraudulent purposes.

The sentence was *ten years of labour on the roads*.

The jury had requested that the trial not be adjourned. As this request found mutual agreement, the trial started on the Thursday morning and continued all through the night. When Charles Skerrett was taken to a cell to begin his ten-year gaol sentence, it was four thirty in the morning. It was Good Friday.

⊰ Trial ⊱

For the prosecution, the evidence of Joseph Andrews was certainly the decisive factor in the jury reaching its verdict of guilty. Plunkett presented a number of documents bearing the genuine signature of Isabella Mary Kelly to the court for comparison with those signatures on the Bill of Sale and the Receipt. The jury was able to examine these in reference to Andrews' evidence.

Amazingly, the defence did not question Andrews on a complete reversal of testimony: he had sworn the Kelly signatures were genuine at the committal hearing and sworn they were forgeries here at the trial. Yet there was no challenge to his credibility.

Andrews would claim in later years that he was not completely sure about the signatures at the committal hearing, so he testified that they were genuine to be on the safe side.

For the defence, Margaret Skerrett's evidence had harmed the defence more than it had helped. It just did not ring true. John Dawson, Skerrett's solicitor, had gone into the trial completely believing in his client's innocence, but by the end of the trial, he too believed Skerrett was guilty.

Charles Skerrett had been extremely concerned about his daughter Jane testifying. He thought that the breaking of her leg had been a good solution to his problem, especially by claiming Kelly caused it. Ironically, Manning residents generally believed that she had *not* broken her leg, and that Skerrett concocted the story to prevent a weak testimony like that of her sister Margaret.

Catherine Skerrett's evidence was remarkable, not in what she said, but in what she did not say. She was around when the Bill of Sale was signed, so why did two of her younger sisters sign it and not her? Kelly claimed that Catherine knew it was wrong to sign the documents, and refused to do it. Further, why did the two girls sign at all? Why not William Turner and/or Ann Richards? No explanation had been offered.

Phillip Dew, Sam Turner, John Davis all testified that Miss Kelly had told them she had sold her cattle to Skerrett. Kelly never changed her story – she had only ever told two people, Findlay and Cameron. It was imperative, in such a small community, that people believe Skerrett had bought the cattle from Kelly – they would not buy the cattle from him otherwise. It is likely their evidence was at the behest of Skerrett either as a favour to him, or because they disliked Kelly – or for both reasons.

Kelly denied Samuel Turner's story of her notes being "too heavy". The bush was largely a cashless society, with goods and services bartered. Kelly claimed that when Turner was working on her house, he drew most of his money in rations. He had only once asked her for money, and on that occasion, she said she paid him.[8] There was one time, she recalled, when Sam Turner had been present as a man bought a foal from her for £35, paying with four £10 notes and receiving a £5 note in change. As a woman alone, it was most unlikely that Kelly would give even a hint of having a lot of money with her – she would never have told him her "notes were too heavy".

It is easy to see how Skerrett may have approached Samuel Turner: If Skerrett was found guilty, it would follow that William Turner was guilty of perjury and could face a gaol sentence. On the other hand, if Skerrett was found not guilty, William Turner would be in the clear.

There was one matter, which seemed to gain little attention at the trial, perhaps because of the difficulty it exhibited for both the prosecution and the defence. This was the difference in the Kelly signatures on the Bill of Sale and the Receipt.

Isabella Kelly thought she had made changes to her signature sometime in 1853, but she was not sure. On one occasion when in Sydney, Kelly presented a cheque to a grocer, before gathering goods from around the store and returning to the counter. The grocer showed her a copy of her signature, which he had just made, because, he said, it was so easy to forge. Amazed at its likeness, she decided to change her signature, in an effort to make it harder to imitate, by adding loops to the "y" in "Mary" and "Kelly".[9]

Skerrett had two originals – the lease for Brimbin, and the agreement to muster the cattle – indicating that Kelly's signature on these papers had no loops on the "y"s. But this was *after* she changed her signature. Did she sometimes relapse into the old signature?

Kelly observed another minor difference in the signatures on the Bill of Sale and the Receipt. The former was written with a steel pen, which is what she always used in her house, but the

Receipt was written with a quill pen.[10]

While the Chief Justice, Sir Alfred Stephen, had expressed his agreement in the jury's verdict, the residents of the Manning Valley did not hold the same conviction. Few, other than witnesses, would have attended the trial in Sydney. There were no local papers, and there was only one brief report of the trial in the *Sydney Morning Herald* and reprinted in the *Maitland Mercury*. And Isabella Kelly had few friends to promote her side of the story.

There was one crucial question which would come to dominate the residents' gossip and cause them disquiet: If Isabella Kelly had not sold her cattle to Skerrett, why were there so many people saying *Kelly told them* Skerrett had bought her cattle?

This led many in the Valley to believe that Kelly *did* actually sign the documents agreeing to sell her cattle to Skerrett, but they were not sure why. At the same time, the residents also assumed Skerrett had *not* given her the money as promised – he was not known to have any money.

All in all, it seemed to them, Kelly must have had *some* complicity in the affair. Yet while she was able to continue with her stock business at Brimbin, Charles Skerrett was spending ten years in gaol, leaving his wife and nine children destitute.

11. Fallout

During the twelve months before his conviction, Charles Skerrett had told Joseph Andrews on a number of occasions that Miss Kelly was going mad. Skerrett had said he would not be surprised if she committed suicide, and that "she would be found in a waterhole or hanging from a tree".[1] Andrews was quite dismissive of Kelly losing her sanity, and did not take much notice of Skerrett's remarks at the time.

But shortly after the trial, Andrews was talking with the Rev J. Carter and discovered that Skerrett had said the same thing to the minister.

Andrews became convinced that Skerrett had been considering the murder of Miss Kelly, with the intention of making it appear as a suicide. When he told Isabella Kelly of these suspicions, she related the story of Skerrett following her to Dungog. She was convinced Skerrett intended her harm, but perhaps the presence of young Richard Smith had deterred him.

Joseph Andrews also believed Skerrett had designs on Kelly's Mount George property. He recalled the time when Skerrett showed him the Bill of Sale at his hotel, and asked him what the value of Kelly's remaining horses and the value of her Mount George property. Andrews suggested a certain price of the property to Skerrett, to which Skerrett replied, "It is all mine."[2]

Understanding this to mean that Skerrett intended to buy Mount George, Andrews said to him, "Very well Mr Skerrett, I am very glad to hear it as I shall get rid of Miss Kelly. She was always a troublesome neighbour to me."[3] As a result, Skerrett was very frequently at the hotel after that, believing that Joseph Andrews was a ready ally.

Andrews inferred that with the accidental death of Kelly, a document might have been produced showing that Skerrett had bought Mount George. Kelly's death would also have solved Skerrett's problem of being prosecuted by her.

As always, Isabella Mary Kelly was a woman alone. On her death, who would have disputed Skerrett's ownership of Mount George?

Before the trial Reuben Richards had been a friend and ally of Charles Skerrett. He had taken residence with the Skerrett family at Brimbin sometime during 1854. There he met Frances Ann Andrews, generally called Ann (who appears to have been no relation to Joseph Andrews)[4].

Sometime in the early part of 1855, Reuben and Ann were married, with the wedding taking place at the Skerretts'.[5] Reuben was twenty-three and Ann about twenty. Later the same year, their first child, also named Reuben Richards, was born. Ann would bear another eight children, with the last being twenty-three years later.

The Richards family migrated from Stamford, Lincolnshire, England,[6] and arrived in the colony on the *Blonde* in 1849, moving to Nelsons Plains near Raymond Terrace.

Ann said Reuben did some work for Miss Kelly at Brimbin, but did not say in what capacity or for how long. Asked about Ann, Isabella Kelly said,[7]

> She reads and writes a little. She lived twelve months in my service, but Skerrett induced her to go to him after she had served that time with me …
>
> When she lived with me I had not a [bad] word to say about her. When she went to live with Skerrett, he dressed her out and had a horse (the horses were borrowed from Mr Sullivan) and saddle for her, and she used to ride out with them.

By changing employers, Ann had moved from Kelly's rooms at the Brimbin homestead to Skerrett's section of the house.

Ann's relationship with Miss Kelly after leaving her service was rather stormy, alternating between aggression and remorse. One can imagine Ann may have borne the brunt of Kelly's temper at times. Kelly, on the other hand, seems to have had a soft spot for Ann. There may even have been maternal feelings surfacing, for she would not hold Ann's actions against her and was always forgiving of her actions.

With the conviction of Charles Skerrett, Reuben and Ann Richards had a falling out with Maria Skerrett. It was unlikely that Ann received any of the wages due to her for service to the Skerrett family, as servants were not usually paid until the end of their contract. Maria Skerrett was certainly in no position to pay the money.

Further, the Skerretts had wanted both Reuben and Ann to testify against Miss Kelly at the trial, but they had refused to do so.

Reuben Richards returned to Nelsons Plains with his wife.

Some time after the trial, Maria Skerrett told Miss Kelly that Ann Richards had more than actively supported Charles Skerrett. Maria claimed that, at one time, her husband had wanted to drop the forgery business and take off for the goldfields, but Ann talked him out of it, and urged him to keep on with his scheming against Miss Kelly.

Isabella Kelly wrote to Ann Richards, and included Maria Skerrett's statements in her letter. Reuben and Ann Richards wrote a reply to Miss Kelly, with the letter in Reuben's handwriting and dated "Nelson's Plains 23 July, 1855":[8]

> I must say your letter has kindled a feeling of remorse and anguish, and an excessive pain of mind. I am both provoked and displeased with the absurdity of Mrs. Skerrett; not that she will not deliver up my wife's boxes, etc., but her statement regarding my wife's character. Dear Miss, I spoke the words of affection and candour; you state in your [letter] that Mrs. Skerrett tells you that my wife is equally as guilty as her husband; that she backed Skerrett in his plot, by perjury. And you further state, Skerrett was going to the diggings, but was prevented by my present wife's words, that they wanted to drive him from his wife and family, etc.; and that Davis[9] declares that she was the best active friend Skerrett had, and that she urged him on in his plot, but that you don't believe it is true, not all of it …

The letter confirmed what had been rumoured – that Charles Skerrett had written down on paper the evidence he wanted his witnesses to give in court:

> … I could not swear to the date – but that Mr and Mrs.

Skerrett were both in the parlour a long time, and after their consultation they gave me and Margaret one sheet of paper each. I asked what they were for, and Mrs Skerrett told me that whatever was in them Margaret and I were to learn. What was in Margaret's one I do not know; the one that was given to me I read it; the contents I need not repeat. After reading it I put it into my box; after some dispute arose, and I told Mrs. Skerrett and Margaret I would not learn it, but that when I was called to court I will tell them I know nothing of it; some time after this I went to my box and found it was gone. I made a great to-do about them going to my box without my consent. Margaret kept hers, and read it repeatedly …

One can feel nothing but sympathy for sixteen-year-old Margaret and the invidious position she had been placed in by her parents.

In the letter, there was also an oblique reference to a time when Skerrett tried to break open Kelly's door while Kelly was still inside, but there is no other reference to this incident.

Isabella Kelly said that, on another occasion, Ann Richards also told her personally that Skerrett had written out on a sheet of paper what evidence she was to give in the witness stand. Ann claimed she refused to do it, saying, "If I was to do as they told me, my soul would be forever damned."[10]

Ann added her own message at the end of the letter:

Dear Miss, we have thought ofttimes of you, and fancied something had happened to you. I was glad to hear from you, and shall be glad to see you any time you come down the line. Be pleased to write as soon as convenience will allow.

I remain,
  Yours affectionately,
  Frances Ann Richards

To finish the letter, Rueben Richards made a comment that suggested Mrs. Skerrett had once been "walking the streets of a city" and signed off with "Your sincere friend and well-wisher, Reuben Richards".

When asked if Reuben Richards was educated, Kelly said, "No; that is his letter – you will see by it he cannot spell."[11] (Evidently, the spelling mistakes were removed in the transcription of the letter in 1862). Joseph Andrews also claimed Richards was a bad speller, saying he spelled "situated" as "sutuated", the same way he pronounced it.[12]

Asked if Richards expressed himself well in conversation, Kelly said, "He does, but not grammatically, of course. He speaks in the usual way that a poor man would. But he is a clever fellow, there is no doubt".[13]

Ann Richards is yet another example of the power of Charles Skerrett's personality. Ann's decision to work for Skerrett as soon as she completed her contract with Kelly was a major victory in his campaign against Isabella Mary Kelly. With Ann Richards loyal to Isabella Mary Kelly, Skerrett's conspiracy would have petered out very quickly, as she could have testified how Skerrett deceived Kelly.

With the trial behind her and with Skerrett safely in gaol, Isabella Mary Kelly changed her mind — she was no longer leaving the district. She now resumed her seven-year lease of Brimbin, and continued her stock operations. Kelly now owned Mount George, as well as leasing Brimbin and the A.A. Company run, across the river from Mount George.

As far as Reuben and Ann Richards were concerned, all seemed forgiven. In May 1857, Isabella Mary Kelly agreed to rent them a paddock at Mount George on a two-year lease. The paddock contained the replacement cottage for Kelly's burned house, which the Turners had built for her. As well as running horses there, the Richards decided to offer accommodation to passing travellers. He also gained the Government contract to deliver mail around the district.

Kelly moved into a cottage on the A.A. Company run. Her reasons for doing this are not clear, but perhaps the friction between Joseph Andrews and herself had begun to surface again, and she wished to avoid returning to the previous unpleasantness between them.

While the Richards family settled into domestic life at Mount George, their former friends, the Skerretts, were in much different circumstances. Maria Skerrett and the nine children were now in extreme poverty, with no means of support, and relying on charity.

After the trial Maria Skerrett and the children stayed on at Brimbin for a time. On June 6, the family had been there for twelve months, without paying any rent. Of course they were now living in poverty, with no income. Magistrate Day asked them to leave Brimbin, probably at Kelly's request. Denny Day gave Mrs. Skerrett a sovereign.[14] Day was transferring back to Maitland and offered Margaret a job as a servant in his house there, but she refused.[15] Maria Skerrett and the children seemed to have stayed on in the Manning Valley, but where is not clear.

On September 21, 1855, the eldest Skerrett daughter, Catherine, married William Chapman. Three months later, on December 10, her sister Margaret married Henry Cann, the half brother of William Chapman.[16]

After his conviction, Charles Skerrett was transferred to Cockatoo Island Prison to serve his sentence. Cockatoo Island, just offshore from the inner Sydney suburb of Balmain, was more noted in the twentieth century as a naval dockyard after the closure of the prison.

Over the next few years Maria Skerrett visited her husband in prison on a number of occasions, taking some of the children with her. Occasionally Maria would hire a boat to Cockatoo Island, while on other occasions she used the Police Magistrate's boat, which was free but needed an application to the Magistrate from her.

Many wives would have taken the gaoling of their husband as the end of the road, and resigned themselves to waiting until their husband completed his prison sentence – but not Maria Skerrett. She campaigned tirelessly to have her husband released, writing letters and visiting anyone she thought might have some influence in the matter, always maintaining his innocence.

In particular, she wrote letters and made personal calls on Sir Alfred Stephen, who, as well as being the presiding judge at her husband's trial, was Chief Justice of the Supreme Court and had the ultimate responsibility of recommending any changes to a prisoner's sentence.

As the Attorney General, it was unethical for John Plunkett to make any decision about a case other than from the legal depositions placed before him. Informal personal interviews were out of the question. Plunkett recalled Maria Skerrett's approaches to him:[17]

> "After the trial I knew nothing of Skerrett at all, but I had a great sympathy with his family – his wife and daughters – used to come to my wife to try to get her to interfere on Skerrett's behalf.
>
> I always made it a point that my wife should never speak to me upon any matters of that kind, and I requested that she would not do so, and that she would not allow these people to see her at all. But they absolutely persecuted my wife, and called at my house to urge my wife, for a considerable time, to induce me to do something for the father."

Plunkett was making the point that he had to make his decisions based on depositions that could be tested in a court of law, and not by personal conversation – this could leave to bias.

Maria Skerrett was encouraged by the support of people at all levels in the Manning Valley. In 1857, Maria Skerrett presented a petition to Sir Alfred, requesting the release of Charles Skerrett.

Sir Alfred was astounded, not only by the volume of supporters of Skerrett, but the *quality* of them – *four* of the signatories were magistrates in the Manning Valley.

Magistrates were the leading citizens of any remote community, and their opinions demanded respect. On November 26, 1857, Sir Alfred wrote a letter to the Colonial Secretary (also the Premier of the state), with the petition attached:[18]

> The petition is recommended by above seventy persons … I am perfectly certain that probably *not one* [Justice Stephen's emphasis] of the subscribers knew anything of the circumstances, or had the means of considering the case.
>
> Mrs. Skerrett is a respectable person, with a large family, respectably educated, and in deep distress. It is not surprising, therefore, that she should have many well-wishers; and the more so, when it is remembered that her husband's prosecutrix is extremely disliked, and is in fact, a harsh and most eccentric person, almost always at variance with her neighbours.
>
> My duty, however, is to report most strongly against the petition. I believe Skerrett took advantage of Miss Kelly's habits and unpopularity, to lay against her a deep and clever

scheme of villainy, such as the records of few Courts can parallel. He very nearly succeeded in his plans; and I firmly believe that, had not two or three remarkably intelligent men been on the jury, he would have triumphed in an acquittal ...

It was remarkable that the eldest girl, aged 19, was not a witness to the alleged bill of sale, but the two younger daughters were selected, aged 17 and 15 respectively. It was singular, too, that Skerrett should have had and kept so large a sum as £400 in cash in the bush, which cash nobody saw except his own family ...

I have taken great pains, since the trial, to sift the facts, and my impressions remain unshaken. I cannot find out the prisoner's early history. He has been in all these colonies, and it is rumoured that he came out a convict, but I do not know how the fact is ...

I must truly regret that I cannot recommend any mitigation at present in this case.

Justice Stephen mentioned a Mr Blake, of Balmain, who gave Skerrett a good reference on his pre-colonial days. He was probably a relative, as Charles Skerrett's middle name of Blake was his mother's maiden name.

The Chief Justice received a letter from Magistrate Hawthorne, of the Manning, as well as a letter from Rev. J. Carter, also of the Manning, who wrote to tell him that he had signed the petition, but had never actually met Skerrett. (Justice Stephen would have sent this letter to the Colonial Secretary, except he had misplaced it). The Chief Justice had written back to Carter and Hawthorne but received no further correspondence from them.[19]

Sir Alfred had also borrowed from the Crown Solicitor the two documents, which the whole case revolved around – the Bill of Sale and the Receipt. He examined them closely, particularly in connection with Joseph Andrews' evidence on Kelly's signature.

Sir Alfred, as Chief Justice, was now operating under a new politicised system of Government. New South Wales had been granted self-government and the first elections for the Lower House, the House of Assembly, were held in the previous year, 1856. The Governor now took on the role of a Governor-General, while the Premier also took the office of Colonial

Secretary. Sir Alfred, as the Chief Justice, was given a seat in the Legislative Council, the Upper House. Much of the pressure Sir Alfred now received was *political* pressure — a pressure he was not used to.

Chief Justice Stephen had gone over and over all the evidence of the case in minute detail. He even wrote to John Plunkett and received confirmation that Plunkett "never had any doubt in this case at all".[20]

Sir Alfred held an absolute conviction of Charles Skerrett's guilt.

12. A Window of Doubt

Horses had been the strength in Isabella Kelly's business.

One manager for the A. A. Company had once stated that the Company had shipped horses to India for Miss Kelly, and that her horses were of a better quality than the A. A. Company's — they had fetched higher prices.[1]

In the early 1850s, she had sent eight horses with Captain Goble to Madras on the west coast of India, receiving £200 for them after all expenses had been paid. In 1854, she contracted with Capt Goble to send fifty horses to Madras. This deal appears to have fallen through amid her distraction with Charles Skerrett.

A Mr Peters came from Port Essington, Victoria, to Brimbin, to look over her horses. Peters offered Kelly £4000 for the lot. Kelly said she wanted £4500. She would have taken the £4000, she said, except she may have needed to pay £500 to Captain Goble as compensation for breaking her contract to him. No deal was made.[2]

William Burt ran into Isabella Mary Kelly in Castlereagh Street, Sydney, in August 1855 and again the following January. He told her he was chartering a boat to take a shipment of horses to Calcutta, on the east coast of India, for sale to British cavalry.[3]

Kelly told Burt she had not sent horses to Calcutta before, so she would not send many horses this time, and see how much she received for them. She might be able to send as many as fifty horses after that. Burt assured her she would get better prices for them than she did in Madras.

Burt called at Brimbin in March 1856 and Kelly showed him some of her horses. He told her that he had been to Cundletown and the firm of How, Walker & Co would ship twenty horses with him, and he wanted twenty horses from her. She would have to get the horses to Port Stephens (about sixty miles from

The Trials of Isabella Mary Kelly

Brimbin) by May 8th.

The British Cavalry wanted the horses unbroken so they could be the trainers. Burt required the horses to be "quiet", with the generally accepted definition being that the horses would drink from a bucket and not object to having their tails pulled.

Fifteen horses were made ready by April 10th and left for Port Stephens, under the control of Kelly's stockmen. At Port Stephens one of the horses escaped and consequently only fourteen boarded the *Harkaway* before sailing to Calcutta.

In the following year, William Burt returned from Calcutta and sent Isabella Kelly his account stating she would receive just £45 from the deal.

Burt stated three horses died during the voyage and two after landing. The nine remaining horses sold for £584 with prices ranging from £30 to £110.

Among his deductions Burt deducted £25 for each for six empty stalls on the *Harkaway*, totalling £150, plus the profit he would have made on these horses, claiming Kelly had *contracted* to send him twenty horses, when in fact she only sent fourteen. He charged 5% commission rather than the 2½ per cent claimed by Kelly as the agreed rate.

Burt provided no proof of the death of the five horses. Kelly claimed it was usual to cut out the brands of dead horses and return them to the owner as evidence of their death as Captain Goble did this when shipping her horses to Madras. Burt did not.

Isabella Mary Kelly was furious. She refused to accept the payment of £45 and took court action against William Burt. Burt was about to leave the colony as the warrant reached him, forcing him to post bail and cancel his departure.

The matter was heard in the Supreme Court before a jury of four on Wednesday, April 21, 1858. The judge was the Chief Justice, Sir Alfred Stephen. Barrister Arthur Holroyd, briefed by solicitor John Dawson, represented Isabella Kelly as the plaintiff. (Ironically, these were the same lawyers who defended Skerrett at his trial.) Mr Isaacs, briefed by Stephen Brown, appeared for the defendant William Way Burt.

Isabella Mary Kelly deposed that Burt's commission was to be 2½ per cent. She told Burt she was not sure how many horses she would be able to send as she could not rely on her servants.

She was short of hands, but would try and send as many horses as she could get ready in time. Mr Burt said he hoped she would send twenty horses, and she said he was not to keep any stalls for her. She told Burt she would try and send fifteen, but he must not charge more than $2\frac{1}{2}$ per cent commission. Burt agreed to this saying that as she intended to send more later on, he would be reasonable.[4]

There had been a deal of correspondence between Kelly and Burt before the ship sailed, and some of these letters were read out in court (but unfortunately their contents were not recorded). In particular, after his visit to Brimbin, Burt sent a memorandum of the fees he would charge, but which he had not signed. Isabella Kelly said she refused to sign it, as it was not what they had agreed (but remarkably, took no other action).

After the horses boarded the ship, Kelly received a receipt from Burt, in which she claimed Burt wrote, "I have received on board the *Harkaway*, 8th May, fourteen horses. I sail tomorrow." She had given this receipt to her attorney, Mr Holroyd, but his clerk said it had been lost after he handed it to Commissioner Carter at a pre-trial meeting of the opposing parties.

Burt claimed this receipt acknowledged his custody of fourteen horses as being "part of twenty". The Clerk took the stand to swear that the receipt contained no mention of twenty horses. Kelly said her stockman had brought the receipt to her, but he had since left for the diggings. Carter deposed he remembered nothing about the receipt.

In his evidence, Francis Donahoo confirmed that he and the stockman had delivered fifteen horses to Port Stephens for Miss Kelly, describing the horses as all "quiet" by the time they were delivered.

In his deposition, William Burt stated that he told Miss Kelly he always charged 8% commission. Miss Kelly said she would not allow it, so he said he would only charge her 5%. At Brimbin, Miss Kelly told him she would send him fifty horses. Then she spoke of sending thirty-five. He told her his terms were for twenty – he fixed it at twenty. She did not reply to that statement. Miss Kelly continually changed the subject. She said she was very anxious to send a large number of horses, but she never said not to keep any stalls for her.

The Trials of Isabella Mary Kelly

The horses were knocked up by the voyage, Burt said, as it was a long one, and the weather was boisterous and warm. The horses were not "quiet", even though they could stand having their tails pulled, and drank from a bucket. Some of Miss Kelly's horses required five or six men to keep them in order, and one even kicked a groom's brains out.

Burt said he expected eleven more horses from the Cundletown Company, but he did not have a *contract* with them, only an *undertaking* – there was no binding contract. The ship could have carried 140 horses. He purchased 16 horses in Maitland to make a total of 120 horses shipped.

Sydney Burt, the brother of William Burt, testified that a few weeks before the *Harkaway* sailed from Port Stephens, Miss Kelly called at their Sydney office to talk about a possible sale of her stud on the Manning. Miss Kelly told him she had arranged to sell twenty horses with his brother, William. He saw her again after the ship sailed, and asked her why she did not send twenty horses. Miss Kelly replied that it was because she could not collect them.

Holroyd recalled Isabella Kelly. She had not been in Sydney two weeks before the shipment. The conversation with Sydney Burt did not take place. She had gone to Burt's office *after* the shipment left, but she had no discussion with Sydney Burt about the horses.

After summing up by both Mr Isaacs and Mr Holroyd, Justice Stephen gave his instructions to the jury. The jury returned about thirty minutes later, giving their verdict *for the defendant*, William Burt.

The last sentence of Sir Alfred Stephen's notes read: "A result which is entirely in unison with my own opinion."[5]

There can be no doubt that Isabella Kelly believed she had been wronged. At one stage during the trial, Kelly said Mr Isaacs approached her with an offer to settle the case out of court for £100. Kelly rejected it, saying she wanted £400 or £500 as Burt had told her she would make at least £40 per horse.[6]

Isabella Kelly was not a good witness. A good witness is clear and decisive on the witness stand. Burt was a good witness. Kelly was often vague, got her dates wrong and contradicted herself. One line of evidence in the Judge's notes recorded Kelly as stating, "I can't remember when the defendant first spoke of twenty horses", which the Judge then followed with the bracketed statement, "(Then she says, 'It was at Brimbin'.)"

Kelly did not always make her meaning clear. Some may have interpreted her statement "I did not promise to send him twenty" as they *talked* about twenty horses, but twenty were not *promised*, while others may have interpreted this as meaning twenty were never spoken about, which was clearly false. At another point, the Chief Justice recorded Kelly as saying, "I told him I would try and send him fifteen."

In a civil trial the jury had to decide whether to believe the plaintiff or the defendant – a decision between the two had to be made – whereas in a criminal trial the jury had to be convinced of the defendant's guilt beyond a reasonable doubt.

With Burt's testimony that he had a *contract* with Kelly (but not a signed written contract) and only an *undertaking* with the Cundletown Company, Holroyd contended that Kelly was actually paying for the Cundletown Company's shortfall of eleven horses, making the point that the shortfall of horses was assigned to Kelly because she was a woman, and seen to be an *easier mark* for recovering money.

Stephen Brown, Burt's solicitor, said he thought the case had gone Burt's way because of the contents of a letter written by Kelly to Burt, which was read to the Court. He thought it contained a phrase like, "I had intended to send twenty, but found I could not get them, through the carelessness of my servants", but he could not recall the exact sentence.[7]

Brown thought a second factor was the case of two oaths against one – both William Burt and Sydney Burt had sworn that Kelly had promised twenty horses, in separate individual conversations with her.[8]

Burt offered no proof of the death of Kelly's horses, no confirmation of the ship's manifest and produced no documents of the sale of the horses from the auctioneer, saying the auctioneer did not give them to him.

All of these details depended on Burt's word.

In all her appearances in various courts over many years,

whenever it came down to Isabella Kelly's word against a man's word, the *man* was always believed. In this case there were two men.

Mr Holroyd had asked Sir Alfred to request the jury, in returning their verdict, to give an opinion on whether they believed Burt's account to be an *honest* one. Justice Stephen said he would not "embarrass the jury" with such a question, as "he saw no reason whatever to doubt the perfect truth and honesty of the account, and he had no doubt the jury and everyone else who heard the case, must be of the same opinion."[9]

The Chief Justice had a complete faith in Burt's honesty and integrity.

This leads to the question of how Isabella Kelly was perceived by the various participants in this 1858 case. Was Isabella Kelly seen as a *businesswoman* in the same way as William Burt was seen as a businessman? Or was she seen as a *woman in business*, naïve and one who really had no right to be there?

Crucially, Sir Alfred Stephen's conviction in the honesty of William Burt led him to believe Isabella Kelly had *lied under oath* in this case.

At no stage though, did Sir Alfred ever indicate precisely where he thought she had lied. He said that perjury was rarely proved because two corroborating witnesses to the perjury were needed. He did not have the evidence to prove her perjury – hence he did not charge her.[10] So it came down to belief.

The Burt civil trial resulted in the opening of a window of doubt in the mind of the Chief Justice: *Isabella Kelly might have lied at Skerrett's trial.*

Four months later, Sir Alfred Stephen was once again considering the Skerrett case.

By this time, Maria Skerrett had presented another two petitions to the Chief Justice. Some of the signatories were even more prominent members of society than before – there were signatures from Mr Henry Parkes (later Sir Henry), Mr Thomas Whistler Smith, Mr Tooth, Mr Williamson, Mr John Campbell, Mr G. Thornton and "many other persons of character and station".[11]

Sir Alfred Stephen had lengthy discussions with Thornton

and Williamson but could not get them to change their views.

The Chief Justice went over the evidence again and again, but no matter how many times he went over it, he always came back to the same conclusion – Kelly had been truthful at the Skerrett trial and she had been greatly wronged.

In a letter dated August 5, 1858, Sir Alfred again wrote to the Colonial Secretary, mentioning his doubts about the truthfulness of Miss Kelly: [12]

> I return here the two petitions of Mrs. Skerrett, praying for a mitigation of her husband's sentence. She naturally believes him to be innocent; and it is not surprising that she has found many respectable people ready to adopt her impressions. I am somewhat startled by the assurance, to which many respectable persons have affixed their signatures, that the general impression in the neighbourhood of the occurrence was in the prisoner's favour. Such a circumstance is, unquestionably, not lightly to be regarded in any quarter.
>
> I must admit, also, that I had recently tried a case, in which Miss Kelly, the prosecutrix of Skerrett, was a witness, and that her testimony was contradicted on essential points by the defendant, whom the jury believed; and that, in fact her evidence on that occasion was, in my opinion, false.
>
> Nevertheless, false testimony in support of a litigant's own interests is of frequent occurrence, in cases where the suspicion of perjury is scarcely possible; and the difficulty in Skerrett's case is, that Miss Kelly must have been perjured if she did not speak the truth, and that circumstances were strongly, if not conclusively, in favour of her story …
>
> Neither can I believe in Skerrett's innocence, without believing also in the perjury of Mr Andrews. Mrs. Skerrett represents the latter as a person of questionable character. He has, however, been recently made a Magistrate; and at the time of the trial he kept a public house. …
>
> I cannot think it credible, in opposition to Miss Kelly's oath, that Skerrett kept so large a sum as four £100 notes in the bush, or that he would have been content with a bill of sale witnessed by his own daughters merely. Mr Blake says, indeed, that Skerrett had in his possession, on returning from Melbourne, from 100 to 150 sovereigns. This, however, is far short of £400; not to mention expenditure, for his family and the like, between that period and the date of the bill of sale…
>
> If Skerrett really had possessed four £100 notes, would he

not have been able to prove the fact? Then on the supposition that Miss Kelly really received such notes, how happened it that no effort was made to trace any of them? ... He declared that the money was paid; but he unhappily specified a bank, which never issued £100 notes.

I retain my opinion, therefore, that Skerrett was guilty of the crime laid to his charge. At the same time, if the general opinion be, after fair means of inquiry, that the verdict was either unsatisfactory or wrong, I am far from desiring that the conclusion should be unfavourable to Mr Skerrett. Perhaps a reference to the Manning Bench on that point may be desirable; or an inquiry into any facts, which may appear to be material. And, on the other hand, Skerrett's real character and history should be ascertained.

I wish it to be understood that I still retain my first opinion; but I shall be well pleased to hear that, nevertheless, this prisoner can be released, especially if compelled to quit the colony, consistently with due regard to the interests of public justice and the community.

One magistrate recommends the petition, because he in his wisdom thinks the sentence too severe. My answer is, that if the prisoner was guilty at all, the sentence was a light one; for he robbed an unprotected woman of all she possessed, and then added to the that crime circumvention and forgery, supported by the subornation of perjury by his own child.

Sir Alfred Stephen raised the very pertinent point that if Miss Kelly had lied at the Skerrett trial, then it followed as a natural consequence that Joseph Andrews had also lied, and Joseph Andrews was now a Magistrate (appointed on November 13, 1857). But then *four* other Manning Valley Magistrates had signed one of Mrs. Skerrett's petitions.

In all his deliberations over the evidence presented in the Skerrett trial, the Chief Justice could not accept Skerrett's story of the payment of the £400. This problem would have to be satisfactorily explained to him before he could ever change his opinion.

Chief Justice Stephen still maintained a full belief in the guilt of Charles Skerrett but perhaps, in response to the pressure being exerted, it would be politic to find a means of setting him free. He did not actually recommend Skerrett's release, but he would not oppose it, if Skerrett left the colony upon release.

These matters weighed so heavily on his mind that, the very next day, he wrote a second letter on the same issue to the Colonial Secretary: [13]

> As to Skerrett's case, I have every desire that effect shall be given (if thought right by those on whom the responsibility rests) to the "general opinion" should that opinion be shown to be founded on knowledge of the real facts, and on fair consideration of the reasons *for*, as well as against the verdict. Will, then, those who oppose the verdict say how they reconcile with innocence the circumstances connected with the four £100 notes?
>
> I have shown my first report to ONE of the subscribers, and he retains his opinion against the verdict, because, though knowing nothing of Skerrett, he thinks very ill of Miss Kelly.

Here was one of the few times the prejudice against Isabella Kelly was actually recorded. This same (unnamed) gentleman, Sir Alfred said, was not prepared to examine the facts of the case – his judgement had been formed by his dislike for Miss Kelly.

Sir Alfred had heard the latest theory about the Skerrett case, which was gaining greater momentum in the Manning Valley. It gave a reason for Kelly to sign the Bill of Sale and the Receipt: Kelly had wished to avoid having her property confiscated if found guilty of the charge of cattle stealing (brought by McPherson and Turner). Under nineteenth century law the property of a convicted felon could be appropriated by the State.

This would explain, the speculation went, why Kelly had told so many people Skerrett had bought her cattle. The fact of Skerrett helping to bail Kelly out when she was arrested was perceived as making this theory even more credible.

Pursuing this conjecture to a logical conclusion meant Skerrett had reneged on their supposed deal after Kelly signed the documents, and tried to keep the cattle and horses.

Sir Alfred said that he could not give any consideration to this theory in his deliberations as Skerrett had not used it as a defence at his trial.

There, a concerned Sir Alfred Stephen let the matter rest.

13. A Hidden History

One particular morning as Maria Skerrett was leaving the Supreme Court after talking with the Chief Justice, another lady arrived to see the Sir Alfred. She recognized Mrs. Skerrett and remarked to Sir Alfred that she had first met Mrs. Skerrett in Hobart. With Hobart being a penal settlement, it immediately raised Sir Alfred's suspicions about Skerrett's past. At their next meeting, Sir Alfred asked Mrs. Skerrett if her husband had been a convict in Hobart, and while she did not deny it, Maria Skerrett would give him no details.

Charles Skerrett had been very careful to conceal his personal history.

No one in the Manning Valley seems to have known much of his long history of trouble with the law. While Maria Skerrett had aroused the interest of the Chief Justice in Skerrett's past, Sir Alfred made no attempt to contact officials at Hobart on the matter – no letter of enquiry was written.

If the public had possessed a full knowledge of Charles Skerrett's hidden history, particularly his conviction and transportation to Van Diemans Land, their attitude to Skerrett may have changed considerably.

Charles Blake Skerrett was born in 1816, in the small town of Carnacrow in County Galway,[1] on the west coast of Ireland and on about the same latitude as Dublin, on the east coast. For centuries the Skerretts (alternatively Skerritt or Skerratt) had been one of the famous families in Galway known as the "fourteen tribes". Skerrett was well educated and from a highly respected family. While the family was not overly rich, they were certainly well off.

Because of his background, the arrest of Charles Skerrett for robbery in London in October 1835 caused great interest in the

London newspaper, *The Times*, which gave a full report of his arrest in its Bow Street Police Report:[2]

Yesterday a young man of gentlemanly appearance and well dressed, who gave his name as Charles Blake Skerrett, was brought up in custody by Ballard and Fletcher, the [police] officers, charged on suspicion of stealing from the Bath Hotel, Piccadilly, a jewel-case, containing a gold watch and various articles of jewellery to a considerable amount, the property of a gentleman named Pratt, who had lodged at the Bath Hotel when the robbery took place, and is now at Totton, near Southampton. A paragraph describing the robbery appeared in the papers about a week ago.

It appeared that on Monday, the 19th inst., the prisoner came to the Bath Hotel and ordered dinner, telling the waiter that he should sleep there the night. He was then shown to a bedroom up stairs, where he placed his carpetbag, and went down to the coffee-room, where he dined, and almost immediately, after dinner he called the waiter, paid his bill, and told him that business called him to Birmingham, and he must proceed to that place immediately by the coach. He then went up stairs to the bed-room he had previously engaged, and returned with his carpet-bag, which the porter belonging to the hotel offered to carry to the coach for him, but he declined his assistance, and left the house with the bag in his hand, with the intention, as it was then supposed, of proceeding to the city by the branch Birmingham coach.

Soon after he had gone it was discovered that the jewel-case in question, with the property it contained, had been stolen from the bedroom of Mr Pratt, which was situated close to the one, which the prisoner was to have occupied. An account of the robbery, and a list of articles stolen, appeared in the Police Gazette and the Hue and Cry but no trace could be discovered of the prisoner until yesterday morning, when from information received by the two officers above-mentioned, they proceeded to a respectable board and lodging house in the neighbourhood of Leicester Square, where they found the prisoner, who had assumed the name of Jones.

He turned pale on seeing them enter the room, and learning that they had come from Bow-street, he appeared greatly agitated; but afterwards recovered his self-possession, and acknowledged that his name was Skerritt, telling the officers that they were mistaken in supposing that he was the person they sought, and that they had come on a wrong scent. In reply to a question put to him, he denied that he was at the Bath Hotel on the evening in question, and again assured them that they were mistaken. On searching him, however, they took from his person a gold watch and massive gold chain, and upon examining the former, the initials "J. B. P". were found engraved on the outer case, the inner case bearing the maker's name "Oanthony, Cheapside". The prisoner said that the watch and chain were his, but on comparing them with the description of a watch and chain included amongst the articles stolen, they were found to agree in every particular.

The officers then proceeded to search the room, and in a drawer they found a gold seal, two gold snaps, a pair of tortoiseshell combs set with pink topazes and gold, a gold ornament for the head set with rubies, emeralds, and pearls, together with several pawnbrokers' duplicates forbrooches, earrings, bracelets, &c., and one for a diamond ring pawned for 4/-, all which articles were included in the list of the stolen property. They also found a tin jappaned case, which agreed with the description of that in which the jewels were deposited, and upon examining it the officers found that it had been forced open.

The officers also took possession of a carpetbag, on a brass plate affixed to which was the name of Mrs. Woulfe. The bag contained some pocket-handkerchiefs, marked with the same name. A writing-case was likewise found in the prisoner's room, the name of the person to whom it belonged being obliterated with ink.

The prisoner being placed at the bar, charged as above, the officers requested the magistrate to remand him, to give time for the attendance of Mr Pratt, to identify the property.

The prisoner, who said nothing in his defence, was accordingly remanded until Monday next, when it is expected that other charges of a similar nature will be preferred against him.

He is said to be respectably connected in Ireland, his sister being married to a gentleman who represents in Parliament one of its western counties. He himself is a married man, and according to the statement of a gentleman who said he was his brother-in-law, he left his wife behind him in Ireland, and when she followed him to this country he refused to see her. The same gentleman stated that the prisoner had committed several depredations of a similar description at various hotels in Dublin, from which city he was obliged to make precipitate retreat, the police being after him in all directions.

The prisoner's person was fully identified in the course of the day by the waiter who attended on him at the Bath Hotel, and the porter who offered to assist him with his luggage.

Amongst the articles found in his room were two wigs, the one dark and the other a light colour, and a pair of spectacles with green glasses. These articles were supposed to have been used by the prisoner in order to disguise his person.

In all probability, one of Skerrett's fellow lodgers at the London boarding house reported him to the police. On the following Monday Skerrett was again brought before the Bow Street Magistrate, where several other charges were laid against him. Lieutenant Tracy, the Governor of Tothill Fields Prison, where he had been detained, reported that he noticed Skerrett's demeanour changed after his arrest. *The Times* reported:[3]

> [Lieutenant Tracy] became very uneasy about him, and getting up from his bed in the middle of the night, he called one of the turnkeys, and proceeding to the cell where the prisoner was confined, he found him in a very desponding state. Upon searching his person a knife was found upon him, which must have been given to him by one of the prisoners confined for debt, by having been allowed an indulgence during the day to walk in the debtors' yard, and as no prisoner charged with felony was allowed a knife, it was most likely procured by him in that way. The knife, of course, was taken from him, and he was again locked up in the cell.
>
> The Governor said, however, that he still felt extremely uneasy respecting the prisoner, and after some time he again went to the cell, when he found the prisoner stretched on the floor, apparently in the agonies of death, he having contrived to tie his handkerchief so tight around his neck that he must inevitably have been strangled had not assistance arrived. His knuckles were bruised and cut from struggling on the floor, and his face was black and convulsed. Having with some difficulty cut the handkerchief, the prison surgeon was sent for, and the necessary means having been adopted to restore animation, he at length recovered; but he was still so weak that when Shackell [the warder] arrived yesterday morning to convey him to this office he was obliged to be assisted into the coach.
>
> After the examination yesterday, his wife, a young woman

of rather interesting appearance, who has followed him from Ireland, was allowed to accompany him in the coach to Tothill-fields Prison.

Charles Skerrett was nineteen years old. His wife Maria was seventeen, and their first child, Catherine, had been born earlier the same year. *The Times* reported that Skerrett's solicitor, who had been employed by a friend of the family, said Skerrett was related to an Irish Marquis.

On November 6, Charles Skerrett was again brought to face the Bow Street Magistrate, where he was charged with a second robbery bearing the same modus operandi as the first.[4]

A porter from the Sussex hotel deposed a blue vest and coat were reported stolen from a room at the hotel on October 12. He saw Skerrett arrive on that evening and order dinner, at the same time asking for a bed for the night. Skerrett was shown to a room upstairs. After dinner Skerrett left the hotel and returned half an hour later, asking for a candle to get to his room. Shortly after Skerrett again left the hotel, saying he would return soon, and pay his bill then, but he never returned.

A pawnbroker from Soho produced two coats, which owner identified as his stolen property. The pawnbroker said that Skerrett had pawned them several days after October 12, and had received three shillings and four pence for them.

The arresting officer told the Court that on arresting Skerrett, he searched his room in Leicester Square. Hidden in a secret draw of Skerrett's writing desk, he found duplicates of the pawn tickets for the coats.

The Magistrate indicated there were other stealing charges pending against Skerrett, but this evidence was sufficient to commit him for trial.

On November 26, 1835, Skerrett was brought before Chief Justice Denman in the Central Criminal Court, London (also known as the Old Bailey).[5] When the evidence was outlined against him, Skerrett offered no defence. He made no statements mitigating his actions and no character witnesses were presented on his behalf. The Chief Justice delivered a verdict of guilty and sentenced Charles Skerrett to transportation for life.

Sitting in court witnessing these events, life must have

seemed very bleak for Maria Skerrett – she was now three months pregnant with their second child.

Charles Skerrett, sailed from the Downs on January 20, 1836, on board the *Elphinstone*, one of 238 male convicts, and arrived in Van Diemans Land on May 24. As very few convicts could read or write, it was noted that Skerrett, with his education, could be assigned to work as a clerk or a teacher. Skerrett started his convict life as a clerk.[6]

The day before her husband Charles stepped ashore in Hobart, Maria gave birth to their second daughter in London.

Twelve months later, Maria and the two daughters arrived in Hobart on June 1, 1837, travelling as passengers in steerage on the lower decks of the *Andromeda*, the cheapest fare. There was financial assistance available to the wives of transported convicts to enable them to join their husbands in the colony, and Maria may have received this assistance.

The convict record of Charles Skerrett in Tasmania proved to be quite chequered.

A month after his arrival, on June 20, 1836, Skerrett was charged with stealing a waistcoat, while working as a clerk, and received a sentence of twelve months hard labour.

Three months later, while working on the roads, he was charged with two offences:
- improperly bandaging his leg so he would not be able to work
- striking the Station Overseer.

Skerrett received a total of eight months hard labour as punishment.

Assigned as a constable[7] in 1839, Skerrett was soon in trouble again:
- March 30, charged with misconduct, neglect of duty and disobedience of orders – ten days confinement in a cell on bread and water.
- May 14, charged with neglect of duty and absent from his post without leave – 48 hours Tread Wheel.
- May 31, charged with being drunk – dismissed as a constable.

On June 7 there was a recommendation for a ticket-of-leave for his praiseworthy conduct in the apprehension of a murderer, apparently made before the these last charges were brought against him. This ticket-of-leave did not last long.

In 1841 Skerrett was involved in a number of incidents:
- Jan 15, charged with insolence and refusing to work – fourteen days solitary confinement on bread and water;
- June 30, charged with possession of an illegal weapon – deprived of ticket-of-leave with twelve months hard labour;
- September 1, charged with disorderly conduct – 48 hours solitary confinement.

Skerrett was transferred to the prison at Port Arthur.[8]

On November 18, 1842, Skerrett received a recommendation for his conduct in the pursuit of bushrangers, and regained his ticket-of-leave.

Three years later on October 28, 1845, he was recommended for a Conditional Pardon. Less than a month later on November 21, he was charged with unlawfully inciting a woman to commit perjury, but the charge was dismissed.

Finally, in October 1846 after ten years of life as a convict in Van Diemans Land, his Conditional Pardon was approved and Charles Skerrett became a free man. The Conditional Pardon meant that the prisoner had suffered sufficient punishment for his crimes, and had one limitation only (which the Absolute Pardon did not) – he could not leave the colony of Australia.

Skerrett and his family sailed from Hobart Town to Melbourne on the *Margaret* on January 6, 1847.[9] Three daughters had been added to the family while they were in Hobart.

His movements in Victoria are hard to trace until two and a half years later, when Mr & Mrs. "Skerret",[10] together with a son and six daughters are recorded as travelling from Belfast, Victoria, to Warnamboul and then to Sydney, arriving on board the *Brothers* on August 16, 1849.

Charles Skerrett met Henry Vaughan early in 1850, and went to work for him. Henry Vaughan had arrived in Sydney on the board the *Crescent* in 1840 and established the Albion Brewery in Elizabeth Street, Sydney, with very little money, building up the business quite considerably over the next ten years.[11] Henry Vaughan had been so impressed with the work of Charles Skerrett at his brewery that, at one stage, he considered making him a partner in the firm.

That all changed when Vaughan discovered that Skerrett had stolen one of the firm's horses and sold it. Vaughan took out a warrant and charged Skerrett with horse stealing, but the Magistrate dismissed the charge.

Next, Vaughan discovered that Skerrett had taken some of the firm's equipment and sold it. After working for the brewery for twelve months, Skerrett was dismissed. Vaughan then found that Skerrett had made a parting gesture of visiting the firm's debtors and, after collecting their debts to the Albion Brewery, pocketed the money for himself. Vaughan said he took legal advice, but did not pursue a prosecution because of the cost of such an action. The result was the bankruptcy of the brewery, which forced Henry Vaughan to subsequently turn to barbering for his livelihood.

It is hard to go past this episode without considering the possibility of Charles Skerrett achieving a highly successful career, especially as a salesman, if only he could suppress his criminal tendencies and apply himself fully as an *honest* employee – he had so much potential.

Charles Skerrett soon found another job as an employee of the wine merchants, Price, Favenc & Gwyn. It was not too long before he was in trouble with that firm as well.

On Thursday, August 7, 1851, Charles Skerrett appeared in court to answer charges of embezzlement.[12] The charge sheet listed him as a salesman, but he may have been involved in distilling as well as other aspects of the firm's operations.

John Ryan Brenan appeared as Skerrett's defence attorney, who, ironically, was the same attorney later hired by Isabella Mary Kelly to assist her to convict Skerrett in his trial of 1855. Brenan knew some members of the Skerrett family in Galway. Mr Gwyn's prosecution of Skerrett resulted from three unaccounted sums of money, which had been collected and given to Skerrett, but did not appear in the firm's financial books.

The first prosecution witness, a porter with the firm, testified he delivered a parcel of wine and collected eighteen shillings and six pence (18s. 6d.) as payment. He gave this money to Charles

Skerrett in the office. Another porter with the firm testified he collected two sums of money and gave both to Skerrett on his return to the office.

Skerrett's employer, Mr Gwyn, deposed he had searched through the books and found no record of these sums of money. He added that he had included a fourth charge in the original prosecution, but had quashed it when he later discovered it in the books.

Brenan, for the defence, asked for an adjournment of the Court. This would delay his cross-examination of Mr Gwyn, giving Mr Gwyn an opportunity to again examine the firm's financial books under instruction from his client, Mr Skerrett. Brenan was sure that his client "would be able very satisfactorily to explain the charges of Mr Gwyn".[13]

The Court adjourned.

When the Court resumed on the following Monday, Mr Gwyn was able to report that he had indeed been able to find two of these items. Other employees had been able to account for them. Mr Gwyn was unable to find any trace of the third sum, but said he was prepared to believe that some explanation was possible – hence he was willing to drop the charges against Skerrett.

The prosecutor was pleased to announce the termination of the prosecution, and the Magistrate discharged the prisoner "without the slightest reproach on Mr Skerrett's character".[14]

It defies explanation that it was not until his employer reached the witness box, that Charles Skerrett thought, quite confidently, he would be able to help Mr Gwyn trace the money – notwithstanding only two of the three missing amounts.

That Skerrett was unable to do this in the months before the matter got to court, suggests he was working overtime behind the scenes, organising other employees to help him get out of trouble.

Skerrett left the firm (whether by his own choice or not, is not clear), and together with his nine-year-old son, headed for the Victorian Goldfields. John Ryan Brenan visited the Skerrett home with the intention of collecting his legal fees from Skerrett, only to find Maria Skerrett and her daughters living in poverty with the rent owing.[15]

In Victoria, Skerrett said he worked for a brewery and "was employed in carrying freight between Kilmore and McIvor diggings".[16] When he and James returned from the diggings, Maria Skerrett and the daughters were living in Port Macquarie.[17]

There are some unanswered questions here: How did Maria and family get from Sydney to Port Macquarie? When did she move? How did they survive without their bread-winner?

Now living in Port Macquarie, Skerrett began dealing in horses. He bought horses on the MacLeay River or at Port Macquarie and took them down to Raymond Terrace and Sydney for re-sale. Joseph Andrews said that Skerrett usually called at his Inn with two or three horses in tow, when passing through on these trips. Skerrett told Andrews he was not making much on the horses and that he had "not been successful to any extent at the diggings".[18] It was for this reason Andrews did not believe Skerrett when he said he had given Miss Kelly £800 for her cattle.

Skerrett took a lease of Clifton Vineyard from Major Innes, just a mile and a half out of Port Macquarie. While at the vineyard Skerrett apparently did some illegal distilling, with the result that Major Innes, or his partner, was in trouble with the law.[19]

Innes cancelled Skerrett's lease, and evicted him.

Skerrett sued Major Innes for breach of contract on the lease, taking out the warrant on March 25, 1854.[20] Skerrett claimed he had lost money on a large quantity of goods he purchased for the vineyard, which were rendered useless by the breaking of the lease. The civil trial was scheduled for September 1854. As Skerrett could not get his witnesses, it was re-scheduled for March 1855, but ultimately dropped before his own criminal trial in April 1855.

Charles Skerrett told Isabella Kelly he had inherited £1500 and would buy her cattle. This was another half-truth. The only source is an unpaid account for £36 addressed to Mr Charles Skerrett from a firm of solicitors.[21]

The itemised account detailed consultations made in 1853, of which one item stated, "Very numerous attendances on you conferring and advising as to your claim to property in Ireland under your Father and Mother's settlement and the best means of establishing it and obtaining payment of the amount due."

The expected money appears to have been some form of an inheritance. Skerrett did not make much progress with the claim. A power of attorney was sent to a Mr Carroll in Dublin, but in 1860 Skerrett's solicitors noted that, "ultimately Mr Carroll declined to proceed in the matter".[22]

Wherever Charles Skerrett went, he left a trail of debts behind him. On December 23, 1854 a bailiff travelled from Port Macquarie to Brimbin and served a summons on Skerrett for a Supreme Court Judgement in Sydney. When Skerrett failed to appear, court costs were added in his absence, making the debt £62.[23] The next step would have been a court-enforced insolvency, but this was overtaken by Skerrett's trial and subsequent imprisonment.

Like most of his debts, this one was never paid.

In July 1855, two months after Skerrett's incarceration, John McLerie, the Chairman of the Cockatoo Island Prison Board, wrote to the Colonial Secretary to complain of overcrowding at the prison. Wanting to send thirty inmates from Cockatoo to the Parramatta prison to ease this situation, McLerie wrote: "I enclose a list of the names of 45 men all more or less afflicted, whom I consider unable to perform the heavy work required from them at this establishment."[24]

Number 41 on the list was Charles Skerrett. Despite this listing, Skerrett remained on Cockatoo Island for the duration of his sentence.

Charles Skerrett had been sentenced to "hard labour", but reminiscent of his time in Van Diemans Land when he was caught improperly bandaging his leg to avoid work, it appears he did not do too much of the heavy work.

Isabella Mary Kelly would only ever hear how Charles Skerrett arrived in the colony as a convict; how he ruined Henry Vaughan's business; and that he caused problems for Major Innes at Port Macquarie.

The rest of the Charles Skerrett story would always remain hidden.

A Hidden History

Charles Skerrett told Isabella Kelly he was a Roman Catholic, when in fact his children had previously been baptised in the Church of England. After more than fifty-five years of marriage, Maria and Charles Skerrett would die within two years of each other, and be buried in the Church of England section of Rookwood Cemetery, Sydney.

During their life, there were a number of times when Maria and the children were separated from Charles – sometimes enforced during his prison sentences, sometimes not, as when he cleared out for the Victorian diggings. But she had devotedly followed her husband from Dublin to London, to Hobart, to Sydney, to the Manning Valley and so on.

While one could argue she was completely dependant on him for the support of her nine children and herself, there were other signs of devotion to him. In particular there was her fervent pursuit of her husband's release from prison despite aiding and abetting him completely in his criminal designs on Isabella Kelly.

One descendant[25] of Charles Skerrett, currently living in the Manning Valley, believes there is more to this relationship. Having visited the house in which Charles Skerrett was born, he is quite sure that Charles Skerrett was born in the Catholic faith, and then rebuffed by the Church.

He suggests that as the maiden name of Maria Skerrett was Abrahams, a Jewish name, Maria Skerrett was Jewish. This, he says, combined with Skerrett's intention to marry Maria, could have caused a split between Charles Skerrett and the Catholic Church. Further, Charles Skerrett did not get his inheritance and a Jewish wife may also have explained this.

There is no confirmatory evidence of Maria Skerrett being Jewish at this stage, so it must be considered as conjecture. If it were true though, it would make an even more remarkable love story.

14. The Laird of Taree

One Manning Valley contemporary of Isabella Kelly said of her: "I knew her well. She was rather an intelligent woman to talk to, but seemed rather fond of the law."[1] This reflected the fact she went before the Magistrates so often trying to settle her problems with servants. It also ignored the reality of a woman (and a physically small woman at that) giving orders to her servants, many of them men, with no man to back up her authority.

She had been at loggerheads with George Rowley throughout the 1840s. James Hawthorne became a Community Magistrate in 1851, several years before Rowley left the district. She fell out with both Hawthorne and Police Magistrate Day over her committal on the cattle stealing charge.

Charles Croaker, Hawthorne's son-on-law,[2] also because a Community Magistrate. Asked why she had fallen out with Croaker, Kelly explained:[3]

> Because I did not visit or make friends with him. I never visited his house, nor any of his family. We were not even on speaking terms, because he charged me with having written an anonymous letter about his sister misbehaving herself. I never wrote that nor any other anonymous letter, as I would not be guilty of such a piece of meanness. They accused me of having done so, and we were consequently not upon terms.

One of the general complaints made about Isabella Kelly was her propensity to tell people what she thought of them to their face, making it rather hard to imagine her writing anonymous letters to anyone.

On July 1, 1857, Henry Flett's name was added to the list of Community Magistrates.[4] Flett was taking in more tenants on Tarree and consolidating his wealth, with more time now to spend outside his estate. When Henry Flett was present on the

The Laird of Taree

Bench, he always dominated proceedings and acted as Chairman, more by force of personality than for any other reason.

Flett took every opportunity to rule against Isabella Kelly or to dismiss her case.

Isabella Kelly recalled how a sidesaddle had been sent out to her from England. As she was absent from the district when the saddle arrived, it was left with a storekeeper who let anyone borrow the saddle. When Kelly finally retrieved the saddle, she found it damaged, and that repairs had been carried out in two or three places.

She summonsed the storekeeper for £10, the cost of the saddle, in the Small Debts Court. On the day of the scheduled hearing, the Manning River was in flood and she could not cross the river to get to the hearing. Henry Flett was the only magistrate able to get to the Bench, with the other magistrates flood-bound. Flett dismissed the claim on the ground that Kelly did not attend the hearing.[5]

When a man named Sorrell[6] was taken before Magistrate Flett charged with cattle stealing, Isabella Kelly's stockmen identified the cattle as hers – they had both Kelly's brand and Sorrell's brand on them. Flett dismissed the charges on the ground that it was a case of trover, meaning that the cattle had not been stolen but had accidentally wandered on to the man's property. Trover only applied where the owner of the cattle could not be identified, but Kelly's brand on the cattle clearly showed her ownership.

Isabella Kelly said that there were so many occasions on which Magistrate Flett was hostile to her court applications, that some of her servants in arguing with her would threaten her with, "I will take you before Mr Flett."[7]

One such servant was a stockman named John McKinnon. When Kelly hired him, McKinnon asked for an advance of £3. She gave him the £3 and entered it into her financial books, taking a receipt from him. When he was leaving Kelly's service and settling the wages due to him, Kelly deducted the £3 owing. McKinnon told her he wanted the £3 and, on her refusal to pay, went to Mr Flett at the Court.

Again, a hearing date was set, which Isabella Kelly could not attend because she needed to go to Sydney on business. She went to Mr Flett and told him she would not be able to attend the

The Trials of Isabella Mary Kelly

hearing, but she had a receipt for the transaction, and would be able to produce it to him in Court as soon as she returned. As with all Debt Claims, the defendant had to lodge the money in question with the Court, so it could be paid to the prosecutor if the case was lost – Isabella Kelly gave Flett the £3 bond.

On the day of the hearing, Flett did not postpone the hearing, but gave the decision to McKinnon, who then received the £3 from the Court. Kelly said that when she returned, Flett told her he had given the decision to McKinnon because he was a "respectable young man"[8] about to commence as an overseer on a property at £70 a year. Flett became angry with her, she said, when she told him McKinnon had once been charged with mail robbery.

What could Isabella Kelly – or any citizen for that matter – do in these situations?

In this period the actions of these Community Magistrates did not come under the scrutiny of any newspapers, as there were none in the Manning Valley until 1865, nor did they stand the scrutiny of qualified legal attorneys as there none until 1871.[9]

When Denny Day transferred from Port Macquarie to Maitland in June 1858, he received a citation from 237 Port Macquarie residents, which said, "you have won respect and esteem which always attend the conscientious discharge of duty."[10] His departure left the Manning Valley with no Police Magistrate, a situation that continued for the next twenty-six years. During this period, Justice in the Manning Valley depended entirely on the Community Magistrates – and they had no legal training.

As the Community Magistrates were unpaid, wealthy men were the main applicants. For the Government, it was a cheap means of providing a basic legal system in remote areas of the state.[11] Henry Flett continued his magisterial duties for the next fourteen years, during which time he continued to dominate the Bench, as well as his community.

Flett's arrogance was clearly evident in a case before the Wingham Bench in March 1867, when he chaired a bench of four Magistrates. The defendant, Alfred Marsh, was charged with possession of part of a beast, suspected of being stolen. Constable Coady, who had arrested Marsh, also acted as prosecutor of the case in the Court.

Coady and another prosecution witness gave their evidence.

When Marsh wanted to call a witness for his defence, Flett refused him permission. Chairman Flett announced that the Bench found Marsh guilty and fined him £10 plus costs. A stunned Marsh asked the Bench if he could appeal to a higher Court. Henry Flett replied, "No, the judgement of this court is final and there is no appeal."[12] When Marsh asked for a copy of the depositions, Flett again refused him.

Marsh paid the fine.

Towards the end of his time as a magistrate, Flett came under more criticism from his fellow magistrates, the community, and the local newspaper, the *Manning River News*. When the Bench of Magistrates retired to make their decision in a case, Flett would refuse to return to the Bench to announce the decision, if he disagreed with it.

Joshua Cochrane was a newly appointed Magistrate and a future mayor of Wingham. In giving sworn evidence to a Parliamentary Committee in May 1871, Cochrane claimed he could not believe what Flett said, even when Flett was under oath. Further, Cochrane said, Flett allowed tenants from his Tarree Estate to come to him and talk about their case before they were due to appear before him on the Bench. This practice was considered highly unethical.[13]

Replying to these charges in a letter to the Parliamentary committee, Flett hotly denied that he ever officiated in cases involving his tenants.[14]

At the end of the year Flett retired from the Bench, taking up residence in Sydney, with the *Manning River News* commenting:[15]

> The effect of the absence of a gentleman who used to call himself Chairman seemed to us to be well marked. There was unusual decorum, a total absence of all bluster and a calm dignity, which seemed likely to inspire confidence in the fair administration of Justice. For every decision given on this occasion, satisfactory reasons were assigned and we left the Court impressed with a belief that the Manning Bench will now compare favourably with any other Bench in the colony.

In the latter part of 1857, William Allan (the brother of John Allan) and Joseph Andrews both became Magistrates. William Allan was extremely conscientious and principled, but resigned after three years because of the onerous nature of these duties.

Joseph Andrews was highly respected, with his obituary stating that he was "one of our oldest and most esteemed Justices of the Peace, and was strictly impartial in his judgements".[16]

Others, like Flett, Rowley and Croaker, seemed to have had some difficulty with the truth under oath, when it suited their purposes.[17] Further, having presided over so many court cases where witnesses could give truth quite a battering, they were well placed to know *when* they could lie or twist the truth – mainly in one-on-one conversations or situations, when it was simply their word against the other person's word.

There were four unnamed Manning Valley magistrates who signed Maria Skerrett's petition. Flett, Hawthorne and Croaker were three obvious signatories.

The fourth is less obvious. It is unlikely to have been William Allan, Joseph Andrews or Denny Day (a Police Magistrate and Government employee). It could have been John Croker, of whom there is little recorded information, or even George Rowley, who, although living in Sydney, kept in contact with Henry Flett.

The colony of New South Wales had been granted self-government in 1856, creating a lower house, the House of Assembly, and an upper house, the Legislative Council. Only adult male landholders could vote in the elections for the House of Assembly, and they could vote more than once if they owned land in more than one electorate (with elections held on different days in the different electorates).

Members of Parliament were unpaid unless they held a ministerial position. Country Parliamentarians were particularly disadvantaged by their distance from Sydney, and were of necessity, wealthy men. They needed to attend the sittings of Parliament in Sydney, but had to pay their own accommodation and travel expenses, while at the same time neglecting their family and affairs at home.

The Manning Valley was located in the electorate of Gloucester and Macquarie, covering the area from Raymond Terrace to Kempsey and west to Gloucester, but excluding the Maitland District. Joseph Andrews was the Valley's first candidate.

Politically, Andrews was described as "an out and out radical" by the *Maitland Mercury*. Andrews wanted to "do away with the upper house"[18] and to extend the vote from just male landholders to *all* adult males (aged twenty-one and over). On the election platform, Andrews described himself as honest, an ordinary family man and independent, not some one put forward by the A. A. Company or the Cundletown Company.

On April 10, Thomas Barker of Raymond Terrace was the first candidate past the post, and declared the winner with 163 votes (an expected result as the greater population lived in the Raymond Terrace end of the electorate). Captain James Williamson gained 139 votes, while Joseph Andrews gained 130 votes.[19]

After this election an electoral redistribution took place, creating a new electorate called The Hastings, which covered the MacLeay River (Kempsey), Port Macquarie and the Manning Valley, with the greater population in the Manning Valley.

In June 1859, four candidates – Joseph Andrews and Henry Flett from the Manning, Frederick Panton and James McCarthy from Port Macquarie – contested the election for the second New South Wales Parliament. Although there were no political parties at the time, Flett would be described in modern terms as conservative or on the right wing of politics, whereas Andrews would be on the left wing. The candidates attended a number of political meetings expounding their views.

On Friday, July 1, Henry Flett received 321 votes; Joseph Andrews 278 votes; Frederick Panton 186; and James McCarthy just one vote.[20]

With no polling booth in the fledgling Taree township, Flett won an astounding 81% of the 196 votes cast at Cundletown and 60% of the 141 votes cast at Tinonee, while Andrews won 55% of the 158 votes cast at Wingham and 55% of the 71 votes cast at Port Macquarie.

The correspondent for the *Maitland Mercury* reported that at the declaration of the polls at Wingham and Cundletown, some of Flett's supporters were "roughly handled"[21] by Andrews' supporters.

The *Maitland Mercury* printed the anonymous letter of "an elector", who was supportive of Andrews but critical of Flett. (Because of very slow communications, the letter was printed

Henry Flett – parliamentary photo, 1859

after the election.) The letter accused Flett of changing his policy on State Aid to Religion, depending on which part of the electorate he was in. It also bemoaned Flett's objection to extending voting rights to all adult males, as provided by the new Electoral Bill, as well as criticising Flett's existing political power:[22]

> It is well known that some twenty years ago Mr Flett arrived in the colony as poor as anyone, and now, when Mr Flett finds himself in a higher position, is it generous to turn round and tell the class from whom you sprung that they have no right to enjoy the same political privileges as the laird [Scottish lord] of all Tarree? …
>
> It is well known that two-thirds of the money voted last year for roads and bridges in this district goes to improve Mr Flett's private property. Even the paltry sum allowed between Tinonee and Wingham must be spent on Tarree.

This letter encapsulated the two main allegations made against Henry Flett: arrogance and the use of his power to benefit the Taree township and his own property. Later the same year, the first punt on the Manning River commenced operations from Tinonee across to Flett's Tarree Estate.

At the beginning of December 1860, Henry Flett sat on the Wingham Bench with fellow Community Magistrates, William Cross and Charles Croaker, as he usually did when in the District. According to the Manning River correspondent for the *Empire* newspaper, Flett was out-voted by his fellow Magistrates in a civil case, but then arrogantly asked the losing party, before retiring from the Courtroom, "to see him after Court was over, and he would advise him as to further proceedings."[23] At this insult, Magistrates Cross and Croaker left the Bench in protest.

Flett dealt with the next two cases, both of which were for horse stealing. In both cases, the stolen horse had been captured in the same "trap yard", used for trapping wild horses, but in these particular cases trapping two horses which had strayed from their owners. The original owners of the horses identified them as they were being ridden by their new possessors.

In both cases, Magistrate Flett dismissed the action for stealing, on the grounds that it was a case of "trover" – the horse had come into the man's possession accidentally – despite no attempt being made to return the horses.

On the second dismissal, a man named John Blair addressed the bench. The *Empire* correspondent reported:[24]

> Mr John Blair, a very respectable and intelligent settler on the Manning, came forward and stated that he was in a position to prove that this wholesale system of horse stealing was carried on by the authority and sanction of Mr Flett, and that he (Mr Flett) was as much implicated in the case as the man who had just been tried.
>
> He said it was no secret that this trap yard had been put up by the direction of Mr Flett, for the purpose of catching stray horses, without regard to ownership, and by such acts, he (Mr Flett) was getting himself into great disrepute. Mr Flett immediately ordered the constable to take Mr Blair in charge, and lock him up until the sitting terminated, which was accordingly done.

The Laird of Taree would brook no opposition.

On February 18, 1862, a political meeting was held at the Cundletown Town Hall. The correspondent to the *Sydney Morning Herald* recorded that the notice for this meeting, which had been pinned up around the district, called on Mr Flett to explain his recent Parliamentary behaviour to his constituents.[25]

At the meeting, Flett got to his feet with some bluster, to tell the crowd that the meeting was "perfectly illegal", because they had not gained *his* permission as the senior Magistrate to hold it. After Flett made a second objection to the meeting on the ground that he had only been given two day's notice of the meeting, an interjector called out, "You only live three miles from here, so as many hours ought to suffice."

Flett condescendingly said he would "waive these objections" and allow the meeting to proceed. One of the signatories to the notice calling the meeting, a man named Wilson, had been in the district for only five months. Flett declared that the man had no right to attend the meeting – he was not even on the electoral roll – and if he were not careful he would have him put out of the hall. Wilson called out that he might not be on the electoral roll, but he had every right to be there, and would say what he wanted to say (with the Chairman's permission).

The Chairman gave the floor to Wilson, who asked pointedly why the Government was paying Flett £800 to fence the road running through his Tarree Estate, when they could not get even a small sum like £35 to repair the road from Cundletown to the Lower Manning. Secondly, he had heard that the prison lock-up was now to be built at Taree because Mr Flett had offered the land to the Government. When he looked through copies of the *Sydney Morning Herald*, Wilson said, he noted that Mr Flett always voted with Mr Cowper: did Mr Flett receive the £800 as a reward for that support?

In reply, Flett said he had donated the road to the Government as a public road, and read letters from the Minister for Lands supporting his application to have the road fenced. As for the lock-up, Tinonee, Taree and Cundletown had all applied for it, but only Tinonee and himself had offered the land, with the Government accepting his offer. Further, Flett stated, he would always support the Cowper Government, and Wilson was against Mr Cowper. He had done a lot for the Lower Manning. He had been instrumental in getting the Courthouse for Cundletown.

When, at the conclusion of the meeting, the Chairman said Mr Flett had satisfactorily answered all questions, and that he would move a vote of confidence in Mr Flett, the crowd voted with their feet by leaving the hall. The *Sydney Morning Herald* recorded Flett as saying, "he would not leave the room till the vote of confidence was passed."

Three weeks later a similar meeting was called at the Lamb Inn, Wingham,[26] where those not on the electoral roll were removed before the commencement of the meeting. Flett's actions were strongly defended before a vote of confidence was moved in his integrity. The motion carried unanimously and was followed by three cheers. Flett did not attend the meeting.

The £800 for fencing was an incredible windfall. It allowed Flett to divide his Tarree peninsula into many more farming lots and increased the traffic between Cundletown and Tinonee and passing through Taree, where Flett was selling allotments of land. In the twentieth century this road became part of the Pacific Highway, winding its way up the north coast of New South Wales.

15. Waterview

On February 2, 1858, with the seven-year lease of Brimbin nearly expired, Isabella Mary Kelly bought a 43-acre property, naming it Waterview.[1] It had been advertised in the Government Gazette and was situated further up the Dawson River not far from Brimbin. There she built a cottage and a stockyard, moving onto the property later that year. Her horse and cattle operations continued as before, with Kelly moving between the Mount George property, the Ganget lease and the Waterview property.

About March of 1859, a servant girl of Miss Kelly disappeared from Waterview.[2] The Superintendent of Kelly's Gangat Lease, a man named Corcoran, called in to Waterview and found nobody at home. After staying the night there, he went looking for Miss Kelly, and finding her in Cundletown, reported the girl missing.

Henry Flett said, "It was supposed that she ... had lost herself, and I think for eight days there were from eighty to a hundred people, out in search of her in all directions".[3] It was all to no avail as no trace of the girl was ever found.

This mystery captured the attention and imagination of all the settlers in the Valley. Those who wrote memoirs usually mentioned it. John Allan wrote:[4]

> Everyone had their own theory.
> My theory is that the girl went out for a walk and got lost. It was a beast of a place for any one not knowing the lay of the country to get lost in. If anyone got up the Lansdowne [River], or any of those places, ten chances to one if they ever got out.

Settler Robert Herkes wrote:[5]

> Yes, I remember the girl who was employed by the noted Miss Kelly, and who mysteriously disappeared – in fact, I was one of those who spent several days looking for her. She was

killed, I feel certain of that — but whether by a blackfellow or "whitefellow" it's hard to say. The girl or her remains were never found. Yes, there are some "black" waterholes about Brimbin. Miss Kelly always had a pistol handy, and could use it if necessary.

Her murder by aborigines was most unlikely as there are no recorded deaths of settlers at the hands of aborigines in the Manning Valley.

There were some people who thought Kelly had murdered the girl, despite the evidence to the contrary. Accounting for her whereabouts at the time of the girl's disappearance, Kelly said she had left the girl at Waterview and been away for three days, getting supplies. Neighbour Mr Bates was able to support Kelly's evidence.

Flett said the other magistrates, headed by Charles Croaker, held an inquiry into her disappearance. Some of these magistrates, he said, went to Miss Kelly's cottage at Waterview and "tore up the slab",[6] looking for a dead body. He did not join this inquiry because he thought it illegal — perhaps meaning there was no habeas corpus.

The inquiry went nowhere.

Another report held that the girl eloped with a lover, and there were other reports that she had been seen in Port Macquarie or along the coast, after her disappearance.

Henry Flett thought she had eloped with Superintendent Corcoran, who left for New Zealand a short time after the event, suggesting the motive for her disappearance in this manner being to avoid prosecution by Kelly for breach of contract.[7]

The mystery was never solved.

When construction of the North Coast railway line passed through Mount George in 1912, a skeleton was dug up on Kelly's former Mount George property, producing many wild rumours in the district of convicts having been murdered by Miss Kelly. Settlers immediately recalled the missing girl.

Settler Robert Herkes, who had worked for Joseph Andrews at one stage, gave a simple explanation: he could remember a groom who had been kicked in the stomach by a horse during Miss Kelly's time at Mount George, and died as a result. With no formal cemetery existing at that time, the man was buried in an unmarked grave on the property.[8]

But the rumours persisted.

An anonymous article, appearing in a 1927 edition of the Taree newspaper *Northern Champion* under the headline of "The Notorious Miss Kelly" (and reprinted in Gordon Bennett's *Dungog Chronicle*), reflected the many rumours circulating in the district about her:[9]

> Stories concerning her heartless doings in those wild days have been many, and any particularly villainous tales have easily been attached to this 'Pioneer in Skirts' as she has been called, for she seems to have had very few friends to advocate her cause.
>
> She fought her own battles.
>
> The late Mrs Neal and Mrs Bains, who both knew her and stayed in her house, often spoke kindly of her as being misunderstood.
>
> But everything that has got into print makes her out as a virago, vixen, masculine, evil minded, ill tempered, unnatural sort of individual, who shot down convicts with the two big old horse pistols she carried at her belt; that she murdered her maid servant in her tantrums; ...
>
> Such are the tales in the district today.

In Gordon Bennett's second story for *Smith's Weekly* ("The Man Who Dared Miss Kelly" in 1927), there was the implied murder of two aborigines, who were working for two men trying to steal Kelly's property. Bennett wrote: "Gimbi and his gin were lured into the bush [by Kelly] never to be seen again."[10]

The following year Bennett produced his third story ("Gunwoman of the Manning"), which contained the sentence: "this strange woman, who, single-handed, was said to have terrified tribes of wild blacks ..."[11]

Twenty years later, in "Manning River Amazon", C. K. Thompson had Kelly committing genocide when he wrote:[12]

> Then she [Isabella Kelly] struck trouble with the blacks who annexed a few head of cattle. Off she went down to Dungog and demanded that the Police Magistrate, Captain Thomas Cook, send out an expedition to deal with the aborigines.

Cook refused and Miss Kelly expressed her opinion of him in such violent and abusive terms that he wrote to the Colonial Secretary about it.

Having failed to enlist Cook's aid, Isabella returned to Brimbin breathing fire and slaughter and, armed with gun and pistol, proceeded to reduce the aboriginal population to practically nil.

Of course all the later articles picked up on this drivel and wrote it as fact.

In the 1950s, George Matthews wrote a series of articles on local history for the Taree newspaper *The Northern Champion*. The last two paragraphs quoted above from *Manning River Amazon* appeared word for word in one of his articles on Isabella (without attribution).[13]

If a recognised local historian believed these stories, what hope had the ordinary reader of divining the truth?

Towards the end of 1858, after owning Waterview for less than twelve months, Isabella Kelly sold it to Cooper & Begbie, a partnership consisting of Maria Cooper and her son-in-law Alfred Begbie. The family lived a few miles upriver from Mount George.

Maria Cooper was a remarkable woman. She was born Maria Smirnoff in 1805 and raised in St. Petersburg. Her father, a Russian Consul to Holland, had been murdered in Holland in 1815 shortly after the conclusion of the Napoleonic wars. Her aunt Sarah had married Leonard Cooper, who lived in Madras, India. In 1828, Maria married their son (her first cousin), also named Leonard Cooper, in an arranged marriage at Madras.

After her husband died in 1852,[14] the eldest two boys moved to Australia. Her daughter Sarah married Alfred Begbie. In 1857 Maria Cooper and the rest of the family also moved to Australia, where she and her son-in-law formed the partnership.

At one stage Miss Kelly had employed the Cooper boys for three months, working as stockmen with her cattle on the Manning Flats. In December 1858, Kelly sold all her cattle to Cooper & Begbie, saying she was certain there were at least five hundred head of cattle, and probably six or seven hundred head. The cattle were running wild in the bush, and Begbie would have to muster them.

The Waterview property, on which Kelly built a small cottage and stockyards, was included in the deal with Begbie with the title deeds to be delivered to Begbie when he had made full payment to her. In the meantime Kelly continued to use Waterview as her own.

Kelly included all her milking equipment in the deal as well, presumably to be delivered when she no longer needed them. Begbie never received them.

Begbie was to pay Kelly £1200, with £200 paid in cash the next day. The balance was in the form of two promissory notes for £600 and £400 to be paid in twelve months. As they were friends, Kelly told them, if they found difficulty in paying by the due date, she would give them more time to pay.[15]

Theodor Müller, the Swiss national who had worked for Isabella Kelly, also worked for Maria Cooper for a short period. Müller indicated that Cooper & Begbie might have expected to get more than just six hundred head, when he wrote: [16]

> [Maria Cooper] bought from Miss Kelly a number of horses and over a thousand head of cattle, which were tended by her three sons, the eldest of whom was only twenty years of age. She owned a beautiful farm along the Manning River which, however, could only very slowly be cultivated, as the sons could not, or rather would not, spend much time on it. They preferred to go out stock riding.

Waldemaar Cooper (generally called Waldy) and his brothers were mustering the cattle bought from Isabella Kelly.

Isabella Kelly was on extremely good terms with the family, but this sale would eventually be the cause of that friendship breaking.

This sale of all her cattle was the first step in the retirement plans of Isabella Mary Kelly. She was approaching the age of sixty.

Her next step was to sell the sheep and the horses. There were about four hundred horses, which she was finding difficult selling at the price she wanted. This price was often rather ambitious, but she tended not to sell for less.

The third and final step in the retirement plans of Isabella

Mary Kelly was to sell her Mount George property, after breaking it up into large farming allotments. In 1856, she had tried to sell Georgetown once again, probably in response to the sale of town allotments in Taree and Wingham in the 1854-55 period. Once again it failed, with one of the few sales being to Joseph Andrews, who bought one town lot for £8.[17]

Reuben Richards had started the process of buying two farming lots in 1858, but later withdrew from the deal. At the same time, two other farming lots were sold to John Paton, who move onto them immediately.[18] She was still hopeful of selling the rest of Mount George as farming lots.

The overall plan was to sell everything and return home to London, where there were friends and relatives of the Crowders, with whom she was in regular correspondence.[19]

But it was not to be.

16. The Chief Justice

Sir Alfred Stephen, the Chief Justice, was born in 1802 at Basseterre, on the island of St. Kitts, in the West Indies, and educated in England. He had been called to the Bar in London in 1823, but then decided to migrate to Australia, arriving in Van Diemans Land with his wife, in 1825 on board the *Cumberland*. Although he was headed for Sydney, he decided to take up law in Hobart. In the year of his arrival, he was appointed Solicitor-General and Crown Solicitor, and later, in 1833, the appointment of Attorney General followed. He resigned this position in 1838 due to ill health and the death of his wife in the previous year. In 1839, the invitation to be a puisne judge in New South Wales was accepted and he moved to Sydney, shortly after he married his second wife.[1]

In October 1844, Alfred Stephen was appointed the third Chief Justice of New South Wales, a position he would hold for twenty-nine years until November 1873. He received his knighthood in 1846 and became highly esteemed as the hard–working and dedicated architect of the New South Wales judicial system. There was only one criticism of him – some thought his sentences could be rather harsh.

One day in May or June 1859 (he was not sure which) Sir Alfred Stephen returned home from the Supreme Court to be met by Charles Skerrett, who had been waiting for some time in Hyde Park opposite the Justice's house.

Stephen said he was surprised to meet Skerrett, as he was not aware Skerrett had been granted parole.

Skerrett was released from prison on April 30, 1859, with a ticket-of-leave for the Illawarra District, where his daughter Jane (now married to John Brandswait, the Master of a ship) was living.

Skerrett's prison record showed he received seven days of

The Chief Justice

punishment as he served four years of his ten-year sentence.[2]

Sir Alfred's last consideration of the case had been his letter to the Colonial Secretary of August 5, 1858. The decision to release Skerrett on a ticket-of-leave had been political, made without further consultation with the Chief Justice. No condition of leaving the colony had been placed upon Skerrett.

Charles Skerrett wanted to talk to the Judge Stephen about the evidence of his trial. And he had many complaints to make. Attorney General John Plunkett and John Ryan Brenan, Kelly's attorney at his trial, were particular concerns to him.

Skerrett said Sir Alfred "told me to write out a statement of what I had to say, and then if he could prove my statements to be correct by affidavits and by making enquiries, he would see what he could do for me."[3]

The Chief Justice asked Skerrett to bring his statement to his chambers early in the morning, and he would go over the case with him then, before Court sittings began. For many days they met every morning, in the Judge's chambers, discussing the case in "minute detail".[4]

At these meetings Skerrett would prove to be a master "spin doctor" – always able to re-assign people's motives – and an expert dealer in the half-truth, admitting certain facts to be true, and then able to twist what actually occurred.

Sir Alfred had previously asked Maria Skerrett if her husband was a convict in Van Diemans Land, so Skerrett knew that the Chief Justice would ask him this question. Skerrett answered in the affirmative. He told the Chief Justice that he had been very young when he was convicted, and that he had been found guilty of abduction and bigamy, with the woman being a willing accomplice.[5] The implication of this fabrication was that Skerrett had been a rather naughty young man suffering a rush of blood to the head, but he was not really a *criminal*.

Skerrett said his wife followed him out to Hobart, but never explained to Sir Alfred how she fitted into the bigamy scenario. After he completed his time in Hobart, Skerrett said, he moved to Melbourne. In fact, Skerrett had been in Hobart at the same time as Sir Alfred, but if their paths ever crossed, the Chief Justice did not remember it. It should have been rather simple for Sir Alfred to write to Hobart and ask for Skerrett's record – but he did not.

Skerrett brought new witnesses to these meetings. Thomas Barker, a Member of the New South Wales Parliament, came to the Chief Justice's chambers and made representations on Skerrett's behalf, bringing with him one or two of Skerrett's daughters (Sir Alfred could not remember how many daughters came).[6]

Although Sir Alfred could not recall the daughter, it was almost certainly Jane Skerrett, as she had been unable to give evidence at his trial because of her broken leg. This was new and corroborating evidence of Kelly selling the cattle and horses to Skerrett, as well as correcting the erroneous impression gained at Skerrett's trial, that Jane had not broken her leg.

In talking to Sir Alfred, Skerrett wanted to know why the Chief Justice had not believed his story. It did not take too long for Skerrett to work out that the Chief Justice's main sticking point was the money – the £100 notes themselves and the fact that he *had* so much money.

Skerrett said he had been to the goldfields in Victoria after he had been living in Port Macquarie and just before he moved to Brimbin. He brought a man, purporting to be a settler[7] living in the Manning Valley, who told Sir Alfred that, just before Charles Skerrett bought the cattle and horses from Miss Kelly in June 1854, Skerrett had bought a considerable number of horses from *him*. Not only had Skerrett bought the horses, but he also paid *cash*.

John Kirk was the next witness brought by Skerrett to be interviewed by the Chief Justice. Sir Alfred, by his own admission, said he was "staggered"[8] by the evidence of this man. By coincidence, the Chief Justice knew Kirk from his own time in Hobart, and Sir Alfred knew Kirk as a builder, not as a convict.[9]

Kirk told Sir Alfred that he first met Skerrett in Melbourne in 1842. (A simple check with Hobart by Stephen would have revealed that Skerrett was a convict in Hobart until October 1846). After that, Kirk said, Skerrett moved to Geelong, living there for a few years, before moving to Sydney in 1850. Kirk said Skerrett had "set up as a brewer, which business he carried on extensively".[10] Skerrett had gone to the diggings after moving to Sydney. When Skerrett left Melbourne, he was a man of property and had "plenty of money"[11]. Further, Kirk said, he had never heard anyone say anything bad about Skerrett's character.

Skerrett told the Chief Justice that he had been worth about

£600 or £700 when he returned from the diggings.[12] Skerrett said that on his return, he noticed an advertisement for the sale of cattle placed by Miss Kelly, which resulted in him visiting Miss Kelly and buying her cattle (Kelly had not advertised).[13]

Here Charles Skerrett was re-arranging his history. To convince the Chief Justice he had the money, he needed to have returned from the goldfields *just before* he arrived at Brimbin. In fact he had gone to the goldfields from Sydney then to Port Macquarie and subsequently Brimbin.

Isabella Kelly was well aware Skerrett had arrived at Brimbin penniless. The Rev Thomas O'Reilly, the Church of England Minister at Port Macquarie, stated he thought Skerrett was at Port Macquarie probably eighteen months before his move to Brimbin in June 1854. He said he had little contact with Skerrett, but believed that Skerrett and his family were "quite destitute" while in Port Macquarie.[14] Joseph Andrews said he first met Skerrett probably twelve months before June 1854.[15] Daughter Jane Skerrett thought that her father returned towards the end of 1853, but she was not sure.[16]

The legal action Skerrett took against Major Innes placed Skerrett in Port Macquarie on March 25, 1854.[17] He signed the lease with Kelly on April 29 and claimed to have bought the cattle on June 6. In seeking his inheritance, an invoice to Skerrett from solicitors Holden & McCarthy notes their "very numerous attendances" on him in 1853.[18]

Skerrett stayed at the diggings all through 1852, probably leaving there some time in the early part of 1853.

As far as Sir Alfred Stephen was concerned, John Kirk had now provided a satisfactory explanation of Skerrett's possession of a large amount of money in June 1854.

Skerrett told the Chief Justice that before his trial in 1855, Kelly had the time to find out the name of a bank which did not print £100 notes – this was the Commercial Bank. She arranged for Joseph Andrews to say that Skerrett told him he got the notes from the Commercial Bank. She then sold the £100 notes to Andrews, because she was unable to dispose of them in the Manning Valley (meaning that if she sold the notes to Andrews for, say, £90 each, Andrews would make £10 profit on each note).[19]

According to Skerrett, three people had been unable to give

evidence at his trial because of Kelly. She had deliberately fired a pistol near his daughter, so Jane would be injured and unable to give evidence against her, and Sir Alfred had now been able to personally establish that the leg had indeed been broken.

Secondly, William Turner, the man who had witnessed the Receipt, did not testify at his trial, and *no one* denied his signature on the Receipt was genuine. Skerrett claimed Turner would have been his best witness – Turner could definitely prove that he paid the money to Kelly. Kelly had murdered Turner, or if she had not, she had paid him money to go away, so he could not testify against her.[20]

The third was Charles Langley of the firm of Rich, Langley & Butchart, who was a defence witness at his trial in 1855. Skerrett claimed that when Langley appeared at the trial, the Prosecutor, Attorney General Plunkett, had illegally sent him away.[21] Not only that, but Kelly was a friend of Plunkett. Langley would have been able to testify that Kelly never had any cattle for sale in the hands of his firm, as Kelly had claimed at his trial. As trial judge, Sir Alfred knew that Langley had not appeared at Skerrett's trial, but his respect for the long serving Attorney General was such that he could not accept that John Plunkett would do such a thing.

On June 25, 1859, when Sir Alfred had completed his morning sessions with Charles Skerrett, he wrote to Premier Charles Cowper (holding the office of Colonial Secretary), to advise him he had changed his opinion about the case. Sir Alfred wrote:[22]

> Charles Skerrett having been released from confinement on a ticket-of-leave, has entreated my attention to some points in his case, noted in the enclosed papers; and I have thought it due to humanity, and the cause of truth, to permit him to go through the whole of the evidence with me (morning after morning, before sitting of the Court), and I have interrogated him on various matters connected with his past life, and the transactions with Miss Kelly which ended in his conviction.
>
> I confess myself to he greatly staggered by the explanations and account which he gives; supported as they are (in part) by the papers already mentioned. It was on the evidence mainly of Mr Joseph Andrews, and on the absence of the witness whom he called before the Justices, and the improbabil-

ities of Skerrett's having so much money in notes, and of the documents being signed in the daughters' presence, that that conviction rested.

And since it appears that Skerrett really had a good deal of money, with which he was buying horses, and that Miss Kelly not improbably did ascertain, or certainly had time to ascertain, what Bank did not issue £100 notes, I think it a duty to say that very serious doubts have been excited in my mind as to the prosecution generally; which doubts, added to the verdict against Miss Kelly last year, in a civil case tried before me, in which her oath was utterly discredited, lead me to report my opinion, that the royal prerogative of mercy may, in this case, be not unfitly extended further to Skerrett.

If he be really an innocent man (as, on his own statements, could all of them he substantiated, he would turn out to be), the woman Kelly is the most abandoned perjurer on record. But looking at the whole case, in connection with the papers submitted, I cannot now say that my persuasion of his guilt is by any means what I formerly reported it as being.

The case had been a constant worry to Sir Alfred Stephen.

As Trial Judge in the case, he was convinced of Skerrett's guilt. As Chief Justice, he was under the enormous pressure of popular opinion from the community, from four magistrates in the district, a number of politicians, including Henry Parkes – all of whom had signed petitions, or made representations supporting Skerrett's innocence. Then Sir Alfred had been the trial judge in the Burt case, where he believed Kelly lied under oath. Now Charles Skerrett had given the Chief Justice some plausible explanations to the basic problems of the case which had been gnawing away at him.

As a result Sir Alfred changed his mind – he now believed Charles Skerrett to be innocent, although he did not state it directly.

In Sir Alfred's previous letter to the Premier on August 5, 1858, and in reference to the Burt case, he stated that Kelly's "evidence on that occasion was, in my opinion, false", but in this letter his statement changed to a more vehement "her oath was utterly discredited".

As Sir Alfred pointed out, if it was likely that Charles Skerrett was innocent, then as a consequence, it was likely that Isabella Mary Kelly was guilty of perjury, and logically, Joseph Andrews was also guilty of perjury.[23] Now Skerrett had given a reason for Andrews to perjure himself – he would profit from Kelly's £100 notes.

Sir Alfred Stephen received a letter from an under-secretary of Premier Charles Cowper, asking if he was recommending a pardon for Skerrett. On July 12, Sir Alfred replied, "I beg to say that, under the existing circumstances, and having received a ticket-of-leave, I do recommend a remission of the remainder of his sentence."[24]

The next day Governor William Denison signed the pardon. Charles Skerrett, having now been vindicated by the Chief Justice of the Supreme Court, was *a free man.*

Unlike the conditional pardon, which indicated that the convict was guilty of the crime but had served sufficient of his punishment, the free pardon indicated the convict had been *innocent* of the crime for which he was incarcerated.

Charles Skerrett had turned the Chief Justice.

To put it more brutally, the Chief Justice had been *conned* by the powerful personality and plausibility of Charles Skerrett.

The conversations recorded above between Skerrett and Sir Alfred, are the *recollections* of the Chief Justice of those conversations as he later related them, and certainly not the complete conversations between them.

It is remarkable that any Chief Justice of a Supreme Court would go through this process with a convicted criminal – and certainly one as highly regarded as Sir Alfred. It is even more remarkable that he would take new evidence from witnesses provided by Skerrett and recommend a pardon as a result of this evidence, without seeking any further validation of it, and without consulting with Isabella Mary Kelly, her attorneys, a fellow Justice *or any other person.*

Skerrett's evidence was not taken down under oath in a deposition and consequently could not be tested in a court of law. Skerrett was not held accountable for any statements he made to the Chief Justice, and further, he was free to change or "improve"

The Chief Justice

his story with impunity. This was in complete contrast to the high ethics of Attorney General John Plunkett, who refused all attempts to give him evidence that was not in a deposition.

The Chief Justice may have thought that Charles Skerrett was no longer guilty *beyond a reasonable doubt*, when he said his actions did not mean that he thought Charles Skerrett was innocent, it only meant that he now thought there was more chance of him being innocent than there was of him being guilty.[25] The Chief Justice was quite ingenuous if he thought the general community would accept this.

The *perception* of the general community, and the Manning Valley in particular, was this: There could only be one reason for Sir Alfred to recommend a free pardon for Skerrett – Sir Alfred Stephen now believed *Charles Skerrett was innocent* of the cattle stealing charges brought against him.

Did Sir Alfred ever consider the implications for Isabella Mary Kelly?

Sir Alfred Stephen

17. Committed

At about 4:30 on Saturday afternoon of July 16, 1859, there was a knock on Isabella Kelly's door. She was in Sydney on business for a while, and staying at Mrs. Price's Boarding House in Hunter Street. When she answered the door, it was Inspector Harrison with a warrant for her arrest.

The charge was perjury.

Kelly accompanied the Inspector down to the Police Office. As it was so late in the day, and the next day was a Sunday, no bail could be arranged. She spent the rest of the weekend in a cell at the lock-up in Erskine Street, waiting for arraignment in court on Monday morning. The Darlinghurst Police Description Book recorded her description as: "about 50 years old, short, small face, keeps a farm on the Manning River".[1]

The hearing on Monday morning proved to be something of an anti-climax as no papers concerning her case had arrived. The Magistrate dismissed the case and Isabella Kelly returned to the boarding house.[2]

Charles Skerrett had taken out the warrant for Kelly's arrest. Isabella Mary Kelly had not even been aware of his release from gaol. Skerrett charged Kelly with the perjury of declaring both the Bill of Sale and the Receipt to be forgeries.

The warrant for Kelly's arrest was re-issued about three weeks later, and Kelly was arrested a second time on Thursday, August 11, and given bail. Two days later, Isabella Mary Kelly appeared at Central Criminal Court, for the committal hearing.[3]

The original sworn statements made by Isabella Mary Kelly at Dungog on October 6, 1854, were read to the Court: "I solemnly swear that I never sold any horse, or ever parted with or lent any horse whatever, to the said Charles Skerrett" and "the paper marked No. 2 [the Bill of Sale] I solemnly swear is not signed by me, and is therefore a forgery."

But the crucial documents themselves, the Bill of Sale and the Receipt, were *missing*.

A thorough search had been made at the Crown Solicitor's Office, but they were not to be found. The Chief Justice was the last person to borrow them. An assistant of the Chief Justice deposed that he too had made a search for them, and could not find them. He was quite sure the missing documents were returned to the Crown Solicitor's Office after the Chief Justice finished with them.

Sir Alfred Stephen deposed he was the trial judge who had convicted Charles Skerrett of cattle stealing in April 1855. He had obtained the documents in the case in 1857 when he received a petition from Mrs. Skerrett, but he believed the documents, including the Bill of Sale and the Receipt, had been returned to the Crown Solicitor's Office.

The Prosecutor asked the Court to allow the introduction of *copies* of these documents as secondary evidence. Despite objections from Mr Dalley, Kelly's barrister, this request was granted. The genuineness of these two documents was pivotal to the whole case.

If Kelly had been charged with *forgery*, and with these documents missing, the Magistrate would automatically have dismissed the case then and there. Although the charge against Kelly was perjury, the perjury *depended on forgery*. Perjury on Kelly's part could not be proved unless these documents were proven to be genuine. Surprisingly, no one raised any further objections.

The prosecution called Charles Skerrett, who ran over his story of how he bought cattle and horses from Kelly only for her to accuse him of forging the Bill of Sale and the Receipt. He had bailed her out when she was charged with cattle stealing. He had agreed to let a cottage to her on the Brimbin station for six pence per week. On this agreement Kelly acknowledged that she had sold him her right to the station, cattle and brands. Kelly did not make any charge against him until he found out she had stolen some of his cattle, which she had previously sold to him. He had been released from gaol after four years and had recently received a *free pardon*.

Under cross-examination by Mr Dalley, Skerrett denied he

had told Joseph Andrews he did not have a Receipt. He did not recollect telling Ann Andrews he bought Kelly's cattle for £800, but he did recall telling her that Kelly had offered to sell the cattle to him.

Jane Brandswait (nee Skerrett) stated she remembered signing the Bill of Sale. Miss Kelly had asked her to witness the document. Both her father and Miss Kelly read it aloud to her before she signed it.

Sir Alfred Stephen was re-called. After spending some time outlining the case, as he knew it, the Chief Justice asked if he could make a statement. The Chief Justice said he had heard it rumoured outside the Court that he had recommended a pardon for Charles Skerrett (he was obviously absent from the Court when Skerrett deposed he had received a free pardon), and "he wished it to be distinctly understood, that the grounds of such pardon had nothing whatever to do with the present case."[4]

Was Sir Alfred serious?

Did he really believe that people would accept there was no relationship between the granting of a pardon to Charles Skerrett and a trial of Miss Isabella Mary Kelly for perjury – that these events were not cause and effect?

Dalley moved to have his client, Miss Kelly, discharged on a technicality – when she had preferred her charges against Charles Skerrett, she had not been duly sworn upon the Holy Gospels of God. The motion was denied.

The Magistrate ruled that a *prima facie* case had been established, and committed Isabella Mary Kelly to stand trial on the charge of perjury. Bail was set at £500, with two sureties for £250 each.

Isabella Kelly returned to her cottage at Gangat in the Manning Valley.

She was sick with worry.

In amongst her worries about the trial, Reuben Richards had become a large thorn in Isabella Kelly's side.

His rented paddock at Mount George was about an acre and a half, containing the cottage built by the Turners in 1854, and had been fenced round with saplings.[5] Having completed his two-year lease several months previously (in May 1859), Richards had still not paid the due rent, nor did he appear to have any intention of paying, yet he was still very keen to renew the lease.

Additionally, Reuben Richards wanted to rent a *second* paddock from Isabella Kelly. This paddock, referred to as the Mount George paddock, contained about fifteen acres of good grazing land. Richards wanted to lease the Mount George paddock for his mail delivery horses. Despite Kelly's refusal of the lease, he put his horses into the paddock to graze anyway.

This second paddock, between Richards' current rented paddock and Joseph Andrews' Woodside property, was often occupied with stock belonging to Andrews. Further, Isabella Kelly had been organising another shipment of horses to Madras, and decided to make use the Mount George paddock to stable the horses in preparation for their transportation to Madras.[6] (This was probably partly in reaction to Richards putting his horses there.)

While Isabella Kelly was in Sydney for her committal hearing, she had written back to her Overseer to give written notice to Richards to leave Mount George.[7] To put additional pressure on Richards, Kelly asked her Overseer to notify Richards that she was charging him an exorbitant five shillings per week for *each* of his horses using the Mount George paddock.

This situation became very complicated now Kelly was committed to stand trial. Isabella Kelly wanted Reuben Richards or his wife Ann to be a witness at her trial.

There was the letter,[8] which Reuben Richards had written to Isabella Kelly just after Skerrett's conviction (in 1855), in which Richards detailed how Skerrett had given his witnesses sheets of paper detailing the evidence he wanted his witnesses to give at his trial. A small "hello" message signed "Ann Richards" appeared at the end of this letter. Kelly was desperate to use this letter in the coming trial, as part of her defence. If either Reuben or Ann Richards acknowledged it to be genuine, it absolutely confirmed the guilt of Charles Skerrett.

Kelly did not trust what Reuben Richards' would say in Court, if she called him as a witness. She still had faith that Ann Richards would do the right thing for her, and testify to the genuineness of this letter – if only she could get Ann into the witness box.

She thought Ann was baulking at being her witness, because (as Reuben Richards had stated in this letter) she may have been afraid of Skerrett. Kelly told Ann she was getting a subpoena, and gave her a cheque for £5 to cover her expenses down to Sydney.

On Monday, September 12, Reuben Richards called in at Kelly's Gangat cottage.[9] Kelly had two guests with her, Mr Cosgrove and Mr Manton. At one stage, Cosgrove had been in partnership with Kelly, when they bought a flock of sheep and used the Gangat run to grow wool. Manton, from Port Stephens, was introduced to Richards as a prospective buyer of Kelly's sheep. Richards told Manton the sheep were diseased, and received the expected rebuke from Isabella Kelly.

Reuben Richards asked to examine the letter Kelly wanted to present in Court. Reading through the letter, he admitted he wrote it, but claimed his wife had not signed it, as he had forged her signature – hence, Ann knew nothing about it.

This was despite Ann personally telling Miss Kelly she *had* signed it.

Fearing Richards might decamp with her valuable evidence, Kelly snatched the letter out of his hands, and ordered him to leave and not to come back. Richards visited Kelly again the next day, and the day after.

Towards the end of the week she came down sick and took to her bed. She was so sick she could not write, and only signed some cheques, which another visitor, Alfred Begbie, had written out for her.

On Sunday, September 18, Isabella Kelly was sick in bed all day, with a female servant about the place, looking after her. She received a visit from neighbours, John Paton and his wife, who had bought two farming lots on Mount George, and were close neighbours of Reuben Richards.

Isabella Kelly told them she had refused to re-new the Reuben Richards' lease of his rented paddock. She entered into an agreement for Paton to erect stabling on the Mount George paddock for use in mustering the horses bound for Madras.

According to Paton, Miss Kelly also said that when she returned from Sydney, after her trial, "she would live in a tent in the paddock, until she would eject Richards from the cottage, he then lived in at Mount George".[10]

Next day, Reuben Richards and another man arrived at Gangat on horseback. Kelly, still sick, ordered them to leave. The other man, unknown to Kelly, moved off a short distance and waited, while Richards remained mounted on his horse speaking to Kelly as she stood in her doorway. Richards again asked Kelly not to take Ann to Sydney.

According to Kelly, Richards said, "My wife will do you more harm than good."

Kelly replied, "I don't care, all I want is for her to speak the truth. I have no doubt you are plotting with Skerrett all this time. Kennedy [a farmer further up the valley] has said that you were riding about with Skerrett."

Richards admitted this, replying, "Skerrett has been with me."[12]

Richards had been good friends with Skerrett before his imprisonment in 1855, but had then fallen out with the Skerretts. During this period he had written the letter so damaging to Charles Skerrett. Now, it seemed Richards' friendship with Skerrett had been renewed.

Richards complained to Kelly that no one would cash Ann's £5 cheque. Kelly offered to get it cashed for him. Richards told her Ann had been subpoenaed as a prosecution witness against her – he had written to the Attorney General requesting it.

With the trial imminent, Kelly attempted to leave Mount George on Tuesday, but was still too sick to mount her horse. On Wednesday, September 21, she left in the morning, and travelling slowly, covered twenty-four miles. She stayed at Grant's overnight, and rode nineteen miles to Dungog the next day. From there she rode to Maitland and caught a train.

While in Sydney, awaiting trial, Isabella Kelly received a visit from Alfred Begbie,[12] who had come down from the Manning, specifically to negotiate withdrawing from the deal they had signed in December 1858. Kelly mentioned Begbie was at her Gangat cottage before she left, and that twenty of her horses were mustered in his stockyard, indicating they were indeed on very cordial terms. Their discussions probably started then.

The Trials of Isabella Mary Kelly

Begbie had money problems. He owed Kelly £1000 in promissory notes, but could see no chance of making the payments. Normally Kelly could be expected to be reasonable and defer payment – she was, after all, a wealthy woman. Begbie told her he wanted to sell up and go back to Madras.

Perhaps Begbie was also thinking ahead to the possibility of a guilty verdict against Kelly. This could lead to Charles Skerrett establishing a claim to the cattle he had bought from Kelly. This could include those cattle Begbie had already mustered and sold.

He made an offer to Kelly, which he thought weighed heavily in her favour. Joseph Andrews believed she would gain £300 out of it.

In the offer, Kelly could have all the cash he had collected on the horses already mustered, as well as the 326-acre property, which he owned. She could keep the £200, he had already paid her, and he would try and raise another £50 or £100 from his friends to give her. She would have to take the promissory notes back, as well as keeping the property Waterview and the milking utensils.

The truth was Isabella Kelly needed Begbie's £1000 in *cash*. Her court appearances, and her many trips to Sydney, had been draining the money away. She had sold all her cattle, and with only a few horses sold, there was very little recent income.

Her trial would be expensive. There were not only the legal fees – she employed *two* barristers for her defence – but also the expenses of the witnesses, who always depended on her for their accommodation and travelling expenses as well as compensation for their loss of earnings. Trial postponements increased these expenses.

She also wanted enough money to retire on.

Equally, if convicted at her trial, she faced further loss; a loss of stock to Skerrett by a possible claim of ownership (she still had at least 400 horses); loss of both property and stock from a possible confiscation by the Government, as a convicted felon.

Isabella Kelly refused Begbie's offer.

Just before the trial, in the company of her solicitor, Isabella Kelly went to see William Lennon of the firm of Lennon & Cape.

She wanted him "to wind up her affairs"[13] and sell everything.

Isabella Kelly had another worry: If she were convicted, there was the possibility of the Government confiscating her property as a convicted felon. In retrospect, this was probably only a small risk, as confiscation tended to occur in more settled areas, and applied generally to former convicts who had been found guilty of another crime, especially bushranging.

But Kelly was concerned enough to assign the Mount George property and stock over to Lennon. This should avoid the possible confiscation by the technicality that she no longer owned it.

She also borrowed £320 from Lennon, to be repaid out of the money gained by the sale. There was another problem – the Mount George property had been mortgaged to John Roxburgh for £500 in the previous year.[14] This mortgage was due in another eight months. That £500, plus interest, would also have to come out of the sale.

Isabella Kelly thought there were other added benefits from the deal with Lennon. If she were convicted, they would look after the property to protect their interest of £320. Also, if she were not convicted, and wanted the property back, she could borrow the relatively small amount of £320 from friends, and retrieve ownership of Mount George.

In the days leading to her trial Isabella Kelly had all these worries.

18. Perjury

At 10 a.m. on Thursday, October 5, 1859, the trial of Isabella Mary Kelly began before Mr Justice Dickinson and a jury of four.

Isabella Kelly engaged two leading barristers John Darvall and Arthur Holroyd to represent her, with solicitor Eyre Ellis to brief them. Holroyd had been Kelly's barrister in the civil case involving William Burt, but he had also been Skerrett's defence attorney in his 1855 trial. Apparently no one saw any conflict of interest, despite the extremely close nature of these two trials.

The prosecution was led by the current Attorney General, Lyttelton Bayley, and briefed by Skerrett's attorney, Mr Forbes.[1]

In his opening address, the Attorney General outlined the case for the prosecution. The alleged perjury occurred when the defendant, Miss Kelly, had sworn she had not sold her interest in cattle to the prosecutor, Mr Skerrett, who alleged that the sale had indeed taken place. The result of the defendant's sworn statements was that Mr Skerrett had been sentenced to ten years hard labour on the roads. Mr Skerrett had petitioned for a remission of his sentence and the Chief Justice had recommended a pardon, which was granted.

Bayley called his principal prosecution witness, Charles Skerrett who deposed he was living in Port Macquarie in 1854, when he met Miss Kelly. She leased Brimbin station to him. He bought all her cattle and twenty horses for £800. When he started mustering them, he could only find 300 cattle, so he told her he would only pay £600 for them. His two daughters witnessed the signing of the Bill of Sale, and William Turner witnessed the Receipt.

When Miss Kelly was arrested on two counts of cattle stealing on the Manning, Skerrett continued, he had bailed her out. She had told him that she was the niece of a gentleman he knew in Ireland. He told Miss Kelly she could not stay at Brimbin unless she rented a cottage from him. She rented the cottage for six pence per week, and Ann Richards witnessed the signing of that agreement. Miss Kelly signed another paper authorising him to muster her horses.

He had never told Miss Kelly he bought the cattle from the firm Rich, Langley & Butchart, Skerrett maintained, and he paid her in £100 notes issued by the Bank of Australasia

Under cross-examination from Mr Darvall, Skerrett testified that he never heard the jury at his trial declare these documents were forgeries or that his daughter had perjured herself – he did not believe the jury said it. He gave Kelly a promissory note for £200, Skerrett said, which was to be paid in twelve months with no mention of interest. He had never paid the £200, nor had he been asked to pay it.

Skerrett testified he got the four £100 notes in Melbourne when he was paid £425 for two teams of horses, a cart and sundry articles. He could not remember the name of the man who bought them. Mr Kirk [the next witness] knew that he had the money. At his own trial, he did not look for evidence that he had received £400 in Melbourne. He had never told Mr Andrews, or anyone else, the notes were issued by the Commercial Bank. On the Manning, after leaving Melbourne, he bought some horses from Mr Smith. He paid Smith £120 in sovereign coins.

There was a fire at his place in 1854, Skerrett said, and some papers were burnt – the house did not burn, just a file of papers. Miss Kelly heard that his documents had been burnt. Miss Kelly had once asked him if any important papers had been in the fire, and he replied there had not [indicating that Kelly thought the Bill of Sale and the Receipt had been burnt, and thinking they no longer existed, claimed he had not bought the cattle and horses from her].[2]

The Receipt was read out aloud, Skerrett said, by both Kelly and himself before she signed it. He told Miss Kelly he did not want his daughters to witness the Receipt, and suggested that Turner should witness the Receipt. He had not told Mr Andrews in October 1854, that he did not have a receipt, and that he would get one – he never consulted that man about anything. He had never told Tippin [the constable from Dungog who arrested him] he was a Justice of the Peace in Melbourne. Yes, he arrived in Australia in Van Diemans Land, but he would not answer questions of why he was in Van Diemans Land as it was not connected to this case.

Despite further objections by Skerrett, Darvall pushed on. He had stayed in Van Diemans Land for five years. He was tried in a criminal court in London in 1835. There were two charges: one was bigamy and the other was shooting a Major in the arm. The lady concerned was the wife of the Major. As a result he was convicted of bigamy and transported for life.

Skerrett said he had lived in Melbourne for several years and kept a brewery there. He carried freight between the Kilmore and McIvor digging, receiving £40 for the 40 mile journey. When he sold the horses in Melbourne, the prices were high. He had not been charged with stealing a horse in Sydney – some charge was preferred against him in a dispute about a horse, but the magistrate dismissed it.

Attorney General Bayley called John Kirk who deposed he was a builder living in Melbourne. He came to Australia with Dr Lang (indicating he was not a convict). In 1852 he often saw Skerrett in Melbourne and Geelong. He knew Skerrett well and saw him with money. He saw Skerrett with three £100 notes, but he did not know which banks issued the notes. He had advised Skerrett to go to a bank and get a draft rather than carry the notes.

Cross-examined by Mr Darvall, Kirk said he saw the £100 notes in Skerrett's possession on the wharf at Melbourne, when Skerrett was boarding a schooner to leave Melbourne in 1853. Skerrett had shown him as much as £3000, but Skerrett did not tell him how he got the money.

At this point it was reported to the Court that further searching had not produced the Bill of Sale and the Receipt. Darvall had to admit they could not be found, and was forced to accept that copies of these documents would be used as secondary evidence in the trial.

It completely defused the crucial argument of whether these documents were genuine or not. At Skerrett's trial, the jury, after personally examining the Bill of Sale and the Receipt, in connection with the evidence given by witnesses as to their authenticity, declared them to be forgeries. It precluded the calling of

Perjury

handwriting experts to give opinions on the allegedly forged Kelly signatures. The experts of the time were bank officers, who constantly scrutinised signatures on cheques.

It is remarkable that Darvall did not at least *ask* for the trial to be terminated. The perjury depended on forgery – it was not Kelly's forgery, but Skerrett's forgery. If it were a forgery trial, there would have been an automatic termination here.

The complexity of the trial came down to this: For the jury to have a reasonable doubt on Kelly's perjury, they would have to have accept Skerrett's documents were forgeries, but Skerrett was not on trial here.

The trial continued.

The next prosecution witness, Jane Brandswait (nee Skerrett), gave her evidence much the same as at Skerrett's committal hearing. She had been called in to sign the Bill of Sale. Her father and Miss Kelly both read it out to her. No other persons were present in the room. Her father had been recently living with her, but he had not discussed the case with her.

Sir Alfred Stephen deposed he was the presiding Judge when Skerrett was convicted of cattle stealing. He borrowed the missing documents but was quite sure they were returned, but he had no distinct recollection on the matter. After he reported two or three times to the Colonial Secretary, Skerrett was set free.

Cross-examined by Mr Darvall, Sir Alfred said he did not remember if any of Skerrett's family was in his chambers when the documents were there. He was certain they had not stolen them.

Margaret Cann (nee Skerrett) deposed she had signed the Bill of Sale as a witness. She saw Miss Kelly sign it and heard her say something about the money. Both her father and Miss Kelly read out the document. Questioned by Mr Darvall, Margaret said Miss Kelly called her into the room, and she heard her father say he would rather someone other than his daughter witness the document.

Philip Dew stated he was a farmer on the Manning. In May or June of 1854, he met Miss Kelly as he was driving some cattle. Miss Kelly said she was sorry to hear about his illness, and then told him she had sold her cattle to Skerrett. He had bought two horses from Skerrett at Raymond Terrace, about three months before that.

Under questioning by Darvall, Dew stated that Miss Kelly was on a horse and by herself when he spoke to her. He bought cattle from Skerrett which were some of those Kelly sold to Skerrett.

The Attorney General called Samuel Turner, who said William Turner was his son. He and his son worked for Miss Kelly in 1854. He had not seen his son for five years, and did not know where he went. Miss Kelly told him she had sold her cattle to Skerrett. He had asked Miss Kelly for payment of money due to him, but she said her notes were too heavy, and she would send the money over to him with Skerrett. He had never received the £36. His son William could read and write.

Cross-examined, Turner stated he has been owed the £36 for five years. The Bungay Court would not award him the money, and he could not afford to bring the matter to Sydney. A month after his son disappeared, Miss Kelly told him she had a warrant out for William's arrest. He knew of no reason why his son would leave, unless his son feared the warrant taken out against him by Miss Kelly. Darvall read out part of the evidence which Samuel Turner had given at Skerrett's trial: William knew the warrant was out against him *before* he left. Resuming, Samuel Turner stated he may have said that, but he did not remember saying it.

The final prosecution witness was Ann Richards, who stated she had lived with Miss Kelly as her servant at Brimbin. She remembered Skerrett buying the cattle off Miss Kelly. She afterwards went to work for Skerrett. Her future husband, Reuben Richards, was then living at Skerrett's place. Previous to this her husband had worked for Miss Kelly.

In July 1854, she was called into a room to sign a document. The paper was read over by both Miss Kelly and Skerrett and concerned the renting of a cottage for six pence per week, as well as a sale of cattle and brands. She saw Miss Kelly sign it. On a previous occasion, she remembered Miss Kelly calling William Turner into the house. She also remembered Miss Kelly telling her she had sold all her cattle and twenty horses to Skerrett.

Darvall cross-examined. The paper she signed stated that Miss Kelly rented a cottage from Skerrett for six pence per week, and mentioned that Kelly had sold the cattle and brands to Skerrett. She thought Skerrett wrote it.

Perjury

Darvall handed Ann Richards the letter which Reuben Richards had written to Kelly after the gaoling of Skerrett in 1855, with an added message at the end signed by Ann. Yes, the document had a signature of "Ann Richards" on it, Ann said, but it was not her handwriting as she had never written any letter to Miss Kelly.

At 4:30 p.m., with the prosecution case completed, Justice Dickinson adjourned proceedings for the day. The case for Skerrett was now far stronger than in his 1855 trial.

John Kirk was a most impressive prosecution witness. He had mended a very large hole in Skerrett's story. At Skerrett's own trial, no one believed he could possibly have £400, as he hardly seemed able to feed his family. Yet here was John Kirk telling the court he had seen Skerrett with £3000.

For the defence, Darvall had an impossible task to either shake Kirk's story or his credibility – no one knew him or knew of him. In fact Sir Alfred Stephen was the only person, other than Skerrett, who knew Kirk. Sir Alfred would later admit that during his own discussions with Kirk in the Chief Justice's chambers, Kirk never made mention of seeing £100 notes in Skerrett's possession.

It is notable that at no stage did the prosecution call the valuable witness "Mr Smith", who had told the Chief Justice (in Skerrett's sessions at the Judge's chambers) that Skerrett had paid him £120 in cash to buy horses from him in early 1854. If Skerrett had been able to produce the witness "Mr Smith" to the Chief Justice, why could he not produce him at the trial – or even produce a deposition from him? Who was "Mr Smith"? The more likely answer is: "Mr Smith" was not who he said he was – he would have been readily recognised by other Manning residents at the trial.[3]

As for Ann Richards, she had certainly nailed her colours to the wall.

The cottage rented for six pence per week at Brimbin was for Kelly's Chinese stockman. Ann Richards' statement implied that Kelly wanted the cottage for herself, which led to a further implication that Kelly was a tenant of Skerrett rather than the actuality. This was same document, which Kelly had not read properly after being upset when confronting Skerrett. It contained the phrase, "Brimbin, which station I sold to him with the stock on 6th June, 1854". Kelly believed this phrase had been added *after* she signed it. Even more damning was the fact that this document, which Kelly admitted to be genuine, was definite proof she had allowed Skerrett to write out agreements between them.

Here was yet another witness to say Kelly told them Skerrett had bought her cattle.

Day Two of the trial commenced at ten o'clock, on Friday morning with Darvall completing his questioning of Ann Richards. She did not recollect telling Mrs. Andrews that she had been given a paper with written instructions on what to say at Skerrett's committal hearing in 1854 – she would have remembered if she had.

This concluded the case for the prosecution.

Mr Darvall outlined the case for the defence. It was a most villainous plot that had been laid against Miss Kelly. Her character was unimpeachable, whereas Skerrett was a person of no character. Skerrett could not have been convicted of bigamy, as he had been transported for life, and bigamy was a much lesser crime than that. It was no wonder Skerrett had a large number of supporters, because success in this prosecution would see Skerrett get all the property mentioned in the documents. It was highly improbable that a lone woman like Miss Kelly would tell Turner that her notes were too heavy – rather the opposite, that she had no notes. If Kelly told people Skerrett had bought her cattle, it was because Skerrett told her he had bought them from her agents in Sydney, and she *believed* him.

Holroyd called Henry Vaughan, a barber in King Street. From his knowledge of Skerrett, Vaughan said, he would not believe him on his oath. In 1850, Skerrett had worked for him in his brewery business. Skerrett stole a horse from him, and when he charged Skerrett with horse stealing the magistrate dismissed it. He could not afford to chase the matter through the courts. Skerrett had ruined his business.

Richard Smith, described by the *Sydney Morning Herald* as a "dull looking youth", testified next. He was working for Miss Kelly when Skerrett was at Brimbin. He was then aged about ten

Perjury

or eleven. He heard Skerrett say to Miss Kelly that he had bought her cattle from her agents in Sydney, and that he paid £800 for them. Miss Kelly had about four or five hundred horses. Skerrett had not mustered the cattle or horses.

He remembered riding with Miss Kelly one day, Smith said, and meeting a man named Dew. Miss Kelly asked Dew to fix his stirrup. There had been no conversation between Miss Kelly and Dew about cattle. Richard said he could not read or write. He did not know the name of the present month.

John Tippin deposed that as a constable stationed at Dungog in 1854, he arrested Skerrett on a cattle-stealing charge. Skerrett told him he was a magistrate in Melbourne for nine or twelve years. Skerrett told him he paid Kelly in four £100 notes, two of which were on the Bank of Melbourne and two on the Australasian Bank.

The *Empire* newspaper reported that Tippin "was evidently under the influence of drink", as he then gave contradictory evidence by stating that two of the notes were on the Commercial Bank of Melbourne. Justice Dickinson warned Tippin he could commit him for contempt. Tippin admitted he had been dismissed from the constabulary for drunkenness.

An accountant from the Commercial Bank stated that his bank had never issued £100 notes.

The next defence witness was Joseph Andrews, who had been such a strong witness for Kelly in 1855. He reprised the evidence he had given about the Bill of Sale and the Receipt in 1854, including statements that two of the £100 notes were on the Commercial Bank, and his belief that Kelly's signature on both the Bill of Sale and the Receipt were forgeries.

Andrews deposed that he had seen the letter of Reuben Richards mentioned earlier in the trial. He had received a number of letters from Richards and knew his handwriting. He believed that Richards wrote everything, including his wife's message at the end.

Darvall asked Andrews to read Richards' letter out loud, but the Attorney General objected. In a devastating blow to the defence, Justice Dickinson ruled Richards' letter could not be read, as its authorship had not been established.

Resuming his evidence Joseph Andrews said Skerrett had

The Trials of Isabella Mary Kelly

told once him that Miss Kelly was cranky and that she went out at night with pistols. Skerrett told him he was worried that Miss Kelly might shoot him or that she might commit suicide. He told Skerrett he had nothing to worry about, as there was nothing wrong with Miss Kelly.

Cross-examined by Bayley, Andrews stated Miss Kelly had a remarkable temper and she was a strong-minded woman. He never saw her with pistols but he heard she carried them. He had never been charged with cattle stealing.

Here the Attorney General asked that the depositions made at Skerrett's committal hearing at Bungay Bungay in 1854 be read out, highlighting Andrews' declarations that Kelly's signatures on the Bill of Sale and the Receipt were *genuine*.

Andrews admitted he was under the impression, at first, that the signatures were genuine, but the peculiar formation of the "y" in the signatures had changed his mind. He then went on to tell how Kelly had changed her signature.

Ann Andrews deposed that Skerrett told her he bought the cattle from Kelly for £800. Ann Richards had told her that Mrs. Skerrett gave her a paper to learn off by heart – it was the evidence Ann Richards should give as a witness at the Skerrett trial. Ann Richards told her this in September 1855, after Skerrett was convicted.

John Kingsmill, a teller from the Australasian Bank, stated that his bank had only started to issue £100 notes on August 23, 1853. Their Melbourne branch started to issue them after this date, but when he did not know.

Joseph's brother, William Andrews, corroborated a great deal of Joseph's evidence, stating he was present at the Inn with Joseph and Skerrett when the conversations took place.

Darvall called William McLean, a Wingham storekeeper, who deposed that he had a conversation with Skerrett at Raymond Terrace in November 1854, after Skerrett's committal hearing. Skerrett asked him what he thought of the case, and he replied that the £100 notes worried him, but thought they should be easy to trace. Skerrett then told him he had already traced them to a shop at Brickfield Hill [George Street, Sydney]. He asked Skerrett which bank issued the notes, and Skerrett replied, "the Commercial Bank".

Perjury

John Dawson (there was no mention that Dawson was Skerrett's solicitor during his trial) was called as a character witness for *Miss Kelly*. He said he had known Miss Kelly for fifteen years, and had never doubted her veracity.

That completed the defence.

Although nothing had been heard of William Turner for five years, the deposition he made at Skerrett's committal hearing in 1854 was read to the Court. Turner was present when Skerrett paid Kelly the £400, and then he signed the Receipt as a witness.

The Attorney General summed up. This was an unusual and complicated case. Charles Skerrett had been tried in an adjoining courtroom, found guilty and sentenced to ten years imprisonment. The Chief Justice must have had a valid reason for recommending a pardon for him. Sir Alfred had reported several times that he was not in favour of a remission for Skerrett. But when he was able to collect new evidence, he did recommend the remission and Skerrett was released.

Skerrett was innocent like William Barber, the Attorney General continued, and Barber had just been voted £5000 compensation by the British House of Commons for a wrongful imprisonment. If the jury disbelieved Skerrett's story, then his two daughters and William Turner were also guilty of perjury. The main point was whether Kelly had sold her cattle to Skerrett or not, and this was corroborated by the evidence of Philip Dew, Mrs Richards, Samuel Turner and William Turner.

Mr Justice Dickinson summed up for the jury, taking over two and a half hours. At nine o'clock the jury of four men retired to consider their verdict.

The jury returned an hour and a quarter later with their verdict – *guilty of perjury*.

Justice Dickinson would later say that he was taken by surprise at the jury's verdict. He told Isabella Mary Kelly she had been found guilty, and without rebuking her, sentenced her to *twelve months imprisonment and a fine of £100*.

At half past ten on Friday night, Isabella Mary Kelly was led away to a damp cell in the Darlinghurst complex to commence her twelve months prison sentence.

The Trials of Isabella Mary Kelly

This trial was a re-run of the Skerrett trial held four years previously, except that the prosecution and defence had swapped tables.

The guilt of one was the innocence of the other.

Isabella Kelly could not defend herself without accusing Skerrett. Attorney General Bayley had objected to several lines of questioning, and had been at pains on a number of other occasions, to say that Skerrett was not the one on trial.

Skerrett had very cunningly committed perjury in giving his evidence. With a deft skill he was able to re-assign motives and twist events to his advantage. He even told outright lies in situations where there was no one to contradict him, such as his transportation to the colony had been caused by bigamy.

Almost as staggering were the number of other witnesses prepared to commit perjury on Skerrett's behalf – John Kirk, Philip Dew, Ann Richards and Samuel Turner. Even William Turner's perjured evidence from 1854 was read to the court. Each of these witnesses had perjured themselves for two reasons, and in a varying degree of each reason: loyalty to Charles Skerrett and a dislike of Isabella Kelly.

The inadmissibility of the Reuben Richards letter had been a major blow to the defence. It outlined how Skerrett organised his witnesses to commit perjury at his own trial.

Another major blow had been the loss of the forged Bill of Sale and Receipt documents. This immediately stifled all debate on the genuineness of the Kelly signatures, and made much of Joseph Andrews' evidence about the signatures rather meaningless.

The Attorney General had also been able to diminish Joseph Andrews' credibility by highlighting the about-face in his testimony between Skerrett's committal hearing and Skerrett's trial.

But the greatest factor in the conviction of Isabella Mary Kelly was the shadow cast over the whole trial by the actions of the Sir Alfred Stephen: he was the Judge who had *sentenced* Charles Skerrett to ten years imprisonment; he was the Chief Justice who had *recommended a pardon* for Skerrett.

For Charles Skerrett it was an amazing victory. Within the space of eighteen months he had gone from a prisoner of the Crown with no future, to a free man, legally able to make a claim on Kelly's horses and cattle (now in the possession of

Perjury

Alfred Begbie).

All of this had been achieved because the Chief Justice of New South Wales had been conned by the outrageous fabrications of Charles Skerrett.

For Isabella Mary Kelly her worst fears had come true – although a completely innocent woman, she was now a convict.

On the Tuesday following the trial of Isabella Mary Kelly, the *Sydney Morning Herald* printed an editorial criticising the leniency of her sentence:[4]

> The most remarkable case tried there [Central Criminal Court] has been that of Miss Isabella Mary Kelly, who was charged with perjury. This perjury was declared to have been committed on the trial of one Skerrett, for cattle stealing.
>
> It had the effect not only of branding Skerrett as a felon, but of imputing falsehood to two of his children, who were examined as witnesses on his behalf. Skerrett had been sentenced to ten years' servitude on the public works, and had already endured four years of such punishment, when the residue of the sentence was remitted by the Government on the ground that circumstances recently disclosed went to prove his innocence.
>
> The indictment of Miss Kelly followed as a natural consequence; and the jury after a protracted investigation, have declared her to be guilty. Her sentence, however, was only one year's imprisonment in Darlinghurst gaol and a fine of £100. We cannot understand upon what principle, so lenient a punishment has, in this instance, been awarded.
>
> The guilt of this woman must be taken to have been established, the jury having so declared. If there were any reasons upon which a fair presumption of her innocence could still be founded, they might have been submitted to the executive, with whom rests the power of the responsibility of remitting or of mitigating punishments.
>
> How then stand the facts as his Honour had to deal with them? By wilful and corrupt perjury this woman has blasted the prospects of an innocent man, has subjected him to four years of the most degrading penal servitude, and has kept a charge of falsehood suspended for the same period over the heads of his two children. Should she not have been made to suffer at least the same period of imprisonment as her perjury

has inflicted upon Skerrett, instead of only one-fourth of that time?

The editorial went on to describe the sentence of Baron Alphonse Hainess, who had received three years hard labour for fraudulently receiving money from a cheque:

> Compare these two sentences. We do not say that of the Baron is too heavy; but, if it be not so, surely that of Miss Kelly is infinitely too light. Society must be protected, as far as possible, against the swindling in any and every shape; but it is still more important to protect it against perjury – a crime which, as has often been said, "pollutes the fountain of justice at its very source".

The weekly newspaper, *Bell's Life*, also considered that Kelly had received a light sentence: [5]

> Miss Kelly, who is in her turn duly convicted and sentenced to imprisonment – though it strikes us that her sentence of 12 months is remarkably lenient, considering the misery and degradation which she was the means of inflicting on Skerrett. ...
>
> The liberation of Skerrett and the subsequent conviction of the perjurer, will satisfy the pubic mind in so far as the mere vindication of justice is concerned; but apart from this, it is but right that compensation should be awarded to Skerrett for the heavy loss and trouble to which he has been subjected.

This was an option now open to Charles Skerrett – he could seek compensation from the Government for wrongful imprisonment.

Part 3
The Lie of the Land

"Scenes then occurred which are almost incredible."

— The Sydney Morning Herald.

December 5, 1859.

"What is a forgery but a good imitation?"

— Joseph Andrews.

The Trials of Isabella Mary Kelly

… **Aftermath** …

19. Aftermath

Isabella Mary Kelly entered Darlinghurst Gaol as a privileged prisoner – the prison did not have any other female prisoners of the *quality* of Miss Kelly. The Darlinghurst Gaol Admission Book does not record any of her personal details as it does for all other prisoners, suggesting she was taken straight to her cell, in which she was the only occupant – the cells housed up to four prisoners.

The prison Governor, Mr Beverly, allowed Miss Kelly to walk in his own personal garden within the gaol each afternoon.[1]

At the end of October, after three weeks, all this came to a sudden halt. Complaints had been received that Kelly was getting special treatment, and Governor Beverly was ordered to treat Kelly as he would any other prisoner. This resulted in Kelly being banned from using Beverly's garden. Instead, she would have to go to the small walled exercise yard used by the other prisoners – their only respite from bleak sandstone cells.

On receiving the news, Isabella Kelly made a decision. She would not leave her cell, and she certainly did not want any of the other prisoners to visit her. She would do her prison time in solitary confinement, but it was self-imposed. On the door of her cell the words "solitary cell" were written.[2]

There were some people in the Manning Valley whom Isabella Kelly would not visit for social reasons, how could she possibly socialise with the small number of other female prisoners in the gaol – prostitutes, homeless destitutes, thieves?

Prisoners were not generally permitted to have any communication with the outside world or to have reading materials other than uplifting books such as the bible. Isabella Kelly was allowed to write and receive letters, and sometimes received old newspapers.

The prison provided only a meagre diet with meat provided

The Trials of Isabella Mary Kelly

just once a week. Female prisoners wore a black bonnet and uniform during the day. Again Isabella Kelly seemed to be favoured in these respects, being able to provide many of things using her own money. She said, "I found myself everything whilst I was in gaol – I paid for my washing and everything."[3]

But there were no favours from the environment itself. The cells of thick sandstone walls were unlit with the only light coming from a single, small, barred and glassless window, up high.[4]

After spending many a night in Darlinghurst Gaol during bouts of alcoholism, the poet Henry Lawson wrote a poem about his experience there. It included the line: *And it strikes a chill to the backbone on the warmest summer night.*[5]

Isabella Kelly recalled the sandstone cell as "exceedingly cold and damp – so much so, that the very clothes under me on the bed were mouldy and damp."[6]

It was not long before she developed bronchial problems.

And one can only imagine the mental anguish of an innocent woman of position and intelligence, alone and ruminating on her incarceration while pondering the freedom of her perjurers.

Darlinghurst Gaol and Courthouse circa 1870

The document signing control of Isabella Kelly's Mount George property over to the firm of Lennon & Cape was dated October 11, 1859, five days after her imprisonment, and lodged with the Lands Commission.[7]

It appointed William Lennon as trustee, with an all-encom-

Aftermath

passing power to wind up her affairs: to sell her livestock (about four hundred horses and one thousand three hundred sheep); to sell Mount George at public auction or by private sale; to collect any money owing to Kelly; to pay Kelly's debts, which were listed on the deed as £73 to John Dawson, £500 plus interest to John Roxburgh for mortgage; to take her debt to the firm of £320 plus interest out of the proceeds.

Further, according to this document, Kelly was to bear all costs involved in these operations: Lennon could send up a superintendent to round up the livestock and sell them, paying him a "reasonable"[8] wage; Lennon would take an unspecified "usual commission".[9]

With the power Kelly had assigned to the firm, Lennon, as trustee, had no need to consult her on any decision they made in the winding up of her affairs. As one of their first actions on taking control, Lennon sent a letter of demand to Alfred Begbie for the £1000 owed to Kelly.

Lennon & Cape selected Mr Girard[10] as their superintendent and dispatched him to Mount George to take control. He was French (but spoke good English), a Justice of the Peace and an extremely capable man for the job.

Girard's remuneration of £250 per year, plus a commission of 2½% on all stock sold, was a generous contract signed by Lennon & Cape, but then it was coming out of Miss Kelly's purse rather than their own. At the end of October, Superintendent Girard arrived at Mount George to take control.

Six months previously, in April 1859, Isabella Kelly had signed Tim Leane to a twelve month contract as her new overseer. Leane had only just arrived in the colony. Although employed by Isabella Kelly, Leane was now under the direction of Superintendent Girard, who was working solely in the interests of Lennon & Cape and himself.

With the onset of the lambing season, one of Girard's first decisions was to instruct the shepherds kill most of the lambs – they were "knocked on the head"[11] as they dropped from the ewes. Girard made this decision in the belief that the ewes, without the lambs sucking on them, would fatten quicker, and realise more money – he was, after all, on a commission.

Leane said he complained about the waste – he did not

believe it would make any difference to the ewes. The shepherds counted about five hundred lambs killed in this manner, leaving only about thirty lambs to survive.

When Charles Skerrett returned to the Manning Valley after his release from gaol, he went to stay with Robert Searle and his family.[12]

While he was in prison, Charles Skerrett said his wife had been teaching school (but gave no further details).[13] His daughters Catherine and Margaret had married half brothers William Chapman and Henry Cann, and Robert Searle was their stepfather. Twelve years previously, Searle and Chapman had opposed Isabella Kelly when she successfully prosecuted Branston and Walker for cattle stealing. They now aligned themselves with Skerrett.

Towards the end of 1859, Skerrett took a twelve-month lease of a property in the Manning Valley for £30.[14]

On one particular day when Girard was absent, Charles Skerrett arrived at Mount George and asked Leane if he was in charge. Leane replied that he was when Girard was absent from Mount George. Skerrett said there were thirty of his horses on the run, and he was giving him notice that he would be coming back on a certain day to muster them.

Leane asked Skerrett what brand was on the horses. Skerrett replied it was the MK brand – Kelly's brand. Leane said he did not think Mr Girard would stand for that.

When Skerrett returned some days later, he noted that Leane was riding a horse with Kelly's MK brand, and ordered Leane to get off the horse and give it to him, claiming it belonged to him.

Leane refused.

Skerrett left and went to the Police Office, taking out a warrant for the arrest of Tim Leane for the theft of a horse. Leane was arrested, and appeared before Magistrate Joseph Andrews, who bailed him to appear at Wingham Court of Petty Sessions for a committal hearing.

There Leane came before the Bench, chaired by Magistrate Henry Flett. The Bench dismissed the charge against Leane on the ground that while Skerrett claimed ownership of the horse,

Aftermath

it had never actually been in his possession.

With the gaoling of Kelly for perjury, Skerrett now had a right to make a claim against Kelly. But as he only ever claimed to have paid Kelly £400, he could not expect any more than that from the civil courts.

From a moral and legal point of view, the claim should have been pursued with the trustees Lennon & Cape, in the first place, and through the civil courts in the second place. The missing Bill of Sale and Receipt would be an impediment to Skerrett's civil action, but this would be offset by Kelly's conviction for perjury.

It is obvious from Skerrett's initial actions after Kelly's trial that he aimed to take *all four hundred* of Kelly's horses, despite the fact that his alleged Bill of Sale stated he had bought only *twenty* horses.

Charles Skerrett soon made another strike on Kelly's horses. He came upon one of Kelly's young stockmen out riding, and seeing the boy's horse had the MK brand on it, Skerrett ordered the boy off the horse. When the boy dismounted, Skerrett rode off with the horse in tow, leaving the young stockman to walk home.

On returning home, the boy related the incident to Superintendent Girard. Both Girard and Leane went out looking for the horse, eventually finding it hobbled in Richards' paddock, where both Richards and seventeen-year-old James Skerrett were guarding the horse.

It was quite obvious that Richards was once again fully in league with Skerrett. As Girard proceeded to attach the horse, Richards tried to stop him. The physically strong Girard grabbed Richards round the throat, and half throttled him.

Girard and Leane had come across James Skerrett earlier in the day, and he too had been half throttled when he got in Girard's way. This time James, now in fear of Girard, was content to stand back and watch, telling Girard that his father would not like him taking the horse.[15]

Girard was always prepared to take physical action, and intimidated most who opposed him. James Skerrett also complained that Girard had one of those new weapons called a revolver, which greatly superseded the single-shot pistols currently in use. The revolver was in a case, and while Girard did not take the revolver out of the case and just sat it on his lap while mounted on the horse, it acted as sufficient intimidation. Girard had also manhandled other men who helped Skerrett.[16]

Girard was a magistrate, and was quite happy to let Skerrett know it. He knew the law and was extremely keen to use its full extent to pursue Skerrett. At no time though, did he sit on the Bench in the Manning Valley.

Girard took out a warrant against both Charles Skerrett and his son James, for horse stealing. When the constable went to Robert Searle's house and tried to arrest Skerrett, he met with resistance from Skerrett, who drew a pistol. Eventually the constable was able to get Skerrett to the lockup without shots being fired, and a second charge, that of resisting arrest, was added to the charge of horse stealing.

According to Wingham storekeeper, William McLean,[17] the constable and Skerrett arrived at the Wingham Courthouse at about 6 p.m. on Friday, in company with Robert Searle. Robert Johnston, the Community Magistrate from Dingo Creek, offered Skerrett bail of £40 to be released on his own cognisance and Searle's cognisance, but Searle refused to go bail for Skerrett.

On the other hand, Searle was quite happy to bail James Skerrett. With James bailed, young Skerrett and Searle left the courthouse, with Searle telling Charles Skerrett that bail would be forthcoming on the next day.

On the following day Skerrett's son-in-law, William Chapman, together with his stockman, went to the courthouse to bail Charles Skerrett. Magistrate Charles Croaker refused to bail Skerrett to a servant. On Sunday Magistrate Henry Flett was sent for, and finally on Monday Skerrett was released on bail.

The reluctance of Skerrett's friends to go bail for him was quite noticeable. While Searle may not have had sufficient funds, perhaps Searle's biggest influence was the fact that Skerrett rarely parted with money, and had no conscience about repaying debts.

It is not clear on what conditions Flett released Skerrett. Did Flett pay the bail or (more likely) did he just release him under his own cognisance?

After this, Charles Skerrett made a raid on Alfred Begbie's numerous cattle bearing the MK brand. Maria Cooper, mother-in-law and business partner of Alfred Begbie, claimed that Skerrett took the cattle by force, and produced arms when they tried to resist him.[18]

Skerrett managed to get about thirty cattle, which he then sold at Tinonee.

Begbie, apparently at Girard's urging, charged Skerrett with using threats of violence. At the committal hearing, Philip Dew appeared as Skerrett's main witness, with the result being that Skerrett was bound over to keep the peace. Despite being a witness for Skerrett, Dew was another who avoided becoming bail for him.[19] (There is little source material for this episode.)

On December 2, Attorney General Wise wrote letters to the Magistrates at Wingham, as well as to Charles Skerrett, advising them he declined to proceed to trial on the charge of horse stealing against Charles Skerrett, "because it appears clear to me that there was no felonious intention, but the horse was taken under a claim of right, and any question respecting it should be settled by *civil* proceedings, and not Criminal".[20] Wise said he had not read Skerrett's accompanying letter of complaint, but he would now read it if Skerrett desired him to do so.

In retaliation, Skerrett and Richards saw a solicitor, and charged Girard with assault.[21] Taken before the Bench, Girard was committed and the papers sent to the Attorney General. He dismissed this case also. It set a trend in which there would be suit and counter suit, and *all* dismissed by the Attorney General.

On November 11, 1859, the Member for East Sydney presented a petition to the Legislative Assembly from Charles Skerrett. The petition sought compensation of £1000 for wrongful imprisonment, and outlined Skerrett's imprisonment for cattle stealing; his release after four years; he was granted a pardon; and the recent conviction of Isabella Mary Kelly for perjury. The petition continued:[22]

> That on the occasion when your Petitioner was tried the Bill of Sale, Receipt, and other documents belonging to your Petitioner, which was the only evidence he had of the sale of Miss Kelly's Cattle to him on the 6th June, 1854, were taken from your Petitioner, and that the whole of these documents have since been lost out of the Crown Law Office.
>
> That your Petitioner has thus unjustly been deprived of his liberty for upwards of four years, and not only subjected

to great loss of character and health, and his family to very great deprivation, but that your Petitioner has been most unjustly deprived of the whole of his property amounting at the time of his trial to about £1,000.

That in consequence of the loss of the documents above referred to your Petitioner will be put to great and otherwise unnecessary expense in proving his case in an action against Miss Kelly for the recovery of your Petitioner's property, to say nothing of the possibility of the non-production of these documents having an effect upon the trial detrimental to his interests.

As always, Skerrett was able to put his own "spin" on events. In fact, the missing documents had been one of the major reasons he was convicted in 1855, and their loss certainly helped convict Kelly in 1859.

The next step in this process would be the establishment a Select Committee of Parliamentarians to examine the merits of the case.

On December 3, 1859, *Bell's Life*, the weekly Sydney newspaper, commented on the Skerrett case:

… Skerrett's innocence was subsequently established, and he in turn succeeded in bringing home the crime of perjury to Miss Kelly, who is now undergoing a term of imprisonment for that offence.

Some few weeks since Skerrett proceeded to take possession of the cattle in dispute, when on the information of Miss Kelly's agent [meaning Girard], he was arrested and again committed by the local justices for cattle stealing, and refused bail, although any amount was forthcoming.

After enduring a long confinement in a loathsome watch house [lockup], bail was granted, and Skerrett is now in Sydney to seek redress. We may state that the Attorney General has declined to file a bill against him on the latter charge.

As Skerrett has petitioned the Legislature for compensation, we shall abstain from expressing any opinion upon the matter, beyond stating our belief that the last attempt to criminate him increases his claims to consideration.

Aftermath

Next Monday, December 5, the *Sydney Morning Herald* printed an editorial on the Kelly/Skerrett case. The *Herald* was writing in response to information it had received of events on the Manning, as well as the presentation of Skerrett's petition to Parliament. There was a hint in the editorial that the information came from Charles Skerrett himself.

After running over the case including Skerrett's conviction and release, and Kelly's imprisonment, the editorial continued:

> But her conviction had this further effect; it pronounced the validity of the Bill of Sale and the Receipt, and established Skerrett's right to the cattle; and he was advised by his lawyers to assert his claim.
>
> Skerrett accordingly went to the station, and took possession of a horse in the presence of witnesses, which he declares to have formed part of the stock, which he purchased from Miss Kelly. Upon this he was arrested for horse-stealing, and by a person in the employ of Miss Kelly and two other magistrates [presumably Andrews and Girard] of the same stamp he was committed for trial, confined in a miserable room for a long time – bail being refused by these precious magistrates.
>
> The maltreatment he had received produced such excitement in the neighbourhood, that there was a general disturbance. One man was stabbed, and the proceedings of the Court, having terminated, there was a general drunken orgy. Scenes then occurred which are almost incredible.
>
> After this Skerrett succeeded in obtaining a magistrate from a distance, who took bail for his appearance, and thus enabled him to escape the black hole kind of accommodation which seems, with the excitement, to have made a serious infraction upon his health.

On the following Monday, December 12, the Herald's rival newspaper, *Empire*, also ran an editorial on the Skerrett/Kelly story, commenting on Skerrett's petition to Parliament. *Empire* stated it was using information received in a letter from Charles Skerrett.

The editorial gave the history of the case, including Skerrett's "spin" on a number of events. It also stated that when Skerrett returned to the Manning after his imprisonment, "he found several persons, amongst them one or two magistrates, branding and slaughtering the increase of his cattle". These magistrates had threatened Skerrett not to make any claim on his cattle.

While stating they were unable to vouch for the accuracy of Skerrett's statements, *Empire* outlined Skerrett's version of his arrest on a summons by Girard including: the constable had lied and contradicted himself; the Bench refused to hear Skerrett's witnesses; Skerrett was not allowed to ask Girard any questions.

The editorial continued:

> We are informed that the committal of Skerrett occasioned great excitement at Wingham. A settler named Dew having remarked that Skerrett was justly entitled to the horse, which he was accused of stealing. One of the Magistrates ordered his apprehension. He was immediately seized by the constables, when a scuffle ensued, and Dew was stabbed in the back with a knife. Dew subsequently made a statement on oath of this fact before one of the magistrates on the Manning, and we understand he is determined not to let the matter drop.
>
> In a long written statement, which we have received from Skerrett, the charges of the most serious nature in connection with this case are preferred against certain magistrates on the Manning. The unjust treatment, which he has undergone, may naturally enough have impelled him somewhat to colour this statement – but, making every allowance for this, we are convinced from what we have learned from other and unbiased sources, that the charges he has preferred are in the main correct. We dare not give utterance to these charges [possible slander] …
>
> If all the facts be as they are stated, the case of Charles Skerrett exhibits as gross an outrage on the liberty of the subject, and as unwarrantable a violation of a great principle of English law as it has ever been our lot to hear of in this colony…
>
> Skerrett has suffered in pocket, suffered in health, suffered in reputation, through the perjury of a worthless woman. His wife and family have, of course, participated in his sufferings. That redress and compensation to which, judging by the evidence before us, he appears to be entitled, can be afforded by Parliament alone. An investigation also into the conduct of the Bench of Magistrates at Wingham is imperatively demanded.

Wingham store-owner, William McLean, read the editorials. Exasperated, he wrote a letter of reply to the editor of the *Sydney Morning Herald*, which published it on Friday, December 23.

⇥ Aftermath ⇤

McLean wrote that he had personally witnessed these events, and proceeded to correct the editorials on the facts, as he saw them, of Skerrett's arrest and appearance before the Bench at Wingham, including Skerrett's eventual release by Henry Flett.

He then went on to deal with their statements about Philip Dew:

> I wonder how any respectable journal could be so gulled as to swallow such a wholesale dose of slander and falsehoods. I was present during the whole day, and saw neither the excitement nor the drunken orgy you so graphically described.
>
> The only drunken man in our quiet little township on that day was Philip Dew, Skerrett's principal witness, who, before the business of the Court terminated, was sent to the watch house for contempt of Court, and who on the following morning, when apologising to the magistrates for his conduct on the day previous, stated that he got drunk purposely to avoid being called on to become bail for Skerrett.
>
> This took place during the hearing of a case in which Skerrett was charged with using threats of violence towards Mr Begbie, for which he has been bound over to keep the peace.
>
> The case of stabbing was never heard of here until it made its appearance in the leader of the Herald. I stated before that Philip Dew was sent to the lockup for contempt of court, and on passing the table at which a clerk was standing making a [quill] pen, staggered against him and broke the blade of his [the clerk's] knife. This, I presume, was the case of stabbing.
>
> But if Dew was stabbed at all, it must have been very slightly, as I saw him after being liberated, offering to fight the best man on the Manning for a five pound note – a thing seldom he is known to possess.

One wonders what effect, if any, this letter had in correcting the erroneous views previously presented by the editorials of these newspapers to their readers.

In her prison cell on December 30, Isabella Kelly was given some newspapers several weeks old, one of which was the *Empire* of December 12. After reading the editorial, she too felt impelled to write a letter to the Editor of the rival newspaper, the *Sydney Morning Herald*.

Starting with, "Having by accident seen the leading article in the *Empire* of the 12th instant",[23] Kelly launched into a rambling self-defence, using very little sentence construction. She may have been unaware that the *Herald* had previously written a similar editorial.

In particular she wanted to correct the record on Jane Skerrett's broken leg. Contrary to the editorial, Kelly wrote, she had not fired any pistol, and had in fact spent three days caring for Jane.

She then moved on to a topic that is not sourced anywhere else – the disappearance of her Chinese stockman – with the implication that Skerrett had murdered him. Some time after her return from Sydney in September 1854, Kelly went looking for the stockman.

Isabella Kelly wrote:[24]

> How did Skerrett dispose of my stockman, who had lived in my service above three years? I obtained a warrant for his [the stockman's] apprehension and offered a reward of £10. He disappeared shortly before Skerrett's trial. He would have been my principal witness, but he has never been heard of since.
>
> I went to Brimbin shortly before his disappearance, accompanied by Mr Bates, a Gentleman of the Manning River, to take my stockman away. When Skerrett saw me going to the stockman's hut, he ran after me and would not allow Mr Bates in, threatening him at his peril to enter the hut. Mr Bates stood opposite the window, where he could see into the hut.
>
> I told my stockman I had come for him, [and] to get his things immediately ready to accompany me, as Mr Bates had brought a boat to take him away. On hearing this, Skerrett struck me on my chest [and] knocked me over a form with such force, as the blood rushed from my mouth.
>
> On seeing Skerrett strike me, Mr Bates ran into the hut [and] asked him what he struck me for. He caught hold of Mr Bates by the collar of his coat, and dragged him out of the hut for some hundred yards. ...
>
> As soon as I was able to go to the Doctor, he examined me and stated I had received a dangerous blow. He gave me a certificate to that effect. I obtained a summons from the bench for the assault.

Aftermath

The warrant for the stockman was for the purpose of obtaining a deposition from the stockman. As the stockman looking after some of her horses for three years at Brimbin, this unnamed Chinese man would have been able to give extremely valuable evidence concerning Skerrett's behaviour at Brimbin, as well as the instructions the stockman had received from Kelly during this period.

Kelly made no mention elsewhere of this summons. It was probably superseded shortly after, by the committal of Skerrett for cattle stealing. Both Kelly and Bates evidently fled to the boat moored on the bank of the Dawson River, leaving the stockman behind. Kelly did not see or hear of him again, although she advertised for him in *Hue and Cry*.[25]

Kelly implies in her letter that Skerrett may have murdered the stockman, but that would be unnecessary. After the departure of Kelly and Bates, it would not have taken too much for Skerrett to frighten the man away or for the stockman simply to leave of his own accord.

The letter was never published.

The Chief Justice, Sir Alfred Stephen prepared to take leave and go Home to England for twelve months. He had argued with Parliament, in the first place to get twelve months leave, and then, when it was granted, he argued over his salary while absent. He had threatened at one stage to retire, and collect his significant retirement benefits. The whole process had delayed his departure.

On December 10, the House of Assembly voted 31-17 to allow the Chief Justice twelve month's salary while he was on leave.[26] Many Parliamentarians were against the motion on the ground that his annual salary of £2600 should have been more than enough to sustain him in his leave of absence.

Sir Alfred had been making an all out search for the missing Bill of Sale and Receipt. It was most likely in response to Skerrett's petition to Parliament, where Skerrett stated he had been disadvantaged by the loss of these documents. A Parliamentary Committee of Enquiry could be expected soon, and the newspaper editorials only exacerbated the situation.

After much dedicated searching over several weeks, the Bill

of Sale and the Receipt were found in a drawer in the Banco Courtroom, a room they should not have been in.

Each Justice of the Supreme Court had a drawer in this room in which they stored papers connected to the cases held there, usually on a temporary basis. When Sir Alfred's clerk went through his drawer with "upwards of forty or fifty papers"[27] in it, the documents were found amongst them.

With the recovery of the missing documents, the Chief Justice still declined to take any action.

On January 7, 1860, Joseph Andrews wrote a letter to Miss Kelly. This was his first letter to her since her imprisonment, despite receiving several letters from her. Andrews began by writing there was no good news, and that Skerrett "has been successfully resisted by Mr Girard from taking any horses, but he has succeeded in taking Mr Begbie's cattle, and for the last eight or ten days we have heard nothing of him."[28]

Joseph Giles had recently returned to the Manning and taken employment with Joseph Andrews. Giles told Andrews that when he was working with William Turner in at the time of Skerrett's committal hearing in 1854, Turner had made a confession to him of falsely signing the Receipt and giving perjured evidence before the Bench. Giles had then advised Turner to clear out.

Andrews wrote that Turner had been seen at Maitland races after he absconded five years ago, so there was still every reason to believe Turner was alive and every hope of tracing him.

"Can you get a new trial?", Andrews wrote, fearing that if she had to complete the whole of her twelve months sentence, there would be no chance of bringing Skerrett to justice.

When the Chief Justice found the missing documents, Joseph said, he thought Kelly would have been released immediately, but he had been wrong.

He finished the letter with a message of support, "We are all well; hoping you are so, and under the consciousness of your innocency in this matter, you will bear up against it."

It must have been comforting for Isabella Kelly to know there was at least one person who believed in her innocence.

20. The Disputed Lease

Before her trial, Isabella Kelly had left Mount George and her dispute with Reuben Richards unresolved. Richards had six or seven horses grazing in the Mount George paddock since he gained the mail contract.

Having written to Overseer Tim Leane asking him to notify Richards in writing (as the first step in taking legal action) that she was charging him five shillings per week for each horse grazing in the Mount George paddock, she received a reply back from Leane that he had complied fully with her request. Leane lied.

Leane seemed to be on very friendly terms with Richards, and instead of giving the written notice to Richards, Leane simply showed him Kelly's letter. Leane said he was amazed to find Richards already had a copy of the letter (or at least knew the contents of the letter), suggesting to Leane that Mailman Richards must have been opening Kelly's mail.

Kelly also left instructions with Tim Leane to repair the stockyard and fence of the Mount George paddock, which he did.[1] Andrews had been putting stock in this paddock for a number of years.

On October 7, 1859, several days before Kelly's trial, Richards asked Leane to write him a letter, stating Leane had *not* notified Richards in writing of the five shillings per horse charges. If Kelly was convicted and trustees came to look after her property, Richards said, they would demand the money for the horses from him, and it had risen to a substantial amount.

Leane obliged by writing the letter and, at Richards' suggestion, falsely headed it with a date of "22nd August", and the place of origin as "Waterview".[2] Leane said he wrote this letter because he did not want Richards getting into trouble because of him.

According to Leane, on Monday, October 10, while Kelly's

trial was still continuing, Leane visited Richards at the cottage he rented from Miss Kelly. Repeating the latest (false) rumours about her trial, Richards said to Leane: "Oh! She's all but convicted, because the Chief Justice, Sir Alfred Stephen, has sworn before the Court that she's been guilty of perjury since 1855. I suppose I shall now have to defend an action against her trustees for my horses being in her paddock. I offered Miss Kelly £10 a year for the paddock, and I would willingly give £15 a year for it now."[3]

Richards then added, "Is it not a pity the bloody old wretch would not give me the paddock before she went away."[4]

The next day, Tuesday, with the fence repaired, Leane and a boy tried unsuccessfully to get Andrews' cattle out of the Mount George paddock. Richards said to Leane, "It is useless for you to repair the fence, as Andrews' cattle are always in the paddock."[5]

Richards then lent the boy a horse to help get the cattle out. While the boy removed the cattle using Richards' horse, Richards said he had sent Andrews notices to keep his animals out of the paddock. Leane chided him, saying it was not *his* paddock to be issuing such notices. Richards replied, "whose else could it be, if Miss Kelly is convicted."[6]

Richards said, "I will be obliged to you to go over to Andrews and caution him to keep his cattle out of the paddock, as you are in charge."

Leane said, "I won't go, for I won't incur Miss Kelly's displeasure, because she told me not to interfere with Andrews' cattle."

Richards said, "It's very hard to allow Andrews' cattle to be in the paddock, but if the old wretch, Miss Kelly, had given me the paddock I'd soon make them keep them out."

Leane suggested Richards go and see Andrews himself. Richards said, "If I do, they'd only laugh at me, knowing it's not mine."

On Friday, Joseph Andrews returned home from the trial to find Richards agitating for him to remove his pigs and cattle from the Mount George paddock. A week later Richards sent a note over to Andrews, giving him formal notice to keep his pigs and cattle out of the Mount George paddock.

These two men had been on reasonable terms since Richards' move to Mount George in 1857, but now the friction between them was beginning to warm considerably.

The Disputed Lease

Reuben Richards summons Joseph Andrews with trespass. On Wednesday, December 7, the hearing came before the Bench at Wingham. For the Manning Valley residents it was a most unusual sight for one of the Community Magistrates to appear before three other Community Magistrates (Henry Flett, Robert Johnston and William Cross).

According to William McLean[7] (the Wingham storekeeper attending the proceedings as a spectator), after Reuben Richards formally complained to the Bench of trespass, Joseph Andrews asked him by what authority did he claim possession of the Mount George paddock. Richards replied, "I have a lease of the paddock".

Andrews asked, "Who gave you the lease?"

Richards answered, "That's my business not yours."

Andrews then turned to the Bench and said, "I demand a sight of the lease".

Henry Flett asked Richards to hand the lease to the Bench. After examining the lease, Flett declared, "It's alright – this is a lease of the paddock to Richards from Miss Kelly."

Again, Andrews asked to look at the lease.

Flett gave the lease back to Richards, telling Andrews it belonged to Richards, "he can do with it what he likes."

Persistently, Andrews demanded a sight of the lease. Magistrate Cross sidestepped Chairman Flett, and ordered Richards to give the lease to Andrews, who read the document:[8]

> Agreement entered into this 19th day of September 1859, between Isabella Mary Kelly of the Manning River of the one part and Reuben Richards of the same place on the other part witnesseth that the said Isabella Mary Kelly doth let to the said Reuben Richards all that portion of land situated upon the Manning River and known as the Mount George paddock containing 15 acres more or less and now occupied by the said Reuben Richards for the term of nine years to commence upon the day of the date hereof and the said Reuben Richards shall pay no rent for the first four years.
>
> But shall fence round the farm in a workmanlike manner as an equivalent and for the next five years a rent of six pounds a year payable yearly and the said Reuben Richards shall give up the said land at the expiration of the above nine

years to the leaser her executors administrators and assigns.
   Isabella Mary Kelly.
   Reuben Richards.

On the back of the document, another part of the agreement was written, like an afterthought:
   I hereby agree that the said Reuben Richards take what timber he requires for the said fences round the said paddock from off any part of my land.
   Isabella Mary Kelly.
   Reuben Richards.

The first thing observed by Andrews was that the *whole document*, apart from the signature of Reuben Richards, was purportedly in the hand of Miss Kelly. Joseph Andrews pulled out of his pockets a number of letters written to him by Miss Kelly, and proceeded to compare the writing.

He said to the Bench, "I have letters from Miss Kelly. I believe it [the lease] to be a forgery."[9]

Henry Flett replied, "It is no forgery – I could swear to the document being a genuine one, and anyone who has ever seen Miss Kelly's hand could not be mistaken."

Andrews repeated himself, "I believe it to be a forgery – what is a forgery but a good imitation?"

Flett again handed the lease back to Richards.

Andrews asked the Bench to keep the lease, saying, "I wish the lease to be impounded – I'll challenge it to be a forgery."

Chairman Flett declared, "We have no business to make any such order."

At this point, Magistrates Cross and Johnston left the Bench, and in their absence Flett and Andrews continued debating the impounding of the lease. Of course, being a Magistrate himself, Andrews knew what the Bench could do or not do. Andrews again objected, saying to Flett, "It is a most unusual mode of proceeding to give up an instrument challenged to be forged into the hands of the forger."[10]

When the other two magistrates returned to the Bench, they directed Richards to hand the lease to the Clerk of the Court for impounding.

The Bench made no determination on the trespass, with the

expectation of the lease being tested in a Court of law at a later date.

Joseph Andrews believed the lease to be a forgery for a number of reasons. He had never known Kelly to write a lease like this – she always had a non-interested third party *write* the lease and then to *sign* it as a witness. In fact when Richards signed his original lease on his arrival at Mount George in 1857, it had been written and witnessed by Joseph Andrews.[11]

Further, Kelly had written several letters to Andrews since her imprisonment, and none of them made any mention of a lease to Reuben Richards. Andrews believed the lease was not written on paper Miss Kelly used – since her problems with Skerrett, she had taken using a certain paper containing a watermark. This was not like the paper she had been using. More than that, this paper appeared to be *similar* to one of the warning notices about the paddock, which he had recently received from Richards.[12]

The date of the lease was significant: September 19th was two days before Kelly left Mount George to go to Sydney for her trial. If Kelly had indeed made such a lease, why would she not have told her overseer, Tim Leane, or Andrews or anyone else?

For Henry Flett, it was clear where his sympathies lay. In declaring the lease to be genuine and returning it to Richards, he would have given Richards the opportunity to destroy the lease, making Richards immune from any forgery charges. Further, in any future Court action, Richards could rely on Flett to testify that the lease was genuine. Perhaps Chairman Flett would have enjoyed declaring Joseph Andrews guilty of trespass – it was only five months since he and Andrews had been opponents in the parliamentary election.

But Joseph Andrews was reluctant to test the validity of Richards' lease.

There were many difficulties, not the least being that Miss Kelly would need to testify, and she was currently in gaol for perjury, with nine months of her sentence remaining. Much of the other evidence, which made him believe the lease was forged, could best be described as circumstantial.

On December 22, Mr Girard called in to see Joseph and

convinced him to change his mind and proceed against Richards. Girard even filled out the summons.

The committal hearing came before the Wingham Bench, on Wednesday, January 4, 1860. Richards did not appear. It soon turned into an anti-climax, when it was discovered that the lease had not been retained by the Clerk of the Court, but had been sent to Sydney to the Crown Solicitor's Office. Consequently, the lease was unavailable – case dismissed.

The Bench stated that the case had gone to a higher court and hence, they would not rule on it. Andrews objected stating that he had not received any notification of any action, but was overruled. As far as Andrews was concerned, that was the end of the matter.[13]

Richards would later admit[14] that as soon as he received Joseph Andrews' warrant for forgery on December 29, he immediately travelled down to Sydney – that was the reason he did not appear before the Bench. On his arrival in Sydney, Richards saw his solicitor, Robert Abbott, and asked him to immediately retrieve the lease from the Crown Solicitor's Office.

Abbott obtained the lease, and retained possession of it. Richards directed Abbott not to give it to anyone.[15]

On January 17, 1860, Joseph Andrews received a summons to appear in the Supreme Court to answer charges of slander and malicious prosecution, taken out by Reuben Richards. The slander was alleged to have taken place at the hearing for trespass against Andrews on December 7. The malicious prosecution was the action brought by Andrews against Richards on January 4, for forgery. The case was set down for May, and, as it was a civil issue, there was no committal hearing.

On February 3, Reuben Richards' solicitor, Robert Abbott, registered the lease for the paddock at Mount George with the Lands Commission.[16] This was unusual, in that leases were rarely registered, but it was a very smart move, as the original lease did not have to be registered – only a *copy* of the lease. It meant that there was a legal copy of the lease, which could be referred to at any time, without the need for the original.

The only person who could authoritatively deny the lease, was Isabella Mary Kelly – and she was in gaol for perjury relating to documents she alleged to be forged.

21. The Smear

On February 3, 1860, in the Legislative Assembly, William Arnold, the Member for Paterson, moved a motion to establish a Select Committee to investigate the petition of Charles Skerrett. In speaking to his motion, Arnold gave a brief summary of the case, based on the outline given in the editorial of the *Sydney Morning Herald*, and read a paragraph from that editorial to the House.

Mr Arnold said he had no doubt that Mr Skerrett had been wrongfully convicted, and the Legislature should make some recompense to him. He made reference to the £5000 compensation made by the British Government to William Henry Barber, who had spent a number of years imprisoned on Norfolk Island as the result of a perjury conviction connected with a will, only to have been later proved innocent. Arnold concluded with the comment that although it was the duty of the Government to punish crime, it had a higher duty to protect the innocent from unmerited suffering.

Mr John Darvall, the Member for Hawkesbury, and one of the barristers who unsuccessfully defended Kelly at her trial, noted that it was a most extraordinary case, and requested that the phrase "perjured evidence" in the motion should be replaced by a phrase which did not assume as fact that which the Committee was about to investigate.[1] The amended motion became:[2]

> That a Select Committee, with the power to send for persons and papers, be appointed to inquire into the cases of Charles Skerrett, who was convicted of Cattle Stealing in 1855, and subsequently liberated and pardoned, on the discovery that such conviction had been procured on evidence, which has since lead to a conviction of perjury.

Mr John Plunkett, the member for West Sydney, and the

Attorney General who successfully prosecuted Skerrett in 1855, stated his support of the motion. He suggested that the Select Committee quickly obtain evidence from the Chief Justice before he left the colony, and while all the facts were still fresh in Sir Alfred Stephen's memory. Mr Plunkett also expressed surprise at the leniency of Miss Kelly's sentence, saying that if the verdict at her trial had been justly arrived at, then the maximum penalty should have been applied to her.

The amended motion passed unanimously, with William Arnold, the mover of the motion, becoming the Chairman of this Select Committee.

On Tuesday, February 7, 1860, just four days later, William Arnold held the first meeting of the Select Committee in the committee rooms of Parliament House.[3] The Committee consisted of John Black, John Clements, James Hart, Richard Jones, Andrew Loder, Henry Oxley, Henry Parkes, John Robertson and Robert Wisdom. Several of these members, including Henry Parkes, had signed Charles Skerrett's petition.

The Committee's first resolution summoned Sir Alfred Stephen to appear before them. Two days later, Sir Alfred appeared before the Committee, and proceeded to give an outline of the case right from the start, as most members only knew of the case from what they read in the papers. He tried to explain the complexity of the charges: Skerrett was charged with cattle stealing, but the guilt of cattle stealing depended on the guilt of forgery.

The Chief Justice produced the Bill of Sale and the Receipt, and recounted how the documents had been lost (it was not his fault) and found. The Kelly/Burt civil trial had raised doubts in his mind of Miss Kelly's veracity. He had examined Skerrett in his chambers before recommending a pardon for him.

The Chief Justice said he believed Miss Kelly should be pardoned:

> Mr Wisdom: "If you thought Skerrett innocent, you would think Miss Kelly guilty?"
>
> Sir Alfred: "I could not find Skerrett innocent without finding Kelly guilty of the most aggravated perjury, and Andrews guilty of perjury also."
>
> Mr Hart: "You say that if you were on Miss Kelly's trial for perjury you would acquit her?"

Sir Alfred: "I should return a verdict of not guilty; that in the evidence the charge is not proved, and therefore that she is not guilty."

Mr Hart: "Do you think that she ought to receive a pardon now?"

Sir Alfred: "It follows that I do think so, simply on the ground stated by me, that the case is too doubtful to justify punishment by any human tribunal."[4]

Sir Alfred went to say he had come round to the view (popularly held on the Manning River) that the Bill of Sale was a genuine document. He believed that Miss Kelly had actually signed it to give Skerrett a "fictitious title"[5] to her property in order to protect it from confiscation by the Government if she were convicted of cattle stealing (referring to the malicious summons by McPherson/Turner shortly after she met Skerrett).

If he were a juror in a civil case, and had to make a decision between Skerrett and Kelly, Sir Alfred said he would find for Skerrett. As a juror in a criminal case, he would find Miss Kelly not guilty because the burden of proof needed to be far more rigorous in a criminal case i.e. there was a "reasonable doubt".

The Committee asked the Chief Justice how he changed his opinion of the guilt of Skerrett and Kelly – and found it very hard to follow his logic:

Chairman Arnold: "You refused to recommend a mitigation [of Skerrett's sentence], because you thought the verdict justified?"

Sir Alfred: "Just so."

Chairman Arnold: "But, afterwards, you say that, on again taking the details into consideration, you came to a conclusion in his favour. I cannot understand how you can reconcile that with the statement that you did not recommend a mitigation because you thought him guilty?"

Sir Alfred: "That is a matter on which any man may form his own opinion. In the first instance, I thought him guilty. I retained that opinion until after Kelly's evidence against Burt. After this, and on fresh facts coming out, I doubted entirely about his guilt; and so I altered my opinion; but I never expressed an opinion of his innocence. My reports and recommendations are before you."

Mr Clements: "You lost faith in her evidence?"

Sir Alfred: "Yes; and I no longer hold the opinion that he is guilty. Some may think that inconsistent with my declining to say that he is innocent; but I am content to state the facts."[6]

On the following Saturday night, Sir Alfred Stephen attended a public farewell dinner, attended by many dignitaries of the colony, lavishing praise on his sixteen years as Chief Justice.[7]

On February 14, Justice John Dickinson, who had presided at Kelly's perjury trial, advised members of the Supreme Court he was now the Acting Chief Justice.[8]

The next day Charles Skerrett appeared before the Select Committee, where his allegations caused a sensation.

Skerrett began with allegations against John Plunkett.

He alleged that Plunkett, in his role as Attorney General, had illegally held back the depositions made at his committal hearing, so they could not be used in his trial. Here he was referring to Joseph Andrews' deposition, in which Andrews declared the signature of Isabella Mary Kelly on the Bill of Sale to be genuine, and which he then repudiated at the trial.

Further, Skerrett alleged that Attorney General Plunkett had conspired with Skerrett's own counsel, Mr Holroyd (keeping in mind Holroyd had been Skerrett's counsel in 1855 and Kelly's counsel in 1859), to send away an important witness (Butchart of the firm Rich, Langley and Butchart). Skerrett said that not only did the *Sydney Morning Herald* report that Butchart had been sent home, but Judge Stephen commented on it as well.

> Mr Skerrett: "I saw my lawyer [Mr Holroyd] and Mr Plunkett whispering together; and then they spoke to the witness [Mr Butchart]; and the witness went out of Court and went away."
>
> Mr Parkes: "Do you know by whom the witness was sent away?"
>
> Mr Skerrett: "I cannot say positively beyond what I saw in the newspaper report; but I saw my lawyer and Mr Plunkett whispering together."[9]

This was typical of the smear tactics adopted by Skerrett in giving his evidence: Skerrett accused Plunkett and Holroyd of removing a witness vital to his defence from the trial, but then shied away with a vague answer when asked for more specific evidence.

Skerrett complained that Magistrate Day kept delaying the committal hearing while ever Skerrett's most important witness was available. (Day had postponed Skerrett's committal hearing on one occasion because of Kelly's inability to attend due to illness.)[10]

> Chairman Arnold: "Who was the witness?"
>
> Mr Skerrett: "Mr Turner; he was the man who was witness to my having paid the money, and to Miss Kelly having got the £400. While this witness was there, Miss Kelly would never appear at court. But as soon as he disappeared, she came down and prosecuted me. He has disappeared and has not been heard of since."[11]

Continuing, Skerrett said people on the Manning thought Turner had been murdered by Kelly. A woman had disappeared from Kelly's place, and she too was thought to be murdered by Kelly. People on the Manning were told by Kelly that Mr Plunkett would do anything for her [implying that Plunkett would bend the law for Kelly]. Kelly and Plunkett were in Dublin together, and when Skerrett lived in Dublin, he heard that Miss Kelly was Mr Plunkett's housekeeper.

> Mr Parkes: "Your statement that he was living with Miss Kelly is rather vague. When you used that expression, did you mean to say that she lived in his service as an ordinary domestic?"
>
> Mr Skerrett: "No, as his housekeeper. The saying used to be 'That is Plunkett's housekeeper'"
>
> Mr Oxley: "Do you mean to say that she was living in a state of concubinage?"
>
> Mr Skerrett: "Yes, that was the meaning at the time."
>
> Mr Jones: "Then you assert that you had heard it said at the time that Miss Kelly was living with him as his mistress?"
>
> Mr Skerrett: "Yes."
>
> …
>
> Chairman Arnold: "Did you at that time know Mr Plunkett personally?"
>
> Mr Skerrett: "No, I did not. I was in a much higher position than Mr Plunkett."

The Trials of Isabella Mary Kelly

Chairman Arnold: "Did you know Miss Kelly personally?"
Mr Skerrett: "No farther than her being pointed out to me and being told about her."[12]

The Committee must have been absolutely stunned by these accusations. John Plunkett had been Attorney General of New South Wales for over twenty years, and was highly regarded in both his private and public life – there had never been even a hint of scandal about him.

Skerrett continued with complaints about Joseph Andrews. Not only had Andrews given false evidence against him, but after his conviction in 1855 he had stolen his cattle. Before he was convicted Andrews had no cattle, but now he had cattle with his brand on them. Before he was convicted, Andrews had not even owned a property, and now he did. Skerrett said Andrews had stolen the increase of his cattle and placed his own brand on them.

Mr Clements: "What makes you say he [Andrews] was badly off, when by your own showing [evidence], he was keeping a public house?"
Mr Skerrett: "Because he had nothing. Everybody knows that at that time. Joseph Andrews was a poor, miserable man."[13]

Skerrett continued his evidence with more allegations of a Great Conspiracy against him. He had written letters to the Chief Justice, but Mr Ormsby, the Superintendent of Cockatoo Island Prison had illegally refused to send them to the Chief Justice. Ormsby was a friend of Plunkett; and in Dublin, Ormsby and Plunkett had been spies for Dublin Castle giving information to Major Sirr.

(Major Sirr, who was probably not well known by the members of the Committee, had put down an Irish rebellion, resulting in the death of Irish hero Lord Fitzgerald, in Dublin in 1798 – *before* Plunkett was born.)

The Committee moved on to more recent issues, with Skerrett stating that Andrews and Girard had persecuted him. While he was in gaol, they had killed his cattle. William McLean had also been slaughtering his cattle. (This was to counter McLean's letter to the editor of the *Sydney Morning Herald*.)

Chairman Arnold: "Then whilst you were in the lock-up, they killed your fat cattle?"

The Smear

Mr Skerrett: "Yes, and when I was sent down to stand my trial, they mustered my cattle and sent them off up the country."

Chairman Arnold: "Were you sent down to Sydney in custody?"

Mr Skerrett: "No, I was bailed out. All the settlers round about came to the Court House and said it was a shame I should be so prosecuted. About thirty persons offered themselves as bondsmen for me."

...

Chairman Arnold: "Have you ever got any of the property you purchased from Miss Kelly?"

Mr Skerrett: "No, Andrews has got all the cattle."

...

Mr Parkes: "I suppose you do not consider that it would be safe for you to go up and claim your cattle?"

Mr Skerrett: "No man is safe, it is true. Andrews is a man you are never safe with. He will rob you and then, if you say a word, he will bring a charge against you, and [as a magistrate] send you down to Sydney under committal, and so get rid of you."

...

Chairman Arnold: "What is your object in asking for this investigation?"

Mr Skerrett: "My object in asking for this enquiry is, that I am left without a shilling in the world. Everything I had, all the hard earning of years, has been taken away from me by these persons, and now, me and my family are left nearly destitute.

What I wanted was to get my property back, or else that I should have some means of support given to me and my family. For if I do not get my property back, I shall be left destitute.

My wife has been keeping school and what she has got from that is all I have had to depend on since I came off Cockatoo Island. For whilst I was there, I received a blow on the head, that has left me unfit to do anything.

I have been in ill health ever since, and have been under Dr Bland ever since I have been off Cockatoo."[14]

Of course Skerrett's recent activities on the Manning were in direct conflict with his evidence of ill health. Skerrett's evidence concluded with a rather sardonic observation:

> Mr Parkes: "You never fired off a pistol in Miss Kelly's presence?"
>
> Mr Skerrett: "Never."
>
> Mr Parkes: "Did you ever give her cause to fear that you would murder her?"
>
> Mr Skerrett: "No, if I had wanted to shoot her, I could have done it a thousand times. She gave me plenty of chances. But I would scorn to take that kind of satisfaction and still more, upon a woman – though she should have been shot years ago."[15]

Members of the Committee, like Henry Parkes, who had signed Skerrett's petition, must have left the committee room quite shell-shocked. As for Charles Skerrett, he may have conned many people in his time, including the Chief Justice and the newspapers, but these allegations against the highly respected Plunkett were just too unbelievable for the Parliamentarians. They *knew* John Plunkett.

After this, members of the Committee would often ask other witnesses if they thought Skerrett was mentally unbalanced. It was a point from which Skerrett never recovered – he had lost all credibility with them.

John Plunkett appeared before the Select Committee on Friday, February 17. As a Member of Parliament, he would have been aware of Skerrett's allegations, and may have read the transcripts of the interview. Plunkett answered his questioners with a quiet dignity.

After Chairman Arnold read portions of Skerrett's evidence to Mr Plunkett, the former Attorney General replied: "All that I have to say is that it is a pure fabrication, without the slightest ground, shadow, or colour of excuse for making it. I never knew Miss Kelly in Ireland, and I never saw her face until many years after I came out here."[16]

Plunkett recalled that Miss Kelly had delivered a parcel to Mrs. Plunkett, shortly after Kelly's arrival in the colony, but they had never met socially.

Mr Hart: "As a colonist, have you heard anything of Miss

The Smear

Kelly's singularity of character, which might have drawn her into notoriety?"

Mr Plunkett: "I heard from public rumour, but it also came before me in connection with these many cases of horse and cattle stealing, that she was a most eccentric character – a masculine woman, who used to ride through the country with pistols in her holsters, and who carried on the breeding of horses, and all that sort of business. Altogether what I learned of her was not calculated to impress me very much in her favour."[17]

Here was one of the few occasions when the circulating rumours about Isabella Mary Kelly were explicitly stated. The pistols in the holsters were just not true.

And one can notice Plunkett's distaste of a woman involved with breeding horses.

On February 21, Charles Langley, of the firm Rich, Langley & Butchart, was called into the Parliamentary committee room. He reported that since the events of 1854, the firm had gone into insolvency, with Mr Butchart going to Deniliquin and Mr Rich going to Victoria. Miss Kelly did put about 280 head of cattle in their hands for sale, but he could not remember if it was 1853 or 1854, as the books were with the Official Assignee.

After Langley withdrew, John Dawson was interviewed. As Skerrett's solicitor at his trial, he recalled that he had told Butchart he was not needed for the defence. Mr Plunkett had nothing to do with Butchart leaving.

A week later, Arthur Holroyd, Skerrett's trial barrister was called in. He confirmed Dawson's evidence about Butchart, and denied any influence by Plunkett.

Later that day Miss Isabella Mary Kelly was taken from her cell and appeared before the Committee. She had been summoned to appear several times before, but the Sheriff had failed to produce her on each occasion, probably because of illness.

Kelly would have been unaware of what evidence had already been given. The Committee were very keen to ask about her relationship with John Plunkett.

> Chairman Arnold: "From what part of Great Britain?"
> Miss Kelly: "From London."
> Chairman Arnold: "Was London or England the place of your residence before you came here?"
> Miss Kelly: "My place of birth was Ireland, but I was in England from eight years of age."
> Chairman Arnold: "Do you know any families in Ireland?"
> Miss Kelly: "No."
> Chairman Arnold: "Did you never live in Dublin?"
> Miss Kelly: "Yes, I was taken away by my brother at the age of eight from Ireland. My parents were dead and the late Sir Richard Crowder, who has lately died – his father, Mr Justice Crowder, was my guardian."
>
> ...
>
> Chairman Arnold: "Did you ever know Mr Plunkett before you came here?"
> Miss Kelly: "I never saw him in my life till I came here. I met Mrs. Plunkett's mother in Paris at Mr McHenry, the banker's, Rue de la Paix."
> Chairman Arnold: "Had you any private acquaintance with Mr Plunkett at any time?"
> Miss Kelly: "No, never."
>
> ...
>
> Mr Parkes: "Did you ever state while you were residing on the Manning, that you had been acquainted with Mr Plunkett in Ireland?"
> Miss Kelly: "Never, I could not say so."
> Mr Parkes: "Did you ever state that Mr Plunkett was your friend, and would pull you through any scrape?"
> Miss Kelly: "Never, he is too honourable a gentleman to do such a thing."
> Mr Parkes: "You never said so?"
> Miss Kelly: "No, never in my life."[18]

The Committee continued the examination over a wide range of events. Kelly told of meeting Skerrett and her dealings with him. Above all she maintained her innocence in the affair. Finally she handed in a copy of the unpublished letter she had sent to the *Sydney Morning Herald*.

Isabella Mary Kelly was then returned to her prison cell.

The Smear

On Wednesday, February 29, Joseph Andrews was called before the Committee. After asking him to give his opinion of the genuineness of some signatures of Isabella Mary Kelly, the Committee questioned him about Charles Skerrett.

Andrews stated he knew Skerrett in 1853, when Skerrett occasionally passed through Mount George taking two or three horses for sale to Stroud or Maitland. He did not think Skerrett had bought Kelly's cattle for £800 because he did not believe Skerrett had that much money. Andrews thought William Turner was a foolish young man, and that his signature on the Receipt was genuine, but he did not believe Turner had witnessed Kelly sign the document.

Andrews reprised the evidence about the "Isabella Mary Kelly" signatures, which he had given at both trials. Then, for the first time, Andrews was questioned on his change of evidence from Skerrett's committal hearing to his trial.

> Chairman Arnold: "Do you remember saying on the occasion of Mr Skerrett's committal, 'I have looked at the paper now handed to me marked No. 4 and I believe that signature to be that of Isabella Mary Kelly'?"
>
> Mr Andrews: "Yes, I recollect that too. It resembles her signature and I could not point out the difference at the time. I had not then the opportunity of comparing the signature with any other, but I now see upon comparison that the 'y' and the 'r' in 'Mary' are far too carefully written for Miss Kelly's hasty signature."[19]

At the conclusion of each interview, the interviewee was entitled to read through the transcripts and add any revisionary notes, without changing the original transcript. When looking at the transcripts after the interview had finished, Joseph Andrews wrote:

> I should have stated to the Committee that John Lewis, a carpenter, and Joseph Giles, both still residing on the Manning, were working on the same farm with William Turner, when he absconded. Turner confessed all to them, that he signed the receipt for the £400 at Mount George, and with a great deal of trouble, Skerrett had taught him to sign his name.
>
> Turner admitted to them that he had perjured himself.

They then advised him in that case to off, and he went off accordingly.

On March 1, 1860, the Premier of New South Wales, William Forster, met with the Governor General and tendered the resignation of his ministry. Forster had been Premier for just over four months, but the demise of any administration meant that all Select Committees had to close down.[20]

William Arnold, as Chairman, decided to try and complete the work of the Committee in one day. On March 7, George Rowley was the first of seven witnesses to appear before the Committee. He had left the Manning River early in 1854 and had little first-hand evidence of Charles Skerrett or his affairs.

Rowley stated he had met Skerrett several times when Skerrett was passing through Bungay Bungay, taking horses to be sold. They were very fine horses, and prices were very high then.

> Chairman Arnold: "Can you give any idea of what was the value of these horses at that time?"
>
> Mr Rowley: "Horses at Melbourne at that time were very high."
>
> Chairman Arnold: "I am not speaking of Melbourne. You say he sold them at Stroud?"
>
> Mr Rowley: "Horses at that time were not of very great value here – I suppose £30 or £40 would have been thought a very high price, but they were worth a great deal more for the purpose he alleged. He said he was taking them to Melbourne."
>
> Chairman Arnold: "What do you think was the value of them at that time here?"
>
> Mr Rowley: "I did not get much for mine at that time; they were not of much value in that part of the country."
>
> Mr Wisdom: "What do you think they would have brought?"
>
> Mr Rowley: "From what I repeatedly heard, they would have brought a very high price in Melbourne."[21]

Skerrett had testified at Kelly's trial that he received the money to buy her cattle by selling his two brewery teams of horses in Melbourne, and insisting that prices for horses there were high at the time. Skerrett never suggested he took any horses from the Manning to Melbourne, but Rowley, as a spectator at

Kelly's trial,[22] may have gained that impression.

As a long-standing opponent of Isabella Mary Kelly, Rowley was very keen to support Skerrett. Rowley told the Committee about the Brislane/Connolly case in which he had stated in the witness box that he would not believe Kelly's oath. The Committee did not seem to approve of Rowley's action.

> Mr Parkes: "We want to know the actual facts on which you based the opinion?"
>
> Mr Rowley: "I cannot bring to my mind any particular occurrence. I recollect one occasion, for instance, a case that was brought before me and a brother magistrate against Miss Kelly. It was a case for wages brought by a servant who had been with her and who was then with Mr Andrews …
>
> I forget the defence but Miss Kelly pleaded poorly; she said she could not meet the wages due to her servants, cried, and pretended to be in great distress. I interceded for her with the person who brought the charge. Miss Kelly said she had some fat bullocks to sell in a short time, and when she had received the money for them, would be in a position to pay.
>
> The plaintiff withdrew the case, if I recollect right. However, it was arranged, and I said 'In what period will you pay this?'
>
> She said, 'In some three or four weeks', and the matter was left in my hand.
>
> I said I would send the constable at a certain time, mentioning the day, and he should receive the money and bring it to me.
>
> The matter was arranged, Miss Kelly declaring most solemnly that she would pay at the time appointed. In course of time, the constable proceeded to her residence, and she then repudiated everything, and said she did not intend to pay."[23]

> Chairman Arnold: "Do you know any instance in which Miss Kelly swore that to be true which you knew to be untrue?"
>
> Mr Rowley: "I do not know that I can tax my memory. A person may live in the neighbourhood with an individual and form a general knowledge of that individual, without being able to remember —"

Mr Hart: "Some people form strong prejudices?"
Mr Rowley: "People are apt to form prejudices. I aver that I made this statement deliberately. I was asked the question and could not have stated otherwise without falsehood."
Mr Parkes: "Did it occur to you, that you had an advantage over her from your position, she being a lone woman without friend, while you were holding Her Majesty's Commission as a magistrate?"
Mr Rowley: "I considered nothing of the sort. I was asked a plain, straight forward question by a learned barrister upon the floor of the Court and I answered it."
Mr Parkes: "Do you not think the circumstance of you being a magistrate, gave weight to your testimony?"
Mr Rowley: "No, it would not have done with me, had I been a juryman, and it certainly did not then, for the man was sent to Maitland gaol for twelve months."
Chairman Arnold: "The jury believed Miss Kelly's evidence?"
Mr Rowley: "I do not know what the jury believed. That was the result of their verdict."[24]

George Rowley stated that he had been subpoenaed to appear as a witness for Skerrett, in the Kelly trial, to testify on "Miss Kelly's character", but ignored the subpoena, despite attending part of the trial as a spectator. Ignoring a subpoena, particularly by a man who now practiced as a solicitor, was quite unethical.

The second witness of the day was Thomas Weedon, who stated he was a solicitor from Port Macquarie. He represented Charles Skerrett, when he had sued Major Innes over the lease of a vineyard. He thought Skerrett had a good chance of success in that case, but the matter lapsed after he was charged and convicted of cattle stealing.

The next witness, William Mullen, had represented Miss Kelly at Skerrett's committal hearing.

Mr Parkes: "When you say both characters were upon a par do you mean they were reputed for the same kind of qualities, the same kind of conduct or merely that they were both disliked?"
Mr Mullen: "I mean that Miss Kelly was not much liked for her eccentricity of character, she was a litigious woman."

The Smear

Mr Hart: "Disagreeable, litigious, unfeminine was she not?"
Mr Mullen: "Yes."
Mr Parkes: "Did you ever hear anything affecting her character morally?"
Mr Mullen: "No, never."
Mr Parkes: "As to dishonesty?"
Mr Mullen: "I have heard some stories about stray calves, or something of that sort, more than once."
…
Mr Hart: "Did you read the account of the trial?"
Mr Mullen: "I did not. It created a great sensation at the Manning River. It was just over as I passed through, and as far as sympathy went she had the whole of it."
Mr Parkes: "You say public opinion was in her favour there?"
Mr Mullen: "Strongly."
Mr Parkes: "Not withstanding she was a very disagreeable and quarrelsome woman?"
Mr Mullen: "Not withstanding all that."[25]

Appearing next was Mrs Jane Brandswait (nee Skerrett,) who stated: she and her sister, Margaret, signed the Bill of Sale. She had not been able to testify at her father's trial because Miss Kelly fired a pistol, which resulted in her receiving a broken leg. Miss Kelly did not attend to her after the accident. She did not see Miss Kelly fire the pistol, but it must have been Miss Kelly as no one else lived near them.

Mr Parkes: "Did you ever see Miss Kelly use firearms?"
Mrs. Brandswait: "Never."
Mr Hart: "Were there any stockmen about the place?"
Mrs. Brandswait: "No, there were no men on the place at the time."
Mr Parkes: "You say Miss Kelly did not attend upon you?"
Mrs. Brandswait: "She did not. She forced her way into the room and insisted that the leg was not broken, that it was just a false report. I was three days and my leg was not set."[26]

Henry Flett, the Member for Hastings was the fifth witness of the day. He told the highly improbable story that Miss Kelly had called at his Tarree property in 1854 seeking his advice.

The Trials of Isabella Mary Kelly

Chairman Arnold: "What do you know of the matter?"

Mr Flett: "I recollect about the time this alleged purchase took place, Miss Kelly called at my house one day and got Mrs. Flett to send to the field where I was engaged with some men. She said she wished particularly to see me. When I got up, she said she had become tired of living on the Manning and a gentleman was going to lease her stock but before doing so she asked to take my advice whether it would be safe.

I said, 'Who is the party?'

She refused to tell the name and said he was person of high character and a very honest man and she thought she could trust him. I said it would not be safe to lease the stock to him. She was to have leased the stock for five years – unless she could put confidence in him.

I said, 'If you cannot do so you had better sell the cattle to him and have done with it at once'.

She went away and some time after, I heard that Skerrett had purchased the whole of the stock. In fact it became the common talk of the Manning from the top to the bottom that she had sold the good will of Brimbin Estate, which she had lived on for the term of her lease."[27]

Flett stated that the common talk on the Manning River was the sale was a *bona fide* one. If Skerrett was selling her cattle she must have known it.

Mr Parkes: "You only infer from the notoriety of Skerrett's acting that Miss Kelly must have known it if everybody else knew?"

Mr Flett: "Yes."

Mr Parkes: "You have no facts to state of your own knowledge?"

Mr Flett: "No."

Mr Parkes: "Do you know of no case where Mr Skerrett sold cattle in her presence?"

Mr Flett: "No."

…

Mr Hart: "Do you know whether Skerrett acted as agent for her in the sale of cattle?"

Mr Flett: "No I never heard that. I rather think he has never done so. However he was the party alluded to when she spoke of leasing her cattle."

The Smear

Chairman Arnold: "Have you a very clear recollection of the circumstances of this time?"

Mr Flett: "Perfectly clear of what I have stated now."

Chairman Arnold: "I do not know whether you see the difference between her stating to persons who applied to her to purchase cattle that she had disposed of them to Skerrett, and her acquiescence in the sale of them by Skerrett, he receiving the money?"

Mr Flett: "No, as I understand she stated that she had sold all her cattle to Skerrett, and that led me to infer that she had acted upon my advice. He was the reputed owner of the cattle."

…

Chairman Arnold: "I suppose being her next neighbour you had a good opportunity of forming an opinion [of her character]?"

Mr Flett: "She never had a good character."

Mr Parkes: "Will you be kind enough to explain what you mean?"

Mr Flett: "I want to say that she was litigious, constantly bringing her servants before the Court. In fact I know that for years she never had a servant that she did not bring up on some charge or other."

Mr Parkes: "She was an eccentric person?"

Mr Flett: "More than eccentric, not very honest, for I have known her to bring many of her servants before the Court before their time had expired, as I would imagine to do them out of their wages."

Mr Parkes: "You imagine that towards the end of their engagements she trumped up charges with a view to evade the payment of their wages?"

Mr Flett: "Yes."

…

Mr Wisdom: "What reputation did Skerrett bear upon the Manning?"

Mr Flett: "I never heard anything against him farther than it was thought at the time to be merely an arrangement between himself and Miss Kelly. I was rather astonished to hear Mr Mullen's evidence, for Skerrett had not been on the Manning more than a few months, and could not have been very well known beyond being occasionally met when driving horses over.

Indeed he was not long living at Port Macquarie, and Mr Day

could not have known much of him, for he was Police Magistrate not more than twelve months during the time of Skerrett's residence, if I recollect rightly.
I never heard anything against Skerrett's character till I went to the Supreme Court [Kelly's trial]."[28]

As he continued his evidence, it was obvious Flett had either been listening to the evidence given by other witnesses to the Committee or reading the transcripts. Flett said he had heard Miss Kelly boast of her influence with Mr Plunkett many times — she was very intimate with Plunkett.

Andrews had declared Richards's lease of Kelly's paddock to be a forgery before even looked at it. He had read the lease, and it was definitely in Miss Kelly's writing.

There was a girl, a servant of Miss Kelly at Waterview, who went missing. He had refused to sit on the Bench because the girl might be found, but Joseph Andrews had insisted on the inquiry going ahead.

Mr Flett: "... I said, 'I decidedly refuse to sit [on the Bench]. I have come up to hear'.
'You do not believe then', said Mr Andrews, 'that she is murdered?'
I said, 'Decidedly not'.
'I firmly believe Miss Kelly has murdered her', said Mr Andrews.
'I am sorry to hear you say so', I replied, 'What makes you believe so, what could induce her to perform such an act?'
He said, 'You do not know Miss Kelly as well as I do, she would murder her for the £7 wages she owed her'.
After that Mr Andrews became her particular friend — I was her friend up to that time."
Mr Parkes: "What do you mean by her particular friend?"
Mr Flett: "He has been doing all in his power to assist Miss Kelly."[29]

Even at the lowest ebb of his relationship with Isabella Kelly would Joseph Andrews have ever suggested Kelly was guilty of murder, let alone for the sum of £7.

The interview ended with Flett declaring that Joseph Andrews had illegally committed a man for horse stealing, and the Attorney General had dismissed the case. Flett did not mention the man's name was Skerrett.

Like George Rowley, Henry Flett had no direct knowledge of the case – he had come simply to attack Kelly's character. And he had no qualms about lying under oath (but always in one-on-one situations).

Robert Blake deposed that Skerrett had returned from the goldfields with a lot of sovereigns – probably about £100 or £150.[30] The final witness, seventeen-year-old James Skerrett, deposed he had gone to the goldfields with his father. He had been present when his father sold the brewery horse teams for about £600 or £700.

The last sentence recorded by the Committee was: "Committee deliberated and adjourned."

Usually a Select Committee produced a report for Parliament, with the transcripts of the interviews presented to the House for members to read, eventually being printed in *Votes and Proceedings*, the record of the House of Assembly. But a report was never produced.

Consequently the transcripts of the proceedings did not reach the floor of the House, nor did the newspapers get wind of them (they have never been published to the present day).[31] It can only be assumed that the main reason for this non-reporting by the Committee was to conceal the smearing of John Plunkett's reputation by Charles Skerrett – his Great Conspiracy was untenable.

Skerrett's petition was never pursued under the new Robertson administration, nor does Skerrett seem to have made any attempts to revive his claims for compensation.

On March 6, 1860, three days after the fall of the Forster administration, and with the demise of the Select Committee, Acting Chief Justice John Dickinson wrote a report to the Governor concerning the case of Miss Isabella Mary Kelly.

After relating the legal history of the Kelly/Skerrett case, his main points were:[32]

- As the presiding judge at Kelly's trial, he had expected a different verdict – a 'not guilty' verdict. At the same time, after

reading the notes he took at the trial, he did not feel that he had reason to be dissatisfied with the verdict of jury, considering the evidence placed before them.
- Now that the Bill of Sale and Receipt documents had been found, he believed there was a reasonable doubt as to Miss Kelly's guilt. When he examined these documents in conjunction with reading the evidence given by Joseph Andrews at the trial, he found they strongly confirmed Andrews' evidence.
- If the jury had been able to examine these documents, they may have believed the evidence Andrews gave, deemed there was a reasonable doubt, and acquitted Miss Kelly. They might also, under the same circumstances, have concluded she was innocent.
- Miss Kelly should also be acquitted because the Chief Justice, Sir Alfred Stephen, when testifying as a witness, erroneously told the Court that the Receipt was "for £400, and also, I think, for the bill", when it was only for £400. [This was a technicality.]
- He believed Miss Kelly's trial had been prejudiced by the loss of the Bill of Sale and the Receipt documents. He recommended to His Excellency that Miss Kelly be immediately released from prison, and her fine of £100 remitted.
- He made these recommendations *ex abundanti cautela* (from an excess of caution to avoid misinterpretation). In so doing, he did not offer any opinion as to the actual guilt or innocence of either Charles Skerrett or Miss Kelly.

A week later, the Governor, Sir William Denison, ordered the immediate release from prison of Isabella Mary Kelly – she was *pardoned*.

Isabella Kelly had been imprisoned for five and half months.

The £100 fine had never been paid – it was not requested, nor had it been offered.

As prison officials went to discharge Isabella Kelly, they found her too ill to be moved, and it was not until the next day she finally left Darlinghurst Gaol. Describing her departure, Isabella Kelly said:[33]

After the first month [of imprisonment] I never had my

The Smear

health, and when I left I had to be carried out and lifted into the carriage that took me away. In fact, when my discharge came, I was too ill to leave, and it was not till the following day that I could be got into a fit state to be moved.

I then had to be carried out to the carriage, and one of the women went with me to assist me, for I was not able to sit upright by myself.

Isabella Kelly was taken to Mrs. Hoare's boarding house, where she would remain for months, very slowly recuperating, and unable to exert any real control over her affairs.

But she was free.

22. A Worried Man

Joseph Andrews was a worried man.

As the trial date drew closer, Joseph was becoming more concerned at the rising costs as he conferred with solicitors and organised his witnesses. At first Andrews felt that Richards would not be game to pursue the slander court action to a full conclusion, as he would have to produce the lease – he thought Richards was just trying to make him expend a lot of money consulting solicitors.

Reuben Richards was playing a dangerous game. He would have to produce the lease in Court and that could end with a charge with forgery if things did not go his way – the Court could impound the lease. Kelly could be a witness, but Richards did not think that as a convicted perjurer she would be permitted to give evidence, or if she did that a jury would believe a perjured woman. According to Philip Dew, Richards thought he could get as much as £500 in damages from Andrews.

What concerned Joseph Andrews was Miss Kelly's lack of action. On her release from gaol, he had expected Kelly to return to the Manning and evict Richards and charge him with forgery (as well as take action against Skerrett). But she had been out of gaol for a month now, and there was no sign of her in the Manning Valley.

Andrews was unaware of the seriousness of Isabella Kelly's illness, and that she was only recovering very slowly.

He reasoned that his current problems with Richards, and the money it was costing him, had all eventuated because he had stood up and defended Isabella Kelly and her property. In a letter to Isabella Kelly dated 14 April, 1860, Andrews wrote:[1]

> We hope you will not spare any one of the conspirators. Your friends expect this, and justice demands it. You say that you have heard that Richards has absconded – he has done

A Worried Man

nothing of the sort, but is far more impudent and daring, and has circulated all over the district that *you have bolted and that you cannot be found* in all Sydney.

It was thought by all here that as soon as you were liberated you would pounce at once on this villain, and thereby have saved me from all this expense and trouble. It is sickening to think how I have been treated in defending your property. Such scheming is disgusting. It will prevent anyone for the future in interfering on your behalf. You will have heard no doubt by this time that the case is set down for trial on the 14th May next.

I am glad to know that I will be able to justify my cause by one that Richards took into his confidence, even if you were dead, which event your enemies devoutly wish for. I think, somehow, that Richards will not appear; but evidently he is taking all the caution possible to put me to all the same expense as though he should appear – and at the last moment he will be off. The course he is pursuing convinces me of this. I fear therefore he will escape after all.

Why not take out a warrant for him at once, for perjury and forgery, and secure the villain, before he makes his escape. Richards knows well, for he told Dew that his lawyer told him, unless he could prove the lease genuine, he might not expect to go back to the Manning, and that he would not take the case unless he would refer him to some respectable person…

Andrews had been talking to Tim Leane, and Leane was prepared to be a witness for him. Leane could testify that Richards told him on October 10, that he did not have a lease of the Kelly's paddock, despite Richards claiming to have signed the lease on September 19.

Having failed with the petition to Parliament, Charles Skerrett changed tack. On March 26, he filed for insolvency. After filling in his insolvency schedule, the deficiency between his assets and liabilities was just £15 – surely one of the smallest deficiencies in the history of the Insolvency Court.[2]

But Skerrett had an ulterior motive.

In his schedule, Skerrett noted that, "The Insolvent has no stock in trade or furniture or money." Under "Personal

Property", Skerrett wrote:

500 head of Cattle	£300
20 head of Horses	£100
Total	£400

He added the note: "These cattle are not in the possession of the insolvent, but are running chiefly on the Manning Flats – Manning River." These, of course, were the stock bearing the MK brand of Miss Kelly – the cattle now owned by Alfred Begbie and the horses owned by Isabella Kelly.

Skerrett listed Samuel Wooller of George Street, Sydney, as owing him £23 for the sale of 19 head of cattle, but noted that Wooller may have a "layer claim" against him, meaning that (at the bottom line) Skerrett probably owed him money.

Skerrett listed £435 in debts to creditors including solicitor Greer for £100, solicitor Weedon of Port Macquarie for £73, and £200 owed to Miss Kelly. It is ironic that Skerrett's insolvency listed this promissory note of £200 to Miss Kelly as his major debt, when Kelly claimed it did not exist. The inclusion of this debt also lent credibility to her "sale" of the cattle to him. One suspects though, there were many more creditors Skerrett could have used.

On April 10, Robert Sempill was appointed the Official Assignee to handle the insolvency. Sempill was very experienced, and his first action, on the same day as he received his appointment, was to go to Court and obtain a warrant to take possession of the cattle and horses, listed as Skerrett's assets.

Skerrett now returned to the Manning River, and armed with a court order to sequester the cattle and horses, began posting notices around the district.

It was only six days since Joseph Andrews had last written to Isabella Kelly, but he penned another with a much more desperate tone:[3]

> Since I wrote you last I hear that Skerrett has posted up notices everywhere, cautioning everyone against interfering with his cattle, horses, &c. I have no doubt but that he will drive off what he can, when he finds that there is no one to protect your property.
>
> What do you mean to do?
> There is somebody at fault.
> I would say to you: Act on your own judgment – com-

mon sense is the best lawyer. If you wait until the lawyer thinks it time to act, you may find that the whole of your horses are gone; and what redress will you have for that loss?

A warrant should have been issued at once to take him [Skerrett] up for forgery and perjury.

If you think of coming up before Richards' case comes on, be quick; there are only two Magistrates now acting on river – Cross and myself. If Mr Cross refuses you a warrant, I will grant you one, and try the case myself; you have plenty of evidence in the first instance without me. This course, I think, is the only one that will effectually stop Skerrett from plundering you while the lawyers are looking on.

Skerrett I hear is determined to have a draft [take all] of your horses at all risks, and you know he has got plenty to assist him. He is making many believe that you can do nothing against him, and that the cattle are still his. At any rate, he will take what he can in the meantime, if not arrested at once.

Mr Girard has left the Manning about a week ago with your sheep, and Skerrett is aware of that. T[im] Leane must he in Sydney by the 14th May, on this case of Richards, and if Skerrett is not secured before that, there will be nobody to see to your property at all.

Decide therefore at once what you should do. I have given you all the information I can.

The suggestion of Andrews trying a case against Skerrett is an indication of the desperation Joseph Andrews was feeling, particularly as it would have been tainted by a conflict of interest.

Charles Skerrett approached Girard and showed him the court order. Girard simply ignored it, and continued to resist any attempt made by Skerrett to take possession of Kelly's horses. With his experience as a magistrate, Girard believed he could afford to disregard the court order on the basis that Skerrett had never at any stage had the horses in his possession – possession was everything.

As far as Girard was concerned, if Skerrett wanted the horses, he would have to go to the Supreme Court and take *civil proceedings* against his employer, William Lennon, and then Girard would then have no choice but to abide by the result of such a case.

There were two very good reasons Skerrett not to take this action. Firstly, apart from the doubt of winning such a case, the

Bill of Sale and Receipt would once more come under scrutiny – a scrutiny that could result in criminal proceedings against him. Secondly, by the Bill of Sale he was only entitled to twenty horses, but he wanted to take all four hundred.

One of the debts claimed against Skerrett in his insolvency received was £13 from Edward Cory, a solicitor engaged by Skerrett. Corey was another in the long list of solicitors to represent Charles Skerrett, most of whom (if not all) were not paid.

The first item on Corey's invoice to Skerrett, dated December 14, 1859, was, "attending you and your son, long conference as to your remedy against Girard and others for stealing your cattle."[4] There were also mentions of "attending you and Richards", indicating the depth to which Richards was involved with Skerrett. When the Attorney General refused to proceed to trial after Girard's committal, Solicitor Cory, at Skerrett's request, wrote a letter of complaint to the Attorney General, but received no reply.

The invoice stated that Skerrett asked Corey to write a letter to Dodds and Co of Maitland about Begbie and Cooper, presumably warning them not to sell any more cattle on Begbie's behalf.

—⁕—

Tim Leane went to the Bench to obtain an order for rations (flour, meat, sugar, tea) for the workers on Mount George. Miss Kelly had left the store locked, and Leane did not feel entitled to break open the lock. Joseph Andrews was on the Bench for his application, and granted an order to obtain the supplies.[5]

Tim Leane had completed his twelve-month contract on April 28, and seemed, initially, to be in two minds whether to continue as overseer. But on May 8, he wrote to Miss Kelly, tendering his resignation, and left Mount George. Girard had suggested Leane join the police force, and wrote him a reference for his application, which proved successful.

The Richards/Andrews court case had been postponed until May 30, but seemed certain to go ahead. At the beginning of May, Joseph Andrews went to Sydney to continue preparations for the trial. At the same time, his wife Ann was seven months pregnant with their fourteenth child.

A Worried Man

Tim Leane agreed to give evidence at the trial. Joseph Andrews regarded him as his best witness.

David Baxter had an extraordinary story to tell relating to the Richards/Andrews case. On September 23, 1859, two days after Isabella Kelly left her Gangat Station to stand her trial in Sydney, David Baxter visited Reuben Richards in connection with his mail. Baxter was a recent settler in the Manning Valley, having married a schoolteacher in the previous month.

He and Richards talked about the Kelly case.[6] In particular, Richards spoke about the letter from Richards, which Kelly had been so keen to use as evidence at her trial. Richards said Kelly would have a hard time proving that it was his handwriting, because he was always changing his handwriting.

Richards said he was very good at imitating other people's handwriting. He had only one problem – he was a poor speller. Richards said he could imitate anyone, and wrote "Isabella Mary Kelly" several times. Richards asked Baxter to write his signature, and then proceeded to copy it. It was very good. Baxter said he could not distinguish between his own signature and the copy.

When Ann Richards came into the room, she said to her husband, "You're a fool – you know nothing about him [Baxter] – you'll make yourself a second Skerrett."[7]

Reuben Richards told his wife to go and mind her own business.

Baxter said he and Richards were relative strangers, ands they had only ever spoken on two or three occasions.

Baxter was prepared to be a witness for Joseph Andrews

Perhaps in response to Joseph Andrews' last letter, Isabella Mary Kelly went to the Police Office in Sydney, and took out a warrant for the arrest of Charles Skerrett on a charge of forgery. The Magistrate decided to await the outcome of the Richards/Andrews civil case before holding a committal hearing.

Immediately before the trial, Andrews made the Emu Inn his headquarters. Witnesses, including David Baxter, William McLean, Tim Leane and Philip Dew, stayed there and discussed the case, with Andrews paying for the accommodation. Mr Girard went to the Inn and was involved in the discussions, but surprisingly did not appear as a witness at the trial.

Although still not fully recovered, Isabella Kelly visited the Emu Inn in anticipation of being a witness for Joseph Andrews.

23. Slander

On Wednesday, May 30, after a number of postponements, the civil action between Reuben Richards and Joseph Andrews commenced in the Banco Courtroom, of the Supreme Court, before the Acting Chief Justice, John Dickinson. Ironically, this was the same courtroom in which those other allegedly forged documents were found, and this was the same Judge who had sentenced Isabella Mary Kelly to gaol and later released her.

Sir William Manning, briefed by Mr Matthew Stephen, prosecuted the case against Andrews on behalf of Richards. Mr John Darvall, who defended Kelly at her trial, represented Joseph Andrews and was briefed by Mr Butler.

There were three actions against Joseph Andrews upon which Sir William Manning asked the jury of four to award damages to Reuben Richards:
- trespassing on Richards' paddock (called the Mount George paddock)
- slandering Richards' name in declaring the lease to be a forgery
- maliciously charging Richards with forgery.[1]

In Andrews' defence, Mr Darvall stated there was *no* trespass:
- Andrews acted with the consent of the paddock's owner, Miss Kelly
- the lease was a forgery
- Andrews took Richards to court for the public benefit.

As the plaintiff, Reuben Richards was the first witness called and spent the entire day and the next morning in the witness box.

Richards deposed he asked Andrews to remove his pigs from the Mount George paddock because he needed the grass for his mail horses. He threatened Andrews with legal action.

He told Andrews he had a lease of the paddock from Miss

John Plunkett

John Darvall

Sir William Manning

Arthur Holroyd

Sir Lytleton Bayley

John Hargrave

Kelly. Andrews said, "If you take proceedings, I'll say it's a forgery" before he even saw the lease. Andrews said he was sure Miss Kelly would swear it was a forgery also. When he charged Andrews an impounding fee of three pence per head of cattle, Andrews' son paid the fee, and he gave Andrews a receipt.

He charged Andrews with trespass and Andrews said the lease was a forgery while he was still getting it out of his bundle of papers. He gave the lease to the Magistrates. When they read it to the Court, Andrews said, "I still say it is a forgery."

At the hearing Mr Flett said, "Mr Andrews, I am astonished at your conduct, that you should swear the lease a forgery when you have not seen it." Mr Flett asked him if he had any objection to Andrews looking at the lease and he said he did not. Andrews read the lease and said, "I still pronounce it a forgery."

Andrews' men knocked down the fence around the Mount George paddock, and threatened to beat him up. Andrews laughed when they made the threats.

Under cross-examination by Mr Darvall, Richards deposed he knew Charles Skerrett, and he had heard Skerrett was mixed up with Miss Kelly. The Mount George paddock was not included in his original lease from Miss Kelly in May 1857, but she had given him a verbal lease of that paddock at the same time.

In September 1859, he wanted a written lease of the Mount George paddock because Miss Kelly threatened to have him off the whole farm. He had arranged with Miss Kelly to sign the lease on September 19. She agreed to have a witness there, and he would bring a witness with him.

On September 19 he went to Kelly's station and was there between noon and four o'clock. He brought Nicholas Binkin with him as his witness, but she did not have her witness there, and Binkin left.[2] Miss Kelly signed the lease but no one else was present when she did. He had not wanted Kelly to sign the lease without her witness present.

He brought a draft of the lease with him, and she copied it, but not exactly. She said she would write out the lease because everyone would know her writing.

Re-examined by Sir William Manning, Richards stated Kelly had quarrelled with him before May 1859 because he was too friendly with Andrews. She wanted him to prevent Andrews from

The Trials of Isabella Mary Kelly

putting his pigs in the paddock.

When Miss Kelly was charged with perjury, she wanted his wife Ann to testify at her trial. Miss Kelly said to him, "I am willing to give you a lease of the Mount George paddock, but I hope you will influence your wife to contradict her depositions in 1854, in Skerrett's case".[3] Kelly said his wife would be "exonerated from blame" for changing her testimony if Ann said she had been afraid of Skerrett. She then agreed to give him the lease.

(Richards had presented a complete rationale of events: although Kelly was arguing with Richards and may have appeared unlikely to give him a lease, she had offered the lease in exchange for his wife's testimony at her perjury trial. Kelly then wrote the lease. When his wife testified *against* Kelly, she repudiated the lease. It sounded very much like a Skerrett "spin".)

The next morning Richards was asked to go through quite a number of papers containing his own writing, Miss Kelly's writing, as well as others. When Darvall noted that his signature seemed to vary from paper to paper, Richards gave a reply heard in another courtroom, "I have different ways of signing my name … Miss Kelly told me to alter my style of writing as mine was so simple anyone could imitate it."

Henry Flett, M. L. A., supported Reuben Richards and confirmed the evidence given by him of the events at Andrews's committal hearing for trespass. Flett said he asked Richards to produce the lease. As Richards was getting the lease out, Andrews said, "If he has a lease, it is a forgery". He said to Andrews, "I am surprised you, a magistrate, should say so before you see the document".

Under cross-examination, Flett said he had no bad feelings towards Miss Kelly. Mr Darvall made the point to him that with Andrews as a probable candidate at the next elections, Flett would like to see Andrews lose this case. Flett replied that he had no political differences with Andrews.

Darvall called Philip Dew in support of Joseph Andrews.

Dew said he had gone to Richards' place on November 22, where they discussed the lease. Richards showed him the lease and said, "I got the lease the day Miss Kelly went down to Sydney for her trial." He said to Richards, "That was on 21st September".

Some people may think the lease a forgery, Richards had said to him, what did he think of it? He replied, "I think it looks

Slander

heavy for a lady's hand." Richards said Kelly would not be allowed to give evidence in Court under oath as she had been convicted of perjury. If she could not appear in Court, who would prove the lease was a forgery?

Richards came to his place on another day, Dew stated, and asked him, "What day was it I told you I got this lease?" He replied, "The morning Miss Kelly left the station for Sydney." Richards said, "That was a mistake, it was on the 19th I told you."

He told Richards that was not the day he had said. Richards replied, "It makes no difference as long as it was only to you I said it."

Cross-examined by Sir William Manning, Dew stated he warned Andrews because Richards said he would get £500 out of Andrews. He told Andrews it would ruin him.

(Philip Dew might have been a great friend of Charles Skerrett, but he was certainly no friend of Reuben Richards. Dew's evidence could well have been true, but he had given false evidence on more than one occasion in connection with Isabella Kelly.)

David Baxter deposed that he had called at Richards' place on September 23 to discuss his mail. In a conversation about Miss Kelly, Richards told him, "I can imitate any hand" and then wrote the name 'Isabella Mary Kelly'. Baxter said he wrote his own signature. Richards imitated it so well he could not tell the difference between the two signatures.

Sir William Manning suggested, in cross-examination, that as Baxter was a relative stranger to Richards, and Richards would be most unlikely to take Baxter into his confidence in this way.

Tim Leane deposed that on October 10, nearly a month after the date on the lease, Richards told him he did not get a lease of the paddock. Richards said he had offered Kelly rent of £10 p.a. but would give £15. Leane said the first he knew about a lease was in December at the Wingham Bench, when Richards charged Andrews with trespass.

Cross-examined by Sir William Manning, Leane stated that Mr Girard recently recommended him to be a policeman. Kelly wrote to tell him to give notice Richards of a charge of five shillings per week for each horse using the paddock. He did not write the notice until October 7 and then he put a false date of

August 27 on it. He did this because he did not want Richards to suffer because of his mistake and because he had a summons against Miss Kelly for breach of agreement. (Leane later admitted there was no summons.[4])

William McLean deposed he was present as a spectator at the Andrews trespass hearing. When Andrews demanded to see the lease, Richards refused but handed it to Mr Flett, who looked at the lease and said, "It's all right".

Flett then handed it back to Richards, saying, "It is his own – he can do with it what he likes". Mr Cross ordered the lease to be handed to Andrews, who compared it to some letters belonging to Miss Kelly. Andrews then said, "I believe it to be a forgery".

Flett had replied, "It is no forgery – I could swear to the document being a genuine one". Andrews demanded the lease be impounded, but Flett refused. Mr Cross ordered it be handed to the clerk for impounding.

Cross-examined by Sir William, McLean said Andrews did not declare the lease to be a forgery before looking at it. He believed Mr Flett had said to Richards, "I'll see that you get the lease back again".

Isabella Mary Kelly deposed she had been convicted of perjury for declaring documents to be forged. Several months ago, she was released and pardoned.

Richards came on September 19th in the company of another man, but remained mounted on his horse. She did not sign a lease. She had no conversation with Richards about a lease on September 19. She had no paper of the kind on which the lease was written.

Under cross-examination, Kelly was given a number of documents and letters in which she was asked to identify her writing and confirm their contents. One was a receipt written out to Richards with her signature on it, for the payment of two-year's rent on Richards' rented paddock. Kelly said, "I never gave that", indicating this receipt was a forgery.[5] A page of a letter written by Kelly to her overseer, Tim Leane, was read to the Court, in which she told Leane she was "desirous of keeping on good terms with Richards."[6] (This was in support of the argument that Kelly had given the lease to Richards in return for his wife's testimony.)

Kelly said she did not believe Andrews had said he would not believe her oath in the Connolly/Brislane case (in 1851). She never told Richards that his wife could say she was frightened of Skerrett. In September 1859 she arranged for a ten-stall stable to be erected in the Mount George paddock.

Joseph Andrews deposed, as he looked at the lease, he did not believe that it was Miss Kelly's writing. He knew Richards' writing, and believed the body of the lease was written by Richards. As he looked at the 1855 letter Richards had written to Kelly (incriminating Skerrett), Andrews said he believed it was in Richards' writing.

Andrews said he had not heard anything about a lease until a month after Miss Kelly's conviction. Leane told him he had been asked by Kelly to put up stabling in the paddock. Girard said there was no documentation about any lease. Dew warned him to be on his guard, saying he thought it was a plot hatched by both Skerrett and Richards.

Andrews said he did not think Miss Kelly had any paper like the paper the lease was written on. Richards had given him trespass notices on paper similar to the lease.

Sir William Manning's cross-examination of Andrews was devastating. Andrews was forced to admit that at Skerrett's committal hearing in 1854, he had said the signatures to Skerrett's documents were the *genuine* signatures of Miss Kelly. At Skerrett's trial and Kelly's trial he had sworn they were *not* her signatures. In between, Andrews said, he had more means of improving his acquaintance with her signature.

Sir William Manning recalled Henry Flett, who said he knew Miss Kelly's writing. As he looked at the lease, Flett said he had no doubt Miss Kelly wrote the whole lease.

He had known Miss Kelly for twenty years, Flett said, and he had many opportunities to judge of her character. He would not believe her under oath. He and Miss Kelly used to visit, but that was over fifteen years ago. He had not been at her house for five or six years.

When he gave evidence before the Select Committee of the Legislative Assembly, she made no charge against him or to him. The differences he had with Miss Kelly were caused by his dislike of her character. He had known Richards for two years, and had never heard anything bad about him.[7]

The Trials of Isabella Mary Kelly

Sir William called George Rowley, who deposed he had formerly been a Magistrate on the Manning River. He knew Miss Kelly's writing, Rowley said as he looked at the lease, and he had no hesitation in saying it was entirely in Miss Kelly's writing. The words 'Mount George' and many other words were unquestionably her writing. He was quite familiar with her writing peculiarities.[8]

Rowley said he had many opportunities to form a judgement of Miss Kelly's character, and he would not believe what she said under oath.

He could recall the trial in 1851 when Andrews gave evidence. Andrews was asked by Attorney Purefoy if he would believe Miss Kelly under oath, and Andrews said he would not believe her unless someone else confirmed what she said.

When Sir William put it to Joseph Andrews that he had indeed sworn this, Andrews weakly replied that he did not recollect doing so.

Sir William called Mr Goold, a seller of stationary. He deposed that the paper on which the lease was written, was a slightly different tint to the paper of the notice Richards had given Andrews. Cross-examined by Darvall, Goold admitted this slight difference could have been caused by one of the papers being left out in the sun.

On the morning of the fourth day, Mr Darvall summed up for the defence. The jury should decide that Richards had not made out a sufficient case. On the issue of slander, Andrews was justified in using the words at the time. On the malicious prosecution, Andrews had reasonable grounds. The circumstances of the signing of the lease were incredible, in that Richards said nothing about the lease until Miss Kelly was helpless in gaol.

Richards had tampered with evidence with Leane. If Miss Kelly was as clever as they said of her, then she gave away her property for nothing, as the first four years of the nine year lease were rent free, followed by £6 p.a. Richards said he prepared the draft of the lease without a book or any other help, yet it had all the marks of a legally composed document.

Mr Flett had been indecisive in determining Miss Kelly's writing from the letter he gave him. Flett's conduct at the Wingham Bench in giving up a document thought to be a forgery was quite improper, and this deprived Andrews of the chance to vindicate himself.

When Skerrett went to Parliament for compensation, it resulted in the release of Miss Kelly from gaol. Dew had confirmed that Richards fabricated the evidence. It was a conspiracy against Miss Kelly, and the last step in this conspiracy was to bring in witnesses, who said they would not believe her oath. Andrews had only been trying to prevent injustice.[9]

In the afternoon, Sir William Manning made his final address to the jury on behalf of the plaintiff. The case was more between Richards and Kelly than it was between Richards and Andrews, he said. There was not a word that could be said against the reputation of Mr Richards, but the same could not be said of Miss Kelly. Sir William then went through the complete history of the Skerrett/Kelly case.[10]

Andrews had no right to take Richards to Court for forgery, as the forgery was not against him. Andrews did it because he was in dispute with Richards. Andrews even pronounced the document a forgery before he saw it. The Magistrates had no right to impound the lease.

The reflections made on Mr Flett and Mr Rowley by the defence were unfounded, said Sir William. Mr Flett had confirmed that Miss Kelly always spelled Mr Richards' first name as "Ruben" instead of "Reuben". Mr Richards always spelled his name correctly, and, remarkably, in the Mount George lease it was spelled "Ruben".[11]

Miss Kelly was known for years as a litigious person whose neighbours did not regard her as a safe person to deal with. Miss Kelly, far from being the victim in this case, was the one who sought to victimise others.

Justice Dickinson instructed the jury to return a verdict on each of the charges, and if the verdict was guilty, to specify the amount of damages for each count.

The jury of four retired to consider their verdict at a quarter-past-five and deliberated for over five hours. They spent most of their time comparing the writing of the lease with the many papers and letters of Miss Kelly, entered as evidence, before eventually concluding that the lease was *genuine*. It then took little time then to assess the amounts of the damages.[12]

At half past ten, the jury returned to the Court, giving their verdict:
- Yes to trespass by Andrews – damages of £30
- Yes to slander by Andrews – damages of £50
- Yes to malicious prosecution by Andrews – damages of £20.

Reuben Richards would have been very happy with the verdict, but probably not so happy with the amount of damages – the total of £100 damages was certainly not the £500 Dew claimed Richards hoped to get.

There had been a doubt about the trial going ahead, at one stage, because Richards could not afford to pay all the advance legal fees. His solicitor, Robert Abbott, said he decided to proceed anyway because he thought there were good prospects of success.[13]

While Andrews believed Leane would be his best witness, Leane's admission he had falsified the date on Kelly's notice to Richards completely negated his credibility.

Once again Isabella Mary Kelly had been put on trial – albeit indirectly – and once again she had not been believed. Not quite three months out of prison, she was an easy mark for a barrister of the quality of Sir William Manning.

Henry Flett was the key figure in this trial.

He was behind the scenes pulling the strings. Robert Abbott (Richards' solicitor) said he had often been in contact with Flett concerning the trial as he briefed his barristers.[14]

Flett knew Joseph Andrews' had an Achilles heel – the Brislane/Connolly trial of 1851 where both Andrews and Rowley made declarations they would not believe Isabella Mary Kelly under oath. Richards would not have known about it. When this was combined with Andrews' change of testimony on the Kelly signatures in the Skerrett trial, it completely negated any claim Andrews made to be able to recognise her true signature.

And Andrews was only too aware he had been beaten by his own testimony.

The prestigious positions of Henry Flett (Member of Parliament) and George Rowley (a solicitor working in the office of the Chief Justice, the judge at the trial) only enhanced their

⋈ Slander ⋊

testimonies. Juror Mark Spence later confirmed this.[15]

It is unlikely Richards knew Rowley, but Flett was on very good terms with Rowley – Mrs. Flett was staying with the Rowley family before the trial.[16]

There was a remarkable similarity in the testimonies of Flett and Richards, which conflicted with the evidence given by McLean and Andrews. This suggests that once Flett told Abbott what evidence he would give at the trial, Richards fell into line with it.

Overall it was a very good result for Henry Flett. Once again he had thwarted Isabella Kelly, and her testimony was not believed. At the same time, Flett had disposed of his political rival: Joseph Andrews would not contest the next election.

There was one matter, which the Judge's notes did not make clear. In his summing up, Sir William Manning referred to a letter written by Kelly to Richards with a date of August 24, 1859 (just before Kelly's trial), which promised Richards a lease of land at cheap rent, and which Kelly acknowledged as being authentic.

There is no record of Kelly being examined any further on this letter. After the trial, Kelly claimed she had written this letter to Richards several years earlier, and it concerned the *first* paddock he rented from her – Richards had simply altered the year on the letter, and she did not notice the change at the trial.

The other document produced at the trial, which Kelly claimed to be forged, was a rent receipt for Richards' two-year lease of the first paddock.

After the trial, George Rowley, as Clerk to Chief Justice Dickinson, returned the disputed lease to Robert Abbott. From this point on, the lease was never out of Richards' control and never again tested before a Court.

Andrews made application for a new trial, but it was quickly dismissed.[17]

Joseph Andrews was a bitter man, firmly believing *he* was the victim in this case.

24. What is a Forgery?

Reuben Richards was a very clever forger. He had not simply forged the signature of Isabella Mary Kelly, but the complete document.

And while Richards made many denials of forging the lease in the courtroom, the evidence of his guilt is overwhelming.

David Baxter's evidence had not been accepted at the trial because it was painted as unbelievable that Richards would reveal these skills to a stranger. As defence barrister John Darvall tried to point out, this occurred *before* Kelly was convicted, and Richards' decision to forge the document came *after* her imprisonment.

There were a number of witnesses who could have given damning evidence at the Richards/Andrews trial, but for one reason or another did not attend the trial.

William Mullen was one such person.

Mullen had been Isabella Mary Kelly's attorney at Skerrett's committal hearing in 1854, and, at various times, had done a lot of legal work over many years on her behalf. Towards the end of October, Mullen was returning to Maitland after attending the District Court in Port Macquarie professionally. Passing through Mount George at about five o'clock in the afternoon, he decided to take overnight accommodation at the Richards' cottage.

During the evening, according to Mullen,[1] Reuben Richards asked him to look at a lease. The document concerned the leasing of a paddock at Mount George by Isabella Mary Kelly to Reuben Richards, with the signatures of both appearing on it.

When Mullen scanned through it, he noticed there was a phrase or sentence in the lease, which he thought was inappropriate. He pointed it out to Richards, who immediately went into another room and brought back a second document. This was ostensibly the same lease, but it contained the more appro-

What is a Forgery?

priate phrase Mullen had mentioned. Not only that, it contained the Kelly and Richards signatures and bore the *same date* as the first lease.

As they talked further on the matter, Richards brought out a *third copy* of the lease, which again slightly differed from the other two. This one also contained the Kelly and Richards signatures, but amazingly bore the *same date* as the other two leases, making it a third copy of the same lease. While two copies of the lease could be expected to be drawn up (one for each party), there could be no legitimate reason for the signatories to sign *three* copies of a lease – and further, for one party to have all three copies.

William Mullen said to Reuben Richards, "Is it not extraordinary that Miss Kelly would sign three leases on the same day for the same property?"[2]

Apparently unperturbed, Richards asked him which one he thought was the best.

Mullen replied, "I can offer no opinion about it."

When Richards asked him if he thought the signature on the lease was that of Miss Kelly, Mullen replied that he did *not* think it was her signature.

Mullen said he had seen Richards sign his own signature so many ways, that he would defy anyone to be able to identify it. That evening Richards confirmed Mullen's comment by saying, "It is an extraordinary thing – I have such trouble to get money for the mails from the Postmaster General. I send so many signatures to Major Christie, that he had to send them to a Magistrate before he could get the money to the vouchers."[3]

After Skerrett was gaoled in 1855, Richards had written a letter to Isabella Kelly condemning Skerrett for suborning witnesses. Later he regretted writing the letter, and adopted many different styles of writing so the letter could not be proved to his hand.

William Mullen only heard about Richards/Andrews trial just before its commencement. He wrote to Richards to advise him of the evidence he could give at the trial, and that he believed Richards had forged the lease. He then wrote a similar letter to Joseph Andrews, but the trial was over before his letter to Andrews could be acted upon.[4]

At the trial, Richards claimed he had written out a draft of the lease and Isabella Kelly had copied his draft. This appears to have been in anticipation of the possibility of Mullen appearing at the trial – he would claim he only showed Mullen drafts of the lease – but drafts would not have the signature of Isabella Mary Kelly on them.

Mullen's evidence was particularly damning, as he was a disinterested third party with a professional reputation to uphold.

Reuben Richards had stated during the trial that he had organised Nicholas Binkin to go to Kelly's property on September 19 specifically to witness the signing of the lease.

Binkin was unknown to Miss Kelly, and unknown to most people in the Valley. It was some years before he was located and able to give his evidence. Needless to say, it contradicted Richards' story.

On September 19, 1859, Binkin recalled, he happened to be riding along the road from Gloucester towards Mount George, when he met Reuben Richards on his mail run.[5] They decided to ride together and Binkin would take accommodation at Richards' place for the night. Several miles further along the road, Richards said to him, "I am going to call at Miss Kelly's station. I want to talk to her about something."[6]

When they arrived at Gangat, Binkin got off his horse and moved some distance away from Richards and Kelly, and had a smoke while he waited. Binkin stated that Richards never got off his horse while he talked to Kelly, and that "Miss Kelly seemed to be in a bad temper".[7] There was a high wind blowing so he could not hear what was being said.

As he waited, Binkin became impatient and called to Richards several times to leave, before moving down towards the creek. Richards joined him shortly after and they left. They were at Kelly's property about three-quarters of an hour (he was not sure) before they left.

Nicholas Binkin was certain that no lease was signed while he was there. If Richards and Kelly had wanted a lease signed, he could certainly have witnessed it, but he was never asked. As they rode away, Richards told him that he and Kelly had been discussing a lawsuit between Miss Kelly and Charles Skerrett.

Both Binkin and Richards then rode the five miles to

What is a Forgery?

Richards' Mount George cottage, where Binkin stayed the night.

During the evening, much to Binkin's admiration, Richards demonstrated his handwriting skills by showing "how he could imitate two or three different hands".[8] The next morning, Nicholas Binkin departed on the next step of his journey through the Valley.

About three months or so later, Binkin was again passing through Mount George and took accommodation at the Richards cottage for the night. According to Binkin the Richards family was in dire straits. Binkin said, "He said his family was in great distress, in fact the place was miserable; they had no rations, in fact I could hardly get enough for my supper and breakfast". (Here was an explanation of why Richards had not paid the rent to Kelly, yet did not want to leave Mount George.)

Of vital importance was the fact that Binkin had spent most of September 19th in the company of Richards. On their visit to Kelly at Gangat, Binkin did not see Richards sign a lease, *nor had a lease ever been mentioned.*

It is simply unbelievable that Kelly would give Richards a lease without it being witnessed by a third party – especially when Binkin was available as a witness.

The only other document she had not asked a third party to write, was the lease to Skerrett for the hut of the Chinese stockman. This she had come to deeply regret, as it was presented as obvious evidence that she did *not* always get a third party to write out the agreement.

Paddy Connolly stayed at the Emu Inn with the other witnesses for the pre-trial conference, but was not called upon to testify. This was probably because Paddy had been gaoled a second time since his imprisonment for assaulting Isabella Kelly in 1851.

In April 1857, Connolly had been convicted of cattle stealing after he was caught butchering a calf.[9] Although he received a four-year sentence, he gained his ticket-of-leave after two years. Despite his convictions, Connolly remained a perennially popular figure on the Manning.

Recalling the Mount George lease was dated September 19, Connolly made the following statutory declaration at Wingham

Courthouse:[10]

On Thursday, the 22nd day of September, I was assisting Mr, Frazer to remove his family from the district up to New England. Miss Kelly had left the Manning for her trial in Sydney, and I stopped at Reuben Richards' house, at Mount George, for the night.

Richards had not returned with the mail from Tinonee, and I asked Mrs Richards' permission to put our horses and bullocks in Miss Kelly's paddock. She said they had nothing to do with it.

In the morning I saw Reuben Richards, and he confirmed his wife's statement, and said I had as good a right as Mr Andrews or any other person to put my horses and bullocks in the paddock, and that he (Richards) had no claim to any place but the house, and the little piece of ground containing about one-and-a half acres, which he fenced round with saplings.

According to Paddy Connolly, three days after Isabella Kelly purportedly signed the lease, Richards and his wife were denying they had any claim to the Mount George paddock.

John Paton, a neighbour at Mount George of both Joseph Andrews and Reuben Richards, did not testify at the trial, but also made a statutory declaration at the Wingham Courthouse at a later date. He recalled how he visited Miss Kelly on Sunday, September 18, to find Miss Kelly very sick. On that day, Miss Kelly engaged him to put up stabling in the disputed paddock. Miss Kelly told him that when she returned from Sydney she would live in a tent on Richards' original paddock, until she ejected him from the cottage, because Richards had never paid her any rent since his arrival at Mount George.

Several days after Miss Kelly was convicted, Paton said, Reuben Richards called at his place and showed him a lease of Miss Kelly's paddock at Mount George. Richards asked him if it looked like Miss Kelly's handwriting, and Paton said he thought it did. Richards then asked him if he would swear in court that it was Miss Kelly's handwriting. He told Richards he would not.

When Paton saw the date of the lease, he told Richards he

What is a Forgery?

was very surprised, as the very day before the date on the lease, Miss Kelly swore she would never give him the lease.[11]

One of the jurors at the trial, Henry Selby, a George Street draper, described how the jury of four reached its verdict:[12]

> We compared every letter that was produced [by Kelly] with the writing of the lease, and not only that, but we compared every letter of the alphabet taken separately ...
>
> Where we could get words or parts of words with two or three consecutive letters the same in both, we examined them very closely, and found that the mode of joining letters was the same in both.

A magnifying glass had also been used to examine the writing.[13] Most of the five hours spent by the jury in deliberating their verdict was spent comparing the lease with genuine writing written by Miss Kelly. Once they had reached their final decision that the Kelly had written the lease, very little time was spent in awarding damages to Richards.

Another juror, John Smithers, a schoolteacher, said he had appeared in six trials of forgery as a judge of handwriting, and on five of those occasions he had "proved to be correct". He said he did not believe anyone could put a forgery over him, and further, no one could possibly forge his name without him recognising it as a forgery.[14]

Mark Spence, another of the four jurors also believed that no one would be able to forge his name.[15]

This was the general attitude of the time to forgery – careful examination by anyone would reveal any forgery. The juries were expected to listen to the evidence at the trial, examine the allegedly forged documents, and then make a decision.

The modern attitude is that *any* signature can be forged, if the forger is good enough. And only a trained expert can pick a good forgery, if then.

Isabella Kelly was constantly asked to identify her signature. Generally she identified her signature as genuine in the context of the document. If there was just her signature by itself, she would baulk at identifying it as hers.

In the witness box, both Flett and Rowley loudly proclaimed

their ability to recognise her writing, but in truth they did not have this ability. For their own spiteful reasons, they were out to injure Isabella Kelly as much as they could.

In cross-examination during the trial, Darvall handed Flett one of Kelly's letter, and asked him to say whether it was Miss Kelly's writing or not. Flett said, "Not her writing I think"; then "It may be"; followed by "the signature is hers"; and finally, "I now think the body is hers – not her usual writing."[16]

One can practically hear Flett comprehending the *context* of the letter as he gives his answers, and realising that the letter was written by Kelly, rather than actually recognising her writing.

William Arnold, as Chairman of the Select Committee enquiring into the petition of Charles Skerrett, carried out similar tests on the leading witnesses Flett, Rowley, Andrews, and Mullen. These were even more revealing.

Chairman Arnold handed an envelope with nothing but Isabella Kelly's genuine signature on it, and asked each man if it was Miss Kelly's signature. Flett said, "No, not hers." Andrews said, "Doubtful, does not appear to be hers." Mullen said, "Never seen the signature so heavy, loops indistinct."

Arnold also handed witnesses a false Kelly signature: Andrews said it was "very suspicious" and he had not seen her signature "exactly like that"; Rowley said, "That looks more like her signature"; Mullen said it looked more like her signature than others; Flett said it did not look like hers.[17]

There were other tests, and Joseph Andrews generally fared better than the others.

Arnold took two genuine Kelly signatures and gave them to Henry Flett. They were the two styles in which Kelly signed her name – one had loops on the 'y's and the other did not. Flett was asked to compare them.

Mr Wisdom: "Do you know Miss Kelly's handwriting?"
Mr Flett: "Yes."
...
Chairman Arnold: "Do you think that is hers (handing No. 2)?"
Mr Flett: "No that does not look like it."
Chairman Arnold: "Do you think that looks like hers (handing No. 1)?"

What is a Forgery?

Mr Flett: "They are pretty much like each other."
Chairman Arnold: "Compare them and I think you will see a striking difference in them?"
Mr Flett: "I cannot see much difference."
Chairman Arnold: "Do you not observe that some have no turns to the 'y's and some have loops?"
Mr Flett: "Yes."
Chairman Arnold: "Is that not a striking difference?"
Mr Flett: "It is a little difference. They are like hers and still are not like."
Chairman Arnold: "You could not form an opinion as to whether they are hers or not?"
Mr Flett: "No I have said they are like hers and yet are not."[18]

At the Andrews trespass hearing, Flett had instantly been able to identify the signature of Isabella Mary Kelly on the Mount George lease as genuine, and then asserted it to all so vehemently.

Joseph Andrews had summed it up most succinctly with: "What is a forgery but a good imitation?"[19]

Once one accepts that Reuben Richards forged the Mount George lease, the next step is not difficult: Reuben Richards forged the 'Isabella Mary Kelly' signatures on Skerrett's Bill of Sale and Receipt.

It could be the reason why Richards had refused to testify at Skerrett's trial: he did not want to appear connected to Skerrett in case he was accused of complicity in forging Skerrett's documents. It could also explain Richards boasting his penmanship to Baxter and Binkin: with Kelly charged with perjury, he considered himself home free.

But this accusation about Richards has never been made in any public arena.

Most people never connected Richards to these two documents in any way, as they did not realise Richards' move to Mount George in 1857 was his *second* arrival in the Manning Valley, not his first.

According to Ann Richards, she met her future husband Reuben while he was living at Brimbin with Skerrett in 1854. After their marriage at the Skerretts in early 1855 and after

The Trials of Isabella Mary Kelly

Skerrett's imprisonment, they moved back to Nelsons Plains where their first child was born. They stayed there two years before moving to Mount George.

John Ryan Brenan, who represented both Charles Skerrett and Isabella Kelly at various times, said there were two ways the forgery of a signature was usually done: tracing it with paper superimposed over an original on, say, a window; or making a freehand copy from the original.

Brenan said he thought Skerrett traced the 'Isabella Mary Kelly' signatures on the Bill of Sale and Receipt, as he did not believe Skerrett possessed the writing skills to forge it freehand.[20]

But Reuben Richards had the skills.

And Richards was a friend of Skerrett at the time the forgeries surfaced.

26. Back in the Valley

While the Richards/Andrews trial was still in progress, Ann Andrews wrote a letter to Miss Kelly, dated June 2, 1860, saying how pleased she was Miss Kelly had charged Skerrett with forgery.[1]

Although Kelly had taken out the warrant against Skerrett for forgery, she did not follow through with Skerrett's committal after the trial, and let the warrant lapse. She had consulted with John Ryan Brenan, the solicitor who had represented her at the Skerrett trial in 1855. Brenan told Kelly that he believed there was little chance of a successful prosecution of forgery against Skerrett without a recanting of the evidence given by William Turner, the witness to the Receipt. Turner had now been missing for nearly six years.

If the jury in the civil case did not believe Kelly when she declared Richards' lease to be a forgery, what were her chances of convicting Skerrett of forgery?

Ann wrote that Skerrett had gone to Sydney with a man named Denny, and they had taken eight or ten horses off Dingo Creek. But as no one in the district would let them put the horses in one of their yards, they took them to Robert Searle's place. She heard that Searle's son, Thomas, was driving the horses.

There had also been a number of raids on Begbie's cattle. On one occasion when Skerrett had gone to Sydney, perhaps causing Alfred Begbie to lower his guard, James Skerrett and some men were able to capture twenty head of cattle belonging to Begbie without any resistance.[2]

On another occasion, Girard and Leane caught Francis Denny and William Ladd with about thirty or forty head of cattle bearing the MK brand and belonging to Begbie. Girard summons both at the Wingham Bench for trespass, but the Magistrates dismissed the case.[3]

The Trials of Isabella Mary Kelly

Skerrett and Denny took one lot of Begbie's cattle to Tinonee and sold them through an auctioneer. Ann Andrews wrote that Mr Begbie had taken out a summons on the people who bought the cattle at the auction.

The *Maitland Mercury* printed an anonymous letter to the editor concerning the hardship of Alfred Begbie.[4] The letter reflected the general indignation held in the Valley against Charles Skerrett and his assistants, Richards and Searle. Alfred Begbie was regarded as nothing less than an honest settler caught up in these circumstances through no fault of his own.

With the buyers before the Wingham Bench on June 6, the Magistrates decided to write to the Attorney General and reserve their decision until they received a reply. The Attorney General was unlikely to have sent the Bench any advice (in another case after this, he wrote to a Bench to say he refused to give any advice to Magistrates).[5]

The Wingham Bench eventually dismissed the case brought by Begbie.

The letter went on to say that the auctioneer at Tinonee had claimed to have received an authority from Denny that Skerrett had a legal right to sell the cattle. While the auctioneer stated he had displayed this authority at the commencement of the sale, the letter-writer complained that the auctioneer had been unable to produce it at the Wingham Bench.

The letter continued:

> In this district, the cattle are looked upon as the bona fide property of Mr Begbie.
>
> It is surely time that the matter should be brought to an issue, and the ownership finally settled, as Mr Begbie has already been subjected to considerable loss in a pecuniary sense – not to speak of the vexation and annoyance consequent on proceedings of this sort. ...
>
> In conclusion, Skerrett, accompanied by numbers sufficient to intimidate, has repeatedly appeared on Mr Begbie's run, and forcibly driven off mobs of Mr Begbie's cattle.
>
> If the law now declines to interfere, and by so doing, tolerates those *cattle raids*, Mr Begbie will be necessitated, in defence of his property, to adopt that course pursued by our ancestors – when such things were common – and *repel by force* – a mode of procedure in a British colony, in the year 1860, rather unusu-

Back in the Valley

al, and not particularly well calculated to increase the confidence of the people in the all-protecting power of the law.

Begbie was now in an invidious position: the local Bench and the Attorney General had both abdicated any responsibility in determining *who* owned the cattle.

The once very friendly relationship between the Coopers and Begbie on one side and Isabella Kelly on the other had now turned very sour.

Before Kelly went to prison, Alfred Begbie and Maria Cooper would supply rations to Kelly's stockman if they ran short while she was out of the district, and she would repay them on her return.

After Kelly had refused to buy back the cattle from Begbie, they declined to supply any rations while she was in prison.[6]

The relationship was about to sour even further. Alfred Begbie was now receiving more threatening letters from Lennon & Cape demanding payment of the £1000 owed to Miss Kelly. If he were given time, Begbie thought he would be able to pay the debt. At the time of the sale, Isabella Kelly had said she would give him that time, but now she appeared to be breaking her promise.

Begbie did not understand that he was now dealing with Lennon & Cape, not Isabella Kelly – he believed it was Kelly demanding the money. And Lennon & Cape were not prepared to give Begbie any latitude.

During June 1860, there was a legal seizure of some forty horses belonging to Miss Kelly. When a settler or company was owed a sum of money, they could go to the local Bench and apply for the money, usually offering some kind of proof of the debt. If approved by the Bench, a bailiff could then go to the debtor's property and sell items belonging to the debtor, in order to raise the amount of the debt.

Usually the settler was present and could at least direct what was to be sold. With Kelly absent, the bailiff sold whatever he liked. In a remote area like Mount George, there were not too many buyers, and the bailiff did not really care how much the items sold for, as long as the amount of the debt was raised.

The Trials of Isabella Mary Kelly

The A. A. Company went to the Bench for the rent Kelly owed on her Gangat run. The sale of the thirty-eight horses raised £46. According to Kelly, some of the horses were "of very superior value."[7] The sales should have been notified to the owner (the debtor), as well as being widely advertised, neither of which occurred.

One particular foal, which Kelly believed she could have sold for £20, was sold for less than £1. The gentleman who bought it gave it back to Kelly, along with another horse he bought, after she finally returned to Mount George.[8] The rest of the horses were bought by neighbours, including Joseph Andrews and one of his workers – though Joseph did not feel obligated to return any of his purchases.

Kelly said there had been a number of these sales. A man named Mangan, who she owed for mustering, went to the sheriff to seize her property for his claim of £50. She also complained about one of her shepherds, who said Kelly owed him £4 for wages, but she claimed she owed him nothing. He went to the sheriff and her furniture was sold to raise the money. Kelly said, "I was not there, and it only realised £13 – all my beautiful furniture that had cost me so much. There was no one there to buy it."[9]

Not only was Kelly paying out large amounts of money for her legal expenses, but the assets of the once very wealthy Isabella Mary Kelly were now being slowly whittled way.

Isabella Kelly had been released from prison in March, much to the mystification of Manning Valley residents. Sir John Dickinson's report to the Governor was never published, and there was no mention of her release in the newspapers.

In fact her release had been prompted more by the justice considerations of a fair trial rather than by a determination of innocence. Isabella Kelly was not released as a ticket-of-leave convict, but given a pardon. Yet the Acting Chief Justice had declined to give an opinion on whether Kelly was guilty or innocent.

Consequently there had been no proclamation of Isabella Kelly's innocence on her release. For many her release after only five and half months had been extremely perplexing considering the outcry that her sentence had been too light.

Back in the Valley

It was enough to start rumours of "friends in high places" helping to get her released, rather than the truth: Isabella Kelly was always a woman alone.

Adding to the mystery was Kelly's non-appearance in the valley. Kelly said her illness had made it difficult to get through the Andrews trial as a witness. As most in the Valley were ignorant of her illness, it seemed very strange to them that by July, four months after her release, Isabella Kelly had still not returned to the Valley.

With Skerrett raiding the cattle of an innocent Alfred Begbie, and Kelly having sold the cattle to Begbie, Isabella Kelly was very much the villain of the piece.

In July 1860, Robert Andrews and his family moved to the Manning Valley, buying a property adjacent to Woodside, but downstream, which he named Maryville. Robert came with his wife Mary, and nine of their ten children, the eldest remaining in Sydney. Because of Mary's ill health, a doctor had advised a move to the country. After eighteen years in George Street, Sydney, as a saddler and landlord, Robert was a wealthy man.[10]

Aged forty-four, Robert was two years younger than his brother Joseph. When George Rowley left the district in 1854, Robert bought or leased a property from him called "No. 1 Station." This run, further up the Valley, was over thirty kilometres miles from Woodside in a much more mountainous and remote region, towards the rugged New England ranges.

Robert brought in his younger brother William to manage this station. For six years William had been the overseer of the cattle and horses bearing the AD brand, which, although originally Joseph's brand, now appeared on the stock belonging to all three brothers.

William Andrews' wife had died on the voyage out to the colony, with no children from the marriage. Aged forty and physically fit, William always took a robust, bull-at-the-gate approach to solving problems, whereas Joseph and Robert adopted a more intellectual approach.

Robert and William were about to aid their brother Joseph through the most difficult period of his life.

26. The Rich Insolvent

After the Richards/Andrews trial, Robert Abbott went to the Supreme Court to recover the costs of the court action for his client, Reuben Richards. On July 13, the Court handed down its Judgement: Reuben Richards was awarded £220 in legal costs, which, added to the £100 won in the court case, meant that Joseph Andrews needed to pay Reuben Richards a total of £320.

A week later, on July 20, 1860, Joseph Andrews took the very drastic step of filing for insolvency. Although Andrews no longer operated as a publican, he was generally regarded as a wealthy man, having contested the elections against Flett just twelve months previously.

In his schedule Andrews recorded his assets to be £1005 and his liabilities to be £1914, making a deficiency of £909.[1]

Under 'Landed Property' Joseph Andrews wrote:

Allotment of land at Tinonee	£10
Allotment of land at Mount George	£20

To anyone who knew Joseph Andrews, there was one major item missing – there was no reference to Woodside with an estimated worth well over £1000. (Five years later Woodside was mortgaged for £1000.[2])

On the same day Joseph Andrews filed his schedule, Robert Sempill was appointed the Official Assignee. As Sempill was also the Official Assignee for the Charles Skerrett insolvency, he would have known something of Joseph Andrews already.

Immediately on hearing of his appointment, Sempill left his office in Wynyard Square, and went several blocks to see George Rowley in Justice Dickinson's Offices, as he was aware Rowley had lived in the Manning Valley for many years.[3]

Rowley was able to give Semphill much background information about Andrews, including the No. 1 Station, and Joseph

The Rich Insolvent

Andrews' ownership of Woodside. Rowley told Sempill "it was a farm of seven hundred and twelve acres, where the Insolvent lived and was very valuable having a good house and improvements and much of the land cleared and cultivated."[4]

According to Sempill, he had only been back at his office half an hour when Joseph Andrews arrived to consult him about his insolvency. Sempill asked Andrews if the £120 listed in his assets as 'cash' was in the bank. Andrews replied that it was not, as he had not kept a banking account for four or five years.

When Sempill asked for the cash, Joseph Andrews said he had sold a small farm to his brother Robert two years before, and this was the balance, which had not been paid to Robert. Sempill asked, "Is the farm called 'Woodside'?"

Andrews said, "Yes."[5]

Having just spoken with Rowley, Sempill was now quite suspicious that Joseph Andrews was playing a completely false game in his insolvency. When Sempill went to the Lands Commission office, he could not find any document conveying land title of the Woodside property from Joseph Andrews to Robert Andrews.

Sempill visited the Union Bank and enquired whether they had a customer named Joseph Andrews. The Bank replied that Joseph Andrews held no current account with them as he had closed his account just three days before, when he withdrew £27. Further, he had withdrawn fifty pounds four days before that, and three months ago he had drawn out £336.

It did not take much to demolish Joseph Andrews' claim he had not maintained a banking account for the last four years. While the £336 was a justifiable withdrawal in that it was probably used for his legal costs in the trial, the £77 withdrawal within the last week from a bank account absolutely confirmed Andrews' dishonest intentions.

Joseph Andrews returned to Sempill's office the following day. He told Sempill a man named Richards had falsely taken out civil proceedings against him had forced him into insolvency. He had lost the case, and was now forced into this situation.

Andrews asked Sempill to give him *time* to arrange his affairs with his other creditors. If Sempill would not start selling his stock or possessions, he would be able to put a financial package together, which most of the creditors would find acceptable.

Semphill said he would.

Andrews left the office fully convinced Sempill had agreed to his request.[6]

Joseph Andrews had a plan.

Sixty percent of the money stated as owed to the creditors in Andrews' schedule came from his relations and Alfred Begbie, all of whom were highly sympathetic to him – brother-in-law George McPherson, £232; Robert Andrews, £400; William Andrews, £120; Alfred Begbie, £390. Many of the minor creditors were also sympathetic with Joseph Andrews, and could be expected to accept any proposal Joseph put forward. When the majority of the creditors accepted the financial package, Joseph would borrow the money, and pay everyone.

But there was a *hidden agenda* to the plan. The major creditors would out-vote Richards and accept a package very favourable to Joseph. Joseph's rich brother Robert would ostensively lend him the money to pay the creditors, and hence the insolvency could be resolved without the necessity to sell any of Joseph's assets. Any money owing to creditors, other than Richards, could be paid in full at a later date.

The net result meant Joseph Andrews would pay Reuben Richards *a small percentage* of the £320 he owed him.

But Sempill had lulled Joseph Andrews into a false sense of security.

After Joseph Andrews left Sempill's office on Saturday, July 21, Robert Sempill, as the Official Assignee of the Andrews Estate, immediately went to the Insolvency Court and obtained a warrant appointing Arthur Kingsmill as Special Messenger of this Insolvent Estate. The warrant empowered the Special Messenger to enter the Insolvent's property, and seize any stock or possessions he wished, selling them to raise funds to be distributed to the creditors.

The Official Assignee was on a commission for the amount of money raised from the sale of the Insolvent's assets, usually 5%. Because the Official Assignee deducted all his expenses before allocating any funds to the creditors, many creditors were beginning to question this process, in which the main beneficiary of

The Rich Insolvent

any insolvency was often the Official Assignee. Further, the Official Assignee was the sole arbiter of what constituted an expense — he had no need to justify his expenses.

As a very experienced Official Assignee, Robert Sempill knew it was important to act with speed, before the Insolvent had a chance to hide his assets. He immediately wrote to Arthur Kingsmill in Newcastle, attaching the warrant and the list of property, which Andrews had stated he possessed. Sempill wrote: [7]

> Mr Andrews has given me this information but I am informed otherwise that he has much more property and that if you apply to Mr Richards of Mount George to assist in the collection of stock, he will be able to give most efficient aid and information.
>
> Please act without loss of a day if you can go — and report progress to me and take care that your letters are posted by safe hands. I think perhaps you could hire a horse in Newcastle.
>
> Please be very cautious in your communications with other parties or an endeavour will, I fear, be made to keep property out of sight. Mr Andrews has two brothers there. He sold his farm of 705 acres and other lands to his brother Robert (he says) some time ago — but I find there is no conveyance or written agreement.
>
> The cattle are in the charge of his brother at a station. The cattle as collected must be herded — and so carefully as not to lose their condition. Make careful enquiry about the number of pigs — and about cows (milkers) horses and any other property — and report progress as you can. If you write me that you can go, I will send a letter for you in a day or two to the Post Office at Manning River [Tinonee].

Sempill wrote this letter as an "official letter", keeping in mind that if he later charged Joseph Andrews with fraudulent insolvency (and already he must have considered this to be a distinct possibility), any correspondence between himself and his Special Messenger could be produced in Court as supporting evidence. Hence, for example, the sentence "The cattle must be herded — and so carefully as not to lose their condition." was included for the benefit of a possible future Court action.

Appended to the front of this letter was a cover note, which warned Kingsmill that the Andrews brothers were very smart people. Sempill asked Kingsmill to go and see Reuben Richards and get any information and help he could from him. It was a very smart move on Sempill's part to use Reuben Richards, who, apart from living adjacent to Joseph Andrews, could be relied upon (in his own interest) to ferret out all Andrews' assets.

On the following Monday, Sempill met with another of his insolvents, Charles Skerrett. Knowing that Skerrett was an enemy of Andrews, Sempill decided to use Skerrett's knowledge of the Manning Valley as well as Reuben Richards. He sent Skerrett to Arthur Kingsmill with the following "official letter" of introduction, dated July 23rd, in which he made no mention of Skerrett's past connections with Andrews, and portrayed Skerrett as a businessman rather than an insolvent:[8]

> Mr Skerrett – the bearer of this – is, he informs me, about to go up on business to the Manning River – and being very intimately acquainted with that district, may be able to be of assistance in giving you information of value in the business on which you are presently engaged for me.
>
> He says he will be glad if he can be of service to you in any way in that business, and I shall be glad if you will avail yourself of his experience of the country in the collection of stock, etc.
>
> He says he can inform you of those who know the runs well and who have horses and men at your service, if you require them, and who – from a very intimate acquaintance with the property of the neighbourhood – can give you most valuable information.

Until he reached Raymond Terrace on the following Thursday, Joseph Andrews seemed in no rush to return home to the Manning River. There he learnt that Arthur Kingsmill had been appointed Special Messenger in his insolvent estate and, together with Charles Skerrett, had already left Raymond Terrace on his way to the Manning River to seize his assets.

Andrews suddenly realised how seriously he had underestimated Robert Sempill. He left Raymond Terrace at a gallop, and reached Woodside the next day, just two hours before Kingsmill arrived.

Kingsmill entered Woodside alone. He asked Ann Andrews if she would go through the house, and take an inventory of the

The Rich Insolvent

furniture and any other assets. At the same time Kingsmill noted the quality of the furnishings, and immediately began to form the opinion that Joseph Andrews was a man of considerable wealth.

In another official letter to Sempill, Arthur Kingsmill wrote "every item was given to me with the greatest reluctance by Andrews."[9] Kingsmill finished the letter with his judgement of Joseph Andrews: "If I were not to be on good terms with him, I think we would stand but a poor chance of getting the cattle in."

Reuben Richards, on his rented Mount George property less than a kilometre from Woodside, informed Kingsmill that Andrews had driven sixteen bullocks across the Manning River in the two hours between his arrival home and Kingsmill's appearance at Woodside.

Richards also gave him a list of assets owned by Joseph Andrews: Two farms at Tinonee; 1 kiln of bricks; Woodside Estate and residence; three farms adjoining Woodside on which there were 3 kilns of bricks; cedar, milkers and cattle at No. 2 Station further up the valley; a farm and horses at the Washpool (on the Manning River); an allotment of land at Harrington; eight working bullocks; a dray; farming implements, etc.[10]

Kingsmill notified Andrews of his intention to go to No. 1 Station, and collect the cattle there. Skerrett warned Kingsmill the terrain at No. 1 Station was quite mountainous, and the current wet weather looked like making the task of getting the cattle from No. 1 even more difficult.

On the following Monday, Arthur Kingsmill left for No. 1 Station, taking with him one of Joseph's sons, Waldy Cooper, who had recently been acting as Joseph's overseer, and three hired stockmen.

When the hired stockmen realised that Kingsmill intended taking Charles Skerrett with them to No. 1 Station, they refused point blank to go. Not only was Skerrett notorious on the Manning for his treatment of Alfred Begbie, but Begbie was married to Waldy's sister. After Kingsmill re-directed Skerrett to go to Reuben Richards and assist him instead, the stockmen resumed their duties.[11]

Kingsmill wrote to Sempill telling him he believed Andrews was "a regular shuffler". Andrews should be made to pay twenty shillings in the pound (meaning he could afford to pay every debt to the full amount). Further, Andrews had so many assets he could afford to pay *one hundred* shillings in the pound. Once he removed the cattle were from No. 1 Station, Kingsmill threatened he would attach all the items Andrews had *not* put in his insolvency schedule, and charge him with all the concomitant expenses.

Joseph and Robert Andrews travelled to Sydney to repeat their objections to Robert Sempill personally, but all to no avail. In a letter to Kingsmill, Sempill wrote:[12]

> I received your letter last night. Mr Andrews and his brother came to me yesterday and said it would cost all the cattle were worth, to get them in. They shall be got if it costs three times that. He will see that Insolvent business will be done well in his estate.
>
> If he does not change his intentions towards his creditors, he will find it a hard matter. I have been kept all day at Darlinghurst Criminal Court till now, nearly post hour, prosecuting a man for fraudulent insolvency …
>
> Please use every energy in collection of the property and tomorrow I will send you directions officially and you will get my letter by mail that leaves Sydney on Thursday under cover to Mr Richards.
>
> Andrews has no notion of releasing his estate. Believe him not and do not let him assuage you by his statements. Move everything, except household furniture, to Mr Richards or some safe place, and all stock, horses, cows, bullocks, etc., away from Andrews' residence.

This letter signalled the determination of Sempill, not only to seize Joseph Andrews' assets, which now appeared to be very large, but to punish him for his transgressions by making it a very costly exercise – keeping in mind that all costs of the insolvency were charged to the *Insolvent's* Estate, not to the Official Assignee.

While Arthur Kingsmill was absent at No. 1 Station, Reuben Richards reported to Robert Sempill that large quantities of cedar were being removed from Woodside and taken next door to Robert Andrews' property.

Sempill immediately went to the Insolvency Court and obtained a warrant appointing Reuben Richards as a Special Messenger, able to collect the assets of Joseph Andrews.[13] With

The Rich Insolvent

Richards a major creditor of Andrews, one would have to regard this as rather unethical although quite legal.

On August 13th, armed with the warrant, Richards went to Woodside and conducted his own inventory. Among the page after page of items listed by Richards on that day were: twenty thousand feet of sawn timber (cedar), twenty four thousand shingles, 24 boxes of bees, about 200 pigs both tame and wild, 1300 head of cattle at No. 2 Station, all horses branded AD, etc. Richards also included "1 gold watch & chain lately owned by the Insolvent and not to be found now."[14]

It must have been most galling for Joseph Andrews watching Richards as he went from room to room, leaving no article unrecorded. In the first room, the library, Richards recorded, "1 table, 1 chest, 8 packets [of] washing powder, 1 cloth basket, 1 tea tray, 240 books & music books, 1 bookcase, 1 hat case, 2 chairs, 1 map of Mount George."[15]

And so it continued for another nine rooms.

Charles Skerrett also made a few visits to Woodside, as an assistant to Special Messenger Reuben Richards. If Joseph Andrews had any doubts about the wisdom of going into insolvency, they must have begun to surface by now.

Arthur Kingsmill spent five weeks collecting the cattle and removing them to Maitland. As Joseph had told him, the wet weather and terrain made it extremely difficult, particularly as the cattle were widely scattered. Costs kept increasing.[16]

William Andrews made it very clear he resented Kingsmill's presence at No. 1 Station. On one particular day William Andrews challenged Kingsmill that two of *his* cattle had been collected. Kingsmill refused to release them. William told him he "would rush the mob",[17] and scatter them in all directions. Kingsmill gave him the two cattle. Despite this, Kingsmill collected about 250 head of cattle.

The cattle belonging to the three Andrews brothers *all* bore the AD brand, which had originally been exclusive to Joseph's stock. Since the beginning of the year, Joseph asserted, his cattle had the AD brand and a circle on the ribs, while William's had the AD brand and a 5 on the ribs, while Robert's only had the

AD brand. This, of course, made it impossible to know how many cattle Joseph really owned.

On the way to Maitland, Kingsmill wrote to Sempill reporting that Alfred Begbie had informed him of a meeting held on the Manning by most of the creditors, which had decided to accept a settlement of Joseph Andrews' insolvency. Kingsmill told Begbie that such a meeting *without* the Official Assignee was illegal, and therefore of no consequence.[18]

When the stock reached Maitland in the first week of September, they sold for £526. Arthur Kingsmill resigned as Special Messenger, leaving Reuben Richards as the sole Special Messenger to attach the Insolvent's Estate.

Ironically, as Richards and Skerrett were working for Robert Sempill, who passed all his costs onto the Insolvent's Estate, Joseph Andrews was now indirectly paying Richards and Skerrett to attach his own assets.

On October 19, William Andrews appeared before Police Magistrate Edward Denny Day and Community Magistrate Dodds, in Maitland, charged with forcibly rescuing two horses from the possession of Reuben Richards, who had attached them for the Insolvent Estate of Joseph Andrews.

Reuben Richards had attached the two horses but allowed them to stay on the Woodside property. Later on, William Andrews took the two horses claiming they were *his* horses, not Joseph's.

Robert Sempill instigated the prosecution, probably in retaliation for the harassment Richards was receiving.[19] John McGarrigle, an employee of Joseph Andrews, charged Richards with perjury at the Wingham Bench on September 5, but the case was dismissed.[20] Joseph Andrews said that this perjury charge by McGarrigle had nothing to do with insolvency, indicating that it probably concerned evidence given by Richards in the Richards/Andrews trial.[21]

On another occasion, Richards was charged with the theft of a pair of saddlebags, which he had attached from Woodside. Again the Wingham Bench dismissed the charge, but Sempill maintained these were nothing more than malicious prosecutions designed to interfere with the sequestration of Joseph's Estate.

The Rich Insolvent

Sempill claimed William Andrews had abused Richards, and then thrown him from a ferry into the river, where he almost drowned.[22]

William Andrews had written a letter to Dodds & Co., in Maitland, giving notice in advance that he was bringing a herd of cattle down to their saleyards from No. 1 Station.[23] Richards rushed to Sydney to tell Sempill, who went to Court and took out a warrant for William Andrews' arrest, sending it with Richards to Maitland, and instructing Richards to attach the cattle to the insolvent estate.

Nineteen-year-old Waldy Cooper and Robert Herkes, aged twenty-seven, were drovers with William Andrews. They were relaxing at Bluford's Hotel at Hinton, not far from Maitland, when William was arrested, and forced to spend the night in the lock-up. The cattle were attached to Joseph's insolvent estate, and the two horses, which William had allegedly rescued, were impounded, but the mare disappeared overnight.

At the committal hearing, Reuben Richards deposed that he, accompanied by his brother William Richards, had visited Woodside to attach property and showed Joseph Andrews his warrant as Special Messenger. He attached two horses in the presence of William Andrews and Joseph Andrews, and other members their family.

Later on William Andrews took the horses from him. He tried to stop him, but William Andrews threatened him by saying he would kick him to hell and lock him up when he got there. One of the horses had been used by Joseph Andrews, or his servants, for the last two or three years. He had seen both Joseph and William riding the horse. William did not ride it more than he did any other horse as he did his work or business for Joseph Andrews.[24]

This last statement by Richards encapsulated the whole case – did the horse belong to William Andrews or Joseph Andrews?

For the defence, Robert Herkes deposed that he knew the horse William Andrews was riding. It had been in William's possession for four or five years. It was bred by Joseph Andrews, but for the last four or five years he had never seen Joseph Andrews use that horse.

Herkes said he lived about nine miles from Mr Andrews, and was often at his station. William Andrews lived at No. 1 Station, and had cattle there belonging to himself and his brother Robert. Joseph Andrews' brand has an O on the ribs as well as the AD brand – the O was introduced last January or February.

Waldy Cooper deposed that William Andrews has his own brand – the number 5 on the ribs as well as the AD brand. He could swear that none of the cattle driven down to Maitland by William Andrews belonged to Joseph Andrews. He could swear that the horse belonged to William Andrews. He was not present when William bought the horse, but William told him about a year ago that he had bought the horse.

With the hearing of evidence completed, the two Magistrates disagreed on whether to commit William Andrews or not. Magistrate Day took the most unusual course of writing to Attorney General Hargrave, seeking his advice in the case.

Eight days later, the committal hearing resumed with a reading of the reply from the Attorney General, who stated that he did not "think it right to advise magistrates as to the course to be taken, pending further enquiry before themselves."[25]

With William Andrews facing a possible three-year prison sentence, Magistrate Dodds said he believed that the horse had clearly been proved to belong to the prisoner, and he should not be subjected to "the ignominy of committal".[26]

Day, on the other hand, was quite certain a *prima facie* case had been made against William Andrews. Only one Magistrate needed to hold this view for the prisoner to be committed. The Bench committed William Andrews to take his trial at the next Circuit Court to be held in Maitland, setting bail at £200 with two sureties of £100 each, with the next Circuit Court not due until February/March 1861.[27]

Attached to the depositions taken in the committal hearing, and sent off to the Attorney General, were *two letters*. These letters had been found on William Andrews on the night of his arrest, when the arresting constable searched him, before locking him in a cell for the night.

Although no mention of these letters was made at the committal hearing, the actions of Magistrate Day seem to indicate his concerns about these letters. They were probably the reason Day wrote to the Attorney General and then stubbornly insisted on a committal.

The Rich Insolvent

The first letter, written by Ann Andrews to her son John, seemed very innocent:[28]

> Johnny if it is possible for you to cut off the blue heifer, that is off the Manning Flats – she is the only one that is left of Nowandoc's breed, and she is not broke in.
> Your mother,
> Ann Andrews

Placed in the context of a fraudulent insolvency, this letter confirmed that cattle were being hidden at Nowandoc, not far from No. 1 Station.

The second letter was unsigned, but even more incriminating, being a set of instructions on how to answer questions about the ownership of the cattle and horses. It read (in its entirety):[29]

> Dear Sir
> As Richards has gone to Sydney in great haste, we understand it is his intention to inform Semphill of you, and to seize the cattle. We wish to put you on your guard, if examined by the court, and questioned about brands.
>
> You can explain to them that when your brothers and you went into partnership, your brother Joseph put in all his cattle as his share in the station, agreeing that his children would be allowed the use of the dairy cows for themselves, and the young cattle branded 'AD' conjoined and 'O' are the increase of those cows last year, and when we dissolved partnership, my brother Robert and I gave them to the children as a gift, and they should not have been sold with the other cattle, and I came to Maitland to purchase them back, being superior bred cattle; but they were not sold as advertised.
>
> If asked about the horses, you can say that there were five horses and four mares given at the same time with the cattle, and are now the property of my brother Robert and myself. If you are asked the number of calves given to the children, you say you don't know at present, but that you think there were about forty head.
>
> If Waldy is questioned on the matter, tell him to be cautious what he says, but that he had charge of the cattle that Mr Kingsmill took away, and understood all along that 'No. 1' station belonged to William and Robert in January last, and that the cattle he had in charge belonged to Joseph, and that the calves given by Mr Begbie and branded AD conjoined, was to be branded with the circle O as soon as the stockyard

could be put up and the cattle collected; the yard was completed in June. Herkes of course knows nothing of our affairs, but what he understood from us that No. 1 is yours and Robert's since January, knows nothing about whose horses they were; that Mr Joseph Andrews had very few horses, and always rode one of his daughter's horses.

This unsigned letter, with its clear evidence of a conspiracy to commit fraud, was written by Joseph Andrews. While trying to write the letter in the third person, Joseph used the phrase "my brother Robert and I" in the second paragraph, making the authorship of the letter quite clear.

According to the letter, the evidence given by Robert Herkes at William's committal hearing was not so much what he actually knew about the Andrews family, but rather what they told him. Outside the Andrews Clan, only one family appeared to know that the insolvency was fraudulent – Waldy Cooper, Alfred Begbie and Maria Cooper.

For Magistrate Denny Day, if Joseph Andrews were passing through a false insolvency, this would increase the probability that William Andrews had illegally rescued the horses. Without the letters, it was no more than a case of Richards' word against Andrews' word, which probably meant no case.

Fortunately for Joseph Andrews, few people – Richards and Sempill included – seem to know of the existence of these letters.

Since filing his insolvency schedule, Joseph Andrews was required to attend meetings in Sydney, and make statements about his affairs under oath. At one of these meetings, Joseph proposed that his insolvency be resolved with a settlement of "2/6 in the £" (or $12\frac{1}{2}\%$). Joseph claimed he had approached the major creditors and they would all agree to this settlement except *one* – Reuben Richards. For his £320 debt, Richards would only get £40 by this settlement.

Robert Sempill rejected the offer out of hand, knowing this had been Joseph's primary object all along.

Arthur Kingsmill had asked Joseph Andrews in July how

many cows he possessed, and Joseph Andrews answered two. At the beginning of November, Robert Searle, under instructions from Robert Sempill, drove a herd of forty-eight milking cows and fifteen calves, from the Manning River to Maitland. Richards had attached these cattle to the Insolvent Estate. On reaching Maitland on November 19, the herd sold for £164, but the complete cost of the operation was £167.[30]

Sempill was beginning to make his point.

Robert Searle put in his account for his services to Sempill, dated from October 1, and claiming 48 days service at £1 per day.[31] In fact Searle had spent, at most, a fortnight in collecting the dairy herd and taking them to Maitland.

In a sworn affidavit, stockman Malcolm Shaw stated that after driving the cattle to Maitland for Kingsmill, he had been employed by Robert Searle to drive a second lot of cattle to Maitland. He and another stockman had been detained on the property of Reuben Richards at Mount George for about a month, during which time they did nothing but were paid at the same rate as when they were driving cattle. Searle went to Mr Andrews' place in November and spent five days collecting the cattle and five days on the road driving them to Maitland.[32]

Joseph and Ann Andrews visited Sempill towards the end of November to complain bitterly of the growing expenses Sempill was incurring. Joseph particularly complained that Searle had illegitimately claimed forty-eight days pay when he had only taken ten days.

Sempill flippantly suggested Joseph charge Searle with fraud.[33]

27. Confession

On August 26, 1860, William Turner was arrested on the Dawson River, near Rockhampton, and escorted down to Darlinghurst Gaol, Sydney, where the twenty-five year old was charged with perjury.

Isabella Kelly had received information on Turner's whereabouts in Queensland, and immediately contacted John Ryan Brenan, who sought, and was granted, a warrant for William Turner's arrest. Kelly did not name the source of her information, but one possibility was Turner's mate, Joseph Giles, who had returned to the Manning and was working for Joseph Andrews.

On Turner's arrival at the prison, Brenan interviewed him in the presence of the prison Governor and the head warden (to prevent any suggestion of tainting of evidence). In this interview, Turner admitted that he had falsely signed the Receipt – he was *not* at Brimbin on June 6, 1854, nor did he see Skerrett pay any money to Miss Kelly.

Brenan was quite confident that a charge of forgery against Skerrett could now succeed, as Turner agreed to give evidence. Brenan returned to Turner's prison cell some time later, and with the aid of a Magistrate, took down a formal deposition, after which Turner was given bail.[1]

Brenan went to the Police Court in Sydney to take out a warrant for Skerrett's arrest, but said he experienced a great deal of difficulty because of prejudice against Miss Kelly. This is one of the few references to the general prejudice against Isabella Mary Kelly, generated by her gaol sentence and various newspaper reports supporting Skerrett while she was in gaol.

One Magistrate refused to issue the warrant. Brenan returned on another occasion, only to find the same magistrate in deep conversation with Charles Skerrett.[2]

Confession

On October 8, 1860, Brenan was able to get Magistrate James Murphy to issue the warrant for forgery. A week later, Charles Skerrett appeared before this Magistrate for his committal hearing. The Bill of Sale and the Receipt were presented as exhibits, with John Dawson (Skerrett's solicitor at his 1855 trial) identifying them as the correct documents.

Brenan called Isabella Mary Kelly as the first witness. She spent most of the first day in the witness box, with much of her evidence a repeat of the evidence given at Skerrett's 1855 trial, her trial and the Skerrett Select Committee.

In cross-examination Skerrett's defence attorney put it to Isabella Kelly that she had sold all her cattle to Begbie & Cooper *after* Paddy Connolly told her Skerrett was about to be released (implying she knew they were Skerrett's cattle, so she sold them). Kelly denied this. When asked if she knew a man named Reuben Richards, Kelly said she thought she could see him in the courtroom – he was a friend of Skerrett's.

William Turner spent most of the next day in the witness box. Turner deposed that he had become friendly with Charles Skerrett, and on one particular day Skerrett sent for him. He had been drinking before he arrived at Skerrett's place. Skerrett told him he had bought some cattle off Miss Kelly but he needed a witness on the Receipt. He told Skerrett he did not want to sign it, but Skerrett pressed him hard to sign it, and he did.

Looking at the Receipt, after it was read to the Court, William said he now remembered Skerrett saying something to that effect. He could not read writing, but he thought the signature on the document was his – he could not swear to it, but he thought it was his. Skerrett told him he paid Kelly £400 with four £100 notes on a Melbourne bank. He had lied when he said he saw Miss Kelly sign the Receipt, and he actually signed the Receipt towards the end of July 1854.[3]

Turner made no mention here that Skerrett had trained him to write his signature, as stated by Joseph Giles. But then he did expect to take his trial for perjury, and would not be keen to show any premeditation of the false witnessing, preferring to blame it on liquor.

After he gave this evidence at Bungay Bungay, William said, he ran away. He came to Court today because he had been led astray, but he did not understand that at the time. It was less than a fortnight after the Bungay Bungay hearing when he left the Manning, and he did not see Miss Kelly during that time. She had never threatened him with imprisonment if he did not clear out.

Recalled to the stand, Isabella Kelly said she had never signed any document with William Turner as a witness. She had made efforts to find Turner before Skerrett's trial, but had been unsuccessful. She even wrote to Magistrate Denny Day trying to find him.

Kelly said Turner was at Brimbin the day after her stockman had drowned (three weeks after Skerrett's arrival at Brimbin). Turner was with Skerrett on that day, and she saw them together after that quite often. After Turner gave his evidence at Bungay Bungay, she called him a perjurer.

In cross-examination, Skerrett's attorney asked was he the William Turner who signed the Receipt? Did he give evidence to the Bungay Bungay Bench? Was he the William Turner who swore at Bungay Bungay that he saw Skerrett write out the Receipt and saw Skerrett pay Kelly the money? To all these questions William Turner answered in the affirmative.

Charles Skerrett made an astounding accusation: "I never saw that man."[4]

Skerrett claimed the witness named William Turner, who was giving evidence at this hearing, *was not the William Turner who had signed the Receipt as a witness.*

The committal hearing came to an abrupt and dramatic halt.

Brenan was rather perplexed at this most unusual situation. How could he prove that this William Turner was *the* William Turner? Turner's signature would be easily challenged – it was very rough (if he remembered how to write it). Depositions from various witnesses could be contested and only extend legal argument.

Brenan then thought of Samuel Turner, William's father. Samuel Turner had testified about his missing son in both Skerrett's trial and Kelly's trial – his identification of William Turner would be undeniable. He thought of getting depositions from Turner Senior, but decided it would be better if Samuel Turner came to the Sydney Court and gave his evidence *in person*.[5]

Ryan Brenan asked for an adjournment, which Magistrate Murphy granted.

Confession

It took a month for the committal hearing to reconvene.

Samuel Turner immediately took the stand and declared that the William Turner now in Court was his son. In 1854 he and his son had been employed by Miss Kelly to build a cottage. His son was a witness for Skerrett at Bungay Bungay. He did not speak with his son after the hearing. His son then ran away, and he did not see him again until after his arrest.[6]

Charles Skerrett made no further denials of William Turner's identity.

Cross-examined by Windeyer, Sam Turner stated that one day when he was at Brimbin, Miss Kelly told him Skerrett had bought her cattle. He had sworn that in Court when Kelly was tried for perjury. After she came back from Sydney in 1854, she told him she thought Skerrett had bought her cattle, but Skerrett did not.

With William's perjury now out in the open, there are indications here that there has been a small shift in Samuel's testimony from the former evidence he gave in both the Skerrett and Kelly trials. But Samuel Turner must have been only too aware that if he were not careful, he too, like his son, would be charged with perjury.

The next witness, Joseph Giles, deposed that he had been a spectator at the Bungay Bungay Bench, when William Turner gave evidence. Afterwards he had met Charles Skerrett, who then offered him a £20 bribe to back up William Turner's evidence, but he had refused the offer.

Charles Langley, the former part owner of the insolvent firm of Rich, Langley & Butchart, produced an account from his firm to Miss Isabella Mary Kelly, dated November 2, 1854. This account referred to a loan of £300 given by the firm to Miss Kelly on February 14, 1854. It included a commission and the cost of advertising 280 head of cattle in *Sydney Morning Herald* and *Empire* on six occasions.

The account confirmed Kelly's story that the cattle were in the hands of the firm during 1854. Kelly had previously stated that because she had borrowed money from Rich, Langley & Butchart with the cattle as surety, only this firm had authority to sell her cattle. Skerrett had claimed at one stage to have a letter from the firm stating that the cattle were never in their hands.

The next morning, the committal hearing entered its fourth day. Ann Andrews reprised the evidence she gave at Kelly's trial. Joseph Andrews once again took the witness stand and went through the same evidence he had given under oath on three previous occasions.

Andrews probably expected to be challenged on why he reversed his testimony on the 'Isabella Mary Kelly' signatures from Skerrett's committal hearing in 1854 to his trial in 1855. He rather adroitly answered the question with:[7]

> I had a doubt as to these signatures ... in 1854, I said I believed them to be Miss Kelly's. I said that on oath. Subsequently I said they were not. I changed my opinion from circumstances which came to my knowledge. My first impression is, that when I first saw the signature I challenged it. In comparison of the signatures, I saw there was a resemblance of the signatures, and I gave the benefit of the doubt to Skerrett;
>
> I was not on friendly terms with Miss Kelly in June, July or August, 1854. In October, 1854, I was a friend by turns with both parties. I remember first talking to Miss Kelly about the agreement in September, 1854. I believe she, at that time, abandoned an action which she threatened me with, and I made friends with her.

This was close as Joseph Andrews ever came to admitting his 1854 testimony on Kelly's signature was generated by ill feeling towards Isabella Kelly.

Finally, Magistrate Murphy asked Charles Skerrett if he had anything to say in his defence, and received no reply. Murphy committed Skerrett to take his trial for forgery. Bail of £200 was granted with two sureties of £100 each.

The depositions were sent to the Attorney General.

On November 30, Attorney General John Hargrave wrote to Magistrate Murphy to advise him that he *declined to prosecute* Charles Skerrett for forgery, but gave no reasons.[8]

Questioned some years later on his decision, Attorney General Hargrave indicated the reason was double jeopardy.

It came back to the complexity of the original charges

⊰ Confession ⊱

against Charles Skerrett. In 1855 Skerrett was charged and convicted of cattle stealing. Because the cattle stealing involved forgery, the conviction on cattle stealing also meant Skerrett had been convicted of forgery – and the jury had stated they believed the documents were forged.

Hence, in essence, *Skerrett had already been convicted of forgery*. More than that, he had also been pardoned for it.

This committal hearing on forgery charges was a complete fiasco.

Ryan Brenan was a very capable and experienced solicitor, how did he not see this?

Skerrett could have been charged with the perjury he committed at *her trial*, as this was a new offence committed *after* he had received his pardon. There was, of course, no guarantee of success for this action.

The Skerrett forgery committal had been a very expensive exercise for Isabella Mary Kelly, and when viewed from this perspective, was doomed to failure.

The failure of the forgery charge was not complete. Isabella Kelly had a moral victory with William Turner establishing once and for all, that Skerrett had lied about the Receipt. It also followed logically that Skerrett had lied about the Bill of Sale, and so had his daughters.

But for Isabella Kelly there was no exoneration.

As far as the general community was concerned, the charge of forgery against Charles Skerrett had been thrown out by the Attorney General's refusal to prosecute.

Most residents of the Manning Valley still went back to the old question: Why did Isabella Kelly tell so many people she had sold her cattle to Charles Skerrett, if she did not?

According to Ryan Brenan, on William Turner's release on bail, friends of Skerrett pursued him and tried to get him to reverse his confession. On one occasion he was taken to a hotel, where Reuben Richards persistently tried to induce him to resume the original evidence he gave at Bungay Bungay. William Turner rejected all these attempts, but became frightened to go to Sydney.[9]

One can see the concerns of Reuben Richards: With the establishment of Skerrett's guilt in forging documents, a charge of forgery against Reuben Richards gained much more credibility.

Isabella Kelly dropped the pending perjury charges against William Turner, and he was free to go. Once again Turner disappeared. This time he told Ryan Brenan he could always be found through his father, who was now living at Dungog.[10]

Isabella Kelly visited the Crown Law Office on December 30, seeking a copy of the depositions in the Skerrett forgery case. Speaking to Attorney General Hargrave, she told him he should have put Charles Skerrett on trial, so she could clear her name. Kelly wrote:[11]

> The Attorney General remarked to me, "Your character is unimpeached."
>
> I replied, "It may be so in your eyes, but I want the world to see it also. Give me an answer, yes or no, about the depositions."
>
> He said, "Send your attorney to me, and I will talk to him about it."
>
> I then told him I had no money left to fee lawyers, as I had been robbed of all my property by Charles Skerrett, since he had been liberated from Cockatoo Island."

There was no doubt that the once wealthy Isabella Mary Kelly, while not penniless, was definitely feeling the pinch.

28. The Trust of the Trustees

Lennon & Cape, the trustees for Isabella Kelly, continued to pursue Cooper & Begbie for their debt of £1000 with Miss Kelly. In a letter dated September 21, Begbie received a final demand from the trustees.

Perhaps drawing inspiration from Joseph Andrews, Alfred Begbie became a new insolvent on October 25. John Morris, appointed as Begbie's Official Assignee, proved to be a far more co-operative Official Assignee than Sempill had been in the Joseph Andrews' insolvency.

Begbie listed Isabella Mary Kelly with a debt of £1087 (the original £1000 plus interest) and one minor debt of £5.

Under 'Landed Property' Begbie listed his own 363 acre farm as worth £408, and the 43-acre Waterview Farm as worth £86, noting that the title deeds were "in the hands of Miss Kelly."[1] Without the title deeds Waterview could not be sold.

Under 'Personal Property' his assets totalled £232, which included 100 head of cattle worth £150 and two horses worth £20.

Begbie had a deficit of £361, with debts of £1092 and assets totalling £730.

This insolvency had some dubious aspects

There was no mention of the Cooper & Begbie partnership in the insolvency papers. There are numerous statements by various people, including Isabella Mary Kelly, that *Cooper & Begbie* bought her cattle, rather than just Begbie. Theodor Müller, the Swiss traveller who stayed briefly at the Coopers in 1859, talked of the Cooper boys out every day rounding up these cattle and of the cattle belonging to Mrs. Cooper.[2] Joseph Andrews, when giving evidence in another matter, stated he heard Begbie "state upon oath that he and Mrs. Cooper did purchase Kelly's cattle for £1200."³

By splitting the partnership, Begbie was able to minimise his assets.

Joseph Andrews, in his own insolvency schedule, listed *Cooper & Begbie* as creditors for £390 – this was for cattle formerly belonging to Isabella Kelly. Just before Begbie became insolvent, this amount was officially reduced to £262 for Alfred Begbie and £84 for Waldy Cooper.⁴

The land Begbie listed as worth £408 was legally owned by Cooper & Begbie, but as no buyers could be found for part-owned land, Begbie's assets were reduced by £408 (and the land retained by the Cooper family).

Three months after filing for insolvency, Alfred Begbie brought to the Insolvency Court an affidavit made by Maria Cooper before a Magistrate.⁵ Mrs. Cooper claimed Begbie owed her a total of £450 from four debts, none of which were mentioned in Begbie's schedule. In his written explanation to the Official Assignee, Begbie claimed the debt was left out of his schedule because he did not then know the exact amount, and he did not expect Mrs. Cooper to prove the debt.⁶

The addition of this debt meant that not only would Mrs. Cooper gain a dividend of about 30% from the final distribution, but Miss Kelly (or rather, the trustees) would now receive only 70% of the final distribution.

This debt, highly beneficial to both Cooper and Begbie, seems more than a little suspicious, especially as Insolvents were only required to enter the *approximate* amounts of moneys owed to creditors in the initial schedule, with all debts having to be "proved" later by statutory declarations.

According to Maria Cooper, they had only been able to muster 250 head of cattle bought from Kelly, while Kelly stated that Begbie had taken 380 cattle from Brimbin and 200 from Mount George. There was another 100 head at Waterview, but Kelly did not say if Begbie took them.

Overseer Tim Leane claimed he heard Begbie say at one stage he had mustered about 400 head.⁷ The Andrews insolvency showed he made a sale of about 300 to them. When facing his insolvency, it was in Begbie's own interest to minimise this number.

The Trust of the Trustees

In the Manning Valley all sympathy was for Alfred Begbie. The Manning River correspondent, in an occasional report for the *Empire* newspaper, gave an outline of the Skerrett/Kelly case, followed by sympathetic comments for Alfred Begbie:[8]

> The people of the Manning are sorry to observe the insolvency of Mr Begbie – a gentleman whose honour and integrity are unimpeachable. In an unlucky moment he purchased Miss Kelly's cattle from that lady …
>
> [Skerrett] immediately, as everybody knows, instituted proceedings against Miss Kelly, for perjury, and she, in her turn, was convicted, and after a short period released on what grounds nobody knows …
>
> Mr Begbie was really to be pitied. On the one hand, annoyed and robbed by people running and driving off his cattle, and, on the other, pestered by Miss Kelly for the purchase money of the said cattle, which were evidently disputed property.
>
> I understand that Miss Kelly is the sole creditor, which incontrovertibly proves Mr Begbie to be an honest man; for, a short time ago, to avoid being pestered any more by her threatening letters, he offered her cattle back – his stock of horses, his landed property here, and £50 in cash, if she would give him a receipt in full of all demand.
>
> Besides all this, he, some time ago, had paid her £200 of the purchase money. She cavalierly refused to give him the receipt, and so forced him to file his schedule in the Insolvency Court.

On April 7, 1861, the Insolvent Estate of Alfred Begbie was finalised and a clearance certificate granted.

In a much simpler insolvency than that of Joseph Andrews, the assets raised £309, most of which came from the £262 received from Joseph Andrews (in payment for the cattle which originally belonged to Kelly). Only £47 was raised from Begbie's other assets. The expenses amounted to £39, of which £16 went to the Official Assignee as his commission.[9]

This left £270 to be split between the two creditors, with £80 going to Maria Cooper, and £190 to Lennon & Cape (Isabella Mary Kelly).

Maria Cooper complained long and hard that Kelly had bankrupted Begbie. She wrote in one letter, "Miss Kelly was placed in gaol, and by her false and wicked representations, she completely ruined Mr Begbie and family."[10]

In particular, Maria Cooper complained that the retention of Waterview and the milking utensils by Kelly was basically dishonest. Begbie paid only £200 of the contracted £1200. But the resolution of the insolvency meant Kelly received a total of £390 for the £1200 debt. The question was quite rhetorical: Why should these items have been handed over to Begbie to compound her losses to him?

Kelly eventually sold Waterview for £45.

For Alfred Begbie, the insolvency had a highly beneficial result – it had cost him £300 to clear a £1000 debt, as well as giving his mother-in-law an £80 present.

If Kelly's financial affairs were in her own hands rather than the trustees, it seems most unlikely she would have forced Cooper and Begbie into insolvency. Kelly had much more chance of getting her money by giving Begbie time to pay. After all, Begbie seems to have been generally honest and honourable in his business dealings, and creditors in any insolvency were extremely lucky if they got more than 20% of their money.

Maria Cooper complained, and while she did, many of her neighbours listened.

At the end of October, Lennon & Cape sent an account to Isabella Mary Kelly, detailing their activities on her behalf. After twelve months at Mount George, Mr Girard had completed his operations and left the district.

The horses had been sold for £460. Kelly had four hundred horses when she went to prison. Even Skerrett had valued twenty of her horses to be worth £100.[11] Kelly believed that, in her hands, she could have got at least several thousand pounds for them.

Girard sold the sheep for only £300 – about five shillings each. Two years previously, Kelly had spent £2000 buying the sheep for eleven shillings each. While she was in prison the shepherds had not looked after the sheep very well, and the flock reduced to about 1200. In the twelve-month period before her imprisonment, she had received a wool clip from them realising

The Trust of the Trustees

£228.[12]

Added to this, Girard had killed five hundred lambs. Girard had been well-paid at £250 for his services together with 2.5% of the £760 he raised in selling the stock.

The net result of selling all the stock, the firm informed Kelly, was a reduction of her £320 debt to £140.[13]

Lennon & Cape spent £760 to reduce her debt by £180.

By forcing Begbie to insolvency they collected only £190 of his £1087 debt.

One suspects this to be another example of the general prejudice against Kelly of being a woman convicted of perjury.

The firm had not yet sold her property, which was under an overdue mortgage of £500. If Kelly wanted to take her affairs out of the hands of Lennon & Cape, she could not – not unless she paid all the money she owed them, including the £500 mortgage, plus all their expenses.

And Isabella Kelly had been worried about Skerrett stealing her horses.

29. Assault and Battery

At the beginning of November while Skerrett's committal hearing was adjourned for a month, Isabella Mary Kelly returned to the Manning River.

When she arrived at Waterview, Isabella Kelly became extremely upset to discover that the cottage had been broken into and ransacked, and most of her possessions removed.

In particular, the lock on a box containing many of her personal papers and studbooks had been broken, and most of the contents taken away. These papers were documents and copies detailing her business transactions over a period of twenty years.[1]

Before her arrival at Waterview, Isabella Kelly must have had some inkling of the break-in at her cottage, as she had already seen a document which she knew should have been locked in her box at Waterview.

During the Richards/Andrews trial, Richards had presented many papers as exhibits to the Court, with one of these being a copy of a lease which she had given to a man named Purcell in the early 1850s (before Skerrett or Richards arrived on the Manning). On a visit to the offices of Richards' solicitor, Kelly had pointed it out to Ryan Brenan because it was *not* the original document (which Richards may have been able to obtain from Purcell) but the *copy* she had written for her own record – and she knew it was kept only in her locked box at the Waterview cottage.[2]

Kelly claimed Richards forged the Mount George lease using this document as a model because of the many similarities between the two documents. Further, she said, Richards needed the Purcell lease because of his bad spelling – he did not want misspelled words to appear in the lease.

Richards' possession of this paper suggests he may have been a party to the break-in at Waterview.

Assault and Battery

On Monday afternoon, November 5, Isabella Kelly decided to visit her Mount George property, taking young Andrew Mort with her. Andrew was about twelve years old, and had been a servant of Miss Kelly for the last three years.

Kelly did not state her motivation to going to Mount George.

When she reached Mount George, Kelly was surprised to see five or six horses with her MK brand on them standing *in Richards' stockyard*. As she angrily approached the stockyard, Reuben Richards came running up from the cottage, shouting abuse at her.

According to Kelly, when she asked Richards why her horses were in his stockyard, he told her to get out, and knocked her down, dragging her out of the yard. Richards then seized her around the throat, threatened her with a pistol.

Isabella Kelly and Andrew Mort fled the Mount George property, with two pistol shots fired as they left. They went the short distance to Woodside, where Ann Andrews comforted Isabella, before she proceeded on to Wingham.

On Wednesday Isabella Kelly went to the Wingham bench, but was initially refused a warrant against Richards (probably Magistrate Cross). She could not pursue the matter any further at the Wingham Bench because of her need to return to Sydney for the resumption of the Skerrett committal hearing. When she rode past Reuben Richards, who happened to be standing on the road, they ignored each other.

Isabella Kelly returned to Sydney, leaving Andrew Mort at Hinton to look after horses.[3]

Having returned to Sydney, Isabella Mary Kelly took out two warrants against Reuben Richards. One charged him with assault and battery on November 5 at Mount George, and the other charged him with forging the lease of the Mount George paddock.

On November 21, at the Central Police Court, Reuben Richards appeared for a committal hearing of the forgery charge. In a rather brief hearing, solicitor Abbott, for Richards, stated that the document, claimed by Miss Kelly to be a forgery, was in his possession, but it was not in his client's interests for him to produce it, and consequently he would not do so – his client would not allow him to produce it.[4] (Why go through the expense of a trial with the possibility of a conviction, when it could all be avoided?)

Ryan Brenan, for Kelly, said he would approach the Supreme Court for a Court Order directing Abbott to produce the lease. The Magistrate adjourned the case, awaiting the reply.

A week later, Ryan Brenan admitted defeat. His subpoena against Abbott to produce the lease had been unsuccessful.[5] Without the lease itself the Magistrate had no alternative but to dismiss the charge.

The next day, November 22, Reuben Richards appeared before Magistrate James Murphy, for a committal hearing of the charge of assault and battery, also brought by Isabella Mary Kelly.

Isabella Mary Kelly, again represented by Ryan Brenan, deposed that she had gone to her property at Mount George, where she saw five or six of her horses in Richards's stockyard. Richards told her to "come out of there" and knocked her down. As she got up, he grabbed her round the throat, and, pulling a pistol out of his pocket, said to her, "be off from here or I'll blow your head off."[6]

She went over to the stockyard fence, and as she leant on it Richards struck her on the hand with a stick. He then knocked her down three times and dragged her out of the stockyard. As she was leaving, he fired a shot at her, and she said to the boy, "Come on." Richards fired a second shot.

Under cross-examination Kelly said Richards had struck her on the chest. She thought the pistol was double-barrelled. She was so sore after the incident that, for three days, she would not allow her horse to go into a canter. Yes, she had been found guilty of perjury, and Ann Richards had given evidence against her in that trial. Yes, she had given evidence against Richards in the Richards/Andrews trial, and the jury gave its verdict to Richards.

Re-examined by Brenan, Kelly said she was pardoned on the charge of perjury. The stockyard was her property, and Richards had no right to be there. She believed Richards forged the lease to her Mount George paddock.

Magistrate Murphy adjourned the hearing waiting for Andrew Mort, who was still at Hinton, to give evidence. Bail was given at £20, with two sureties of £10.[7]

Assault and Battery

A week later, the hearing resumed with young Andrew Mort in the witness box. Andrew said he went with his mistress, Miss Kelly, to Mount George on the afternoon of November 5. There he saw Miss Kelly's horses in the paddock.

Richards took down the sliprail to let Miss Kelly out of the stockyard. Miss Kelly picked up the sliprail and refused to go. Richards put his foot on it and knocked it down again. Richards said, "Don't you touch this stockyard – this stockyard is mine".

Miss Kelly said the stockyard was hers, and Richards said she had no stockyard. He then called out for his sister Charity. Mrs. Richards came and poked faces at Miss Kelly. Richards knocked Miss Kelly down and when she got up, she was crying. [8]

Andrew said Miss Kelly refused to go out of the stockyard and Richards shoved her down over the sliprail. Miss Kelly got up and had a stick in her hand. Richards snatched the stick out of her hand and hit her on the hand with it. Her hand was on the sliprail at the time, and it left a black bruise.

Richards called Miss Kelly 'whore', 'bitch' and other names. Richards said to Miss Kelly, "Come in here and see what I will do to you", and pointed into the brush as he said this. As he and Miss Kelly walked away, Richards fired a shot. Andrew said he turned round and saw the smoke. Richards then fired a second shot.

Cross-examined by Mr Windeyer, Andrew said he had not spoken with Miss Kelly about the case before he came to court. She had told him to say nothing but the truth. Miss Charity and Mrs. Richards were there when Richards asked Miss Kelly to go into the bush. They were present when he fired the shots. Richards struck Miss Kelly on the chest with his fist and knocked her down. From the time Richards first spoke to Miss Kelly up to the time the second shot was fired, about an hour and a half elapsed.

With the completion of this deposition, Magistrate Murphy committed Reuben Richards for trial on the charge of assault, and sent the depositions to the Attorney General.

Reuben Richards wrote on his "Statement of the Accused" sheet: "I am not guilty of the charge – not having had a pistol in my hand."

On Tuesday, December 4, the trial of Reuben Richards for

assault and battery commenced before the Acting Chief Justice, John Dickinson, who must been rather familiar with the background to the case by now, have presided at Kelly's trial and the Richards/Andrews trial.[9]

Mr Isaacs and Mr Windeyer, appearing for Reuben Richards, were briefed by Robert Abbott, with Ryan Brenan briefing the Attorney General, John Hargrave, who prosecuted the case for Isabella Kelly.

Hargrave called Isabella Kelly, who gave her evidence much as she had done in the committal hearing. Richards had ordered her out of the stockyard but she refused to go. He had threatened her with a pistol saying, "I'll blow your head off if you don't come out of the stockyard". Richards knocked her down three times, and fired the pistol at her twice.

On cross-examination by Mr Windeyer, Kelly admitted she had been gaoled for perjury in 1859, and Mrs. Richards, the defendant's wife, had testified against her. Also, she had testified against Richards in the Richards/Andrews case.

Questioned by Judge Dickinson, Kelly said she was accustomed to hearing guns and pistols go off, but she could not tell whether the pistol was loaded or not. (This was a crucial point — these were single shot pistols, which could be fired without a ball being discharged. If a ball had not been fired, a much different interpretation of Richards' actions could be found.)

The next prosecution witness, Andrew Mort, was vital to the case, as he was the only witness corroborating Kelly's evidence. He heard Richards say to Miss Kelly, "Come. I'll take you under my arm". Richards then rode his horse up quite close to her, as if to run over her. Miss Kelly said to Richards, "You'd better be civil". Richards ordered her out of the stockyard.

When Mrs. Richards and Miss Charity came up, Mrs. Richards tried to strike Miss Kelly, but Mr Richards rode his horse in between Mrs. Richards and Miss Kelly. When Miss Kelly went over to the sliprail they followed her. Miss Kelly was knocked down three times. Richards pushed her down over the sliprail.

Cross-examined by Mr Windeyer, Andrew said he did not know how old he was till Miss Kelly told him yesterday. He could not read, but he could say his prayers. He saw Miss Kelly knocked down beside the stockyard. Richards shoved her down without beating her. All three times Richards knocked her down with a shove. He did not see Richards strike her, and he did not see Richards drag Miss Kelly out of the yard. Miss Kelly struck Richards just before he called to his wife and sister.

Ann Andrews deposed that Miss Kelly had come to her house between two and three in the afternoon. She saw Miss Kelly's hand, and it was swollen and slightly discoloured. Her daughters cleaned Miss Kelly's dress.

Cross-examined Ann Andrews admitted she was the wife of Joseph Andrews, who had lost an action brought against him by Mr Richards. Yes, her husband had become insolvent since the court case.

Joseph Childs, servant of Joseph Andrews, deposed he lived at Woodside. He had heard two reports from a pistol at about five o'clock. He saw Miss Kelly with her hand swollen and discoloured, and her dress was very dirty.

The next morning, the defence outlined its case before calling Harriet Charity Richards. Miss Richards stated her brother told Miss Kelly to go away but she refused. Miss Kelly took down the rails of the fence, saying she would pull the fences down and burn the rails.

Miss Kelly took a bone and hit her brother. She then took a stick and hit him on the hand. She called him a perjured villain, and said she would have him gaoled. Miss Kelly pulled up her brother's jacket and said to Andrew Mort, "Do you see that pistol? I'll make you swear Richards has been beating me and threatening to shoot me".

Miss Kelly took a limb of a tree and struck Richards with it. When Richards snatched the branch out of her hand, Miss Kelly said to the boy, "See how he has hurt my hand. I'll make you swear he has been beating me". Her brother did not fire his pistol as Miss Kelly was walking away, he fired it later at about four o'clock. Her brother did not knock Miss Kelly down.

In cross-examination, Hargrave was unable to shake Charity Richards' testimony in any way.

Alexander Cameron testified he was a stockman. He heard the pistol go off, but Miss Kelly was nowhere in sight.

Alderman John Smithers deposed he knew Miss Kelly, and he would not believe her on her oath. Under cross-examination, he

The Trials of Isabella Mary Kelly

said he had never spoken to her until five or six months ago. He had been a juror on the Richards/Andrews trial, and from the evidence she gave in that trial, he would not believe her on her oath.

With the completion of the defence, the Attorney General replied for the prosecution before Justice Dickinson summed up for the jury.

The jury retired to deliberate, but were only absent several minutes before returning with a verdict declaring Reuben Richards *not guilty*.

The evidence of Charity Richards, with the distance of time, sounds like pure Victorian melodrama, with much of it most improbable. But there was one basic truth to it, and this was borne out by the evidence of Andrew Mort: Kelly was absolutely refusing to leave the stockyard.

The key to this incident comes from the committal hearing, where Andrew Mort stated that he estimated Miss Kelly was at the stockyard for an hour and a half. He would not have owned a watch, but even if this length of time was an exaggeration – say Kelly was there for at least forty-five minutes or an hour – during that time, she refused to leave.

This was not a sudden unprovoked attack by Richards on Kelly – she was *challenging* Richards to throw her out of the stockyard, and it was played out over a lengthy period of time. This stemmed from her dispute with Richards over the leases – this was *her* property, *not his*, and he had no right to be there, as he had not even paid the rent.

Richards did assault Kelly, but while he knocked her down three times and fired a pistol twice (probably not loaded), and while he tried to intimidate her by being crudely suggestive, he did not act to *maliciously* injure her. According to Andrew Mort, when Ann Richards tried to strike Miss Kelly, Reuben Richards interposed his horse between them to prevent it.

The quick verdict of the jury came from Andrew Mort's evidence, where he contradicted Miss Kelly's evidence on three major points: Richards had *shoved* more than hit Miss Kelly to the ground; he had not seen Richards drag Miss Kelly from the stockyard; he had seen Miss Kelly hit Richards with a stick (but

Assault and Battery

whether this was accidental or deliberate was not stated). Andrew Mort's evidence was quite credible in that he was an uninvolved observer, while Isabella Kelly, on the other hand, was not only emotionally involved, but in the centre of the action.

It was absolutely astounding that Alderman Smithers, a man of standing in the community, should come forward and give character evidence against Isabella Kelly when his only contact with her was as a juror in a trial in which she was a witness. Further, he was giving evidence on behalf of the plaintiff in that case.

Here was another example of the prejudice against Isabella Kelly as a convicted perjurer, despite being pardoned.

Once again Ann Richards had proved her enmity of Miss Kelly, and once again Isabella Kelly had said nothing detrimental about her, despite it.

A month later, on January 2, 1861, Isabella Mary Kelly once again appeared at the Central Criminal Court charged with wilful and corrupt perjury. Reuben Richards, in an action parallel to Charles Skerrett, claimed Isabella Kelly committed perjury at his trial for assault.

Not many details of the committal hearing have survived other than a brief newspaper report. The *Sydney Morning Herald* reported Reuben Richards as giving evidence that Miss Kelly had made false accusations against him at his trial.[10]

Wife Ann and sister Charity Richards also gave evidence.

The Magistrate committed Isabella Kelly to stand her trial, but Attorney General Hargrave declined to proceed with the case. This should not have been entirely unexpected, as he had prosecuted the assault charges against Reuben Richards, and knew the case intimately. Perhaps Richards anticipated the general prejudice against Kelly would see him win the case.

Isabella Kelly had charged Reuben Richards with forgery and with assault, and failed on both occasions. She had charged Charles Skerrett with forgery and failed. It had been a very expensive exercise. This road had now been exhausted.

30. Judgement

At an insolvency meeting conducted by Official Assignee Robert Semphill in November, Joseph Andrews moved to pay all his creditors twenty shillings in the pound – he would pay all his debts in full.[1]

In an affidavit to Chief Commissioner Purefoy, Joseph stated he was obliged to the kindness of his brother Robert in coming forward to pay all his creditors in full, as he would not have been able to make any payment on his debts otherwise. At the same time Andrews complained that so many of his assets "had been needlessly and recklessly sacrificed without any benefit to my creditors."[2]

This was one reason for the urgency in resolving the insolvency. The other reason was the letter found on William Andrews when he was arrested. This letter attested the complete fraudulence of Joseph's insolvency, and if it were to surface, criminal charges against Joseph could result.

Robert Andrews offered to pay each of Joseph's creditors 25% of their debt in cash immediately, with the balance coming in three equal instalments at three-month intervals. All creditors accepted this offer except one – Reuben Richards – who would only agree to an immediate payment of the entire amount.

Consequently, on December 8, Robert Andrews paid Reuben Richards the full amount of £320. The money was paid to Richards' solicitor, Robert Abbott, who deducted the outstanding legal fees and remitted the balance, at most £100, to Richards.[3]

On December 13, Robert Andrews appeared in the Insolvency Court requesting a release from sequestration of Joseph Andrews' estate on the grounds that all the creditors had reached agreement with settlement of their debts, and each had subsequently received their first payment.

⚜ Judgement ⚜

In this deposition, Robert complained that "after repeated applications both verbally and by letter",[4] he finally received an account from Robert Sempill, the Official Assignee, stating that the sale of Joseph's assets raised £691.

But Sempill had expended £705 to raise this £691.

Included in the costs was £90 in wages to Reuben Richards.

Robert Andrews's deposition complained bitterly of the "reckless unnecessary expenses"[5] incurred by the Official Assignee, and requested an investigation into the matter by the Insolvency Court.

The next day Joseph Andrews applied for release of his estate from sequestration, with Robert Sempill opposing the motion. The Chief Commissioner, William Purefoy, ordered the Official Assignee "not to proceed any further in realising the assets of the estate", and invited affidavits from both parties within eighteen days.[6]

The issue of costs in insolvencies was a festering sore that burst when a letter to the Editor was published in *Empire* with the headline "Insolvency Of Mr Joseph Andrews."[7] This letter outlined the particulars of the insolvency starting with the Richards/Andrews court case, and highlighted the fact that the Official Assignee expended £705 in raising £691 for the creditors.

The next day *Empire* published a reply from Robert Sempill, who said it appeared, in the early stages of the insolvency, that the creditors would only get a small dividend, but because of his energy and perseverance as the Official Assignee, the creditors had been paid the full amount.[8]

A flood of letters and editorials followed, spilling over into the *Sydney Morning Herald* and the *Maitland Mercury*.

On January 4, 1861, John Butler, the solicitor representing Joseph Andrews, asked the Chief Commissioner in Insolvency, William Purefoy, to release Andrews from sequestration. Sir William Manning, who had represented Richards in the Richards/Andrews case, and here represented Robert Sempill, opposed the release of the estate.[9]

Sir William presented a number of affidavits to the Court, arguing that the Andrews brothers had obstructed the insolvency.

Butler objected strenuously to the costs of the Official Assignee, and presented the Chief Commissioner with a number of affidavits from people living on the Manning, declaring how much more cheaply the cattle could be driven from the Manning to Maitland.

Herbert Renwick stated he could drive 200 to 300 head of cattle from the Manning to Maitland for £30; Waldy Cooper said he could drive two mobs of cattle for £50 and make a "handsome profit"; Alfred Begbie claimed he had driven a herd to Maitland in two weeks for £25; Magistrate Charles Croaker could take 200 head for £20; Robert Herkes could do it for £40; and William Johnson could take 200 to 300 head for £25.[10]

Sir William Manning, in an unprecedented move, asked the Court *not* to release the Andrews Estate, even if all creditors had been paid, while an investigation was made into the case. Justice Purefoy said he would investigate the costs of the Official Assignee and make a ruling on them on January 31.[11]

A clerk for Joseph Andrews' solicitor personally served notice of this order on Robert Sempill, who angrily told him not to waste his time going to the Manning to get more affidavits about costs. Sempill said Andrews had no right to challenge any expense if he had a receipt for it. Further, if Kingsmill spent £20 buying a bonnet for Mrs. Andrews, and he as Official Assignee permitted it, the Court had no power to overturn that cost.[12]

This was the nub of the problem, and this is why there had been such an outcry in the newspapers. These comments by Sempill were written down in an affidavit by the clerk, and later placed before the Court in evidence.

The newspaper *Empire* published a Letter to the Editor from Wingham storekeeper, William McLean, who wrote bitingly of the Insolvent Law: "In my unsophisticated simplicity, I always understood that particular institution to be for the protection of Insolvents and benefit of creditors, but now I see it is for the exclusive benefit of Official Assignees and their friends."[13]

McLean included a break-up of income and expenditure, as well as all the affidavits of the Manning residents presented to the Insolvency Court on January 4. Among Sempill's expenses was £48 for the cost of criminal proceedings against William Andrews – *Joseph* was to pay for William's prosecution.

Judgement

On February 1, the Chief Commissioner handed down his judgement, taking the extraordinary step of disallowing the Official Assignee's commission of £150 in its entirety, on the grounds that his expenses were "so reckless and unjustifiable."[14]

Chief Commissioner Purefoy also reduced Kingsmill's wages from £92 to £60; halved Searle's wages from £92 to £46; disallowed all Richards' and Skerrett's expenses; disallowed Sempill's expenses of £48 in prosecuting William Andrews.

The net result of these deductions meant that the Official Assignee now owed £350 to the Insolvent Estate of Joseph Andrews.[15] The Chief Commissioner could not have missed the controversy this insolvency had aroused in the newspapers, and there may have been some re-action to this in his judgement.

Sir William Manning, for Robert Sempill, immediately moved to appeal the decision. While Robert Sempill *knew* the insolvency was fraudulent, he was unable to prove it.

The *Empire* editorialised that the Insolvency Court was "still torturing the unfortunate Mr Joseph Andrews", adding "he had been made to suffer, and is still suffering."[16]

On February 5, 1861, the *Maitland Mercury* gave a single-sentence report: "We are given to understand that the Attorney General has declined to prosecute William Andrews."[17]

Having been cleared, William Andrews took the offensive.

On Monday, August 13, 1861, Reuben Richards, aged twenty-nine, appeared in the District Court at Maitland charged with perjury by William Andrews. The committal hearing had taken place at the Manning Bench in early July.[18]

This was a tit-for-tat prosecution by William Andrews, similar to Richards' prosecution of Isabella Kelly for perjury in January. The perjury allegedly occurred when Richards swore out the warrant for the theft of the two horses, result in William's committal hearing.

Co-incidentally, the Judge in this perjury case was William Purefoy. The former Chief Commissioner in Insolvency, who was very familiar with the Andrews insolvency, had resigned during the first half of 1861 and accepted the appointment as the District Court Judge for the Hunter.[19]

As an indication of the low state of his finances, Richards decided to defend himself rather than employ a solicitor.

William Andrews deposed he had been present at Woodside when Richards attached two horses, which were saddled and bridled and standing near the verandah. As Richards approached the horses, he said to him, "Don't you know those horses are mine, and if you interfere with them, I'd think precious little of kicking you to the lock-up at Wingham".

Joseph Andrews confirmed his brother's evidence. Richards was sitting on his horse when William warned him he owned the horses. Richards attached the two horses later. The horse with the AD brand had belonged to his brother William for years.

Both Ann Andrews and Robert Bryant, a stockman for Joseph Andrews, deposed they were present when William Andrews warned Richards that the horses belonged to him, and that the horse had belonged to William for a number of years.

Robert Mills, a stockman employed by both Robert Andrews and William Andrews, deposed that he commonly rode the second horse without the AD brand, and it belonged to William and Robert Andrews. He always worked with William Andrews at No. 1 Station.

As his own attorney, Reuben Richards cross-examined William Andrews on an entry of £120 in Joseph Andrews' insolvency schedule, which stated Joseph owed William the money as *salary* (the point being that if William worked for Joseph, then legally the horse belonged to Joseph). William answered that he had been in partnership with his brother Robert Andrews for five years, and the £120 was for work done before the end of 1859.

As Richards prepared for his trial, he examined the depositions taken at William Andrews' committal hearing in October 1860, and *found the incriminating letters* – one written by Joseph informing William how to answer questions about the cattle being driven to Maitland, the other by Ann Andrews to son John.

Throughout all the legal wrangling between Joseph Andrews and Robert Sempill, there had never been any reference to these letters – Sempill did not know of their existence. With the dropping of the horse stealing charge against William Andrews, the letters had remained buried in the Crown Law Office, attached to the depositions taken at William Andrews' committal hearing.

Judgement

Until now.

In the courtroom, Richards caught William Andrews off-guard as he produced the letter and him how he got it. William answered that the letter came by post, when he was about to sell a mob of cattle in Maitland. No, he did not believe his brother Joseph had written the letter.

Richards re-called Joseph Andrews. Yes, he wrote the letter. (Joseph must have realised there was little use in denial – it could be easily proved to his hand.)

Reuben Richards called only one witness for his defence. Samuel Steele, the Maitland District Court Bailiff, deposed that he had attached the cattle, which William Andrews had taken to Maitland.

The *Maitland Mercury* reported that Reuben Richards, as his own attorney, addressed the jury, "introducing a great deal of extraneous matter, and revealing very much bad feeling between him and several of the witnesses."[20] The basic problem for Richards was he had no witnesses (other than the Bailiff who contributed little) to defend him – not even a character witness.

After a reply by the Crown Prosecutor, and the summing up from Judge Purefoy, the jury retired, returning twenty minutes later with a verdict of *guilty*.

Judge Purefoy seemed not to have expected this result, and having concerns about it, delayed sentencing. Two days later, Judge Purefoy sentenced Reuben Richards to *twelve months imprisonment* to be served at Maitland Gaol. At the same time the Judge "reserved a point of law"[21] for the consideration of the appeal judges, if Richards appealed the decision.

Did Richards know the horse was William's and took it to spite him? Did the Andrews family, including Ann Andrews and their workers, give false testimony, as had been given in Joseph's insolvency?

Even today with the advantage of hindsight, the key question of *who* owned the horse – Joseph or William – cannot be answered with any certainty. At William Andrews' committal hearing before Magistrate Day, Richards admitted he had seen William riding the horse – a most unlikely admission if he were lying about the ownership of the horse.

This leads to a third possibility: Richards *believed* the horse belonged to Joseph, but the horse, in fact, belonged to William.

From the evidence presented at the trial, it is difficult to see how the jury found Richards guilty *beyond a reasonable doubt*, other than the combination of the number of witnesses supporting William Andrews and Richards' poor performance as his own counsel.

The compromising letters had wide reaching ramifications. Judge William Purefoy must have realised how much he erred in his judgement of Joseph Andrews, in his former position of Chief Commissioner of Insolvency. With his own knowledge of this insolvency (which the jury did not have), he obviously believed the jury had reached the wrong verdict.

Richards' appeal was heard in the Banco Court before the Chief Justice, Sir Alfred Stephen, and Justice Wise, on October 25, with Richards represented by a solicitor on this occasion.[22]

Richards' appeal was upheld on two grounds.

The first was purely technical, in that there were doubts that Richards had been correctly sworn before giving his evidence to Police Magistrate Day at William Andrews' committal hearing. Secondly, even if Richards had been correctly sworn, the Supreme Court Bench ruled that the evidence produced in Court did not sustain a charge of *wilful* perjury, in that there were grounds for Richards to genuinely believe that the horses belonged to Joseph Andrews. The Supreme Court ruled that Reuben Richards ought to have been acquitted at his trial, and ordered his immediate release.

After two and a half months of imprisonment, Reuben Richards walked free from Maitland Prison.

In the Andrews Insolvency, Chief Commissioner MacFarland who replaced William Purefoy, performed his own examination of Sempill's accounts and delivered his ruling on September 18. MacFarland had taken further affidavits and depositions, and as a result, disallowed a further £90 of Sempill's expenses on top of the £350, which former Chief Commissioner Purefoy had disallowed.[23]

⊰ Judgement ⊱

This report only strengthened Robert Sempill's resolve, and in an affidavit to the Court dated October 19, he made a detailed allegation against Joseph Andrews that the Insolvency was fraudulent right from the start.

Many of the allegations Sempill made about Joseph Andrews were quite true, but Sempill also demonstrated an ability to put his own "spin" on events. Sempill's October 19 document, claimed Kingsmill resigned at the end of the cattle drive because he declined "to risk his life"[24] any further. Two years later at another hearing, Sempill admitted Kingsmill had resigned because he was moving to Tamworth for business reasons.[25]

On Reuben Richards' release from prison at the end of October, he visited Sempill and informed him of the existence of the letters. Sempill obtained them from the Crown Law Office, and submitted a new affidavit to the Court on November 7.[26]

Armed with the letters, Sempill was able to outline a very convincing case against Joseph Andrews in an affidavit dated November 7. This affidavit also contained some wild and exaggerated allegations against William Andrews, which were obviously inspired by his arrest for rescuing the horses. For example, Sempill claimed William resisted arrest in Maitland and needed to be restrained by handcuffing, whereas the arresting constable's deposition indicated nothing more than a co-operative arrest.[27]

In another distortion, Sempill maintained that Isabella Mary Kelly had instigated her prosecutions against both Richards and Skerrett only as a favour to Joseph Andrews, in order to divert them from attaching Andrews' assets.

Joseph Andrews wrote an affidavit to the Insolvency Court trying to explain the damning letters (adding a little of his own colouring):[28]

> ... My said brother and the said Cooper and Herkes being quite ignorant of the expressed malicious vindictive intentions of Richards, and ... being also little acquainted with the said facts, and both young men of little experience, it was considered by us that these parties should be advised against being entrapped by the malicious proceedings of Mr Semphill's agent, whom we well knew would not hesitate to seize the stock then in their charge under the pretext that they belonged to my estate.
>
> This was for the purpose partly of informing them, and

partly reminding them of the actual state and disposition of the property referred to, so that when questioned on the subject, as it was expected that they would be in Maitland, they should not be taken by surprise, and that the said Reuben Richards should not thereby obtain an advantage over them.

If I had any other object I say that I could have easily given the same information to my said brother, and the said Cooper and Herkes, before writing the said memorandum, having met them with the same cattle on their way to Maitland on the day previous to my return home, and two days previous to my writing the said memorandum...

All statements contained in the said letter or memorandum are true in substance and fact ...

Joseph Andrews did not explain – nor could he explain – why, if his insolvency was legitimate, he would write such a letter to his brother addressed as "Dear Sir" and then not sign it.

With the other letter found on William (written by wife Ann to son John), Joseph was on firmer ground, claiming it had been written without his knowledge, and "many months prior to the date" of the other letter.

A week later Joseph followed this affidavit with another, which went through Robert Sempill's affidavit of November 7, refuting Sempill's statements point by point.[29]

All in all, it was totally unconvincing.

On February 10, 1862, Justice Wise, on behalf of the Full Bench of the Supreme Court, delivered the Judgement in the Sempill versus Andrews appeal completely *in favour of Robert Sempill*.

Of Joseph's infamous letter to William, Justice Wise stated:[30]

> Such a document written by an insolvent suspected of concealing the true state of his property – his brother, whom he yet addresses as "Dear Sir", and which letter he does not sign, is stamped with such internal evidence of fraud, that it is scarcely possible to imagine a state of circumstances in which an honest man could have written it. ...
>
> As we are satisfied that the insolvency was intended to defeat Mr Richards' debt, so we are convinced that but for the vigorous and determined conduct of the Official Assignee, the object would have been attained.

Judgement

The Judgement went on to restore the wages and expenses paid by Sempill, which had been disallowed by Chief Commissioner Purefoy, excepting those of Kingsmill and Skerrett. Sempill's commission of £150 was restored, but not the expenses of prosecuting William Andrews.

The Court also accepted as true Sempill's accusations that Isabella Mary Kelly had taken out the prosecutions against Richards and Skerrett merely to deflect their efforts in attaching the assets from Joseph Andrews. Sempill genuinely believed this at the time, but would later accept her actions as genuine.[31]

Joseph Andrews could also consider himself lucky not to be have been charged with fraudulent insolvency. The Supreme Court judges seemed to consider the expenses he incurred as sufficient punishment, taking into account that such cases were not always easy to prosecute.

The *Empire* newspaper, which had editorialised and supported Joseph Andrews over the previous twelve months, printed barely more than a paragraph on the Judgement. The opposition newspaper, the *Sydney Morning Herald*, printed the numerous columns of the Judgement in its entirety.

For Robert Sempill it had been a hard fought battle, with the end justifying the means. For Joseph Andrews, who had shown such a lack of judgement in adopting this course, the costs must have astonished him. When the costs of the insolvency were added to his legal costs and the costs of the many trips of witnesses and himself to Sydney, they must have totalled at least £1000 – and all of this trying to avoid the payment of £320 to Reuben Richards, which was eventually paid anyway.

Once again Joseph Andrews had been undone by his own actions – if the Andrews family had not prosecuted Richards for perjury, the letters would have remained buried, and Andrews would most likely have won his case against Sempill. Until these letters were produced, two Chief Commissioners disbelieved Sempill's protestations of a fraudulent insolvency, and a major daily newspaper campaigned in support of Andrews.

There were many supporters like William McLean, who had faith in Joseph Andrews and believed throughout in the legitimacy of the insolvency throughout. One wonders what they thought of the Supreme Court ruling.

The Trials of Isabella Mary Kelly

Joseph Andrews, who once trained to be a Presbyterian Minister, was always regarded in the Manning Valley as a man of honesty and high integrity. But a plethora of lies and false depositions grew from the one basic lie used by Joseph Andrews to counter what he believed to be an injustice against him.

A beaten Joseph Andrews returned to the Manning Valley to lick his wounds.

Part 4
Where the Truth Lies

"He has proved his spite."

— Isabella Mary Kelly

The Trials of Isabella Mary Kelly

31. Petitions

With the fall of the John Robertson Administration, a general election ensued, with the Hastings electorate set down for voting on December 21, 1860.

Joseph Andrews was a notable absentee on Nomination Day, when Henry Flett and Goulburn Panton (from Kempsey) both attended the Port Macquarie court-house at noon to nominate themselves. Scott Ross and Isaac Aaron, both resident in Sydney, were nominated in absentia but were not considered a real chance of election.

Flett addressed the meeting telling electors that he had not intended standing for re-election, but when he saw the names of the other candidates and what they stood for, he felt obliged to come forward. Flett said he had always supported Charles Cowper and would continue to do so. He was a firm supporter of a national system of education, and was against state-aid for churches. He would now vote for the 13th clause of Robertson's Land Bill, which he regretted having voted against previously.

In questions from the floor, Henry Flett said he was against Chinese immigration, and in favour of an elected Upper House (a change from the last elections). Most electors present were very impressed with Flett's address, and after this meeting his re-election was generally expected.[1]

The election resulted in Charles Cowper becoming the new Premier of New South Wales, and the re-election of Henry Flett with 278 votes; Panton received 191 votes, Ross 40 and Aaron 8. In the Manning Valley Flett gained 88% of the vote at Cundletown, 90% at Tinonee, and 52% at Wingham. Panton's vote was highest at the Kempsey end of the electorate.

After the election, the Manning River correspondent for the *Maitland Mercury* commented that only 270 of the 800 registered voters in the Manning Valley actually voted, following a state-wide trend. The correspondent (obviously not a Flett voter himself) noted that "few men dragged from obscurity know how to bear their honours with meekness, and unfortunately for Mr Flett, he is no exception to the rule."[2]

If Joseph Andrews had been a political opponent for Henry Flett, the election may have aroused a lot more interest in the Manning Valley.

On October 22, 1861, the Rev. Dr John Dunmore Lang, a fellow passenger to Sydney with Isabella Mary Kelly in 1834, presented a petition bearing the signatures of 372 persons who were the "Inhabitants of the Manning River and vicinity", to the Legislative Assembly.

The names of the signatories were not printed, and there was no indication of who organised the petition, other than the fact of Dr Lang presenting the petition suggesting it came from Joseph Andrews. (Lang, Andrews' sponsor to the colony, had visited Andrews at Woodside two years previously.)[3]

> That whereas on the 6th day of April, 1855, in the Central Criminal Court, Sydney, Charles Skerrett was convicted of cattle stealing from Isabella Mary Kelly, and was sentenced to ten years' penal servitude, the Judge regretting at the time that he could not give him a longer sentence;
>
> And whereas, in 1859, Skerrett was liberated from Cockatoo, on the recommendation of the Chief Justice – the grounds of said recommendation having never transpired;
>
> And whereas Isabella Mary Kelly was convicted of perjury, in August or October, 1859, the alleged perjury being her oath that the signatures to certain documents produced on Skerrett's trial were forgeries; but was afterwards – on the 15th March, 1860 – and liberated, owing to the recommendation of His Honour the Acting Chief Justice, who tried the case, and who had made himself acquainted with circumstances that warranted this interference;
>
> And whereas Isabella Mary Kelly has been subjected to much injury and annoyance – pecuniary and otherwise – through loss of property, false imprison and loss of character;-
>
> Your Petitioners humbly implore that your Honourable House will cause an inquiry to be made into this case, to the

Petitions

end that the ownership of the property may be finally settled, and if it be found that the said Isabella Mary Kelly is the rightful possessor, that a sufficient recompense may be made to her for the injuries she had sustained by loss of property, character, and false imprisonment, and by which she has been reduced to penury.

It was an unusual show of support for Isabella Mary Kelly, but there can be little doubt the petition was gathered more in a climate of anger against Skerrett for his raids on Alfred Begbie, as well as Skerrett's work with Richards against Joseph Andrews, rather than any indignation felt by the community for Skerrett's treatment of Isabella Kelly. As can be seen, the petition mainly requested the Government to decide *who* owned the cattle and horses, and "sufficient recompense" for Isabella Mary Kelly came a clear second.

On December 6, 1861, David Buchanan, the Member for Morpeth, presented a personal petition from Isabella Mary Kelly to the House, detailing the circumstances of the Kelly/Skerrett case, and seeking redress for her imprisonment as well as protection from Skerrett's raids.[4]

On January 20, Buchanan placed a motion on the agenda of the House to order the printing of the petition, but this agenda item was not reached. In subsequent meetings of the House, newer motions kept pushing Buchanan's motion down the agenda list until this Parliamentary Session came to an end, without the motion having been dealt with.

Kelly printed a single-page pamphlet to support her application, which bore the date of June 28, 1862. The circular gave a brief, basic history of the case, ending with:[5]

> While in gaol I completely lost my health, by sleeping in a cold cell, and by fretting at my unhappy position. My constitution became so completely undermined that I have been subject to fits ever since – a visitation, which I was never subjected to before. I am now a perfect wreck, both in health and pecuniary means, all of which date from my incarceration in Darlinghurst Gaol.
>
> I can prove everything in this circular is true and unvarnished, and many of my friends are fully aware of it.

David Buchanan, the Member for Morpeth and regarded as a

firebrand by the House, was quite willing to promote Isabella Mary Kelly's case for compensation in the House of Assembly, but events overtook him when he was forced to resign from Parliament in September 1862, after unsuccessfully pursuing a libel suit against the *Sydney Morning Herald* causing him great financial difficulty.[6]

Buchanan asked William Allen to take over the promotion of the Isabella Mary Kelly Petition. Born in Ireland in 1812, the son of a farmer, William Allen arrived in Sydney in 1842, and built a successful business from the production of soap and candles, before entering Parliament as the Member for Williams in 1860.[7]

Allen, who knew little of the case at the time, rather reluctantly adopted the cause of Miss Isabella Mary Kelly, and presented the petition to the House. Very capable and dogged, Allen would prove to be an excellent choice on the difficult road ahead.

The petition sketched the history of the case from Skerrett's arrival on the Manning to the release of Isabella Kelly from gaol by Justice Dickinson, before asking for compensation:[8]

> ... That during the time of your Petitioner's imprisonment the said Charles Skerrett, taking the sentence passed upon your Petitioner as a proof of the validity of the forged Bill Of Sale seized and took away a number of cattle which had belonged to your Petitioner, and had been sold by her to Messrs Begbie and Cooper, on the Manning River, in consequence of which Messrs Begbie and Cooper became insolvent, and your Petitioner lost eleven hundred pounds, due to her from them for the said cattle, and interest.
>
> That the said Charles Skerrett was committed on the charge of stealing the cattle sold by your Petitioner to Messrs Begbie and Cooper, in November, one thousand eight hundred and fifty-nine and afterwards, on the nineteenth October, one thousand eight hundred and sixty, was committed on a charge of forgery, for falsely signing your Petitioner's name to the above-mentioned Bill of Sale; but, in both instances the Attorney General declined to prosecute him.
>
> Taking advantage of the impunity allowed him, the said Charles Skerrett has continued to appropriate to his own use your Petitioner's property, which, at the time of her imprisonment, was estimated to be worth fifteen thousand pounds, and by the said Skerrett's long-continued and successful attempts to injure your Petitioner, she has been reduced from comparative affluence to absolute penury.

Petitions

> Your Petitioner therefore humbly prays your Honourable House to take the premises into your consideration, and to grant your Petitioner such protection against further aggression, and such redress, as may seem just to your Honourable House.

The main point being that with the refusal of the Attorney General to prosecute Skerrett on a number of occasions, Kelly had been unable to prevent Skerrett stealing her stock. By refusing to prosecute, the Attorney General gave Skerrett a quasi ownership of the cattle and horses.

But the £15000 was a best-case amount, and included all her legal expenses (lawyers, witnesses, accommodation, travel, etc.,) generally believed, at the time, to be inadvertent expenses and not claimable; the losses she had sustained because her imprisonment and subsequent illness prevented her maintaining her business; the indirect losses sustained when most of her property had been sold off well below its true value. All these losses, Kelly maintained, had been caused by her false imprisonment for perjury.

On September 23, William Allen moved that a Select Committee be appointed to enquire into the matter. Dr Lang seconded the motion, expressing the desire for the Committee to find the facts of the case. Premier Cowper supported the motion, stating that he was puzzled by this difficult case, but if Miss Kelly had been unjustly treated, then it was only right she should receive redress.[9]

The ten members of the Select Committee consisted of William Allen as Chairman, William Arnold, James Cunneen, James Dickson, Henry Flett, William Forster, Joseph Harpur, John Morrice, Augustus Morris and Robert Stewart. William Arnold, the Chairman of the Skerrett Select Committee of 1860, was also included in the motion as a member of this Committee, but did not attend any meetings.

The other Committee members were probably unaware initially that Henry Flett had not declared a conflict of interest – he had been one of the prosecution witnesses whose testimony on the character of Isabella Mary Kelly had helped convict her.

Finding where the truth lies is the mission of any Select Committee, but Henry Flett was not interested in a search for the truth about Isabella Kelly – his mission was to stop her receiving any compensation.

32. The Select Committee

Only three members attended this first meeting, which took place two days later in the Parliamentary Committee rooms, where Allen, Cunneen and Morris discussed the course of action to be taken by the Committee. At no meeting of the Committee were all nine members present.

Isabella Mary Kelly was called before the Committee on October 3, but asked for an adjournment until she could obtain papers from her former solicitor, John Ryan Brenan. On October 22, the examination of Isabella Mary Kelly began in earnest before six Committee members. Most of the Committee, unfamiliar with the events of the case other than what they had read in the papers or the gossip they heard, asked Kelly to give her version of events right from the start. Henry Flett, on the other hand, knew most of the details of the case. Chairman William Allen knew the basics of the story (obviously from consultation with Isabella Kelly) and led the questioning.

As always, Kelly was not a good witness, and sometimes confused Committee members with her answers in this very complex story. She could go off on a tangent to the question asked of her, or confuse events. For example, when asked the name of Skerrett's trial Judge, she answered "Sir John Dickinson", before answering "Sir Alfred Stephen" when the Chairman repeated the question.[1]

Henry Flett asked Isabella Kelly a few innocuous questions, before the first signs of friction between them surfaced with the subject of William Burt, whom she had unsuccessfully sued in the Civil Court in 1858.

Mr Morrice: "What was the result of this trial?"
Miss Kelly: "He offered £100 to my attorney to have done
   with any further proceedings; but I told Mr Dawson that
   I would not accept any such thing."
Chairman Allen: "You consider you should have had £400 or

£500?

Miss Kelly: "Yes"

Mr Flett: "Are you asking for compensation from Mr Burt, too?"

Miss Kelly: "I am asking —"

Mr Flett [interrupting, and completing Kelly's sentence for her]: "Compensation for the losses you have sustained through him – is that one of your grievances, Miss Kelly?"

Miss Kelly: "Not at all. I am not grieving about that. I am stating the circumstances of the case."[2]

The hostility increased when the topic of McPherson charging Kelly with cattle stealing, despite Kelly giving her neighbours notice of the branding.

Mr Stewart: "Were any of the neighbours present?"

Miss Kelly: "No."

Mr Flett: "Will you tell me the names of any two of the parties you gave notice to on that particular day?"

Miss Kelly: "Yes, to Connolly and Mrs. Joseph Andrews, and to McPherson."

Mr Dickson: "Were they verbal notices?"

Miss Kelly: "Verbal to Mrs. Andrews, but written to the others. I sent my stockman over."

…

Chairman Allen: "Is it a very extraordinary thing in the Manning River District for things of that sort to occur in branding time?"

Miss Kelly: "It is quite a common thing. Why, Mr Flett, there, branded four or five of mine."

Chairman Allen: "In mistake?"

Miss Kelly: "In mistake – mistakes are occurring every day."

Chairman Allen: "You have mentioned Mr Flett's name?"

Miss Kelly: "Yes."

Chairman Allen: "How many cattle has he branded by mistake – young cattle of yours – do you suppose?"

Miss Kelly: "I have been informed that he branded at one time, I know, two; and the second time he branded one; and the third time Mr Harkness, and those who informed me of it, said he branded two in the yard at Killawarra."

Chairman Allen: "And he wrote to you about it?"

Miss Kelly: "No."[3]

Kelly had certainly made her point. So much so, Flett asked

the Committee to remove part of Kelly's testimony from the record, presumably where she said Flett had branded her calves mistakenly and had not given her notice of the branding. The Committee asked Kelly to leave the room, while they discussed Flett's motion.[4] After some debate, the motion was defeated.

The Committee resumed its examination of Isabella Kelly, but it was not long before. Flett raised another objection to the answers Kelly was giving. Once again, Kelly left the room while the motion was discussed. This time the Committee acceded to Flett's request, and removed the offending questions and answers.

Isabella Kelly handed in the letter (as well as its post-stamped envelop) written to her by Reuben Richards in 1855 after Skerrett's conviction, in which Richards claimed Skerret issued papers to witnesses with the evidence they should give when called as a witness in his trial. This letter had been excluded as evidence at her own trial. In an attempt to confirm Richards' handwriting, Kelly also handed in a number of letters written by Richards to different people.

Isabella Kelly claimed she had evicted Richards from Mount George.

> Mr Morris: "You accused Richards of having forged the lease?"
>
> Miss Kelly: "I did. He would not produce the papers. They were not impounded. I then took forcible possession of the place, in order to bring him up to show his lease. I took possession of the whole place, and I have got it still.
>
> 'Now,' I said, 'If you can show me your lease, just show it — I take forcible possession.'"[5]

The Richards family moved to Mitchell's Island, further downstream in the Manning River delta.[6]

As the examination continued, Isabella Mary Kelly refused to allow Henry Flett to badger her with his questioning.

> Mr Flett: "One or two questions have suggested themselves in reading from this petition. Did you ever, at any time, ask Mr Faucett to recommend Skerrett as a proper person to be placed on the Commission of Peace [to be made a Magistrate]?"
>
> Miss Kelly: "I did."
>
> Mr Flett: "What reason had you for doing it?"

Miss Kelly: "He told me he had been nine years a Magistrate at Port Phillip, and I thought he was a fit person to be placed in the Commission of Peace."
Mr Flett: "Was that your only reason?"
Miss Kelly: "That was the only reason. I had no knowledge of it. I know that of the Manning River Magistrates there were none of them that understood much, and I thought a clever man like that was a fit and proper person to be placed on the Bench. I did not know his character, but he told me he had been nine years a Magistrate."
Mr Flett: "Was he living at your place at the time?"
Miss Kelly: "He had just come to live there at the time. He had been there a week or so I think. That was in June 1854 — No — I think that was in June 1854. I do not know exactly the month, but it was before I knew anything about him at any rate."
Mr Flett: "It was about April you recommended him?"
Miss Kelly: "It was in or about June."
Mr Flett: "That was about the time he came to your place?"
Miss Kelly: "I cannot say exactly, without referring —"
Mr Flett [interrupting]: "I wish particularly to know that."
Miss Kelly: "Then I cannot tell you."
Mr Flett: "You also said to me, at my own house, that you thought he would make a great acquisition to the Bench?"
Miss Kelly: "I think you make a mistake."
Mr Flett: "I only ask you the question."
Miss Kelly: "I never said that to you. I never told any person until it came out in evidence."
Mr Flett: "I am merely putting the question to you – I shall not say whether you did it or not."
Miss Kelly: "It is not true."[7]

This clever line of questioning by Henry Flett, while allowing Kelly to deny she told Flett about recommending Skerrett as a Magistrate, gave the subliminal message to the rest of the Committee that Kelly was actually lying about it (and being a gentleman, he was not calling her a liar). Otherwise, why ask the question?

Kelly's claim that she never told anyone of her writing to Peter Faucett in 1854, recommending Skerrett to become a Magistrate, is borne out by the fact that it was never mentioned at Skerrett's trial or Kelly's trial or the Select Committee into

Skerrett's petition in 1860. Her vague statement that "it came out in evidence" probably refers to Skerrett's trial for forgery in December 1860, when Peter Faucett appeared as Kelly's barrister, although no mention of it was made in the Court Reports of the trial in the newspapers.

One thing is certain, if either Skerrett or Flett had any knowledge of this recommendation, they would have used it when giving evidence on these previous occasions — and they did not.

The Committee wanted to know how much money Miss Kelly had lost due to her imprisonment, and more particularly the value of her property (meaning her stock as well as her land).

> Mr Flett: "What property had you at the time when you were put in gaol, on the Manning River — you say here £15,000?"
> Miss Kelly: "I was worth that at the time Skerrett first commenced with me. I refused £4,000 for my horses. I wanted £4,500. I dare say you know that."
> Mr Flett: "I know nothing whatever about it. And at what did you value your cattle at the time — I see you sold them to Begbie and Cooper — you valued them at £1,000?"
> Miss Kelly: "I sold them for £1,200."
> Mr Flett: "Was Mount George your property at that time?"
> Miss Kelly: "It was."
> Mr Flett: "Not encumbered in any way?"
> Miss Kelly: "No."
> Mr Flett: "Is it your property now?"
> Miss Kelly: "It is mortgaged."
> Mr Flett: "Is it your property at all now?"
> Miss Kelly: "I suppose it still is. I am living on it."
> Mr Flett: "I wish you to give me an answer."
> Miss Kelly: "I cannot. It is so far my property until it is sold."
> Mr Flett: "Is it your property now?"
> Miss Kelly: "Yes."[8]

If Isabella Kelly's answers on the status of her property in the hands of Lennon & Cape seemed more than a little vague, it only reflected her own uncertainty. The Mount George property was for sale, but the mortgage money would be deducted from the sale price, whatever that price may be. Kelly had returned to the Manning, and resumed residence in the district at Waterview and Mount George.

The Select Committee

Mr Cunneen: "You said in answer to Mr. Forster, that you considered your property to be worth £10,000 at the time of your imprisonment?"

Miss Kelly: "Yes, at the time of my imprisonment."

Mr Cunneen: "Do you mean to say you have sustained a loss of £10,000 or that was merely the value of your property then?"

Miss Kelly: "I wanted to get Mr Dodd's accounts of landed property sold by him in Maitland."

Mr Cunneen: "Have you any idea of what you consider your actual losses on account of having been imprisoned on this occasion?"

Miss Kelly: "As far as my own calculation has gone, I believe firmly that I have lost about £10,000 through my being knocked about, and my property all sacrificed."

Mr Cunneen: "Do you think you have sustained that loss in consequence of transactions you have had with Mr Skerrett as a private individual, or on account of any act of Government officer in mislaying any documents?"

Miss Kelly: "I believe I have lost it through those documents being mislaid."[9]

While claiming a loss of £10000, Isabella Kelly was very short on the detail the Committee wanted. She knew what she was worth before her imprisonment and she knew what she was worth now, but she could not produce *itemised accounts* of her losses.

Kelly rounded off this section of her evidence with the statement, "I have lost my health, which is worse than all."[10] The Committee, on the other hand, seemed only interested to establish her *monetary* losses *while* she was in prison.

William Allen approached the Speaker of the House of Assembly seeking the transcripts of the Skerrett Select Committee of 1860. The House voted 24–10 to release them to the Committee, expressing reluctance.[11]

On Wednesday, October 29, John Ryan Brenan appeared before the Select Committee. Brenan had the unusual connection of defending Skerrett in his 1851 trial for embezzlement and representing Kelly in her prosecutions of Skerrett for cattle stealing in 1855 and forgery in 1860. After going through his evidence, particularly that of the arrest of William Turner and the evidence given by him at Skerrett's trials, Brenan gave his assessment of Kelly's character.

> Mr Brenan: "From the first day I prosecuted Skerrett until now, I have been of the opinion that Miss Kelly was victimised, beyond all doubt. Although Miss Kelly has a rather short and disagreeable temper, yet I always considered her to be a woman of truth, and straightforward and honourable in every respect. I say this, notwithstanding that we fell out about my bill of costs."[12]

Isabella Kelly had taken objection to one of Brenan's bills for services rendered, and refused to pay it. Brenan reacted by gaining a Supreme Court Judgement in his favour in October 1860, ordering Kelly to make payment on this bill. At the same time Brenan continued to represent her. Kelly steadily ignored the Order, and two years later the bill remained unpaid. Yet despite this conflict, Brenan still considered Kelly as a "woman of truth."

The Select Committee examined Jane Brandswait, the married twenty-two year old daughter of Charles Skerrett. In a rather lengthy interview, Jane's most common phrase was "I do not recollect" as Committee members tried to elicit details of the signing of the Bill of Sale by Jane and her sister, Margaret.

At a later date, the Committee obtained a copy of Sir Alfred Stephen's notes on the deposition given by Margaret Skerrett at her father's trial in 1855 as well as her deposition taken at the Bungay Bungay Bench at Skerrett's committal hearing in 1854.

Not only was the Committee struck by the conflicting differences between Margaret's two depositions, but also their differences with the deposition Jane gave before the Committee.[13]

A week later the Committee interviewed the former Attorney General, John Hargrave, who had declined to prosecute a number of cases involving Isabella Kelly, including the Skerrett forgery case. But Hargrave had little to say.

> Mr Hargrave: "... I have no other recollection of the case except that Skerrett called at my office, and wanted to tell me a great deal about the case; but I stopped him, and said I could know nothing about it except what was in the

depositions. Miss Kelly also, I think, called and wanted to tell me her grievances, and I gave her the same answer." [14]

Like his predecessor, John Plunkett, and unlike Sir Alfred Stephen, Attorney General Hargrave had refused to see Skerrett, judging the case purely on depositions. Hargrave said, as a matter of principle, he never gave any reasons for declining to prosecute any case, and he knew of no Attorney General who did – the basic assumption should be that he considered there was insufficient evidence for the prosecution to be successful.

William Allen asked Hargrave about the legal aspects of Kelly's trial where the missing Bill of Sale and Receipt were replaced by copies of them as secondary evidence.

> Chairman Allen: "Did I correctly understand you to state that it was necessary, in a prosecution such as Miss Kelly underwent for perjury based on forgery, that the documents alleged to be forged should be produced?"
>
> Mr Hargrave: "… I cannot conceive of a Judge admitting secondary evidence in an indictment for perjury, in reference to a forged document, which was missing. When a case turns upon a document of this kind, it [the original] ought to be produced." [15]

Yet this was precisely what occurred at Kelly's trial – *copies* of the original documents were used to convict Isabella Kelly.

Mr Peter Faucett, the Member for Yass Plains, followed Hargrave into the Committee room. He was the barrister hired by Kelly to assist prosecute Skerrett in his forgery trial. He was also present at Skerrett's 1855 trial and gave the Committee his impression of that case.

> Mr Faucett: "Yes, it struck me most forcibly, that several of the witnesses brought forward by Skerrett so glaringly contradicted themselves and one another, that I myself had not the slightest doubt they were committing perjury.
>
> There were two or three children – I think two girls, daughters of Skerrett [Margaret and Catherine], that were examined as witnesses in his behalf, and I was at the time, clearly under the impression, from the manner in which they gave their evidence, and the efforts they made to

evade questions put to them on cross-examination, that there was not the slightest doubt they were telling a story that had been prepared beforehand.

I scarcely ever knew a case in which I formed so strong an opinion …"[16]

When asked his opinion of the missing documents, Faucett stated he thought it "dangerous" for any charge of perjury to proceed unless the allegedly forged documents were present in Court. He added that it would be too easy for two people to concoct a perjury case if they did not have to produce the forged documents on which it was based – the writing of the document needed to be compared with the writing of the alleged author.

The Rev Thomas O'Reilly, the Church of England Minister at Port Macquarie at the time Skerrett lived there, deposed he seldom came in contact with his parishioner Charles Skerrett.

Chairman Allen: "What circumstances was he in?"

Rev. O'Reilly: "I cannot pretend to say. I believe he was in very low circumstances indeed when he came down. I am under the impression that he was quite destitute."

Chairman Allen: "What character did he bear?"

Rev. O'Reilly: "Nearly as bad as it is possible for any man to bear. I never heard of a redeeming trait in his character."

Chairman Allen: "You would be surprised, I imagine, to hear that he had at that time £600?"

Rev. O'Reilly: "Of course I cannot pretend to know what the man's circumstances were, but I had no idea he was possessed of any money."[17]

On Wednesday, November 12, the Select Committee examined four witnesses.

The first was the former Attorney General, John Plunkett who had prosecuted Skerrett when convicted of cattle stealing, and believed Skerrett had received a fair trial. The Committee was very tactful and asked no questions, either here or later, about the scandalous allegations made against John Plunkett by Skerrett at his own Select Committee in 1860.

The second witness, Thomas Findley, was almost certainly

The Select Committee

called by Henry Flett, as he led the questioning. Findley deposed that Miss Kelly told Mr. Cameron and himself that Skerrett had bought her cattle. (Kelly confirmed this was true, as at that time she really believed he had – but they were the *only* people she told.)

Findlay was also asked about the character Skerrett and Kelly.

> Mr Forster: "Do you know anything of the character Skerrett bore in the district?"
>
> Mr Findley: "Latterly he did not bear a very good one, but whether it was true or not I could not say. I had no acquaintance with him further than I have said."
>
> …
>
> Mr Flett: "… I will ask you now what sort of character Miss Kelly bore on the river?"
>
> Mr Findley: "I cannot say anything about the lady, for or against. I have always received hospitality from her when I have called. If I went her way and called in, I was entertained. I have been several times to her residence while at Brimbin and Mount George – only once at Mount George."[18]

Findley seemed nothing less than an honest settler, reflecting the general disquiet of the district about Miss Kelly and Skerrett. Adopting the same tactics as Skerrett used against Kelly, Flett was seeking to show four main themes with witnesses:

- Kelly told *many* people she had sold her cattle to Skerrett;
- Kelly had a bad reputation on the Manning;
- Skerrett was of good character.
- Kelly had never possessed much in the way of assets.

If this last proposition were true, Kelly would have lost very little when sent to gaol. With these four themes in mind, Flett hoped to lead the Committee to one final conclusion:

- Isabella Kelly did not deserve to receive *any* compensation.

Phillip Dew, probably appearing at Flett's instigation as well, repeated the allegations he had made against Kelly at the 1855 trial and the 1859 trial, with some embellishment. Kelly told him, in June 1854, she had sold her cattle to Skerrett. He had not asked to buy her cattle, she had just volunteered the information to him. As a result of this conversation with her, he bought five bullocks and a horse from Skerrett. But after the disturbance between Kelly and Skerrett, she took them back.

Questioned by Flett, Dew said he had known Skerrett for some time, and he was not aware of anything bad in Skerrett's character. He believed Skerrett was possessed of money, as he had seen £5, £10 and £20 notes in his wallet. He had been seen Skerrett with £200 worth of horses. Miss Kelly had lost only one horse and a few cattle to Skerrett. Miss Kelly sold between 500 and 700 cattle to Mr Begbie, but Begbie never obtained half that number.

Dew said he was an excellent judge of the value of livestock, and Kelly had vastly overvalued her property.

> Mr Flett: "Will you put a value on her horses, cattle, Mount George, and other property?"
> Mr Dew: "I think Miss Kelly would have made a good sale if she had sold all she has on the Manning for £1,500."
> Mr Flett: "Have you ever told that to Miss Kelly herself?"
> Mr Dew: "Yes, I told her a few days before she left, when she was at my house. I saw a paper there where she had put down £15,000."
> Mr Flett: "Miss Kelly, you say, was at your house?"
> Mr Dew: "Yes, she called on Sunday and left on Tuesday."
> Mr Flett: "How long is that ago?"
> Mr Dew: "About three weeks ago; I paid very little attention to what she said."
> ...
> Mr Flett: "Did she positively ask you to value her property at £15,000?"
> Mr Dew: "Yes. I told her I would scorn the very idea of seeing such a thing in print."[19]

By his questioning, Henry Flett seemed to be already aware of this highly implausible story of Kelly visiting Dew seeking his support in the evaluation of her assets.

Why would Kelly expect any support from a man who had given so much evidence against her in both Skerrett's trial and her own trial? It is not conceivable she would even visit his home, let alone stay there for three days.

> Mr Morrice: "Were you examined in both cases, Miss Kelly's and Skerrett's?"
> Mr Dew: "Skerrett subpoenaed me at the time of his trial when he was convicted, but I did not attend."

Mr Morrice: "Why?"
Mr Dew: "I did not."
Mr Morrice: "What was running in your mind that induced you not to attend?"
Mr Dew: "I thought by his selling the cattle to me I had lost enough, without running about after his business any more. I think that was a very good reason."[20]

This was a lie – Dew *did* give evidence at Skerrett's trial in 1854. Perhaps Dew was trying to distance himself from Skerrett, in an effort to make his attacks on Kelly appear more credible.

Dew finished his interview by discrediting Kelly's most prestigious horse, Calendar.

Chairman Allen: "Do you know the name of a horse called Calendar?"
Mr Dew: "I know Calendar very well."
Chairman Allen: "What sort of horse is Calendar?"
Mr Dew: "I set him down as not worth anything."
Chairman Allen: "Is he broken down?"
Mr Dew: "He is not the stamp of a horse – he is hip-down; in short, he is a horse that no one except Miss Kelly would allow to run with mares."[21]

This was certainly not the opinion of other settlers in the Valley. Settler George Hill said, "Miss Kelly had a celebrated horse named 'Calendar' and in my boyhood days a horse tracing his descent from 'Calendar' was always highly prized." Another settler, Robert Broomfield, wrote, "A horse of hers – Calendar – had a big reputation from a stud standpoint."[22]

It was clear Philip Dew was not only hostile to Isabella Kelly, but also prepared to give false witness against her.

Joseph Andrews, the fourth witness of the day, gave his evidence about Skerrett and Kelly much as he had on the numerous previous occasions.

Andrews handed a letter to the Committee, dated at "Woodside" from Maria Cooper, complaining that Miss Kelly had driven her son-in-law into insolvency by her lies to him.

Henry Flett questioned Andrews about aspects of the Begbie cattle sale, with both coming to the conclusion Kelly had not actually lost £1000 in this deal – she could have accepted Begbie's buy-back offer of £300 with the cattle being returned to her.[23]

The Trials of Isabella Mary Kelly

Henry Flett reminded an exasperated Joseph Andrews of his past relationship with Miss Kelly, forcing him to admit he had once said he would not believe her under oath.

The examination concluded with Flett and Andrews agreeing that there had been an extraordinary length of time – three months – between the day Kelly found out Skerrett had not bought her cattle and the day she charged him with cattle stealing. Neither took into account their benefit of hindsight, and that Kelly could have no suspicion Skerrett was about to claim ownership of her cattle by producing forged documents.

On November 19, a further three witnesses were questioned by the Select Committee.

Charles Langley came from the newly insolvent firm of Rich, Langley and Butchart. Langley produced a document which showed Isabella Kelly had repaid her lien (secured loan) with his firm on November 10th, 1854.

A basic part of Skerrett's defence had been that the cattle had not been in the hands of Langley's firm in June 1854 when he claimed to have bought the cattle from Kelly. This evidence by Langley was a vital confirmation of what Kelly had always professed, the cattle *were* in the hands of Rich, Langley and Butchart in June 1854, but no one knew anything about the lien which prevented such a sale.

Skerrett had even claimed to have a letter from this firm stating the cattle were not in the firm's hands during this period. Henry Flett went in hard on Langley.

> Mr Flett: "Do you recollect writing a letter to Skerrett dated 22nd November, stating that, to the best of your belief, Miss Kelly had taken the cattle out of your hands for sale about April or May in the same year?"
> Mr Langley: "I never did."
> Mr Flett: "You never wrote such a letter?"
> Mr Langley: "I never wrote such a letter."
> Mr Flett: "You had better say you do not recollect."
> Mr Langley: "It may have been written by someone else in the office – I never wrote it."[24]

By giving a date to the alleged letter, and by telling Langley

The Select Committee

to use the phrase "do not recollect" (Langley could avoid committing perjury without answering the question), Flett was calling Langley a liar. Flett could have presented any such letter to the Committee, but did not.

Flett pursued the statements by Kelly that she believed Skerrett bought her cattle without Skerrett showing her any documentation to that effect.

> Mr Flett: "From your knowledge of Miss Kelly, do you think, judging by her antecedents, that she is a woman likely to allow any man to do such a thing with her stock?"
>
> Mr Langley: "Suppose you were Miss Kelly (excuse my impertinence for making that remark), and a man came and represented to you that he had made arrangements with your agents, and came up as an accredited purchaser, would you not take notice of him?"
>
> Mr Flett: "Not unless he brought a document from my agents, I would not allow him to sell a beast."
>
> Mr Langley: "He might sell them on her account, until she saw her agents and arranged the matter."
>
> Mr Flett: "Five months is a long time."
>
> Mr Langley: "Yes."[25]

The second witness of the day was John Dawson, the occasional solicitor of Miss Kelly over many years. Dawson, as the solicitor representing Skerrett when he was convicted in 1855, had to be careful he gave ethical answers to the Committee's questions without compromising any knowledge gained from Skerrett when defending him.

Dawson told the Committee that up to a certain point he had believed in Skerrett's innocence, but by the end of the trial he thought "the conviction was just".[26]

The Chairman handed Dawson the Bill of Sale and the Receipt to examine. Dawson said he had once believed Kelly's signatures on them were authentic, but he no longer held that belief – not so much from the signatures themselves, but from Skerrett's trial.

Another of Kelly's solicitors, William Mullen, was the third witness of the day. He told the Committee of his staying at the house of Reuben Richards and being shown *three* copies of a lease purportedly signed by Isabella Mary Kelly, each with the

337

same date and each with different content in the body of the document. He said he knew Kelly's signature well, and he did not believe she had signed the leases.

> Chairman Allen: "Do you know anything of the character of Skerrett?"
>
> Mr Mullen: "From the reputation of the man I believe him to be the greatest blackguard in the country – from what I know of him from people on the Manning, and up and down."
>
> Chairman Allen: "By common repute?"
>
> Mr Mullen: "By common reputation."
>
> Mr Flett: "Where did you hear that, sir – was it on the Manning?"
>
> Mr Mullen: "Yes, and at Port Macquarie. The fact of the matter is, there was hardly anything else talked about for twelve months."[27]

The interview concluded with Mullen telling the Committee that Reuben Richards had been convicted of perjury in the previous year and sent to prison for twelve months, but was released from prison after two months. Further, Richards had been found guilty by the jury but released on a "point of law"(a technicality).

Henry Flett vainly tried to promulgate a false story for Richards' release from prison: not even the Andrews family believed the evidence used to convict Richards.

> Mr Flett: "Did it not come to your knowledge afterwards that the evidence then given against Richards was not believed by the Andrews family?"
>
> Mr Mullen: "Certainly not."
>
> Mr Flett: "And that it was on that ground he was liberated?"
>
> Mr Mullen: "Certainly not. I could not have heard that which was not fact. I heard the evidence in Court."
>
> Mr Flett: "I knew the whole case before it went to Maitland."
>
> Mr Mullen: "You knew more than I did. I only know what I heard in Court. I was unexpectedly called as a witness."[28]

Mullen had built up a large legal practice, and was highly respected. The Committee was greatly impressed with Mullen's evidence, and it would become the cornerstone of their doubts about the validity the Mount George lease.

The Select Committee

On Wednesday, November 26, Laurence Spyer and John Smithers, jurors from the Richards/Andrews trial, appeared before the Committee. Henry Flett failed to attend this Committee meeting although he summoned these two witnesses. Spyer returned again on the Friday, but again Flett was absent. Examined in Flett's absence, both jurors were of the opinion, in giving their verdict to Richards, that the Richards lease was genuine, but if they had heard the evidence of Mr Mullen during that trial, they may have been swayed by it.

On another day, with Flett present and leading the questioning, Henry Selby, another Juror from the Richards/Andrews trial, maintained that the Richards lease was genuine and could not be swayed to any other point of view. When Mr Stewart referred to the lease as "this forgery"[29], Selby corrected him. If he had known of Mullen's evidence, Selby said, it would not have changed his opinion that Kelly wrote the lease.

Flett had been diverted from the Select Committee by the need to appear as the defendant in a civil court case, in which the Rev Thomas Watt charged Flett with libel and slander, seeking damages up to £2000.

Earlier in the year, Flett had gone to the Post Office Hotel, where he often stayed when in Sydney. The publican told him of an inebriated man named Watt, returning to the Hotel after midnight with a woman so drunk she could hardly stand. Watt claimed the woman as his wife, but the publican believed her to be a prostitute.[30]

From the description of the man, Flett believed that it was the Rev Thomas Watt, who had recently vacated a £150 per year position on the Manning River, and applied for a £300 position in the Shoalhaven district. Flett told a number of people of the minister's behaviour, and wrote to the Presbyterian Synod about the matter, causing the minister to be passed over for the appointment.

In a trial lasting three full days, the jury of twelve men found for Henry Flett, when it was proved beyond all doubt that the minister lied, and had in fact been the man at the Post Office Hotel. At the trial's conclusion, Justice Wise asked court officials to arrest Watt and charge him with perjury.

Several weeks later, Rev. Watt was convicted of perjury and sentenced by Sir Alfred Stephen to five years gaol on the roads. In handing down the sentence, Sir Alfred remarked on the rising prevalence of perjury in current law courts, and of the difficulty of securing successful prosecutions, mentioning two recent cases where he believed enough evidence had been provided to secure a conviction, but the juries had found the men innocent.[31]

Sir Alfred made no mention of the Isabella Mary Kelly case, where a woman innocent of perjury had been found guilty.

On December 10, 1862, the Select Committee examined Robert Sempill, the Official Assignee in the insolvencies of Joseph Andrews and Charles Skerrett. In answer to Flett's questions, Sempill stated that he knew of nothing adversely affecting Skerrett's character. Sempill went through the Richards/Andrews case as well as the Skerrett insolvency.

What gained more of the Committee's attention was the fact that Sempill had once worked in the office of the Chief Justice as a legal clerk to Sir Alfred Stephen. Sempill found it difficult to believe that the missing documents could have remained missing so long in the drawer in the Banco Court, as they had been regularly cleaned out in his time there.

The next day, in a final examination of Isabella Mary Kelly, the Committee wanted to determine the amount of her losses caused by her imprisonment. Kelly handed the Committee letters written to her by Joseph Andrews while she was still in Darlinghurst Gaol, to show she had "been robbed"[32] during her imprisonment and subsequent ill health.

Kelly deposed that while imprisoned, she "had a severe attack of bronchitis" and she "was subject to fits ever since" her release.[33] These were certainly not fits as the word would imply in modern language, but more likely bronchial or asthmatic attacks.

Kelly stated that when she returned to the Manning, she found her property destroyed and everyone who had had a chance to rob her, did so. She tried to take out a summons against Reuben Richards for the perjury of claiming the Mount George lease to be genuine, but none of the Magistrates there would grant her a summons – Mr Hill, Mr Flett and Mr Croaker all refused her. They told her that, even if they granted the summons, the Attorney General would refuse to file a bill on it.

She sold the cattle and Waterview to Mr Begbie for £1200, but Begbie was not to receive the title deeds to Waterview until complete payment had been made. She thought she had about 600 or 700 head of cattle with a minimum of 500 head. Begbie was anxious to make the purchase from her. Begbie took 380 head from Brimbin and about 200 head from Mount George, and there were about 100 head at Waterview.

Kelly claimed she was worth £15000 and had lost £10000, but seemed carried away when she included the burning down of her house (which happened in 1851, long before these events). The Chairman corrected her, saying this event had no bearing on her compensation claim. Not always clear in her meaning, Kelly further explained that with the rebuilding of her cottage in 1854, just before Skerrett was gaoled, she had refurbished the new cottage replacing the many items burned, and consequently knew she was worth £15000 at the time.

She complained of paying large legal fees to lawyers, and the expenses of witnesses, which she paid three times over for one trial, because of Court postponements.

Kelly claimed a number of people went to the local Court and gained orders to seize her property for sale to pay alleged debts she owed them. A man named Mangan seized for £50. The A. A. Company seized for the unpaid rent of her Gangat lease. A shepherd seized for £4, and all her expensive furniture sold for only £13 to pay him.

Thirty-eight horses had been seized and sold for £46, and this included a foal she would not have sold for less than £20. These horses were bought by neighbours including Joseph Andrews. Another man bought two of these horses and gave them back to her afterwards.

She could not give the Committee itemised details, Kelly said, because her account book her journal and her stud book had been stolen from her house while she was in gaol, but she did have some papers and bills she could show them. The offer of £4000 to sell her horses had been in 1855. When she went to gaol, in 1859, she valued the horses at £6000 despite horse prices not being as high.

Mr Cunneen: "During how long a time after you were released from prison were you incapacitated by sickness from attending to your business?"

Miss Kelly: "During four or five months."

Mr Cunneen: "Can you prove that during the five months you were imprisoned you suffered any special loss?"

Miss Kelly: "My losses all occurred at that time."

Mr Cunneen: "What was your loss during that time – losses occasioned by your not being able to attend to your business?"

Miss Kelly: "About £3000, and since then I have been living upon what means I had by me. I had money in the bank, both at Maitland and Sydney, and since then I have spent it all. Altogether my losses have amounted to quite £10000."

Mr Cunneen: "I wish you to perfectly understand the question – what I require is, that you will take into consideration no losses that you have sustained before or after your imprisonment, but that you will confine yourself strictly to an estimate of the losses experienced during the time you were in gaol – during the five months and a fortnight – you surely could not have lost £10000 in that time?"

Miss Kelly: "I am sure that, at the very least, I have lost £7000."

Mr Cunneen: "During the time you were imprisoned?"

Miss Kelly: "I could not say that, but I know that all my losses either occurred during the time I was incarcerated, or were caused by that incarceration."

Mr Cunneen: "Can you give the Committee any calculation to show how you make out that these losses were sustained during that time?"

Miss Kelly: "I have nothing on which to make them. All my books were taken away."

Mr Cunneen: "Have you made no such calculation?"

Miss Kelly: "I have not done so."

Mr Cunneen: "How long does this account that you have laid before the Committee extend over?"

Miss Kelly: "During 1860. I was for twelve months unable to attend to my business, what with the trial and the imprisonment, and my subsequent illness. And then when I recovered my health, I became subject to fits. I am sometimes for weeks after one of these fits unable to attend to business."

...

Mr Cunneen: "But without referring to papers, can you point out in the same way as you have done with respect to the cattle, any other special loss sustained in consequence of your imprisonment?"

Miss Kelly: "I am not competent to make such a statement. I have bought up with me my accounts of everything that has been sold, and hoped that the Committee would look over them."

Mr Cunneen: "It must be evident to you that the Committee cannot connect these accounts with any losses you have sustained, and it is for that reason that I would wish you to particularize any such loss beyond the cattle mentioned in your petition."

Miss Kelly: "I cannot do so in any other way than by putting these accounts before you."[34]

The Committee was demanding to know her actual monetary losses *while she was in prison*, rather than the losses *caused* by the incarceration. Further she was unable to produce itemised accounts of such.

As the examination neared its end, Flett accused Kelly of lying.

Mr Flett: "You said that Newman seized your horses and sold them?"

Miss Kelly: "Yes."

Mr Flett: "Now did you not drive them into Maitland yourself, and have them sold on your own account?"

Miss Kelly: "No they were seized and sold by Thurlow, through his agent."

Mr Flett: "I say they were not seized."

Miss Kelly: "You are mistaken. They were ordered to be seized and sold by Mr Thurlow."

Mr Flett: "He could not do it."

Miss Kelly: "He did. He sued me in the Supreme Court and got judgement against me, and ordered them to be sold in execution. He wrote to Mr Dodds in Maitland, and directed their sale."[35]

The Trials of Isabella Mary Kelly

The next day, December 12, the final two witnesses appeared. Stephen Brown was the solicitor representing William Burt when Kelly took civil proceeding against Burt concerning a shipment of horses to Calcutta. Brown gave an outline of the case, stating that it revolved around "two oaths against one" – Burt and his brother's oaths against Kelly's oath.

Henry Flett had summoned the last witness, William Cape of the firm Lennon & Cape. Flett began with a question, which would be termed (in modern courts) as leading the witness.

> Mr Flett: "Miss Kelly stated here yesterday, that during the time that her stock was under the management of your superintendent they were completely destroyed and lost by mismanagement – that the sheep were sold at half their price – that the lambs were killed so that the ewes might be fattened, driven to market, and sold – that her horses were sold – and that, in fact, the whole estate was wracked and ruined during the time she was in gaol – have you any knowledge of these facts?"
>
> Mr Cape: "None whatever, except for the fact of certain parties in the neighbourhood throwing every impediment in the way of our overseer, to prevent him from collecting her property and selling it. There is no doubt it did not raise so good a price as if she had been there to look after it herself. I never heard of the lambs being killed."[36]

Cape said his firm as trustees had spent over £900 in recovering Kelly's debt of £320. If Kelly had control of Mount George at the time she would have saved the costs of the superintendent – perhaps some other costs as well. Miss Kelly appeared to be in "affluent circumstances" when she borrowed the money. They still had her unsold property in their hands.

The last Select Committee meeting was held on Tuesday, December 16, with only four members attending – Allen, Flett, Harpur and Stewart. Chairman Allen produced a draft report, which he had written, and asked the Committee to read it.

Mr Stewart apparently left before the end of the meeting,

The Select Committee

leaving only three Committee members. Stewart later said that only a few members attended this final Committee meeting as there had been many other committee meetings on at the same time, all trying to complete their business before the upcoming election.

Harpur moved that Allen's draft be adopted as the Report of the Committee.

Flett voted against it.

Allen used his casting vote as Chairman to support the motion. The draft became the Report of the Select Committee by two votes to one.[37]

Two days later, William Allen presented the Report to the House of Assembly, together with the transcripts of their examination of witnesses, the documents appended, and the minutes of their meetings. The House ordered that they be accepted and printed.

In the Report, Allen recorded the circumstances under which Skerrett went to Brimbin and was imprisoned for cattle stealing, with the Bill of Sale and Receipts documents declared as forgeries by the jury. The Report then went through the release of Skerrett from gaol, the conviction of Miss Kelly for forgery, and the "conflicting and contradictory nature of the evidence given" by Margaret and Jane Skerrett

The Report outlined the Kelly/Burt trial and the Richards/Andrews trial. The Committee had interviewed three of the four jurymen in latter trial, two of whom said they would probably have changed their decision if they had heard William Mullen's evidence. The fourth, Mark Spence, was due to appear on the last day but was unable to attend. Miss Kelly had since taken possession of the paddock, without objection from Richards. As a result the "Committee are of opinion, that neither of these cases invalidates Miss Kelly's claim for compensation."

The Report valued Miss Kelly's assets at the time of Skerrett's release at £10350 (with the break-up being: stock animals – £1200; Begbie & Cooper – £1150; Horses – £6000; the Mount George property – £2000). No consideration was given to her Maitland properties, as they did not sustain losses.

The Committee formed three main opinions:
• The Bill of Sale and Receipt were forgeries.

- Their loss before Kelly's trial had seriously prejudiced her defence.
- Sir Alfred, in giving his evidence at the trial, had misled the jury (this was a technicality).[38]

The Committee recommended the House accept Miss Kelly's claim to compensation was valid. In deciding how much compensation Miss Kelly should be awarded, the House should take into consideration:

- The money she had lost as a result of her unjust conviction
- Her loss of health and liberty.
- The injury sustained to her reputation.

Members now had the opportunity to peruse the documents before the case came before the House of Assembly for consideration.

33. Question 843

The nine-page Report of the Select Committee into the Petition of Isabella Mary Kelly was printed in its entirety in *Empire* on January 15, 1863, and followed up five days later with an editorial.

Empire gave a synopsis of the entire case, before referencing two trials. In the Kelly/Burt trial where "there was no written evidence; the statements were contradictory; and the jury gave a verdict for the defendant",[1] *Empire* said it would not comment. But in the Richards/Andrews case for slander, where Miss Kelly had been called as a witness and disbelieved by the jury *Empire* said, "the evidence laid before the committee proves beyond all doubt that the lease was a forgery".

In conclusion, *Empire* stated:

Miss Kelly has proved her case.

We have carefully gone through the voluminous evidence published by the committee. We consider it overwhelming. There is no doubt in our minds but that Miss Kelly has been victimised and ruined; and that her ruin is owing to the rascality of Skerrett backed up by the blunders of our legal authorities.

Her trial and conviction for perjury was a scandal to the administration of justice. She has a right to claim compensation from the country. …

And while we assert this, we cannot forbear alluding to the part taken by Sir Alfred Stephen in this case. We should like to know whether it is usual for an English judge to descend to personal communication with the outcasts of the law?

Is it usual with our Chief Justice to give morning sittings to unsatisfied felons, and to allow himself to be earwigged by every artful scoundrel?

If it is not usual, what merits did he see in Skerrett's case, that could induce him to so forget himself?

The Trials of Isabella Mary Kelly

The *Maitland Mercury* printed the Report on January 24, 1863, but without an editorial. Neither the Report nor editorial comment appeared in the *Sydney Morning Herald*.

Empire may have led Isabella Mary Kelly to believe she was almost past the winning post, but for Henry Flett the race was far from over.

Rev Dr Lang   Thomas Garrett

On June 26, 1863, William Allen placed notice of a motion to bring the Select Committee Report on Miss Isabella Mary Kelly before the House for debate on June 30, 1863. But Allen failed to attend the House on that day, and his motion lapsed. On the same day, Henry Flett placed his own notice of motion about Isabella Mary Kelly on the agenda.[2]

The next day, Henry Flett rose in the House of Assembly and moved that the Report of the Select Committee into the petition of Miss Isabella Mary Kelly be referred to a *new* Select Committee for consideration.[3] He suggested that the same Members should form this new Committee with the exception of Mr Dickson, who should be replaced by the Member for Monaro, Mr Garrett.[4] (Dickson had only attended one meeting.)

Last December, when the Parliamentary session drew to a close, Flett said in speaking to his motion, he still had more evi-

Question 843

dence to bring before the Committee. At the same time he had a case pending before the Supreme Court and was unable to attend some meetings and examine his witnesses. He intended to give personal evidence, as well as documentary evidence. The Report from the last Committee had only been accepted by the Committee on the casting vote of the Chairman, as there were only two other members present.

Mr Allen rose and objected. He thought it most extraordinary that another Committee should be set up. He had undertaken the case without any previous acquaintance with Miss Kelly, and warned Miss Kelly that if her allegations were not borne out by the evidence presented to the Committee, he would abandon the case. The recommendations of the Report were based on evidence. All the necessary evidence had been obtained, and another Committee was unnecessary.

Committee member Morris supported Mr Allen. He could see no reason for another Committee. More than half the witnesses brought before the Committee were considered to be unsympathetic to Miss Kelly, yet the evidence as a whole was not adverse to her. This indicated justice had been done.

Mr Garrett rose and supported Mr Flett, stating he had read the Report and believed that a large sum of money was to be asked in compensation. Consequently it was in the public interest that the House listen to those members wanting another Committee. It was well known that petitions were being gathered in the Manning district seeking further enquiry.

Quite a number of Members then rose to support Flett's motion. The House roundly condemned Mr Dalgleish when he referred to the actions of the Chief Justice as "criminal negligence" leading him to retract the slur. Mr Harpur was satisfied that the documents in the case had been forged, but did not object to a new Committee.

In his right of reply as mover of the motion, Mr Flett stated he would not have made this motion if he did not have fresh evidence to present to the Committee. The Report was based on the unsupported evidence given by Miss Kelly. Some of the witnesses had been examined in his absence.

The motion was put to the House and carried.[5]

This was unprecedented.

The Trials of Isabella Mary Kelly

Effectively, this would be the *third* Select Committee to enquire into these matters – the Skerrett Select Committee of 1860, the Kelly Select Committee of 1862 and now the Kelly Select Committee of 1863.

Garrett seemed to touch a nerve with many Members of the House with his claim of a large amount of compensation being sought. While the Report stated that Kelly had losses of £10000, members would be very loath to award her such a high amount of compensation. Yet a precedent had been set by the House of Commons in England, when they voted William Barber compensation of £5000 in 1859 for wrongful imprisonment on a perjury charge.

Thomas Garrett, the Member for Monaro, joined the new Select Committee at their first meeting, two days later on Friday, July 3, under the chairmanship of William Allen. Garrett was a youthful thirty-two years of age, and at the start of a long and distinguished political career.[6]

Flett and Garrett were friends, and whenever they were in Sydney for Parliamentary sessions, they would take lodgings together. Having been nominated by Flett, Garrett completely supported Flett both in the questioning of witnesses and in the Committee voting throughout the Committee meetings of 1863.

Garrett seemed to genuinely believe what Flett told him about Kelly.

The first of Flett's witnesses for the 1863 Kelly Select Committee was Robert Abbott, the solicitor for Reuben Richards. Abbott admitted that at one stage the Richards/Andrews trial had been unlikely to proceed because of Richards's lack of funds, but Abbott had pushed on with a firm belief of winning the case.

As requested by Flett, Abbott produced the Mount George lease, but stated he could not let it out of his possession, as his "client's liberty might be at stake." Abbott produced a number of documents, which had been presented at the Richards/Andrews trial, including a receipt, bearing the date September 19, 1859 (the same date as the allegedly forged lease) for the rent of the cottage Richards had leased from Kelly in 1857. Kelly claimed Richards had never paid any rent, and that he forged this receipt also.

Abbott was very keen to defend his client Richards, and professed no doubt that the Mount George lease was a genuine document. The Committee examined these documents and discussed handwriting.

Garrett knew about the way Kelly generally misspelled Richards' first name as "Ruben" rather than "Reuben", and that the lease contained the spelling of "Ruben". (Thomas Garrett could only have known of this small detail through Henry Flett. Throughout this hearing, Garrett was consistently used by Flett in this way – as the second prong of his attack on her.)

Answering Garrett's questions, Abbott argued that as this misspelling was in the Mount George lease, it confirmed Miss Kelly had written the lease.

Allen led the counter argument.

> Chairman Allen: "Supposing a person were going to forge a lease, and the person upon whom he was going to forge had this peculiarity, would he not write the lease in the similitude of the person upon whom he was going to forge?"
>
> Mr Abbott: "It would depend upon his ability. I do not think Richards had enough sense to do it."
>
> Chairman Allen: "I merely ask you as to the likelihood, if a person were going to forge the writing of another, of his spelling according to a peculiar style of the person whose writing he imitated?"
>
> Mr Abbott: "If there were any marked peculiarity in the spelling, and he were a clever forger, he would adopt it."[7]

The subject of Reuben Richards had been raised many times during these hearings, but Robert Abbott was the only person to suggest he was dim-witted.

Cunneen asked Abbott about the integrity of fellow solicitor William Mullen (who told the Committee of Richards having three copies of the lease), forcing Abbott to show his bias towards Kelly.

> Mr Cunneen: "He [Mullen] is a man who stands high in his profession?"
>
> Mr Abbott: "He has a large business in Maitland."
>
> Mr Cunneen: "You believe his statement there as to Richards

producing three leases for the same property, dated the same day?"

Mr Abbott: "I do not believe Mr Mullen would willingly tell — in fact I do not think I am justified in giving an opinion as to Mr Mullen's veracity. I do not think I should be asked such a question."

Mr Cunneen: "Do you think it a likely thing that Miss Kelly would sign three leases of this property, bearing date the same day?"

Mr Abbott: "I think Miss Kelly would do anything in carrying out a plot she had formed. That is my opinion. Of course it is merely an opinion."

...

Mr Cunneen: "As a professional gentleman, and from your experience as such, is it usual for an individual to sign three leases, bearing the same, for the same property?"

Mr Abbott: "Two are always signed."

Mr Cunneen: "Did you ever know an instance of a person sign three leases for the same property, bearing the same date?"

Mr Abbott: "No, I never did."[8]

After Abbott had evaded answering the question, a persistent Cunneen had pushed him into a corner, compelling the admission — albeit indirectly — that there could be no *legal* reason for Richards to have three signed copies of the lease.

As the examination drew to a close, a statement by Abbott stunned the Chairman.

Chairman Allen: "Was there any other document produced at the trial by him?"

Mr Abbott: "Yes, I think there were fifty documents."

Chairman Allen: "On your side [of the case]?"

Mr Abbott: "Yes."

Chairman Allen: "Where are these?"

Mr Abbott: "I have them."

Chairman Allen: "Have you them present?"

Mr Abbott: "*No, I brought all I was told by Mr Flett.*" [author's emphasis]

Chairman Allen: "All that Mr Flett told you?"

Mr Abbott: "Yes."

Chairman Allen: "And you kept back what he told you not to bring?"

Mr Abbott: "I did not ..."[9]

Question 843

Abbott blundered. Flett had asked Abbott to bring specific papers intended to harm Kelly's case, and, by implication, not to bring those that might assist her cause. Here was confirmation to the Committee (probably not needed by now) that Henry Flett was not interested in where the truth lay, but wanted only to crush any claim for compensation by Isabella Kelly.

Under questioning, Abbott also admitted that he had been in frequent consultation with Henry Flett as he prepared for the Richards/Andrews trial, confirming Flett's major contribution to Richards' win.

Chairman William Allen said Flett and Garrett wanted to produce the Mount George lease as evidence against Miss Kelly, but at the same time wanted to retain legal possession of it and prevent Miss Kelly from obtaining it, as they knew she would immediately charge Richards with forgery.

Allen told them, if the Mount George lease were produced, he would impound it.

When Abbott produced the lease, the clerk to the Select Committee retained it, with strict instructions from Allen not to return it to Abbott. Yet despite this directive, the clerk gave Abbott the lease, when Abbott threatened him with legal action unless he did so.[10]

Allen applied to the Speaker of the House of Assembly to determine if the Committee was legally entitled to impound the lease, but was informed by the Speaker that it was not. Allen said the lease was "as barefaced a forgery as was ever attempted to be palmed off on intelligent company."[11]

When Robert Abbott returned to the Committee a week later, he handed in a copy of the Judge's notes in the Richards/Andrews case, but was highly indignant that the clerk had refused initially to give him the lease, and accused Chairman Allen of a "breach of faith."[12] As Abbott failed to retract the accusation, the Committee refused to examine him any further, and he departed in a huff.

It was clear now that William Allen was in a completely opposing camp to Flett and Garrett, with the other members of the Committee spread somewhere in between them.

The Trials of Isabella Mary Kelly

Mark Spence, a Pitt Street draper, was the fourth member of the four-man jury in the Richards/Andrews trial to be interviewed. He had been summoned by Flett to be examined at the last meeting of the 1862 Select Committee, but was unable to attend.

With the 1862 Select Committee reporting that two out three jurymen would have changed their verdict if they had heard the evidence of William Mullen at the trial, Flett was keen for Spence to counter this evidence.

Juror Spence said he had no doubt Miss Kelly had written the Mount George lease. He could not really see how, if Richards had forged the lease, why Miss Kelly would not be able to prove it. He did not think anyone could forge his name.

Mr Rowley, Judge Dickinson's clerk, and Mr Flett had both declared the lease to be written by Miss Kelly, Spence said, inferring that their standing made their statements correct. Miss Kelly said she was ill on September 19, 1859 and could not have signed the lease on that date, yet within a day or two she admitted to riding twenty miles.

He knew from "common report"[13] before the trial began, Spence continued, that Miss Kelly had been convicted of perjury. Here once again is a suggestion of the general public prejudice against Isabella Kelly. And from his answers in the Committee's examination, one can see his attitude to her, as well as the synchronisation of his views with Henry Flett.

Spence also stated that the jury had no doubt of Kelly's guilt and consequently spent most of their deliberating the amount of damages to be awarded to Richards. This was in stark contrast to the evidence given previously by Spence's fellow jurors, who said most time was spent examining handwriting.

Spence said Richards had taken two drafts of the lease to Kelly on September 19, and after writing out the lease itself *signed all three*. (This makes sense in only one context: this was Flett's "spin" to try and explain the three leases. Spence was Flett's witness, and Flett could see how vital Mullen's evidence of the three leases had become. Why would Kelly sign any drafts, especially when each was different from the lease itself?)

Question 843

Leane was Kelly's witness, Spence continued, and she had promised him a job in the Police Force if he gave evidence in her favour. Leane was still working for Kelly at the time of the trial.

Five days later, on July 21, the Chairman called Tim Leane to appear before the Committee to refute the latter statements by Spence.

Leane deposed he was now a constable in the Police Force. Mr Girard, the Superintendent at Mount George, had recommended him for the Police Force – not Miss Kelly. He had resigned from Miss Kelly's service on May 8, 1860, about three weeks before the Andrews trial, and he had completed his twelve-month contract with her.

This was an important point – at the time of the trial Leane was not under any obligation to Kelly – as juries of the period tended to discount the testimonies of employees which was favourable to the employer, on the basis they risked having their employment terminated by giving unfavourable evidence.

Asked about the general opinion of people on the Manning, Leane said that people generally believed Skerrett had not bought Kelly's cattle, but there had been some sort of arrangement between Kelly and Skerrett.

The next witness, Matthew Stephen declared he represented Richards in the Richards/Andrews trial, and never doubted the lease was genuine or that Richards would succeed in the trial. Much time at the trial was spent discussing individual words in the Mount George lease and their similarities to writing admitted to be that of Miss Kelly. One of the jurors had told him after the trial concluded, that they spent most their time comparing Kelly's handwriting with the lease.

On Thursday, August 6, the Committee examined Charles Croaker, the Community Magistrate from the Manning River. He claimed Miss Kelly had told him that she sold her cattle to Skerrett, and, at the same time, she had recommended Charles Skerrett to be a Justice of the Peace; he did not even want to talk to her, but she had volunteered the information as he was overtaking her on his horse.

When pressed for specific details of the encounter, Croaker

became very vague.

> Chairman Allen: "Do you remember the year?"
> Mr Croaker: "No I do not."
> Chairman Allen: "Do you remember whether it was in summer or winter?"
> Mr Croaker: "I think it was in summer, but really I cannot say positively."
>
> ...
>
> Chairman Allen: "You think it was in summer?"
> Mr Croaker: "I do, for I had some men at work at the time at this place – some fencers."
>
> ...
>
> Chairman Allen: "You do not seem to know much of this affair, except this conversation between you and Miss Kelly, and that you say took place in summer?"
> Mr Croaker: "I do not know anything personally. I speak merely from report."[14]

This last sentence, "I speak merely from report", summed up the evidence Croaker gave – he was there simply to malign Isabella Kelly.

Once again Flett had produced a witness (and a Magistrate at that) to make the implausible claim that Kelly told him of her plans to see Skerrett made a Justice of the Peace – implausible because this information had lain dormant without revelation by Croaker for eight years. Further, such a conversation could only have taken place in the *winter* of 1854 – June or July.

Flett stepped in to rescue Croaker with a very clever question.

> Mr Flett: "You say you have no recollection of the time when you overtook Miss Kelly on horseback, and had this conversation about the transaction between herself and Skerrett – was it on or before her trial for stealing calves from McPherson?"
> Mr Croaker: "I think at the very time she was on her way to Sydney when she was under committal for cattle stealing."[15]

The question avoided mentioning that this was actually in winter, and also gave the impression Kelly had actually stood trial for cattle stealing (while Magistrate Day had committed Kelly, the Attorney General refused to proceed further). Flett continued the questioning.

Question 843

Mr Flett: "How long have you been on the Manning?"

Mr Croaker: "Somewhere about twenty years."

Mr Flett: "I suppose you have some knowledge of Miss Kelly from that time till now?"

Mr Croaker: "Yes, Miss Kelly was on the Manning some short time before I went there."

Mr Flett: "In what state was she when you went there, with regard to her landed property – what state was it in?"

Mr Croaker: "If I remember rightly, Miss Kelly was living in a bark hut at Mount George. Very little was done at the time."[16]

This last statement was blatantly untrue – Kelly's house had been no "bark hut". As recorded earlier, John Allan in his memoirs gave a description of Kelly's six-room house before it burned down in 1851, as "such a nice finished house, lined with cedar."[17]

With Flett leading the questioning, Croaker said he had advised Begbie not to buy Kelly's cattle as he thought the cattle were only worth about £500 or £600, and not the £1200 Begbie paid for them. Mr Roxburgh [the mortgagee of Mount George] had offered to sell him the Mount George property for £500 but he did not think it worth nearly that much, and did not buy it. Croaker stated he was not inclined to believe anything Miss Kelly said. He believed Miss Kelly's signatures on the Skerrett documents were genuine.

Flett seemed concerned about his own image with the Committee.

Mr Flett: "Miss Kelly has stated, and the Chairman has stated, before this Committee, that I had a bad feeling towards Miss Kelly – have you ever known, or have you ever heard on the river, that was the case?"

Mr Croaker: "I have thought myself once or twice that you have taken Miss Kelly's part rather more than the opposite, and I have felt annoyed myself."

Mr Flett: "There was a singular thing occurred once with regard to the murder of a woman, and you must remember that I stuck up on the part of Miss Kelly, and even asked the Magistrate not to put her in the lock-up at the time she was committed."

Mr Croaker: "I am quite aware that you took Miss Kelly's part, and were favourable to her with respect to the missing servant girl."[18]

Flett was desperately trying to show he had no bias towards Kelly, and delivered a patent twisting of facts, only to prove his prejudice: the missing girl was upgraded by Flett to a murdered girl, and Kelly "committed" for her murder.

    Chairman Allen: "About the servant girl that Mr Flett was so
        kind as not to have Miss Kelly hanged."
    Mr Croaker: "I am not aware of that at all."
    Chairman Allen: "Was there any servant girl murdered?"
    Mr Croaker: "I am not aware of any. There was one missing."[19]

There were ten members of the Committee in attendance on this day, and they could hardly have missed the harmonisation between Henry Flett and his fellow Manning Valley Magistrate, Charles Croaker.

A week later, when the Committee asked Isabella Kelly about her relationship with Charles Croaker, she said he was one of her enemies – Croaker falsely accused her of writing anonymous letters injurious to his sister.

On Friday, August 14, Isabella Kelly once again faced the Committee, apparently at the request of Henry Flett, who presented one document to the Committee, and had quite a number of other documents spread out in front of him. Flett had evidently been reading the transcripts of the evidence given by Kelly to the Committee in the previous year, and anticipated he could catch Kelly lying to the Committee.

Flett began with events of over twenty years ago, asking how many cattle she originally bought, from whom she bought them and how they reached Mount George. Kelly answered as best she could (given the time span) before Flett gave her one of the documents.

    Mr Flett: "You admit that is your handwriting?"
    Miss Kelly: "Yes, but what has that to do with the quantity [of
        cattle]?"
    Mr Flett: "It is a pass to a Government man [convict] to bring
        seventy-three head of cattle – forty-seven cows and twen-
        ty-six calves, from Maitland, and is dated 4th December,

Question 843

1840."

Miss Kelly: "Yes, but this has nothing to do with the first lot of cattle."

Mr Flett: "You say you do not recollect when you first mortgaged to McGuigan?"

Miss Kelly: "No, I do not."

Mr Flett: "I will tell you – it was on the 1st March, 1841."

Miss Kelly: "Very probably."

Mr Flett: "Who did you mortgage to after that?"

Miss Kelly: "I do not know."

Mr Flett: "You do not recollect?"

Miss Kelly: "No."

Mr Flett: "Did you mortgage to Mr George A. Crowder?"

Miss Kelly: "No, I never mortgaged to him."

Mr Flett: "Had you any money from him?"

Miss Kelly: "No, I did not receive the money, and therefore I did not mortgage to him."

Mr Flett: "Did you not get the sum of £595 from Mr George A. Crowder, or from his attorney?"

Miss Kelly: "No, not a shilling."

Mr Flett: "And do you affirm that you never got any money from Mr Crowder?"

Miss Kelly: "I do, not a shilling."

Mr Flett: "I produce here a release from George A. Crowder to Isabella Mary Kelly for £595."[20]

An exultant Henry Flett presented this document firmly believing he had finally ambushed Kelly and caught her out in a *lie* to the Committee. When Kelly gave her explanation, Flett refused to accept it.

Miss Kelly: "Yes, that release was executed because I had executed the mortgage deed, though I never got the money; and because I had executed the mortgage deed, my property could not be sold until we got this release."

Mr Flett: "Is that your signature?"

Miss Kelly: "If I am allowed to hand in Sir William A'Beckett's letter, that will explain how the thing occurred. I had the mortgage deed prepared, intending to borrow money from Mr Crowder, but the money was never paid."

Mr Flett: "But this deed is executed."

Miss Kelly: "It is. I say that I executed it when I was about to borrow the money. I was in Sydney, and executed the deed previous to going up to the Manning, leaving my attorney to get the money, but the money was never paid."[21]

Kelly had intended to mortgage to George Crowder, and had the mortgage document drawn up by her solicitor. When Sir William A'Beckett lent her £500 (with no interest), she no longer needed the mortgage money from Crowder, and cancelled the mortgage. Even though the mortgage money was not paid, a cancellation (or release) document needed to be drawn for legal reasons, to void the mortgage.

Flett pursued his strategy of showing that the Mount George property was of little value, and certainly not worth the £3000 or £4000 Kelly claimed.

> Mr Flett: "Did Mr Dodds ever offer your property – the Manning River property [Mount George] – for sale in Maitland?"
> Miss Kelly: "I say that it was put into his hands for sale."
> Mr Flett: "Did he not put it up for auction, and was not able to get a single bid for it?"
> Miss Kelly: "That I do not know."
> Mr Flett: "Did he sell it?"
> Miss Kelly: "No, but he received an offer of £2000 for it, and I told him not to sell at that price."
> Mr Flett: "Do you know that Mr Campbell has bought it since for £500?"
> Miss Kelly: "No, I did not know who bought it."
> Mr Flett: "But you know that it was bought for £500?"
> Miss Kelly: "Yes, I do know that, and I know also that you were the cause of it being sacrificed."
> Mr Flett: "I beg to say that I was nothing of the kind."
> Miss Kelly: "I know that you were, and that all my misfortunes were through you."
> ...
> Mr Garrett: "But if it was mortgaged for £500 only, and it was, as you say, worth £3000 or £4000, surely you had notice of the foreclosure, you could have taken some steps to have the property redeemed, supposing it to be worth so much more?"
> Miss Kelly: "Yes, of course, if I thought they were going to sell, I would have borrowed the money from some of my friends, who would have redeemed it for me. But I never

knew of it until it was sold.

When I heard that the mortgage was to be foreclosed, I wrote to Lennon & Cape asking them to interfere, but their answer was, that I had spoken so ill of them that they did not like to interfere any further in my affairs.

I called upon them afterwards, and asked them to tell me who it was that had informed them that I had spoken ill of them, and they said it was Mr Flett who had called and told them so."

Mr Garrett: "But for what purpose did you conceive that you got the notice of foreclosure unless to give you an opportunity of paying the money, if you did not wish to give up the property?"

Miss Kelly: "You must understand that I was living on the Manning River, and that everything cannot be done there so speedily as it can in Sydney. After I heard that the mortgage was to be foreclosed, I called on Mr Roxburgh and asked him not to sell my property. He said he had nothing to do with the matter – that it was entirely in the hands of Lennon & Cape. I then went to them and asked them the same thing.

I said, 'I hope you will not allow my estate to be sold. It is all I have left me, and I have set my heart upon it. It will break my heart if it is sold.'

They said they would see what was to be done in the matter, and I left them under the impression that it would not be sold. Subsequently, after they heard that I had spoken against them, I suppose, the estate was sold. …

Mr Cape informed me that it was Mr Flett who had told them, and I may thank him for my property being sacrificed in this way."[22]

The Mount George property had indeed been sold on January 2, 1863, in an agreement between William Lennon and John Roxburgh (the mortgagee) on the one part, and Robert Campbell as the buyer, on the other part.[23] Nowhere on the conveyance document did the signature of Isabella Mary Kelly appear.[24]

The 895-acre Mount George property had certainly sold well below its value, as Joseph Andrews was able to mortgage the 705-acre Woodside property adjoining Mount George for £1000 in March 1865, and mortgage values were usually well below sale prices.[25] The £4000 price tag Isabella Kelly had placed on Mount George certainly seemed an ambitious amount, with the main obstacle to buyers purchasing the property being the remoteness of the area.

It had been over three years between Kelly's release from prison and the sale of Mount George, and still she had made no attempt to regain ownership of Mount George, as she says she intended. One explanation may have been she waited in anticipation of compensation being paid to her.

William Forster tried to determine why Miss Kelly was so unpopular on the Manning. No mention was made of Kelly being an *independent woman* in a male-dominated society or that she was one of a relatively small number of Catholics in a Protestant community, and Kelly herself seems not to have considered gender to be the problem or part of the problem.

Mr Forster: "You seem to have had a great many enemies on the Manning River?"
Miss Kelly: "Yes, I had."
Mr Forster: "Do you know what was the cause of it?"
Miss Kelly: "In a great measure I do."
Mr Forster: "What reason was there, do you think, for this enmity to yourself?"
Miss Kelly: "They envied me on account of my stock – that was one reason. Another reason was that I did not visit my neighbours on the footing that they would have had me do, because I did not consider that they were fitting companions for me."
Mr Forster: "At all events you seem to have made more enemies in your neighbourhood than most other people?"
Miss Kelly: "It is so."
…
Mr Garrett: "You say you have many enemies on the Manning River, and that they envied you?"
Miss Kelly: "Yes."
Mr Garrett: "How do you account for that?"
Miss Kelly: "In the first place, a person being a Magistrate on the river has it in his power to make me many enemies if he is so disposed, and Mr Flett is one of my bitterest ene-

Question 843

mies there."
Mr Garrett: "Who are the others?"
Miss Kelly: "Mr Croaker is another."
...
Mr Garrett: "Any others?"
Miss Kelly: "Those are the principal ones, but I am happy to say that I have many friends as well as enemies."[26]

While Garrett was a friend and ally of Henry Flett, it is highly likely he believed completely what Flett told him about Isabella Mary Kelly, and he was not being duplicitous in his questioning of her, as Flett was.

Like any good interviewer, Flett knew most of the answers to the questions he asked, *before* he asked them, and consequently he knew what questions *not* to ask. When Garrett asked his next question, he probably had no idea of the answer he would get, and Kelly's answer must have exploded like a bomb in the Committee room.

Mr Garrett: "How was it Mr Flett came to envy you?"
Miss Kelly: "I wish to explain that. He proposed marriage to me and I refused him, and he then said that he would be my bitterest enemy if ever I divulged the secret of his having proposed to me. He has proved his spite."[27]

One can only imagine the face of Henry Flett as Isabella Mary Kelly gave her answer, and the electric atmosphere generated in the Committee room. Garrett blithely pushed on.

Mr Garrett: "And your other enemies, why did they envy you?"
Miss Kelly: "Because I was a large stockholder, and they all had stock more or less, and there were always disagreements about cattle trespassing; sometimes their cattle trespassing on me, and sometimes my cattle trespassing on them. This caused enmity, and afterwards ill-feeling."[28]

The examination continued with Kelly stating that she had sold property in Maitland for £1200 to help pay her legal expenses. But she had not kept accounts of the money she had spent on lawyers, witnesses and her own travel and accommodation in Sydney.

Mr Garrett: "You cannot then produce these accounts?"

Miss Kelly: "No. It would be impossible for me to do so, living as I have since these matters commenced, with expenses up and down from the Manning for myself and my witnesses, and having to pay everything for my servants, and living here in Sydney, as well as all the heavy law expenses. I consider that I have a right to claim for it."

Mr Garrett: "If you spent the money through your false imprisonment then you would have, but you do not show this."

...

Miss Kelly: "... I kept no account of the claims that came in on me and that I had to meet. These were very heavy, for my case was postponed two or three times, and there were several trials."[29]

If Isabella Kelly had realised she would be facing a Select Committee at a later date she may have kept these accounts. Garrett would pursue this line right to the end – Kelly should not receive compensation as she had no accounts to verify any expenditure caused by her imprisonment.

As the examination was concluding, Flett turned his attention back to the Sheriff selling her goods at Mount George to pay her debts while she was in prison, quoting her answer to a question from the 1862 Select Committee.

Mr Flett: "You say that the Sheriff sold off things for a trifle you owed a shepherd – that you were not there, and all the property was sacrificed – all your beautiful furniture that had cost you several hundreds of pounds realized only £13, because there was nobody there to buy?"

Miss Kelly: "I said that I had been both robbed and plundered in every possible way; that everything of value was taken in my absence, and that things were sold in this way at a sacrifice."

Mr Garrett: "Did you ever get an account of this sale?"

Miss Kelly: "No, I was not there at the time."

Mr Garrett: "Did not the Sheriff furnish you with a list of the articles sold, and what they realized?"

Miss Kelly: "No, never."

Mr Flett: "Were not the articles sold a number of dishes and utensils, and an old horse?"

Miss Kelly: "No, the utensils could not have been sold,

because I gave them to Mr [Waldy] Cooper as a present. The horse you speak of was one I was offered £20 for, and refused to sell him, and he was sold by the Sheriff for 12s. 6d. [less than £1]"[30]

A rather emotional interview concluded.

The Committee met on the following Wednesday, August 19, with the Chairman and seven members (including Henry Flett) present. The minutes of the meeting record Mr Garrett as moving the motion that: "Question and answer No. 843 be expunged from the evidence given by Miss Kelly on Friday last."

All questions and answers given in the Select Committee were numbered to enable referencing. In Question 843 Kelly had revealed Flett's proposal of marriage to her.

When Chairman Allen put the motion, it was defeated with Garrett the only person voting to remove the question – Stewart, Morris and Cunneen opposed the motion, while Flett, Harpur and Morrice abstained from voting as, of course, did the Chairman.

At no stage did Flett ever deny a proposal of marriage to Kelly. And he obviously regretted this very public pronouncement of it – these transcripts would eventually be printed for the House to read, and then be available to the public through *Votes and Proceedings*.

There was great irony in this situation: Henry Flett was the one who demanded this third Select Committee, and it was his friend Thomas Garrett who asked Question 843.

On August 26, the Committee met again, with eight members present. A letter from Mr Mullen stated he was unable to attend at this time because of commitments at the Circuit Court in Maitland.

Chairman Allen proposed that the Committee examine Nicholas Binkin, whom he had summoned and was currently waiting outside the room. Henry Flett proposed that Binkin's interview be postponed to another day, suggesting either he did not want Binkin to give evidence (this was the last day witnesses were interviewed) or he had been caught unprepared to counter Binkin's evidence.

The Trials of Isabella Mary Kelly

Flett would have had some idea of the evidence Binkin would give. In the Richards/Andrews trial, Richards claimed a man named Binkin accompanied him to Kelly at her Ganget lease, on September 19, 1859, specifically to witness the signing of the Mount George lease.[31]

Flett's motion was defeated, and Binkin brought in and examined.

Binkin deposed he was travelling from Gloucester towards the Manning Valley on September 19, when he happened to meet Richards, who was delivering mail. Richards said he could take (paid) accommodation at his place for the night, and they then travelled along the road together, calling in at Miss Kelly's.

Richards had remained on his as he spoke to Miss Kelly, standing in her doorway. She seemed in a bad temper, and he waited about half an hour before he left with Richards. He stayed with Richards that night and left the next morning, but at no time had Richards ever spoken about a lease with Miss Kelly.

But Richards had demonstrated his handwriting skills to him.

> Chairman Allen: "Did Richards ever say to you that he could imitate almost any handwriting?"
>
> Mr Binkin: "Yes. He showed me one night that he could imitate two or three different hands, and I said, 'I wish I could write as well as you.' He was bragging about his writing."[32]

This evidence was completely damning to Richards.

All Flett could do was to ask Binkin where else he stayed on the Manning. When he replied that he stayed at Ned Duncan's place, Flett asked him for Duncan's address, which he was able to give.

When the interview was completed, Nicholas Binkin asked the Committee to pay him expenses for attending. Flett replied, "Perhaps the lady will pay you",[33] indicating Miss Kelly. And she did.

While Binkin's evidence was compelling, it did not carry the same weight with the Committee as William Mullen's evidence. As far as the Committee was concerned, Binkin was an unknown with unknown allegiances, whereas Mullen was a respected legal identity.

Question 843

After Binkin had withdrawn, Isabella Mary Kelly was called in for what would prove to be the Committee's final interview. Garrett resumed questioning Kelly on her expenses, but once again she could provide no documentation of her expenditure on legal fees and Court expenses.

William Allen then moved on to her relationship with Flett. Having revealed Flett's marriage proposal to the Committee at her previous interview, Isabella Kelly seemed in a much more confident and aggressive mood.

Chairman Allen: "You stated on a former day when you were before the Committee, that you did not get fair play from the Bench of Magistrates at the Manning?"

Miss Kelly: "Yes."

Chairman Allen: "Can you particularize any case or cases that you can remember?"

Miss Kelly: "When I sold my cattle to Begbie and Cooper, I offered £50 reward for the apprehension of any parties who had branded any of my cattle, as some of my cattle had been branded previously to their purchase."

Chairman Allen: "Branded by whom?"

Miss Kelly: "By a man of the name of Robert Sorrell."[34]

Chairman Allen: "Was he brought before the Bench?"

Miss Kelly: "He was, by Messrs Begbie and Cooper, and my stockman identified the cattle, but Mr Flett dismissed the case."

Chairman Allen: "Was your brand on them?"

Miss Kelly: "Yes, and Robert Sorrell's."

Chairman Allen: "You complain of the Bench for having dismissed the case?"

Miss Kelly: "Yes, as it was fully proved."

Chairman Allen: "On what ground was it dismissed?"

Miss Kelly: "That it was a case of trover [the cattle wandered accidentally onto the property] or something."

Mr Flett: "Have you the depositions?"

Miss Kelly: "No."

Mr Flett: "Were you in the Court yourself?"

Miss Kelly: "Yes."

Mr Flett: "Was there any other Magistrate besides me?"

Miss Kelly: "You were the principal."

Mr Flett: "Why was I the principal?"

Miss Kelly: "You took it upon yourself."

Chairman Allen: "Who else was on the Bench?"

Miss Kelly [speaking to Flett]: "If I really speak plainly, you bounced them all about it."

Mr Flett: "Will you speak the truth?"

Miss Kelly: "I state nothing but the truth. Then there was another case. Seven of my men were taken up on warrants granted by the Sydney Bench. They were handcuffed, and were to be brought down to Sydney, on a charge merely of protecting my cattle and property."

Mr Harpur: "Were they so brought to Sydney?"

Miss Kelly: "They would have been, only the other Magistrates would not allow Mr Flett to forward them on to Sydney, whence the warrants were issued."

Chairman Allen: "Who were the Magistrates on the Bench along with Mr Flett?"

Miss Kelly: "That I cannot say – I do not know."

Chairman Allen: "Were the men sent to Sydney."

Miss Kelly: "They were not – the other Magistrates overruled him. They said the men were to be tried where the offence was committed, and that the case should be heard by the Manning Bench."

Chairman Allen: "Who were the Magistrates on the Bench along with Mr Flett?"

Miss Kelly: "That I cannot say – I do not know."[35]

Isabella Kelly related her total frustration in trying to obtain justice on the Manning.

Miss Kelly: "The district constable came to me, about the time I brought this case of the saddle into Court, and said, 'Miss Kelly, I can tell you where a horse of yours is, which was stolen from you – will you come to the police boat and identify it? I have three witnesses who can prove that it is yours. The man thought he had defaced the brand, but it can be proved that it is yours. It was stolen from the Manning Flats by a man of the name of Ladd, who has now got two years for stealing.'

I said in return, 'What is the good of my going to look after anything that is stolen? I will get no satisfaction from the Bench. Let the horse go.'

So I never went after the horse. Then Kennedy gave me information of another horse, and I said, 'I will never go

Question 843

before the Bench while I live, so let them steal away!' "[36]

Kelly complained that a man named Avery, a tenant of Flett, killed some of her cattle and they had been killed on his premises.

Chairman Allen: "What was done with them after they were killed."

Miss Kelly: "I heard that the beef had been taken in a boat to a place called Tinonee — that Avery took the beef in boats."

Mr Flett: "Was it in my stockyard they were killed?"

Miss Kelly: "I only go by hearsay."

Mr Flett: "I will not go by hearsay."

Miss Kelly: "You told me yourself."[37]

Chairman Allen turned to the papers Flett had been presenting to the Committee, and using to cross-examine Kelly.

Suspicions had been aroused about these papers when the Committee interviewed Isabella Kelly a fortnight previously. On that occasion Flett had produced papers, which were marked as A, B, C, D, and E, and handed them to Kelly, asking her if they bore her signature or if they were in her handwriting.

Identifying these papers more by the context in which they were written rather than the actual handwriting, Isabella Kelly answered "yes" to some and "I think" to others, but Paper D really perplexed her.

Mr Flett: "Is that yours [the handwriting] (paper produced, marked D)?"

Miss Kelly: "That I cannot say. I have no recollection of it."

…

Mr Garrett: "Is this in your handwriting (paper D shown to witness)?"

Miss Kelly: "I have been looking at it, and I cannot understand it."

Mr Garrett: "But with regard to the handwriting, is that yours?"

Miss Kelly: "It looks like mine, but my writing has been so often imitated, and I do not remember this. A number of persons have forged my signature, and I would not speak to this without knowing the paper."

Chairman Allen: "Do you know, or have you any means of saying from the document itself, whether this is your handwriting?"

> Miss Kelly: "I know that I wrote a notice stating that I was going to take my cattle [the 100 milch cows] out of the hands of Charles Skerrett, and that this notice was drawn up by me in the presence of Mr Cosgrove – but it is the date I am looking at …
>
> I know that I gave notice to that effect, but I cannot conceive how it could have got into Mr Flett's hands. If it is a copy of the notice that I gave, then it was in a box in my house, and was locked up, and must have been stolen from there when so many of my things were taken away. It was not the original notice for that was unde the hand of Mr Cosgrove."[38]

It was quite feasible that these were *original* documents, which Flett could have obtained from the people concerned in the documents. The cause of Kelly's bewilderment was the eventual realisation that paper D was *not* an original document, but may have been the copy which she had made for her own record, and was last seen by her *in her locked box at Waterview*.

If paper D was this copy, then it was stolen from Waterview while she was in prison, and Flett was presenting a *stolen* document to the Committee.

Apparently unperturbed, Flett pushed on.

> Mr Flett: "All I want to know is whether the signature is yours?'
>
> Miss Kelly: "I cannot say that it is, though it is like mine. If it is mine it ought not be in your hands at any rate, for if so, it is a copy of the notice I gave, and was left in my desk at the Manning, and must have been stolen. …"
>
> …
>
> Mr Flett: "Is the paper in your handwriting?"
>
> Miss Kelly: "Really and truly I will not say. It may be or it may not be. I will not say positively."[39]

Since that interview, two weeks ago, Kelly had obviously inspected the other documents produced by Flett, and confirmed with William Allen that were in fact stolen documents. In this, the last interview with Isabella Kelly, the Chairman decided to tackle Henry Flett on the issue.

> Chairman Allen [handing a number of papers to Miss Kelly]: "Here are some papers handed in by Mr Flett – will you

> look through them and say how you parted with these documents?"
>
> Miss Kelly: "There never was a document of these out of my hands."
>
> Chairman Allen: "Did you ever part with any of them?"
>
> Miss Kelly: "Never."
>
> Chairman Allen: "There is one, a pass to a Government man [convict], what is the date of that?"
>
> Miss Kelly: "1840."
>
> Chairman Allen: "To whom did you part with those papers?"
>
> Miss Kelly: "Not a single paper of them had any right to be out of my possession, for all of these little things were in my possession."
>
> ...
>
> Chairman Allen: "These you had along with your private papers in a box?"
>
> Miss Kelly: "Yes."
>
> Chairman Allen: "This box was left, where?"
>
> Miss Kelly: "At Waterview."
>
> Chairman Allen: "At your cottage at Waterview?"
>
> Miss Kelly: "Yes."
>
> Chairman Allen: "When you were convicted and sent to Darlinghurst?"
>
> Miss Kelly: "Yes."
>
> Chairman Allen: "And these papers were then in your possession?"
>
> Miss Kelly: "Yes."
>
> Chairman Allen: "How did these papers come out of your box?"
>
> ...
>
> Miss Kelly: "My box was broken open, and these papers were taken out."
>
> Chairman Allen: "These papers were taken out of your box, and brought up here in evidence against you?"
>
> Miss Kelly: "No doubt of that. I never heard of such a thing as that before."[40]

Now it was out in the open – in his attempts to catch Kelly lying to the Committee, Flett was presenting stolen papers to the Committee. And while it was never suggested that Flett stole the papers himself, he could never claim to be completely innocent of any knowledge of their origin – he must have had some idea how they were obtained.

The most likely source of the documents was Reuben Richards. Just before the Richards/Andrews trial, Kelly had seen such a document while visiting the office Richards' solicitor in the company of her own solicitor John Ryan Brenan. Although she drew Brenan's attention to it, the issue was not pursued.

Flett never made any statement on how the papers came into his possession.

At the end of Kelly's examination, there was a discussion about Reuben Richards and an incident for which there are no other sources.

> Chairman Allen: "Was Richards ever brought before the Bench at the Manning for being connected with a mail robbery?"
>
> Miss Kelly: "Yes."
>
> Chairman Allen: "What were the circumstances under which Richards was brought before the Bench?"
>
> Miss Kelly: "He was tried for attempting to cash a cheque drawn by the Bishop of Newcastle in favour of the Rev Mr Newman. This cheque had been stolen, and he went to get it cashed. Mr Flett said, before the court, that Reuben Richards was a perjurer, and was as guilty as the man they had just then committed."
>
> Chairman Allen: "How did Richards get out of the charge of attempting to pass this cheque?"
>
> Miss Kelly: "I do not know."[41]

After the humiliation suffered throughout the day, Henry Flett did not attend any further Committee meetings, leaving Thomas Garrett to fight a lone battle.

Perhaps it was related to those occasions on the Manning Bench, when out-voted by his fellow Community Magistrates in a case, Flett would refuse to return to the Bench to announce the Bench's decision even though he was Chairman.

On September 22, 1863, Statutory Declarations by John Paton and Patrick Connolly were appended to the Report. Paton declared Miss Kelly had engaged him to erect stabling in the

Question 843

Mount George paddock just two days before the lease was supposedly signed, and that she never negated that agreement.

Connolly stated that when he stayed at the Richards cottage several days after the September 19 date of the lease, both Richards and his wife told him separately he could do what he liked in the Mount George paddock, as it had nothing to do with them.

On October 6, Chairman Allen issued a draft report for each of the Committee members to read. A week later the Committee went through the Report paragraph by paragraph to decide on the final wording. A pattern soon emerged of Thomas Garrett voting one way (as Henry Flett would have done if he were present), and the rest of the Committee voting the other way.

Finally the Report was agreed upon.

This Report was very similar to the 1862 Report, but it now spoke of "the improbability of Miss Kelly having made the lease" with Richards, before giving its major findings:

- The Bill of Sale and Receipt were forgeries.
- Miss Kelly was wrongfully convicted of having committed perjury.
- The Chief Justice mislaid the Bill of Sale and Receipt, and in consequence her defence was seriously prejudiced.
- Miss Kelly was in prison more than five months, and her health and constitution suffered severely.
- During her imprisonment and afterwards, Charles Skerrett seized and sold any horses bearing Miss Kelly's brand, which he could obtain. He also seized, where he could, the cattle she had sold to Begbie and Cooper.
- Skerrett was committed for stealing some of these cattle by Begbie and Cooper, but the Attorney General refused to prosecute.
- Charles Skerrett was committed for forgery by Miss Kelly, and the Attorney General refused to prosecute.
- As a result, Miss Kelly was prevented from protecting her property and, without any fault or neglect on her part, Skerrett was permitted to prey on her property until she was reduced to ruin.
- Miss Kelly had made out a complete case for public redress and an absolute pardon.

The Trials of Isabella Mary Kelly

There it was in black and white – "an absolute pardon" – the Report declared Isabella Mary Kelly completely innocent. Although the Report recorded her losses as £10000, it made no recommendation of the amount of compensation – again this was left for Parliament to determine.

Isabella Mary Kelly now waited for the Report to be debated by Parliament.

34. A Final Decision

On October 20, 1863, William Allen presented the nine-page Report to the House of Assembly, including the transcripts of their interviews and the many appendices, and the House ordered the Report to be printed.[1]

The fourteen points enumerated as the findings of the Select Committee, together with the three recommendations, were printed in *Empire* on October 31 and the *Maitland Mercury* on November 3, but nothing appeared in the *Sydney Morning Herald*.

On November 26, Allen gave the House of Assembly notice of a motion for the House to adopt the Report of the Kelly Select Committee, to be placed on the agenda for Tuesday, December 8. On that day, with Henry Flett absent from the House, Allen moved the adoption of the Report. In supporting his motion, Allen once again outlined the history of the case, and in doing so criticised the actions of the Chief Justice, Sir Alfred Stephen.

Allen declared that upon Skerrett's release from prison, Skerrett went to see the Chief Justice. There morning after morning Skerrett was allowed to make statements to the Chief Justice, behind Miss Kelly's back, until the Chief Justice came to believe his story. Allen argued that if convicted men were able to have their verdicts overturned by talking to the Chief Justice, then no man was safe. He thought the Chief Justice was a kind man, but "his kindness perverted his judgement by warping his feeling."[2]

The missing documents had been found in the Chief Justice's drawer in the Banco Court – in this case their loss was his fault.

Whoever was to blame, Allen continued, it was certainly not Miss Kelly, and yet she had been made to suffer. Miss Kelly's health had been so shattered by her five month imprisonment that she had to be carried from prison on her release. She now came to the House to remove the infamy and disgrace that was still upon her. Miss Kelly had made a triumphant case for pardon, and deserved full compensation.[3]

He had read the House of Commons Report on William Henry Barber, Allen said, and believed Miss Kelly should receive an amount similar to the £5000 Barber was awarded for his wrongful imprisonment on a charge of perjury.

The Speaker ruled Allen's motion out of order on the technicality that the Report included the recommendation of a monetary compensation to Miss Kelly. Allen consequently moved that the House move into a Committee of the Whole (committee mode) on the following Friday to determine the amount of compensation, not exceeding £5000, for Miss Kelly.

Mr Darvall stated he had been counsel for Miss Kelly in her court case, but he had a problem setting precedents for compensating people in these situations. He knew Miss Kelly had been hard done by, but he did not join in the censure of the Chief Justice. Mistakes in the court system were inevitable, but only in the very extreme of these cases should anyone be compensated for any such mistakes.

Mr Faucett stated he agreed with the Report entirely. Skerrett had perjured himself at Miss Kelly's trial. In listening to the evidence of Skerrett's three children at his trial, it was obvious that Skerrett himself had suborned the children. It was likely that if the Chief Justice had not lost the documents, Miss Kelly would not have been found guilty of perjury.

Dr Lang said that he agreed with the Report. Miss Kelly had sustained losses as the result of mistakes in the administration of justice. He had met the family of Skerrett and had formed a favourable opinion of the wife and children involved in the case. He had been a fellow passenger with Miss Kelly when she came out from England. He continued to hold a good opinion of Miss Kelly and would support the motion.

Mr Dalgleish, the Member for East Maitland, declared Skerrett used his superior ingenuity to enrich himself at Miss Kelly's expense. She had been sent to prison as a perjurer and lost her property. The Chief Justice may have been humane in releasing Skerrett when he believed Skerrett to be innocent; but the Chief Justice had shown weakness in allowing himself to be earwigged by criminals.

A Final Decision

Mr Flett had not come out of this case with clean hands, Dalgleish continued, Flett had shown his prejudices against Miss Kelly, and it did him no credit. Flett ought to have let the House decide the matter after the 1862 Select Committee. Instead he pretended he had more information to bring forward, with his only intention to delay the matter so he could injure Miss Kelly.

Mr Dalley said he too had been a counsel for Miss Kelly. He believed that Miss Kelly had been wrongly persecuted and punished but he could not agree to the condemnation of the Chief Justice. The loss of the documents had been accidental. Unfortunately Miss Kelly seemed have no friends supporting her other than those she paid for – her lawyers. Skerrett, on the other hand, with his superior cunning and ability, seemed able to make many friends and was even able to deceive the Chief Justice.

Garrett reiterated his constant theme that Kelly had suffered but she had failed to prove any *particular* losses.

Dalgleish interjected with, "She lost twelve month's liberty."[4]

Garrett replied that this was true, but he could not support any motion for compensation until he was informed of Miss Kelly's *actual* losses.

Garrett claimed Dalgleish was helping to bring the administration of justice into contempt by the public, because Mr Dalgleish wanted to overturn the verdict of juries – this was even more dangerous than criticising judges. (According to this logic, any mistakes in the justice system should not be admitted – a person wrongly convicted of a crime should stay convicted, and certainly receive no compensation – and the public would have more confidence in such a system.)

In his right of reply, Mr Allen said everything had gone wrong for Miss Kelly because of the maladministration of justice by the Chief Justice. In answer to one question put to her, Miss Kelly had answered, "When I was a young woman Mr Flett offered to marry me, and I would not have him. On which he said he would persecute me to death for it."[5]

This last statement by Allen was greeted with cries of "Oh; oh!" and laughter.[6]

The Speaker chastised Allen for assigning unworthy motives to a member of the House. Mr Darvall said Allen should refrain from any unworthy reference to the member for Hastings, as he was not in the House. Perhaps Henry Flett had not attended in anticipation of such a reaction.

The motion was put to the House and carried – the House would go into a Committee as a Whole to discuss the amount of compensation to Miss Kelly on the following Friday, three days later.

The *Empire* newspaper, owned by Henry Parkes, had no qualms about criticising the Chief Justice, whereas the *Sydney Morning Herald* printed much less of the criticism in its political report of this motion than *Empire* did. *Empire* ran an editorial highly critical of the Chief Justice's actions, but never critical of his integrity:[7]

> Miss Kelly was victimised right and left.
>
> She was first victimised by the plausible cunning of Skerrett, and she was then victimised by the unaccountable delusion of a judge. Between the two, she lost everything that makes life valuable – health, liberty, property and character. ...
>
> Is it an uncommon thing for judges to feel grave doubt as to the credibility of certain witnesses, or of the guilt of certain prisoners?
>
> We should imagine that few things can be more common. It might be said to take place every day. But is it usual for Judges to cast aside the trammels of routine in every case, which they consider doubtful?
>
> Is it usual for them to take up the case of a convicted criminal with as much zeal as if they had been specially retained for the purpose?
>
> Is it usual for them to give a series of morning sittings, like cheap photographers, to felons who consider themselves aggrieved by a verdict of guilty?
>
> Is it usual for them to lend their ears, day after day, to such characters; to listen patiently to every plausible story, and every artful lie they may concoct; and at the same time to take no note of what might possibly be said on the other side?

Commenting on former Attorney General John Plunkett's decision to deal only with the depositions in the case and not to have interviews with Skerrett, the editorial continued:

> Had the Chief Justice acted in the same way [as Plunkett],

A Final Decision

we would have heard nothing of this case. Charles Skerrett would have been peacefully engaged in smoothing the rugged crudities of Cockatoo [Island Gaol]. Miss Kelly would have remained in undisputed enjoyment of the fruits of her industry and enterprise.

The Chief Justice was the colony's foremost law officer, yet he had not upheld the standards required of law officers. And while no one suggested the Chief Justice had a corrupt motive, Sir Alfred Stephen had allowed his own personal feelings about Isabella Kelly (from the Burt case) to override his professional standards and interfere with his professional judgement.

There was no editorial in the *Sydney Morning Herald*, and the most likely reason was a reluctance to criticise the Chief Justice.

Although placed on the agenda of the House of Assembly for Friday, the Committee of the Whole topic of Isabella Mary Kelly's compensation was not reached.

On subsequent days, other agenda items were inserted above it, so that the Isabella Mary Kelly compensation debate continually appeared on the agenda for each day Parliament sat, but the item was never discussed.

It is apparent when reading through *Votes and Proceedings*, the House had a high volume of business to consider, but the appointment of Thomas Garrett by the House to be responsible for the scheduling of Committee of the Whole proceedings may have been a greater factor in causing the continual postponements.

This delay was quite fortuitous for the anti-Kelly forces, as it enabled a petition to be gathered from the Manning. On February 5, 1864, two months after the House had failed to make a final decision on Isabella Kelly, Thomas Garrett presented a petition to the House of Assembly demanding that *no compensation* be paid to Miss Kelly.

No one asked why the Member for Monaro (from the south of the state) presented the petition rather than the member for The Hastings (in the north of the state), in whose electorate the Manning was situated. Once again Flett was absent from the House as it dealt with a matter relating to Isabella Mary Kelly.

While the organiser and none of the signatories were

named, the arguments used in the petition were certainly similar to those used by Flett at the Select Committee hearings, and there can be little doubt Flett was connected to it.

The petition itself revolved mainly around Maria Cooper and played on the sympathy in the district for Alfred Begbie being forced into insolvency. Despite the dubious aspects of the Begbie insolvency, the district held the general opinion that Begbie had been hard done by, and Isabella Mary Kelly was responsible.

As for her wrongful imprisonment, the petition maintained Kelly had brought that upon herself by going around the district telling people that Skerrett had bought her cattle. This was even believed by settler John Allan, whose family had been on friendly terms with Miss Kelly when she lived at Mount George. Allan wrote that "Miss Kelly got into a mess with a man named Skerrett and somehow he got round her and got her to make a false sale of all her cattle to him".[8]

The petition was signed by 215 "Inhabitants of the Manning River".[9]

> That your Petitioners have heard with no small degree of surprise, the Report adopted by a Select Committee appointed by your Honourable House, to inquire into the claim made by Miss Kelly for compensation, for losses and injuries said to have been sustained by her in consequence of her incarceration in Darlinghurst Gaol, after a conviction for perjury but from which confinement she was liberated before the expiration of her sentence.
>
> Inasmuch as the conclusions of your Select Committee, with regard to the value of Miss Kelly's stock, &c., have been deduced from the unsupported assertions of Miss Kelly, whose estimation of the value of her property and the extent of her losses, and other injuries received by her, is altogether, to use the mildest terms, most exaggerated, and at the same time most inconsistent with that weight of evidence which tends to show the actual value of Miss Kelly's property, the extent of her losses, and the very doubtful character of very many of her transactions.
>
> That although nothing definite was stated by Miss Kelly as to the actual number of horses she possessed at the time of her incarceration, yet your Committee have valued such, for the most part imaginary, stock at the incredible sum of six thousand pounds.

⤝ A Final Decision ⤞

That, although your Committee have valued the equity of redemption of the Mount George Estate at two thousand pounds, yet it has been sold to a *bona fide* purchaser for five hundred pounds, a sum insufficient to satisfy the claims of the mortgagee.

That, in Miss Kelly's transactions with Messrs Begbie and Cooper, she made false representations respecting the number of cattle; she never handed over the milking utensils to them, nor the deeds of the estate Waterview, of which she claims possession to the present day; therefore, considering the amount Miss Kelly received, she was no great loser, but, on the other hand, Begbie was the great sufferer, and much more entitled to compensation than Miss Kelly. (*See Mrs. Cooper's letter*).

Also, that your Petitioners believe that Miss Kelly's sheep were sold for their market Value.

Also, that whatever way have been Miss Kelly's losses, injuries, or inconveniences, from her incarceration, your Petitioners cannot but be of opinion that they are more attributable to her own wilful conduct than to any other cause, inasmuch as she propagated and circulated the report or assertion that she had sold her cattle to Skerritt, in such a manner that if she did not know it to be true, she must know it was calculated to deceive others; and your Petitioners are also of opinion that Miss Kelly's transactions with Skerritt were of a very doubtful character, and no clear proof has been produced showing that her connection was an unjust one, or to establish her innocence.

That your Petitioners are actuated to memorialize your Honourable House entirely from a desire for public justice, being deeply impressed that, in the investigation before your Select Committee, Miss Kelly has failed to make out a fair or just claim for compensation at your hands, and that if compensation were granted upon such claim it would be a direct violation of all principles of public justice.

Your Petitioners therefore pray that your Honourable House duly consider these statements when weighing the evidence furnished by your Select Committee, and should you agree with them, that you will refuse to adopt the Report, and also dismiss Miss Kelly's claim for compensation at your hands.

Mrs Cooper's letter, as referenced in the petition, had been written to the 1862 Select Committee, and claimed Miss Kelly had "completely ruined Mr. Begbie and family"[10].

The crux of this petition comes with the proposition that everything that happened to Kelly was "more attributable to her own wilful conduct", with the subtext being that Isabella Kelly had really brought all this on herself — she may have been wronged but if only she had stuck to popularly designated *women's* activities, these events would never have occurred.

This petition from members of the Manning Valley community was a direct challenge to the findings of the Report, and William Allen's motion to adopt the Select Committee's Report in the House on December 8. They were shocked to think that Kelly could receive as much as £5000 in compensation. There was no one standing up to defend Isabella Kelly and propound her side of the story. Even Joseph Andrews, who knew Kelly to be innocent, had distanced himself from Kelly and supported Cooper and Begbie in their claims Kelly should receive little by way of compensation.

And it was met with silence — silence from the press, silence from Parliament.

The silence in the press came down to perjury. Here was a case where it was obvious much perjury had occurred at the hearings, but the perpetrators could not be clearly identified.

Many of the witnesses, especially those provided by Henry Flett, were unable to provide any first hand evidence — their evidence was either to say Kelly told them she sold her cattle to Skerrett or to denigrate her character, saying they would not believe her under oath. This was the evidence of hearsay, but many believed it.

The silence of Parliament came down to the combination of criticism of the Chief Justice and the amount of compensation Kelly appeared likely to receive. £5000 was an extraordinary amount to award in compensation in the young colony, but the precedent had been set by the House of Commons to William Barber. Yet in the Kelly case, the evidence of mistaken imprisonment was not as clear cut as the Barber case, with the petition adding further to the hesitancy of Parliament.

Still Isabella Mary Kelly waited for a final decision.

A Final Decision

In between her many trips to Sydney concerning the Select Committee hearings, Isabella Kelly had re-built her operations with horses in the Manning Valley to such an extent that she was able to put 300 horses up for sale on July 7, 1864, with a Maitland auctioneer. But with echoes of when she sold her cattle to Begbie in 1858, most were running wild at four different locations across the Manning, with their increase unbranded.

Together with the horses, the buyer would also receive the rights to her brands MK and K. With this action, Kelly indicated that she was retiring completely from the horse business. The advertisement in the *Maitland Mercury*, under a heading of "Great Monster Horse Sale", was selling all her horses and brands, and "estimated at the very least to number over 300 head."[11] The advertisement referred to the suitability of the horses for police or cavalry purposes, and for exportation to India, where she had previously sent horses and received "good prices with flattering recommendations in return."

The sale was a result of "the inability of the proprietress to attend to their proper management through injured and declining health." But more pertinently, she was aging.

There are many unanswered questions here. Where did the horses come from? Did she buy horses with some of the money she received from selling her last allotments of land in Maitland? After Girard's departure from Mount George in 1860, was Kelly still able to round up some remaining horses? Did she borrow money in anticipation of her compensation claim?

The horses and brands were bought for an undisclosed amount.[12] As well as her own property at Waterview, Kelly seems to have re-leased the Ganget run from the A.A. Company, as well as a run at Gun Gully, Wingham.

Having sold the horses, it is possible that she retired to Waterview with a few cows and a vegetable patch, dropping these other leases, while she waited on the House of Assembly to make a decision.

On April 22, 1864, more than five months after the Isabella Mary Kelly debate had initially been set down for discussion by the House, the current Parliamentary session ended with the matter of compensation for Miss Kelly still unresolved.

The House of Assembly resumed on October 18, but only lasted three weeks before the Governor prorogued Parliament for a general election.

The Election Day for the Hastings electorate was scheduled rather inconveniently for December 24, Christmas Eve. Fifty-three year old Horace Dean, an American-born Tinonee storekeeper of several years, had declared his intentions early and held political rallies at Wingham on November 22, and Port Macquarie on November 29.

Henry Flett seemed hesitant and made no declaration of candidacy. On December 10, 1864, candidates had to nominate for the up-coming election at the Port Macquarie Courthouse. Flett nominated using a second, but did not travel to Port Macquarie as he did for previous elections, and may have been unaware that a third candidate, William Forster, had also nominated at the last moment.

The forty-six year old Forster had lost his East Sydney seat in an electoral redistribution, and now faced the difficult task, as a non-resident, of winning a seat from a sitting member. A committee, formed at Kempsey to support Forster's election, was told that Forster could not attend the nomination because of lumbago.[13]

Forster's only link with the district was ownership of a pastoral property outside of Port Macquarie in the early 1840s,[14] but he had a high profile from his five months as Premier of New South Wales in 1859 and his other ministerial commitments. As a Committee member on both of the Isabella Mary Kelly Select Committees, Forster may have believed Flett was vulnerable in his own electorate.

Having nominated, Flett made the strange decision to run a non-campaign, and appears to have attended very few rallies, if any. Either he was supremely confident, or he feared the competition Forster presented, and did not want to be seen competing for a post he would not win.

Both Dean and Forster (but not Flett) appeared at an election rally called at Wingham on December 14, chaired by Joseph Andrews, who, after his insolvency fiasco, had put aside any thoughts of a political career for the time being.

The poll was declared at Port Macquarie on January 2, with

A Final Decision

both Dean and Forster attending. William Forster won the election with 530 votes to Flett's 328 votes and Dean's 260 in the first-past-the-post poll.

Flett had overwhelmingly won Taree with 109 votes (96% of the vote) and gained 104 votes (52%) at Cundletown, while Dean won his hometown, Tinonee, with 88 votes (76%) and Forster won Wingham with 69 votes (56%).[15] The clear and decisive factor in Forster's win were the 259 votes (76%) gained in the Kempsey area, where Forster's committee had actively campaigned throughout the district, and provided steamboats for voters on polling day, making it a picnic day.

In defeat, Horace Dean stated that he was glad Forster had been elected in preference to Flett.[16] Dean now turned to newspaper publishing, and in April 1865 produced the first edition of the *Manning River News* from his base in Tinonee. As editor, Dean produced a first-class political commentary on State politics, as well as reporting local events.

For Henry Flett, his political career had come to an end. He contested the next election but was beaten by Horace Dean. Flett continued in the Manning Valley as the Senior Magistrate on the Bench, as well as President of the Show Society.

Not only had Henry Flett been swept from office, but so too had William Allen, when he ran third in his electorate of Williams. Consequently the prime supporter of Isabella Mary Kelly and the prime opponent had *both* been removed from Parliament. This presented a problem for Isabella Kelly in that she needed some Parliamentary Member to pursue her case in the House of Assembly or the Report of the Select Committee would simply sit and gather dust on some Parliamentary shelf.

The Rev. Dr John Dunmore Lang took up the cause of Isabella Mary Kelly, whether by his own initiative or at Kelly's instigation, is not clear. Many would regard this as a rather incongruous pairing – this single Catholic lady, who had been a settler in her own right in the remote Manning Valley and known to have a temper, and the militant Presbyterian Minister, who was not averse to anti-Catholic sentiment on occasion. But they had met thirty years earlier as fellow cabin passengers on the *James* on its voyage to Sydney, and Lang had presented her first petition to Parliament. Kelly needed a politician with Lang's high profile.

On May 5, 1865, eighteen months after the House had first failed to debate the Select Committee's Report, Dr Lang rose in the Legislative Assembly and moved that the House go into a Committee of the Whole to consider the Report of the Select Committee on the Petition of Isabella Mary Kelly. In committee mode the House would discuss the Report and form a resolution, which would then be put to the House as a formal motion on a later occasion.

In speaking to his motion, Dr Lang said he had been asked by certain Members of the House to defer his motion, but the Lady, who was the subject of his motion, moved in a very respectable class of society, and had been possessed of a large amount of property. Miss Kelly had been deprived of her property, and been imprisoned on a charge of perjury, of which she was altogether innocent. He hoped that the Members would not be so ungallant as to postpone this matter any further.[17]

After a successful vote on the motion, the house moved into committee mode. Dr Lang outlined the history of the case from Kelly's arrival in the colony as a woman of wealth to her conviction for perjury and eventual release from prison. Miss Kelly had been in possession of £10000 before her imprisonment and this had all been expended, and she had been reduced to penury. Miss Kelly was currently ill in St. Vincent's Hospital.

Lang read out the fourteen findings of the Select Committee Report, before moving that Miss Kelly receive "a sum of money as compensation ... for the loss of health and property sustained in consequence of her unjust conviction and imprisonment for perjury."[18]

The *amount* of money was not included – this was the question most Members dreaded. William Forster, the new Member for Hastings who had attended both Select Committees, said he believed Miss Kelly had suffered some injustice but did not think the amount of compensation should be as large as some members seemed to think it should be. Forster's comments were received with numerous "hear, hear"s.

Another Select Committee Member, Mr Cunneen said he

did not think Miss Kelly should receive compensation by reason of the property she had lost while she was in gaol, but she should be compensated because documents (the Bill of Sale and the Receipt) had been lost by a "public officer" (a euphemism for Sir Alfred Stephen).

The decisive speech came from John Darvall, Kelly's former defence barrister. Nothing could be given to the lady which would truly compensate for her loss of property and health, he said, these losses had occurred through a most unhappy miscarriage of justice. He thought in this case she deserved some monetary compensation, and would suggest to the House that £1000 be inserted into Dr Lang's motion.

"Hear, hear" resounded around the Chamber – £1000 was an amount that most Members could accept as an adequate cost of putting an end to the matter.

In speaking to his motion, Darvall said he thought Miss Kelly had been treated most cruelly, and no amount of compensation could restore her health or be in proportion to the losses she had sustained. But he did not believe she had an absolute right to come to the House and ask for compensation, as this should only be given in extreme cases.

After outlining the case involving Skerrett, Darvall said Miss Kelly had been convicted and incarcerated. While she was imprisoned in a cold wet dungeon, the scoundrel Skerrett took every opportunity to steal her property. After her release, she returned to the world with her character maligned, in bad health and a beggar. Since Miss Kelly's release she had been living on charity and had received aid from St. Vincent's Hospital. Her health was now ruined and there was no hope of recovery. In the short time left to her, it would be of some consolation to her if the House showed itself to be sensitive to the injustice and cruelty suffered by her. This was surely one of the most distressing cases to come before any committee.[19]

With agreement reached on this resolution, the committee mode was terminated, and the resolution was placed on the Order of the Day to come before the House in the following week.

Eleven days later, Dr Lang rose once again and moved the agreed Motion to the Legislative Assembly.

Thomas Garrett rose and addressed the House, stating that it was not his intention to oppose the Motion, but he did want to make some statements about Mr Flett, the former Member of the Assembly. Mr Flett had been a Magistrate on the Manning Valley for many years. Mr Flett sat on the Select Committee inquiring into these matters, Garrett continued, and during the hearings, Miss Kelly took every opportunity to impugn the character and conduct of Mr Flett as he carried out his duties as a Magistrate. Mr Flett denied all these allegations, but his denials did not appear in the records of the Committee.

Here Garrett produced papers, which he said were copies of the proceedings of all the cases on the Manning in which Miss Kelly had been before Mr Flett. Garrett said these papers would completely exonerate Mr Flett from all of the charges Miss Kelly made against Mr Flett. Any Member of the House would be welcome to read these papers and see for themselves that only one side of the charges against Mr Flett had been heard.

Further, Garrett said, Mr Skerrett had not been given the chance to go before the Committee and clear his name. Miss Kelly had never given the Committee any substantial evidence of the damages she had suffered. In committee meetings, Garrett said, he had repeatedly questioned her on this point, but had been unable to get anything definite from her. Miss Kelly's evidence was most inconclusive. He believed the compensation was being extorted from House, rather than given on the grounds of justice.

Mr Buchanan interjected, "Not at all." (Buchanan, the original promoter of Kelly's petition in 1861, had returned to Parliament at the last election in a different electorate.)

Garrett replied that the honourable gentleman knew nothing about the case, and if he took the trouble to read the evidence he could see she had not made out a case for compensation – she should not even receive a farthing. Garrett said he did not doubt she had suffered damages, but her evidence had been most unsatisfactory on the point.[20]

Henry Parkes (who had been a member of the Skerrett Select Committee) rose and said it was *Mr Garrett* who had shown by his comments that he knew nothing about the case. Cries of "hear, hear" supported Parkes.

Mr Arnold had moved for a Committee to examine Skerrett's petition in 1860, Parkes said, and Miss Kelly had no

A Final Decision

influence on that Committee as she was utterly helpless in prison. It was notable that Mr Justice Dickinson, who had tried and sentenced Miss Kelly, ordered her liberation as a result of the Skerrett Committee's investigation. If the House passed this motion, Parkes continued, they were doing tardy justice to an injured lady, who would now not derive much benefit from it.[21]

David Buchanan was more direct, not using any euphemisms in his speech to the House, saying the negligence of the Chief Justice in losing documents caused Miss Kelly to be found guilty and imprisoned. Even this amount of money was poor compensation for what Miss Kelly had been through. The loss of her property was insignificant compared to the personal injuries Miss Kelly had suffered.

Thomas Garrett replied that in reference to Miss Kelly's original Petition to Parliament, where she claimed loss of money as result of her imprisonment, she had not *proved* any pecuniary losses at all.

The motion awarding Kelly £1000 was put to the House and passed *unanimously*.

Kelly had finally won through to victory – she had ultimately cleared her name and received compensation, albeit not the £5000 she may have expected, but certainly, with good reason, believed she deserved.

Henry Flett's campaign had not been a complete failure.

But Isabella Kelly had won a pyrrhic victory.

In the eyes of the public, Isabella Kelly's reputation was never restored.

Apart from the political reports, which detailed the passage of Kelly's compensation through Parliament, neither *Empire* nor the *Sydney Morning Herald* printed any articles, editorials, letters-to-the-editor or discussion of the case in any form.

In the Manning Valley, Horace Dean's fledgling *Manning River News* printed a brief report of the Legislative Assembly in committee mode including the resolution agreed by it on the urging of Dr Lang. But Dean completely ignored the second day when the motion passed through the House, making absolutely no reference to Henry Flett's role in the matter or of Garrett

The Trials of Isabella Mary Kelly

staunchly trying to defend Henry Flett's reputation.

The normally loquacious Horace Dean wrote long editorials about all matters political, and covered a variety of topics in his regular column entitled "Table Talk", but no reference – then or in the future – was ever made to Isabella Mary Kelly. Dean's newspaper was a new and expensive enterprise – he had no wish to risk advertising revenue or readership by offending anybody.

So much mud had been thrown at Isabella Mary Kelly it stuck.

35. Slipping Away

On September 11, 1865, four months after Parliament awarded her £1000, Isabella Mary Kelly sold the 43-acre Waterview property on the Dawson River for £45, ending twenty-seven years of residence in the Manning Valley.[1]

Isabella Mary Kelly was now making preparations to return Home to England.

John Ryan Brenan, her former solicitor, read that Kelly had received £1000 in compensation from the Government, and decided to chase the money she owed him. Kelly had stubbornly ignored the Supreme Court writ, which Brenan had obtained in October 1860, ordering her to pay a £108 bill for his services. This bill had since grown to £164 when Brenan added interest and legal costs.

Born in Ireland in 1798, Brenan arrived in Sydney in 1834 and began his private practice as a lawyer. At various times he held the positions of Superintendent of Prisons at Parramatta, Coroner and Police Magistrate. He often described as controversial and having idiosyncratic behaviour.[2]

Brenan had drifted in and out of the Isabella Mary Kelly story for many years. He defended Skerrett in 1851 against embezzlement charges; he assisted Kelly to prosecute Skerrett in 1855; he had obtained the arrest of William Turner and helped Kelly prosecute Skerrett for forgery in 1860.

In 1864 Brenan was forced into insolvency and sold his 104-acre estate in order to resolve the insolvency.[3]

It seems that Kelly may have expected Brenan to look for her, as Brenan wrote:[4]

> I made due enquiry for her address of her attorney, Mr Eyre G. Ellis, and of several other persons to whom she was known, and I was informed that she refused to allow her

address to be known, and although at that time I made every possible enquiry and used every endeavour to find the address of the said Isabella Mary Kelly or where she could be found, I was unsuccessful.

I also applied to the proper officer at the Colonial Treasury for the address of the said Isabella Mary Kelly and was informed by him that she had not left her address nor had she left any instructions as to where she was to be addressed on the subject of the balance of the said sum of one thousand pounds which she was entitle to receive.

On October 17, 1865, Isabella Kelly had withdrawn £250 of the £1000 compensation, with the possibility that her solicitor, Eyre Ellis, may have advised Kelly that by leaving the remaining £750 in the hands of the Government, it was safe from any legal challenge by Brenan, or at least safer than being in her own hands.

Shortly after drawing the £250, Isabella Mary Kelly slipped out of Sydney and travelled to Melbourne, where, according to Eyre Ellis, she took a ship for England in December 1865. It was about March 1866 before Brenan became persuaded that Kelly had definitely left the colony. He went to Eyre Ellis and demanded the money from him. Ellis showed Brenan the document containing the Power of Attorney, and Brenan noted that Ellis had authority to receive funds on Kelly's behalf, but conveniently had no authority to pay any of Kelly's debts.[5]

On September 25, 1866, Brenan went to the Insolvency Court, seeking a compulsory sequestration of the Estate of Miss Isabella Mary Kelly, which was granted. On October 1, the Sheriff's Bailiff left a summons for Miss Kelly with the wife of Mr William McIntosh in Forbes Street, Sydney, the last known address of Miss Kelly. With Kelly having left the colony, there could only be one source to pay the debts of the estate – the £750 in the hands of Treasury.

A number of Insolvency meetings were held in late 1866 and early 1867, with only one other debt coming forward, that of the David Jones store for £41, which involved items such as lace and buttons, and with the last purchase made in July 1863. With no Insolvency schedule filed by Kelly, the Official Assignee had only one option, and that was to go to the Supreme Court and seek a mandamus to appropriate the debt from the £750 held by the

⚜ Slipping Away ⚜

Government Treasury for Miss Kelly.

Delivering its verdict on September 28, 1867, the Supreme Court ruled against Brenan on two grounds. Firstly, it had listened to the opinion of the Solicitor-General, that the £750 had been voted to Miss Kelly by Parliament, and hence was *payable only to her*. Secondly, the application was refused on the purely technical ground that no warrant had yet been issued by the Governor for this sum of money to be paid to Miss Kelly.[6]

After this decision, the Insolvency proceedings collapsed with nowhere to go. The death of John Ryan Brenan in June 1868 put finality to the pursuit of the debt.

An obstinate Isabella Kelly never paid Brenan's bill.

The last years of the life of Isabella Mary Kelly are as full of mystery as are her early years. While there were many reports of her activities once she left Australian shores, there is only one brief source which can be accepted as fact. This is a letter written by Isabella Kelly from London in August 1867 to "My dear Mrs Mackay" of Dungog, excerpts of which were published in the *Wingham Chronicle* in 1918 – the letter itself has not survived.[7]

Her ill health had continued as she wrote, "No doubt you will think me ungrateful for not writing to you long ere this, but the fact is I was very ill on my arrival in England, and was not able to attend to business for three months."

Isabella complained of not receiving the balance of her £1000 from the Government: "Doctor Lang is doing all he can for me. If I had not good friends here I would be in a sad fix." The money would have been withheld until after the Supreme Court handed down its judgement in the following month (September 1867) denying Brenan's application for a mandamus. There is no doubt she did eventually receive the money.

One section of Kelly's letter was quite puzzling as she described petitioning members of the British Parliament, but gave no indication of *why* she was taking this action. The most likely explanation is dissatisfaction with the amount of her compensation – she may have expected to receive an amount more like the £5000 William Barber received from the House of Commons as a result of his unjust imprisonment. Isabella Kelly wrote:

I got a memorial drawn up by my Solicitor. After it was drawn up I told him it was useless to petition the Secretary of State, as I was sure that he would only send it back to Australia, and there it would end. My Solicitor would insist upon it, that the Secretary of State was the proper person to address. I allowed him to do what he considered best. After a lapse of 10 months, my Solicitor called upon the Secretary of State, who told him that they could not interfere with the Colonial Government.

I was then advised to seek some of the members of Parliament. I lost no time in doing so – I interviewed Sir George Bowyer who is a great man in Parliament. He at once got a copy of the memorial, and called upon the Secretary of State, and told him that my case was a sad one.

He (the Secretary of State) told him that I had better petition the Queen, and I had to get a second petition drawn up. Sir George Bowyer has taken charge of it.

Sir George Bowyer was a prominent English politician who had converted to the Catholic religion and pursued a number of Catholic causes in Parliament. While it certainly displayed Isabella Kelly's stubborn persistence, nothing appears to have come from these moves.

There was also a deep sadness displayed as Isabella wrote of her return to England after an absence of thirty years:

Strange to say that nearly all my friends are dead. There are only two families left out of the many that I knew before I left England for Australia. My friends the Crowder family are all dead, but four.

Mrs Crowder made me a present of a very handsome gold watch which belonged to [her husband] the late Sir Richard Crowder.

I was invited to Reeding for a few weeks. Believe me, with all their kindness, I would feel more at home with you. To see the style and grandeur that they live in is remarkable – coachmen, butlers, and footmen.

Reeding appears to have been the home of the Richard Crowder family.

Isabella Kelly went on to describe the Paris World Exhibition, which was open from April to November of 1867.

> I have just returned from Paris. I have been there for 10 months. I saw the exhibition. It was the grandest sight that has ever been seen. Would that I was able to give you a description of what I have seen in Paris. If you were to see the dolls walking and talking. I saw also the Australian Flag. I am sorry to say it was a poor turn-out. I saw several samples of coal and gold dust; stuffed birds and animals. There were some samples of timber there, too.

Settler George Hill of Bungay Bungay wrote, "Miss Kelly went to England, for the purpose – so she said – of placing her diary in the hands of Charles Dickens, so that he might write a novel with the material."[8] While one can well imagine drawing-room conversations in which it was said her life read like a Charles Dickens novel, it does not appear that such an approach to Charles Dickens (1812-1870) was made. But the Mackay letter confirms the writing of her Journal:

> I cannot publish my Journal until I get a settlement from the Australian Government. There can be nothing done without money. I keep writing every day that I am able to. I have made many improvements in my Journal lately.

The newspaper editor of the *Wingham Chronicle* added a postscript to the Mackay letter: "Miss Kelly, as far as can be learned, never had her reminiscences published." And the mystery of what happened to her Journal persists to the present day.

While overseas Isabella Kelly apparently visited Ireland. In a letter to the editor of the *Wingham Chronicle* in the 1930s seeking information about Isabella Kelly, a "P. Lowry" of Brisbane wrote:[9]

> Miss Kelly was my grand aunt. I remember seeing her in Ireland in 1866, when she making a visit to her sister, Elizabeth, who was my grandmother. I was then nine years old.

This is the sole reference to a sister, and there is only one other reference to a brother.

Isabella Kelly returned to Sydney sometime in the period 1868 to 1870.

During the Select Committee hearings Isabella Kelly had stated that her intention at one time had been to retire Home to England, but this did not occur. There are two pointers from the

Mackay letter of her reasons for returning – her health; and the deaths of so many of her friends in England.

David Buchanan, a member of parliament, said Kelly had visited many specialist doctors while abroad, but without any successful diagnosis.[10] She could well have returned to Sydney to escape the harsh British winters. After all, she had stated that her original arrival in the colony in 1835 had been for health reasons.

The legend writers concerned themselves only with the first few years of Isabella Kelly's life in the Manning Valley, where they were able to creatively extend the rumours that existed about Isabella Kelly in connection with convicts and bushrangers.

Virtually nothing was written by these authors about the main the story in her life, that of Charles Skerrett and forged documents. The following untrue paragraphs dealing with the latter part of her life come from author Bill Beatty in 1960: [11]

> But now there was considerable settlement on the Manning, and newcomers began to squat on portions of the big territory which Miss Kelly claimed was her land. Finding that she could not scare them away, and unwilling to risk the drastic personal action that succeeded in the past when settlers were few, she invoked the aid of the law. That settled her.
>
> The Government appointed a Select Committee to inquire into her title. It was then found that she had no proof that any land grants had been made to her. Furthermore, she had taken no steps to record her title to any of the land.
>
> The reign of Isabella Kelly, the woman who had ruled and terrorized the district for nearly thirty years, was over.

Only one paragraph in all the articles purportedly giving the life story of Isabella Mary Kelly mentions the name of Charles Skerrett, and there was never a hint of people like Joseph Andrews, Henry Flett or George Rowley. The writers had no intention of giving any possible offence to the many descendants of the other parties involved in the Kelly story – that could result in a challenge.

Isabella Mary Kelly had no descendants and probably no relatives of any description in New South Wales. Consequently there was never anyone to guard her memory and protect her good name.

When noted Manning Valley historian, Gordon Dennes, printed part of the findings of the 1863 Select Committee in the *Wingham Chronicle* in 1932 to counteract many of the stories that had been appearing about Isabella Mary Kelly, the name "Skerrett" was replaced with "S——" to hide his identity, in deference to the members of his family still living in the Valley.[12]

Ironically this article, with the name of Skerrett blanked out, was also printed in the *Dungog Chronicle*, the newspaper which, in the previous decade, had been so free and easy in its denigration of Isabella Mary Kelly.[13]

On May 16, 1871, John Dillon, the Member for Hunter, rose in the House of Assembly and moved that "a sum not exceeding £1000, to supplement a sum previously [six years ago] voted by this House as compensation to Miss Isabella Mary Kelly, for her unjust incarceration in one of her Majesty's gaols of this colony."[14]

Dillon, in speaking to the motion, refused to give reasons why Isabella Kelly should receive a second £1000 in compensation, stating he would give them when the House moved to committee mode in the following week.

Mr Stewart, a member of the Kelly Select Committee, asked Dillon to give his reasons *now*, as Miss Kelly had already been paid for the injury done to her. Mr Lucas interjected with, "She got £1000." Dillon said he would only give his reasons with the House in committee mode.

Mr Buchanan seconded the motion, saying while Miss Kelly was in prison in a cold damp cell, she had contracted a serious asthma. She did receive £1000 from Parliament, but she had gone Home to England to consult with medical experts, and all her money had been expended on that journey. After spending all the money trying to regain her health, she was now in a state of absolute starvation. Her illness and her maladies were now greatly aggravated. This was sufficient reason for the House to go into committee.[15]

Mr Forster, the former Member for The Hastings and now the Member for Queanbeyan, and also a member of both Kelly

The Trials of Isabella Mary Kelly

Select Committees, rose and gave a brief summary of the case. After her liberation from prison, compensation was given to her for loss of property sustained while in prison, but he did not recall any evidence given about the state of her health. His impression was that she had received compensation fully equal to the necessities of the case, and if the House were to go into committee on this issue, Mr Dillon needed to offer additional information.

Mr Garrett rose and said if ever a case had been thoroughly enquired into, it was this one. This brought cries of "hear, hear." Miss Kelly had received a thousand pounds as full satisfaction for the injury she had received, Garrett said, and he would vote against the motion.

Mr Driver went further. He had always voted against this matter, he said, and he did not believe Miss Kelly was entitled to one shilling in compensation.

Mr Hart, a member of the Skerrett Select Committee, had reservations saying he thought it desirable to have some explanation. The matter had already been investigated and he was not sure that Miss Kelly was wholly free from blame. "Hear, hear" went round the House. A very generous amount of money had already been awarded to her, Hart said, and it was about time a stop was put to these stale claims. Mr Driver called out, "hear, hear."

In a final statement supporting his motion, Mr Dillon said he did not wish to give his reasons now, as they would only be repeated again when the House was in committee. They may say that she had already been compensated well, but how could £1000 compensate for a £10000 loss. When she was liberated from prison, she had lost everything she possessed in the world. Irreparable injury had been done to her health, and now she was on her death bed. If the honourable members had any consideration for their fellow human beings, they would regard this case favourably.

The motion was defeated nineteen votes to nine.

A final curtain had been brought down on the case of Miss Isabella Mary Kelly.

Editor Horace Dean used only four lines of one column to report Dillon's motion in his *Manning River News*, despite its pertinence to the Manning Valley readership.[16]

Slipping Away

Thirteen months later Isabella Mary Kelly died.

Her death certificate[17] recorded her death on June 24, 1872, was caused by a "decay of nature", with the duration of the illness noted as "some time". A doctor had visited her two days before she died.

Richard Blundell, a friend, reported the death and gave her name as Mary Isabella Kelly, suggesting he probably knew her as Mary Kelly in day-to-day life, rather than Isabella Kelly. The death certificate also recorded her age as "about 70" and her place of birth as "Ireland."

The funeral notice in the *Sydney Morning Herald* on Tuesday, June 25, 1872 stated:

> The friends of the deceased Miss Isabella Mary Kelly are respectfully invited to attend her funeral to move from No. 343 Crown Street, Surrey Hills, 3 doors south of the reservoir, THIS (Tuesday) MORNING, at half-past 8 o'clock, and the Mortuary Station at a quarter-past 9 o'clock.
>
> James Curtis, Undertaker, 59 Hunter-street.

Isabella Kelly was buried at Necropolis, now known as Rookwood Cemetery, and unfortunately, no record exists of who attended the funeral. Apart from the paid funeral notice in the *Sydney Morning Herald*, there was no obituary or remarks on her passing in the newspapers – Isabella Kelly had slipped away.

Settler Robert Cox, who knew Isabella Kelly, said that after Kelly returned to Sydney she died "in one or other of the Catholic Institutions of the day".[18] Cox was the only source for this statement.

Settler George Hill was quoted as saying that Miss Kelly "was seen shortly before her death – by a relative of my own – living in extreme poverty".[19]

How extreme this poverty had become, one cannot be certain. Isabella Kelly had come to Sydney as a wealthy woman, and was always regarded as rich. Towards the end she may well have been receiving monetary assistance from friends, which, if it were the case, would have gone very much against the grain.

During the 1863 Select Committee, Isabella Kelly stated two

aunts of Sir Richard Crowder had sent her money to help her through her difficulties. When asked if she had requested the money from them, Isabella replied:[20]

> No, I never dreamed of asking for such a thing. The money was sent to me without any request on my part. They were friends of mine, and I frequently had money sent out by my friends. Here is a letter showing that £100 has been sent out lately, in order to support me in my trouble. I never sent Home [England] for that, nor thought of doing so.

Of course the legend writers had a different take on the death of Isabella Kelly. In 1963, James Holledge wrote in *Australia's Wicked Women* that:[21]

> In her later years Isabella Kelly sank to penury and was a familiar figure haunting the wharves in the Sussex Street area of Sydney. She lived by begging and lived to a great age.
>
> They found her dead one morning in 1897 in the foundations of a warehouse – where in a rat infested cubbyhole she had long made her home.

The year 1897 approximated the year of Kate (sister of Ned) Kelly's death.[22] Even the National Library of Australia records the death of Isabella Kelly as 1897.

At the end of her life, Isabella Kelly may well have been in poor circumstances, but she did have a roof over her head, and she does seem to have made provision for her own funeral, which was carried out by an undertaker who placed a paid funeral notice in the *Sydney Morning Herald*.

She was not buried in a pauper's grave.

One can imagine a Catholic priest conducting a graveside service, but who else came?

Appendix 1
Completing the lives of some characters

Joseph Andrews

Joseph Andrews seemed to recover from his insolvency debacle with his reputation intact. Ever active in the community and leader of the rather large Andrews clan resident in the Valley, it was not until 1880 that Joseph Andrews, aged sixty-six, realised his ambition of being elected to Parliament.

During one of his many absences in Sydney representing the Hastings and Manning electorate, Ann, his wife of forty-six years, died. When his three-year term was completed, Joseph did not re-contest the seat, but simply returned to the farm.

In 1888, at the age of seventy-four, Joseph married a thirty-year-old widow, Pauline Keogh, who together with her two sons went to live with Joseph across the river from Woodside. Joseph had met Pauline in Sydney, and it was less than four months in this remote district, before she and the boys packed their bags and left. The fact that most of Joseph's children were older than Pauline may well have been a contributing factor.[1]

Joseph Andrews died in January 1901, the day before his eighty-seventh birthday, and was buried at Woodside beside Ann.

John Brislane

John Brislane died in October 1902 at the age of 102, and was buried on his own property. His obituary in the Wingham Chronicle stated that "Brislane had a considerable amount of property in Ireland, but he left all to come to Australia to try and make his fortune".[2] His eleven children were unaware that he had come to the colony as a convict until well after his death.

Patrick (Paddy) Connolly

Paddy Connolly died on September 18, 1901, aged ninety-five. In the articles written about Connolly in the years since his death, all record his popularity and offer anecdotes of his revered Irish humour. One described him as a "genial, good-hearted Irishman".[3]

There was never any reference to his arrival in the colony as a convict or his two gaol sentences for assault (1851) and cattle stealing (1858).

Phillip Dew

Phillip Dew drowned while trying to cross the Manning River on May 26, 1863, aged forty-seven. The body, with the head and legs missing, was not recovered until September.[4]

Henry Flett

Henry Flett died on November 15, 1877, aged sixty-seven, at Tarree. He had continued on the Bench as a Magistrate until about 1870, and was active in the community particularly as President of the Show Society and on the Bench.

Henry Flett was a leader in the sugar growing community of the Manning Valley, and fully supported in this activity by Horace Dean in the *Manning River News*, but the sugar industry in the Manning Valley terminated with the heavy frosts of 1872. In the 1870s Flett lived mainly in Sydney, returning to Taree in ill health shortly before his death.

With no local newspaper operating in the Manning Valley at the time of Henry Flett's death, the only obituary appeared in the *Sydney Mail*, and seemed to be searching for a better man. Part of this obituary reported:[5]

> .... in the General Election of December, 1860, Mr Flett was again returned to Parliament, and took part in carrying the land policy embodied in the present law.
>
> He continued to represent The Hastings electorate in the Assembly for four years; when on the rejection of Mr William Forster by East Sydney, Mr Flett retired from the candidature of the Hastings, in order to make way for him, and, by his influence, promoted the election of Mr Forster.

Completing the lives of some characters

He has not since then sought to re-enter Parliament, but has in various ways used his influence for the improvement of the electorate …

Obviously the reporter did not check his facts, and relied on information given to him. As readers may recollect, Flett lost the 1864 election when he received only 328 votes to William Forster's 530 votes. Further, Henry Flett contested the next elections held in December 1869, coming *third* with 307 votes behind Horace Dean's 474 votes and Robert Burdett Smith's 444 votes.[6]

At the time of his death, Henry Flett's image seems to have been well protected.

Reuben Richards

"I was Reuben Richards' neighbour for about two years, and during that period I found him malicious, untruthful, and dishonest, and from a knowledge of his character I would not believe him on oath",[7] said John Paton in a sworn deposition to the 1863 Select Committee – and few seem to have disagreed with him. Richards' prickly nature went with him when he moved his family to Mitchell's Island in the Manning Delta.

In 1867 a school committee was formed to cater for the establishment and running of a school on Mitchell's Island, with Reuben Richards nominated as secretary. School Inspector Allpass noted his regret that one valuable man had refused to join the committee because there was a man on the committee of a "quarrelsome nature", without actually naming Reuben Richards.

In 1874, the second Mitchell's Island teacher, Thomas Hall, called a meeting of parents with Inspector Allpass, to show them letters he had been receiving over the past months from Reuben Richards. Hall described the letters as "offensive, meddlesome and interfering" in the operation of the school. Allpass agreed. In Richards' absence, the meeting unanimously recommended to request the Council of Education to remove Richards from the school committee.

When told of the motion, Richards refused to resign. Consequently the Council abolished the *whole* committee, necessitating a new election, with the result that the new committee did not contain Reuben Richards.

In 1886, Richards wrote to the Department complaining that the current teacher, Mr Govett, was earning a second income (strictly forbidden by the Department) as a lecturer on Ireland. This action originated from Richards' son, who complained that Govett had been publicly objecting to the length of time he and his father were taking to construct a road on Mitchell's Island.

School Inspector Willis stated in his report on the matter to the Department that Mr Govett bore a very high reputation throughout the district, while Mr Richards and his son were "looked upon as a public nuisance." The matter resolved itself when Govett resigned, not, according to the Inspector, because of the complaint.[8]

Reuben Richards, had not lived long on Mitchell's Island, when he filed his schedule with the Insolvency Court in 1864.[9] He listed debts of £96 which surprisingly included a £5 debt to Andrews, dated 1860. Richards said his insolvent state had been caused by his unjust imprisonment for perjury and "the harsh conduct of one of my creditors." (Andrews?)

Richards also stated that while he was in prison a sum of money had been collected for the relief of his wife and children, part of which had been used as "a deposit upon the conditional purchase of forty acres in the name of one of my children." With no assets, the Insolvency went through unopposed.

In 1872 Richards again passed through the Insolvency Court with debts of £86 and assets totalling £22.[10] His losses this time were attributed to the failure of his maize, wheat and sugar crops by floods and other climatic conditions. The owner of the land was listed as Sarah Richards, which probably referred to his sister.

The insolvency passed through unopposed, but as Richards did not pay the necessary bureaucratic fees, no clearance certificate was issued. These fees were paid over twenty years later in 1893, and the clearance certificate was eventually granted, possibly to enable Richards to become a Justice of the Peace.[11]

Ann Richards died in 1890. Reuben Richards died in January 1917 at the age of eighty-four, and was buried on Mitchell's Island.

George Rowley

George Rowley died in 1873 at Berrima, aged sixty-two.

Completing the lives of some characters

After his departure from the Manning, Rowley became a solicitor working in Sydney.[12] Rowley's appointment, as clerk to the Chief Justice was followed by his appointment as Clerk of Petty Sessions at Berrima in September 1860.[13]

Charles Skerrett

Charles Blake Skerrett died on September 14, 1893, aged seventy-seven, and was buried next to his wife Maria in the Church of England section of Rookwood Cemetery, not far from the grave of Isabella Mary Kelly.[14]

Little is known of Charles Skerrett after he left the Manning Valley, other than he went through a second insolvency in 1865 – this time it was genuine. His debts in this insolvency, all dated 1864 or 1865, amounted to £141, mainly for meat, milk, groceries, coal and rent, and oddly enough, included a bill of £6 for the hire of a piano.

In a surprising feature of the insolvency, Skerrett listed his occupation as "Lodging House Keeper" and listed seven people as owing him a total of £113 for board and lodgings, all of which were listed in the bad debts columns as unlikely to be paid. With only £21 in assets (mainly furniture) Skerrett passed through the insolvency rather easily, and was allowed to keep his furniture.[15]

Maria Skerrett died in September 1891, nearly two years previous to her husband.

Appendix 2

The First Story on Isabella Mary Kelly

from Smith's Weekly: August 9, 1924.

The Discomfiture of a Termagant

History records very few instances in which a woman has ventured into the wilderness to develop the land. Some have faced the untrodden paths of the unknown for sheer adventure. Others have been lured by the potent lode-stone of love. A few have quested out to escape the shackling conventions of society.

But Isabella Mary Kelly, who owned Mount George Station, in the Manning River District, in the days when Captain Thomas Cook, of Auchentorlie, Dungog, was virtually Caesar over the vast territory that extended from Port Stephens almost to Port Macquarie, was a pioneer purely and simply.

Romance maybe had touched Miss Kelly's heart in her young days. But in 1840 there were left to her no traces of any of those attributes customarily associated with those who have loved or been loved. Her features were distinctively masculine. Her body possessed no allure. It was bony, gaunt and angular as a tall man's. Her arms were powerfully muscled, her fists like mutton hands. When she spoke, using frequent biting oaths, her voiced as discordantly as any crow's.

The only trait genuinely feminine about the lady was the uncertainty of her temper. Her assigned servants – she worked her property with a considerable body of convict helpers – realised this more fully than anyone else. Their scarred shoulders, torn and wrung from the scourger's cat, proved how grievous

The Discomfiture of a Termagant

were the burdens it imposed.

For years this indomitable woman, by sheer force of character, ruled more than a score of the most rebellious scourings of England's prison hulks, fought off the savage attacks of hostile aboriginals, terrified adventurous interlopers who sought to raid her flocks or squat on her lands, and at last had none to challenge her supremacy.

Scorn For Bushrangers

Miss Kelly's boast that in a decade no one had ever got the better of her, whether in a bargain or aught else, was no idle one. Those who had essayed the task only to retire thoroughly discomfited, were wont to tell shamefacedly of her exploits across the bars of the inns of Dungog. From these highly coloured tales bandied about from lip to lip, added to here, distorted there, the good woman at length came to have an unenviable reputation as a vicious termagant to be left severely alone.

Because Miss Kelly's presence was necessary before the bench of magistrates at Dungog over a matter of the disputed ownership of some sheep, the morning of September 12, 1840, found her camped beside the river below the home of Chief-Constable Thomas Abbott.

Accompanying her was a considerable travelling outfit. Besides her horses there were two bullock drays in the charge of Charles Mathers and Edward Reece, two assigned servants. The reason of this impedimenta was that the chatelaine of Mount George intended to proceed from Dungog to Green Hills, now called Morpeth, to take delivery of a supply of stores for use on the station during the ensuing twelve months. The goods were then waiting in Mr Campbell's shed near the wharf.

After the proceedings in court, wherein she had completely routed the rival claimant for the sheep, Miss Kelly held converse with Capt Cook and his brother magistrate Mr Crawford Logan Brown of Cairnsmore, on the matter of her journey to Green Hills.

Capt Cook had advised her to postpone her departure for a few days as an armed escort of constables would be provided.

"You are carrying a goodly sum of money with you, madam," he pointed out, "and like as not the bushrangers will be on the lookout for you. They are desperate rascals and may do

The Trials of Isabella Mary Kelly

you hurt."

The magistrate could have truthfully added that the most desperate of the outlaws had formerly been in the employ of Miss Kelly and had only taken to the bush because of the harsh treatment he had received at her huge hands.

"Bushrangers, "exclaimed Miss Kelly, scornfully. "A fig for the rascally blackguards. I'm a match for a full score of the knaves. Go I will tomorrow morning."

"If you insist," put in Mr Brown, "Then let me to entreat you to entrust the currency you have to Capt Cook. He will despatch it to Green Hills by the constables who ride thither on Saturday."

Miss Kelly laughed boisterously. "You poor frightened men," she taunted, "I've £125 in bank notes and a brace of pistols. My men are armed with muskets. I am not afraid of any encounter with a few half-starved down-at-heels absconders, even if you are."

Capt Cook bridled instantly at the impeachment of his courage. "You will need the services of my constables before tomorrow's evening," he snapped, "You will find me at Auchentorlie." With that he saluted stiffly and turned abruptly on his heel. Mr Brown followed in silence.

Had the two magistrates been less engrossed over the affront offered them, or Miss Kelly less elated with her small triumph, some one of the three would have undoubtedly noticed that there had been an interested listener to their talk. He was well-set-up man, whose cabbage-tree hat hid his features. After he heard the colloquy he effaced himself with painstaking unostentation.

The listener who had so quietly and quickly betaken himself off was a certain Thomas Buckingham, ordinarily assigned servant and overseer for Mr J. J. Coar of Wallaringa. This worthy, enjoying the confidence of his master and a pass signed by Capt Cook himself, was free to come and go about the district, a circumstance which enabled him to gratify his life-long ambition to operate as a bushranger undetected and unsuspected. In fact, he had brought off several successful coups already, greatly to his own enrichment if to the confusion and ruin of the accomplices of his ventures.

When Buckingham spurred swiftly away from the township, the track he followed led him to the vicinity of that yawning cleft in Pilcher's Mountain which the Jew-boy gang of bushrangers

The Discomfiture of a Termagant

used as a temporary lair when Mr David Dunlop harried them too vigorously in the Wollombi and MacDonald River districts. Although he knew that Davis, the leader, and majority of the gang had ridden to Brisbane Water the day previously, Buckingham was also aware three of the outlaws remained behind through lack of saddles. These, he felt confident, he could enlist for an enterprise that involved the discomfiture of Miss Kelly. Especially as one of the men, Alban, an absconder from her service, had certain debts to pay.

At four o'clock on the following afternoon Miss Kelly, with bitter imprecations, was driving her two servants to desperate efforts to remove a tree that was across the road at the edge of the brush at the foot of Wallarobba Hill. The huge log completely blocked the passage of the drays.

For some minutes she stormed and fumed impatiently, spurring her horse backwards and forwards along the narrow track. At length, infuriated at the futile efforts of her two servitors, she sprang from the saddle to lend her own strength to the task. Seizing an axe from Reece, she prepared to lop the tangled mass of branches.

The She-devil Fights

As she spat on her hands before swinging the broad-bladed axe, something descended over her head and she felt strong arms twined about her body in a vice-like grip. Woman though she was, and handicapped by the sack that had been thrown over head from behind, Miss Kelly put up an astonishingly effective struggle. Her fists swung like flails at three unseen assailants who beset her. The groans and curses that they gritted out proved that the attackers would not go scathless.

Her commands to Mathers and Reece to come to her and went unheeded if heard, for the reason that those two individuals were gazing affrightedly down the barrels of two pistols pointed at them by a tall man wearing a cabbage-tree hat and a muffler about the lower part of his face. Weight of numbers told at last. She was overcome. But as Alban pinioned her arms with a green-hide rope, she raked his thigh grievously with her spurred heel.

"You she-devil," he roared as, as he shoved her roughly against the wheel of the dray.

The Trials of Isabella Mary Kelly

Through the bag Miss Kelly still unconquered in spirit, cursed the bushrangers in hoarse, muffled tones.

"Let me free for just one minute with an axe in my hands," she pleaded, "and I'll chop you up the lot of you, you scurvy cowards."

Helpless though she was, the outlaws were cowed by her very force of character and might have fled had not Buckingham called out.

"She has the money on her. Search her Alban."

Helpless, But Biting

Reluctantly and fearfully, the runaway convict stepped forward to do his leader's bidding. The woman kicked out viciously, but unable to see through the heavy folds of the sack, she overbalanced and fell helplessly to the road. As Alban tore open the bosom of her riding coat and seized the bulging chamois bag hidden there, Miss Kelly ceased to struggle.

"So it's Alban is it?" she said bitterly. "Alban, the poor creature with the heart of a louse." A brave bushranger who used to weep at the sight of the triangles and fell to his knees praying for mercy. A gallant thief who comes to rob a woman when she's helpless. Ah, Alban will be brave when he goes to the gallows, when the greased rope caresses his neck and when the hangman hauls him to the topmost limb of the tree."

The taunts drove the convict to fury, but the feel of the notes in the bag diverted his thoughts from immediate retaliation. He passed the booty to Buckingham. On the log it was divided into five equal parts, the leader taking two shares for himself and the others one apiece.

"Are you satisfied?" asked Buckingham.

"Aye," came the response.

One of the bushrangers then collected three muskets and a pistol from the drays. Besides that he took two saddles, a horn of powder, a bullet-mould and some food.

"She said she had two pistols," said Buckingham, "Where's the other?"

"There was only one," explained the searcher, "I went through everything."

"Well it won't matter," was the comment, "Now let us hurry."

The Discomfiture of a Termagant

As the bushrangers prepared to mount, Alban moved across to Miss Kelly, who was half-reclining against the cart-wheel, still cursing audibly.

"Now you hag," he hissed, "let us hear what you will say when the cat claws you." In his hand he held a greenhide halter, cut into strips and knotted after the fashion of a flagellator's scourge. He raised it to strike, but ere the lash fell, Buckingham's fist crashed on his jaw.

"'Tis bad enough to rob a woman," he said sternly to the prostrate man, "'Tis a coward's trick to beat one."

In ten minutes the bushrangers had vanished over the brow of the hill. Three minutes later Miss Kelly, after roundly cursing her servitors for their cowardice, and their clumsiness in severing her bonds, was spurring after them. In her hand was a pistol that had been concealed beneath the flap of her saddle.

Although the robbers had no misgivings about pursuit, nevertheless they did not linger on their ride to Pilcher's Mountain. Thus they were within a mile of their lair when the sound of galloping hoofs behind caused them to turn.

"My God, here she comes," yelled Alban.

Worth £100

The bushrangers separated, each man spurring with panic-stricken haste into the dense timber. But even as they turned a shot rang out. Alban slumped in his saddle for an instant and something that he had been holding in his hand fell to the ground. A moment later he was out of sight, but one arm hung uselessly at his side.

Miss Kelly reined up, realising the uselessness of further pursuit. Quickly she dismounted and picked up the object Alban had dropped. It was a silk neckerchief wrapped about 25 banknotes. She smiled grimly.

Capt Cook only heard of the robbery a fortnight later when he chanced to meet Mr Denny Day, the Maitland magistrate, on the Green Hills road.

"She did not report the matter," said Mr Day, "but her men talked. Hearing of it I questioned her, but all she would say to me was that it was worth the £100 she had lost to see the look on the faces of those rascals as she charged at them."

Notes

Money

The Colony of New South Wales at the time of this story used the English pound (Sterling) as currency.

1 shilling = 12 pence or pennies
20 shillings = 1 pound
1 guinea = 1 pound and 1 shilling (or 21 shillings)
1 pound 7 shillings and 6 pence could be written as:
£1 7s 6d. or £1/7/6 or £1 – 7 – 6
3/- is read as "three shillings"
3/6 is read as "three shillings and six pence"

In 1966, when Australia decimalised its currency, £1 became $2, and one shilling became ten cents.

In distance: 1 mile = 1.6 km
1 foot = 30 cm

Depositions

The depositions, taken before magistrates and judges (including judge's notes), take the form of never-ending paragraphs containing a multitude of sentences with semi-colons in between them. These are the answers given to the questions asked – but they do not record the questions themselves. Most of the time this does not present a problem, but it does occasionally become extremely intriguing to work out what the question must have been.

Newspaper reporting tended to be much the same.

Select Committees

There were three Parliamentary Select Committees, set up by the Legislative Assembly, mentioned in this book. At a time when Hansard did not exist, Parliament was recorded in "Votes and Proceeding". It did not record what was actually stated in Parliament, but recorded the motions, who moved and seconded them, and the result of the vote, including who voted which way. The phrase "Discussion ensued" appeared often. Newspapers gave a better description of the actual debates, but naturally these were edited.

Select committees, on the other hand, actually recorded what was said, including both the questions and answers. They also numbered the questions so reference could be made easily and distinctly. Fellow Parliamentarians could then read the complete report, and vote accordingly, when it came before the House.

When a select committee completed their investigation, they issued a report, which, together with the transcripts of the meetings, was recorded in "Votes and Proceedings".

The Trials of Isabella Mary Kelly

Abbreviations
IMK – Isabella Mary Kelly
SC – 1860 – Q524-532 means "Select Committee of 1860, questions 524 to 532".

Prologue: The Manning valley
1. *Smith's Weekly*, Apr 23, 1927.
2. James Holledge, *Australia's Wicked Women*, p100-110.
3. *Northern Champion*, Aug 3, 1927.
4. Jim Revitt, Letter to the Editor, *Wingham Chronicle*, Jun 3, 1982. Brimbin crossing is now under National Parks & Wildlife and a re-naming seems imminent.
5. Sir John Coode, *NSW Legislative Assembly, Votes and Proceedings, Report on New South Wales Harbours and Rivers, Manning River*, July 15, 1889.
6. At the time of publication of this book, the Old Bar mouth was again closed up.
7. John Ramsland, *The Struggle Against Isolation*, Chap. 2 covers the AA Company and exploration of the Manning River while Chap. 3 covers the initial settlement of the Valley.
8. Ian McDonell, *The Days of Wynter*. p5
9. Ian McDonell, *The Days of Wynter.*, p7-8
10. *NSW State Records*, Shelf 2/8012, Reel 1200.
11. John Blunt Reminiscences, *Manning River News*, June 2, 1866.
12. Manning Valley Historical Society, *Down to the Sea in Ships*, pp8-9, 52. The *Tarree* traded along the coast of New South Wales and was wrecked on the bar of the Clarence River.
13. John Allan, *The Allan Family*, p8

1: The Settler was a Woman
1. IMK, SC – 1860 – Q524-532.
2. IMK, SC – 1862 – Q238-257.
3. IMK, SC – 1863 – Q765-796.
4. IMK, SC – 1860 – Q527.
5. Receipt for Land, *NSW State Records*, Letter 38/1710.
6. Gordon Dennes, The *Wingham Chronicle*, May 18, 1971.
7. Kimbriki is pronounced kim-bree-ki where the "ki" rhymes with "high".
8. John Allan, *The Allan Family*, p7.
9. Magistrate Gray, *NSW State Records*, Letter 38/11745, Shelf 4/2421.1
10. The note was attached to Letter 38/11745. The letter of complaint by Kelly was not in State Records.
11. SC – 1863 – Q634-653, Q774.
12. This book is being prepared for publication by the Manning Valley Historical Society.
13. The late Gordon Dennes, an avid compiler of Manning Valley historical details, supplied to the Manning Valley Historical Society, a translation of that section of the book dealing with Manning Valley, but not the name of the person who did the translation.
14. *Australian Stud Book*, at website www.studbook.aust.com, 2004.
15. Müller does not always get things one hundred percent correct. English was, after all, a second language for him. There does not seem to be a court case for Kelly in the offing, at this time.
16. 30 miles is about 48 km.
17. The Benevolent Society was located at the end of Pitt Street. It later moved to Surrey Hills, when its buildings had to be demolished to make way for the erection of Central Railway Station and its environs. It had a wide cross-section of welfare people, as well as orphans, and suffered greatly from overcrowding.
18. There is a modern-day parallel with McDonalds. They claim they give young people jobs and training, which they would not otherwise be able to get, in

Notes

return for (relatively) cheap labour.
19. Again, Müller may not be quite correct when he uses the word 'shepherd'. It may have been Tim Leane, an overseer.
20. Advertisement, *The Australian*, February 22, 1842.

2: The Marriage Proposal
1. *Wingham Chronicle*, July 6, 1927, reported that the late Mrs. J. Neal told this story shortly before her death.
2. Ian McDonell, *The Days of Wynter*, p18
3. The *Mary Catherine* passenger list records a Henry Flitt, rather than Henry Flett, as a passenger – an apparent transcription error.
4. Thomas Cook, *NSW State Records*, Letter 37/11643, Shelf 4/2415.2.
5. John Plunkett, *NSW State Records*, Letter 38/1206, Shelf 4/2415.2.
6. Henry Flett, *NSW State Records*, Letter 38/1643, Shelf 4/2415.2.
7. Governor Gipps, as quoted by W. F. Connors, *Pioneering Days Around Taree*, p104.
8. Henry Flett, *NSW State Records*, 2/8732, Insolvency #752.
9. *NSW State Records*, Letter 40/14458, Shelf 2/7858, Reel 1127.
10. IMK, SC – 1863 – Q843.
11. Pre 1860 Pioneer Register, Manning Wallamba, pp122-123
12. *Land Records*, Old system, Book 9, No. 797. Although Henry Flett's mortgage to Carr was not registered, it is cited in the history of the property, in the sale of Killawarra by Carr & Rogers to Edmund Burton for £450 on October 23, 1845. This deal fell through and it was later sold to George Flett for £300. By 1852 George Flett had walked off Killawarra, leaving it vacant, after being unable to repay the mortgage.
13. *NSW State Records*, 2/8732, Flett Insolvency #752.
14. *Land Records*, Old system, Book 11, No. 471.
15. Gordon Dennes, *Manning Valley Historical Society* files.
16. *Land Records*, Old system, Book 11, No. 195 & No. 196. These two documents record a three-way agreement between Henry Flett, Owen MacGreal and John Ryan Brenan, who appears later in this story. Flett paid £100 to Brenan and £150 to MacGreal.
17. *Land Records*, Old system, Book 11, No. 472 and No. 473.
18. Ian McDonell, *The Days of Wynter*, p18
19. John Ramsland, *The Struggle Against Isolation*, pp46-48
20. *Land Records*, Old system, Book 21, No. 738.
21. *Land Records*, Old system, Book 36, No. 423.
22. George Rowley, letter to Mrs. New, May 14, 1855, *Papers of New T. and New T.W*, Mitchell Library.
23. *Land Records*, Old system, Book 39, No. 40.

3: A Woman in Charge of Convicts
1. *NSW Government Gazette*, August 10, 1840. (Gordon Dennes).
2. *Manning Valley Historical Society* Files, Bungay Bungay.
3. *NSW Government Gazette*, 1842, p1183.
4. Warren Cross, *Legal Administration of the Manning Valley*, p11-14, 18-22. The article covers the difficulties of early law administration, particularly in the Manning Valley, but equally applicable to other remote areas of NSW.
5. W. K. Birrell, *The Manning Valley, Landscape and Settlement 1824 – 1900*, p74-75.
6. *Sydney Morning Herald*, April 25, 1843.

415

The Trials of Isabella Mary Kelly

Part of the problem was the remoteness of the Manning Valley from Sydney, but the question still remains: What would have happened if the victim had been a settler rather than an aboriginal?

7. Dungog Bench Book, 1843-1848, May 20, 1843, p63, 83, cited by Gordon Dennes.
8. Dungog Bench Book, 1843-1848, Feb 9, 1843, p69, cited by Gordon Dennes.
9. Capt. McLean, *NSW State Records*, Letter 46/1177, Shelf 4/2732.1, Reel 2265.
10. Dungog Letter Book, 1839-1842, May 7, 1842, cited by Gordon Dennes.
11. *Port Macquarie The Windingsheet*, p205.
12. IMK, *NSW State Records*, Letter 45/11467, (Letter 46/1177, Shelf 4/2732.1, Reel 2265).
13. *NSW State Records*, Letter 45/11467, (Letter 46/1177, Shelf 4/2732.1, Reel 2265).
14. Court Report, *Maitland Mercury*, Dec 14, 1844.
15. John Allan, *The Allan Family*, p7.
16. John Jobson, *NSW State Records*, Letter 45/4402 (Letter 46/1177, Shelf 4/2732.1, Reel 2265).
17. IMK, *NSW State Records*, Letter 45/7356, (Letter 46/1177, Shelf 4/2732.1, Reel 2265).
18. IMK wrote the name Tedsall as "Titzel".
19. Capt. McLean, *NSW State Records*, Letter 46/1117, Shelf 4/2732.1, Reel 2265.
20. George Rowley, *NSW State Records*, Letter attached to Letter 46/1117, Shelf 4/2732.1, Reel 2265.
21. Rowley wrote the name Tedsall as "Teesdale".
22. George Rowley, *NSW State Records*, attached to Letter 46/1117, Shelf 4/2732.1, Reel 2265.
23. John Allan, *The Allan Family*, p7.
24. G. S. Hill, *Peeps into the Past*, p92.
25. "S. C. R.", *Northern Champion*, Aug 3, 1927.
26. C. K. Thompson, *Famous Detective Stories*, p23-26.
27. Frank Hawkins, *Brigalow, Brushbox & 'Blackboys'*, p25.
28. James Holledge, *Australia's Wicked Women*, p100-110.

4: Before the Bench

1. Henry Wynter, *NSW State Records*, Letter attached to 44/9183, Shelf 4/2674.2.
2. George Rowley as quoted by John Gorman, *NSW State Records*, Letter 44/9183, Shelf 4/2674.2.
3. John Gorman, *NSW State Records*, Letter 44/9183, Shelf 4/2674.2.
4. John Gorman, *NSW State Records*, Letter 44/15 to Surveyor General, Reel 3069. These stations, which he called No. 1 Station and No. 2 Station, were legally acquired by him afterwards.
5. John Gorman, *NSW State Records*, Letter 44/55 to Surveyor General, Reel 3069. Copies of the Bench depositions were attached to this letter.
6. Searle received his conditional pardon when he found a bushranger in one of Cann's huts and turned him in. Searle fathered two children to Mary Cann before marrying her in November 1846. As a convict, Searle had been refused permission to wed Mary Cann, and their eventual marriage darkened rumours about the death of her former husband.
7. IMK, *NSW State Records*, Letter 45/7375, Shelf 4/2694.2, Reel 2261. Kelly wrote this letter to the Governor on the same day as she wrote to him complaining about Magistrates Rowley and Cook.

Notes

8. Bids for land were received with the highest being accepted. In modern parlance Kelly may have been "gazumped".
9. John Gorman, *NSW State Records*, Letter 44/58 to Surveyor General, Reel 3069. Edward Bruchett alias Baggott was subsequently fined.
10. Dungog Letter Book, 1847-1851, Oct 22, 1847, cited by Gordon Dennes.
11. Dungog Bench Book, 1848-1853, Oct 29, 1847, p620, cited by Gordon Dennes.
12. Davis' first name was not recorded here, but it may have been John, who was mentioned several times by Kelly on the periphery of events concerning her.
13. Dungog Letter Book, 1847-1851, Apr 10, 1848, cited by Gordon Dennes.
14. *NSW State Records*, Dungog Bench Book, 1848-1853, Reel 668.
15. Court Report, The *Maitland Mercury*, Feb 21, 1849.

5: Trouble with Neighbours

1. Therese Archinal, *The Andrews on the Manning*, p18.
2. *The Australian Encyclopaedia*, Volume V, Australian Geographic, 1996, pp1859-60.
3. Therese Archinal, *The Andrews on the Manning*, p19.
4. John Allan, *The Allan Family*, p5. The official name was "The Traveller's Home" but it was generally known as the "Woodside Inn".
5. The *Maitland Mercury*, Oct 21, 1846.
6. The *Maitland Mercury*, Nov 11, 1846. The third was named Arthur Godwin.
7. The *Maitland Mercury*, Feb 18, 1847.
8. The *Maitland Mercury*, March 6, 1847.
9. Joseph Andrews, SC – 1860 – Q685-687.
10. Therese Archinal, *The Andrews on the Manning*, p21.
11. Joseph Andrews, SC – 1860 – Q710-711.
12. The *Maitland Mercury*, March 8, 1851.
13. *NSW State Records*, Dungog Bench Book, 1848-1853, Reel 668.
14. The *Maitland Mercury*, March 8, 1851.
15. Gordon Dennes, *Manning Valley Historical Society* files.
16. Gordon Dennes, *Manning Valley Historical Society* files.
17. Patrick Connolly, SC – 1863 – Appendix, p10, Letter.
18. *NSW State Records*, Letter 51/4773, Shelf 4/2936.
19. *NSW State Records*, Letter 51/5743, Shelf 4/2936.
20. Article by "Native", *Wingham Chronicle*, February 25, 1911. Brislane and Connolly were not named in the article and referred to as "two Irishmen".

6: Bushranger Stories

1. Richard Smith, *Sydney Morning Herald*, Oct 8, 1859.
2. Joseph Andrews, *Sydney Morning Herald*, Oct 8, 1859.
3. *Wingham Chronicle*, September 6, 1932.
4. Charles Langley, SC – 1860 – Q442.
5. Hawkeye, *Manning River Times*, August 2, 1913. The northern bridge of the Taree bypass off Dumaresq Island is named the *Henry "Hawkeye" Edwards Bridge*.
6. County Kelly, A Story of the Early Manning, Based on the Life of Isabella Mary Kelly, *Wingham Chronicle*, 25 instalments from Feb 7, 1958 to Sep 26, 1958.
7. The first appearance of the Man in the Mask was on May 24, 1919.
8. Dungog local historian, Cynthia Hunter, conversation, March 11, 2004.

9. J. H. M. Abbott, *Castle Vane*, Angus & Robertson, Sydney, 1920.
10. Pilcher's Cave Article, *Dungog Chronicle*, Jan 27, 1925.
11. *Smith's Weekly*, Aug 9, 1924. All three of the Kelly stories were not attributed to the Man in the Mask (Gordon Bennett), but, because of their Dungog detail, appear to have been written by Bennett.
12. *Smith's Weekly*, Feb 18, 1928 and *Dungog Chronicle*, Mar 2, 1928.
13. C. K. Thompson, 'Manning River Amazon', *Famous Detective Stories*, Vol 1, No.8, July 1947, p23-26.
14. Bill Beatty, *A Treasury of Australian Folk Tales and Traditions*, p159-164.
15. James Holledge, *Australia's Wicked Women*, p100-110.
16. William Joy and Tom Prior, *The Bushrangers*, p19.
17. Stories of Australia's History, *The Sun*, July 14, 1975, p12.
18. James Holledge, Our Strange Past, *Sunday Telegraph*, Sep 8, 1985.
19. Monica Heary, Historical, *The Daily Telegraph*, August 9, 1996.
20. W. F. Connors, *Pioneering Days Around Taree*, p100-127.
21. There can be no doubting Wilf Connors' integrity, but it is possible the story, as handed down to him, may have been polluted by the *Smith's Weekly* or *Dungog Chronicle* or *Wingham Chronicle* articles.
22. Les Murray, Poem, *On the North Coast Line*, Quadrant Vol. XLVII, #3 – March 2003.

7: Fire
1. IMK, SC – 1860 – Q613.
2. John Allan, *The Allan Family*, p4.
3. Advertisement, *The Australian*, February 22, 1842.
4. IMK, SC – 1862 – Q1990.
5. F. A. Fitzpatrick, *Wingham Chronicle*, June 24, 1932.
6. IMK, SC – 1860 – Q580-581.
7. John Allan, *The Allan Family*, p7.
8. IMK, SC – 1860 – Q613.
9. Captain Edward Denny Day by Ben W. Champion, *Journal of Royal Aust-ralian Historical Society*, Vol 22, p345.
10. IMK, SC – 1860 – Q613.
11. The *Sydney Morning Herald*, Sep 4, 1850.
12. J. A. Winney, *Wingham Chronicle*, April 13, 1933.

8: Stolen Cattle
1. IMK, SC – 1862 – Q1-111 and SC – 62 – Appendix, pp21-23. The body of this chapter is taken from these two references. Kelly's accounts of these events were taken in sworn depositions over three parliamentary hearings and three trials. Throughout all of these depositions, the story did not change, but some of the finer details appear in some but not in others.
2. IMK, SC – 1860 – Q534-536.
3. Peter Faucett, SC – 1862 – Q1015-1025.
4. William Board, *The Diary of a Pioneer*, recorded in his diary on Nov. 26, 1848, that he called in at Miss Kelly's and then accompanied the "Catholic Priest Dean Lynch" from there to Tuggerabank.
5. IMK, SC – 1860 – Q577.
6. IMK, SC – 1862 – Q44.
7. IMK, SC – 1862 – Q49.
8. Thomas Findley, SC – 1862 – Q1059-1093.
9. Jane Skerrett (Brandswait), SC – 1862 – Q768-771.
10. IMK, SC – 1860 – Q543.
11. IMK, SC – 1862 – Q603.
12. Date obtained from Supreme Court Judgements, 1855 Term 1 #130, I. M. Kelly v. Charles Turner.

Notes

13. IMK, SC – 1860 – Q608.
14. Supreme Court Judgements, 1855 Term 1 #130, I. M. Kelly v. Charles Turner.
15. IMK, SC – 1862 – Q309.
16. In all of Kelly's stated recollections, she never once mentions Charles Turner as involved in this case, only McPherson. Yet the details are recorded in the Supreme Court Judgements, 1855 Term 1 #130, I. M. Kelly v. Charles Turner.
17. IMK, SC –1860 – Q595. With no records surviving from the Bungay Bungay Bench, there is only second hand evidence for this hearing. The legal documents give two different dates for this hearing, July 17 and Aug 7, which suggests there was an ajournment, but Kelly did not attend the Aug 7 sitting.
18. IMK, SC – 1860 – Q574.
19. W. K. Birrell, *The Manning Valley, Landscape and Settlement 1824 – 1900*, p69.
20. Archibald Clunes Innes by Frank O'Grady, *Journal of Royal Australian Historical Society*, Vol 53, part 3.
21. IMK, SC – 1862 – Q49.
22. IMK, SC – 1862 – Q52.
23. IMK, SC – 1862 – Q55.
24. IMK, SC – 1860 – Q546 and Margaret Skerrett, SC – 1862 – Separate Appendix A.
25. IMK, SC – 1862 – Q55.
26. IMK, SC – 1862 – Q55.
27. IMK, SC – 1862 – Q64.
28. Joseph Andrews, The *Sydney Morning Herald*, April 6, 1855.
29. IMK, SC –1860 – Q613.
30. Charles Skerrett, The *Sydney Morning Herald*, October 6, 1859.
31. Supreme Court Judgements, 1855 Term 1 #130, I. M. Kelly v. Charles Turner.
32. IMK, SC –1860 – Q613.
33. IMK, SC –1860 – Q613.

9: Forged Documents

1. Joseph Andrews, SC – 1862 – Appendix pp26-27. Both Andrews and Kelly referred to this legal action on several occasions, but its exact nature was not revealed, nor how far it proceeded. In answer to one question, Andrews (SC – 1862 – Q1374) used the phrase "oral slander".
2. Joseph Andrews, SC – 1860 – Q686-687.
3. Joseph Andrews, SC – 1862 – Q1326-1327.
4. William Turner, SC – 1862 – Appendix, pp23-24.
5. The *Sydney Morning Herald*, July 6, 1854.
6. Samuel Turner, SC – 1862 – Appendix, p25.
7. Joseph Andrews, SC – 1862 – Appendix, p26.
8. SC – 1862 – Appendix, p27.
9. In all the documents written by him, Skerrett spelt "Brimbin" as "Brimbon".
10. Signature from mortgage dated Nov 11, 1843: Book 5, #530.
11. Signature dated Nov 19, 1860, from complaint against Reuben Richards.
12. William Turner, SC – 1862 – Appendix, pp23-24.
13. William Turner, SC – 1862 – Appendix, pp23-24.
14. Joseph Andrews, SC – 1862 – Appendix, pp26-27.
15. Court Report, *Sydney Morning Herald*, August 8, 1859.
16. IMK, SC – 1862 – Q1932.
17. SC – 1862 – Appendix, p27.
18. Ann Andrews, SC – 1862 – Appendix, p26.
19. Joseph Andrews, SC – 1860 – Q699.
20. Joseph Andrews, SC – 1860 – Q706.
21. IMK, SC – 1862 – Q1935
22. IMK, SC – 1862 – Appendix, p22.

23. Joseph Andrews, SC – 1860 – Q712, appended.
24. Margaret Skerrett, SC – 1862 – Separate Appendix A.
25. Joseph Giles, SC – 1862 – Appendix, p25-26.
26. IMK, SC – 1860 – Q607-612.
27. IMK, SC – 1860 – Q609.
28. Marc Hillman, on his web site www1.tpgi.com.au/users/mhillman, May 2003.
29. William Turner, SC – 1862 – Appendix, pp23-24.

10: Trial

1. The *Sydney Morning Herald*, April 6, 1855. The trial comes mainly from this newspaper report. The *Empire* of the same date and the *Maitland Mercury* of April 11, 1855, carried much lesser reports. Minor details have been supplemented from other sources.
2. It was unusual for there to be twelve members of the jury as most trials in this period consisted of a jury of four.
3. Plunkett had been born in 1802 at Mt. Plunkett, County Roscommon, Ireland. He was called to the Irish Bar in 1826 and later to the England Bar; he arrived in Sydney in 1832 and was appointed Attorney General in 1836. In Sydney, Plunkett Street and Plunkett Street Public School are named after him.
4. The *Sydney Morning Herald*, April 6, 1855.
5. Sir Alfred Stephen, SC – 1863 – Separate Appendix A, taken from the Judge's notes on the case. Margaret Skerrett's testimony was the only one, for which Judge Stephen supplied his notes.
6. The *Sydney Morning Herald*, April 6, 1855.
7. Barristers often used the technique of asking witnesses (Kelly in this case) a question and then producing a witness later to contradict their answer. Davis may have been same the same Davis charged by Kelly in 1848 with breach of contract.
8. IMK, SC – 1862 – Q2044-2046.
9. IMK, SC – 1862 – Q117-119. The grocer was Mr. Hughes in Market St., Sydney.
10. IMK, SC – 1862 – Appendix, p21.

11: Fallout

1. Joseph Andrews, SC – 1860 – Q707.
2. Joseph Andrews, SC – 1860 – Q707.
3. Joseph Andrews, SC – 1860 – Q707.
4. Ann Richards' brother, John Andrews, worked for Miss Kelly as a stockman at the same time she did.
5. IMK, SC – 1862 – Q549. The *Pre 1860 Pioneer Register* only gives a "?" on their marriage.
6. *Pre 1860 Pioneer Register*, p169.
7. IMK, SC – 1862 – Q363, Q490.
8. SC – 1862 – Appendix, p17.
9. This is probably the John Davis who gave evidence at Skerrett's trial.
10. IMK, SC – 1862 – Q539-554.
11. IMK, SC – 1862 – Q359-361.
12. Joseph Andrews, SC – 1863 – Appendix p6
13. IMK, SC – 1862 – Q359-361.
14. William Mullins, SC – 1860 – Q822.
15. Jane Skerrett, SC – 1860 – Q942.
16. Marc Hillman, website www1.tpgi.com.au/users/mhillman, May 2003.
17. John Plunkett, SC – 1862 – Q1056.
18. Sir Alfred Stephen, Letter, SC – 1863 – Appendix D No.1.
19. Sir Alfred Stephen, SC – 1860 – Q50-51.
20. John Plunkett, SC – 1862 – Q1056.

12: A Window of Doubt

1. Charles Langley, SC – 1862 – Q1446, stated Mr. Turnbull told him this.

Turnbull also told him her cattle were "superior".
2. IMK, SC – 1862 – Q1953-1956, SC – 1860 – Q599-601.
3. IMK, SC – 1862 – Q260-280.
4. Sir Alfred Stephen's trial notes, SC – 1863 – Appendix B, is the source for the Kelly/Burt trial. It is supplemented by court reports in the *Sydney Morning Herald* and *Empire* for April 22, 1858.
5. Sir Alfred Stephen's trial notes, SC – 1863 – Appendix B.
6. IMK, SC – 1862 – Q278-279.
7. Stephen Brown, SC – 1862 – Q2097-2099.
8. Stephen Brown, SC – 1862 – Q2102-2104.
9. Court report, *Sydney Morning Herald*, April 22, 1858.
10. Sir Alfred Stephen, SC – 1860 – Q121-123.
11. Sir Alfred Stephen, SC – 1860 – Q63.
12. SC – 1863 – Appendix D No.2.
13. SC – 1863 – Appendix D No.3.

13: A Hidden History
1. Dr Wade King, a descendant of Charles Skerrett, has visited Skerrett's birthplace. The house still stands (personal conversation).
2. Court Report, *The Times (London)*, Oct 31, 1835.
3. Court Report, *The Times (London)*, Nov 3, 1835.
4. Court Report, *The Times (London)*, Nov 7, 1835.
5. Court Report, *The Times (London)*, Nov 27, 1835.
6. *Tasmanian Records*, Convict Record, Con 31/40 – Convict 2190 from Marc Hillman, on his web site www1.tpgi.com.au/users/mhillman, (May 2003). Interestingly, Marc Hillman notes that Charles Skerrett's trade is recorded as "farmer" at daughter Jane's baptism, and "writer" at daughter Emily's baptism.
7. Appointing a convict as a constable sounds rather incongruous today, but it was made necessary by a lack of manpower in the colony.
8. *Tasmanian Records*, Convict Muster Ho 10, Reel 80, Piece 51 (Marc Hillman).
9. Argus Passenger Index, p559.
10. *NSW State Records*, Index to Unassisted Arrivals, NSW, 1842-1855, Reel 1276.
11. Henry Vaughan, Court Report, *Sydney Morning Herald*, Oct 7, 1859.
12. Court Report, *Sydney Morning Herald*, Aug 12, 1851.
13. Court Report, *Sydney Morning Herald*, Aug 12, 1851.
14. Court Report, *Sydney Morning Herald*, Aug 12, 1851.
15. John Ryan Brenan, SC – 1862 – Q648-657.
16. Charles Skerrett, *Empire*, Oct 7, 1859.
17. Jane Skerrett, SC – 1862 – Q709-710.
18. Joseph Andrews, SC – 1860 – Q647-657.
19. There are numerous references from a number of people on the trouble between Skerrett and Major Innes, but at no stage is the exact nature of it ever stated. Innes was in partnership with a man named Stokes at this time.
20. Thomas Weedon, SC – 1860 – Q771-783. Weedon was Skerrett's attorney in this matter.
21. Solicitors Holden & McCarthy Account, *NSW State Records*, 2/8995, Insolvency #4853.
22. Solicitors Holden & McCarthy Account, *NSW State Records*, 2/8995, Insolvency #4853.
23. *NSW State Records*, 9/5714,

Judgement Papers #84.
24. *NSW State Records*, Letter 55/7642 (55/8367), Shelf 4/3286.
25. Dr Wade King (personal conversation).

14: The Laird of Taree
1. John Abbott, *Peeps in the Past*, p159.
2. *Pre 1860 Pioneer Register* p26
3. IMK, SC – 1863 – Q837.
4. *NSW State Records*, Magistrate Lists, Reel 3039.
5. IMK, SC – 1863 – Q1025-1033.
6. IMK, SC – 1863 – Q1010-1020. The transcription of Kelly's oral statements gives the man's name as Robert Sorrell, but it almost certainly should have been Robert Searle.
7. IMK, SC – 1863 – Q1087.
8. IMK, SC – 1863 – Q1111-1114.
9. The Manning Valley's first attorney was Phillip Creagh, the son of Community Magistrate Capt. Jasper Creagh.
10. Captain Edward Denny Day by Ben Champion, *Royal Australian Historical Journal*, Vol. 23, p357.
11. Warren Cross, Legal Administration of the Manning River Valley, An Historical Analysis 1828 – 1900.
12. *Manning River News*, March 23, 1867.
13. Joshua Cochrane, Votes and Proceedings 1870, First Report from Committee of Elections and Qualifications, p65.
14. Henry Flett, Votes and Proceedings 1870, First Report from Committee of Elections and Qualifications, Appendix M, p88.
15. *Manning River News*, December 2, 1871.
16. Joseph Andrews obituary, *Wingham Chronicle*, January 12, 1901.
17. This will become apparent later in the book.
18. The *Maitland Mercury*, July 4, 1859.
19. *Sydney Morning Herald*, April 22, 1856.
20. Did McCarthy vote for himself? Probably no, as McCarthy lived at Port Macquarie, and his sole vote was cast at Wingham.
21. The *Maitland Mercury*, July 7, 1859.
22. The *Maitland Mercury*, July 2, 1859. Due to the slow speed of communications at the time, quite an amount of election material like this letter, was published after the election day of July 1.
23. Manning River Report, *Empire*, Dec 13, 1860.
24. Manning River Report, *Empire*, Dec 13, 1860.
25. Manning River Correspondent, *Sydney Morning Herald*, Feb 28, 1862.
26. Manning River Correspondent, *Sydney Morning Herald*, Mar 23, 1862.

15: Waterview
1. *Land Records*, Old system, Book 95, No. 236.
2. This event is dated by Flett stating it was at the time Overseer Corcoran was leaving, and Müller (Chap 1) says Corcoran left as he arrived – in March 1859. Despite the numerous references in memoirs to this incident, no contemporary gave the girl's name. Wilf Connors, *Pioneering Days around Taree*, 1985, gave her first name as Kate.
3. Henry Flett, SC – 1860 – Q1046.
4. John Allan, *The Allan Family*, p7.
5. Robert Herkes, *Peeps into the Past*, p10.
6. Henry Flett, SC – 1860 – Q1046.
7. Henry Flett, SC – 1860 – Q1046.
8. Robert Herkes as stated by G. S. Hill, *Peeps into the Past*, p93.
9. "S. C. R.", *Northern Champion*, Aug 3, 1927.
10. The Man Who Dared Miss Kelly, *Smith's Weekly*, Apr 23, 1927.

Notes

11. Gun-woman of the Manning, *Smith's Weekly*, Feb 18, 1928.
12. C. K. Thompson, *Famous Detective Stories*, p23-26.
13. George Matthews, The *Northern Champion*, Jan 3, 1956.
14. Müller incorrectly wrote that Leonard Cooper died in the Indian Mutiny of 1857.
15. IMK, SC – 1862 – Q1939-1952 and Maria Cooper, SC – 1862 – Separate Appendix E.
16. Theodor Müller, *Neunzehn Jahre am Australien*.
17. *Land Records*, Old system, Book 42, No. 110.
18. *Land Records*, Old system, Book 55, No. 540. These four farm lots were cited as sold to Reuben Richardson (sic) and John Paton, in a mortgage made by Kelly in 1858.
19. IMK, SC – 1862 – Q2035.

16: The Chief Justice

1. The website www.lawlink.nsw.gov.au/history/lah.nsf/pages/stephen – May, 2003.
2. *NSW State Records*, Letter 59/1454, Shelf 4/3401.
3. Charles Skerrett, SC – 1860 – Q288-292.
4. Sir Alfred Stephen, SC – 1860 – Q66.
5. Sir Alfred Stephen, SC – 1860 – Q150.
6. Sir Alfred Stephen, SC – 1860 – Q66.
7. Sir Alfred Stephen, SC – 1860 – Q78. This man is later referred by Skerrett as Mr. Smith.
8. Sir Alfred Stephen, SC – 1862 – Separate Appendix C.
9. Sir Alfred Stephen, SC – 1860 – Q101.
10. Sir Alfred Stephen, SC – 1860 – Q102.
11. Sir Alfred Stephen, SC – 1860 – Q102.
12. Charles Skerrett, SC – 1860 – Q292.
13. Sir Alfred Stephen, SC – 1860 – Q23.
14. Rev Thomas O'Reilly, SC – 1862 – Q1031.
15. Joseph Andrews, SC – 1860 – Q650.
16. Jane Skerrett, SC – 1862 – Q709.
17. Thomas Weedon, SC – 1860 – Q780.
18. Holden & McCarthy Invoice, *NSW State Records*, 2/8995, Insolvency #4853.
19. Sir Alfred Stephen, SC – 1860 – Q78.
20. Sir Alfred Stephen, SC – 1860 – Q86.
21. Charles Skerrett, SC – 1860 – Q174-183.
22. Sir Alfred Stephen, SC – 1862 – Separate Appendix C.
23. Sir Alfred Stephen, SC – 1860 – Q69.
24. Sir Alfred Stephen, SC – 1862 – Separate Appendix D.
25. Sir Alfred Stephen, SC – 1860 – Q66.

17: Committed

1. *NSW State Records*, Police Description Book, Entry #86 and #90, Reel 3041.
2. IMK, SC – 1862 – Q1895-1902.
3. Court Report, *Sydney Morning Herald* and Court Report, *Empire*, both of date August 15, 1859. Most of this section derives from these two sources.
4. Court Report, *Empire*, August 15, 1859.
5. Patrick Connolly, SC – 1863 – Separate Appendix, p10.
6. IMK, SC – 1863 – Q1056-1060.
7. Tim Leane, SC – 1862 – Q387-392.
8. SC – 1862 – Appendix A, p17
9. IMK, SC – 1863 – Appendix A, p5-6.
10. John Paton, SC – 1863 – Appendix C.

11. IMK, SC – 1863 – Appendix A, p5-6.
12. Maria Cooper, SC – 1863 – Separate Appendix E.
13. *Land Records*, Old system, Book 68, No. 184.
14. *Land Records*, Old system, Book 55, No. 540.

18: Perjury

1. The main sources for the trial are the newspaper reports of The *Sydney Morning Herald*, October 6-7, 1859 and the *Empire* of the same dates. They are slightly differing accounts, and complement each other. For example, the *Empire* reporter missed two prosecution witnesses when, obviously, he was absent from the courtroom. At the same time he gives a more detailed report on some witnesses. They both occasionally get names wrong and, in such a complex case, muddle minor parts of the story.
2. The difficulty with the newspaper reports, as with Judge's notes in other cases, is that they never state the questions asked of the witness. Here is a classic situation. The question to Skerrett may have been something like: "Why would Kelly say she had not sold the cattle, when she knew you (Skerrett) had a Bill of Sale and a Receipt".
3. High on the list of candidates for "Mr. Smith" would be Robert Searle, on whose property Skerrett stayed when first released from prison.
4. The *Sydney Morning Herald*, October 10, 1859.
5. *Bell's Life*, October 15, 1859. This newspaper had a heavy emphasis on sport. The article referred to John Skerrett, rather than Charles Skerrett.

19: Aftermath

1. IMK, SC – 1862 – Q1904-1908.
2. IMK, SC – 1862 – Q1910.
3. IMK, SC – 1862 – Q1913.
4. Gaol conditions, communication with John Ramsland.
5. Henry Lawson, *The Song of a Prison*, 1909.
6. IMK, SC – 1862 – Q1907.
7. *Land Records*, Old system, Book 68, No. 184.
8. *Land Records*, Old system, Book 68, No. 184.
9. *Land Records*, Old system, Book 68, No. 184.
10. The different sources spell the name three different ways – 'Gerard,' 'Gerrard' and 'Girard.' The last of these three has been adopted throughout the book. Gordon Dennes lists "Alfred Michael Girard" with Manning Magistrates for the year 1861-1862, although not on the Manning in that year.
11. Tim Leane, SC – 1863 – Q309.
12. William M'Lean (McLean), *Sydney Morning Herald*, December 23, 1859
13. Charles Skerrett, SC – 1860 – Q348.
14. *NSW State Records*, Insolvency 2/8995, #4853. Rented from Croasdil of Newcastle.
15. Tim Leane, SC – 1862 – Q351-358.
16. James Skerrett, SC – 1860 – Q1153-1157.
17. William McLean, *Sydney Morning Herald*, December 12, 1860. McLean's name appears as "M'Lean", with the apostrophe quite common for names beginning with "Mc", in the period. "McLean" has been preferred here, as this became the family name.
18. Maria Cooper, SC – 1863 – Separate Appendix E.
19. William McLean, *Sydney Morning Herald*, December 23, 1859.
20. E. Wise, SC – 1862 – Appendix B, p38.
21. Edward Cory, *NSW State Records*,

Notes

2/8995, Insolvency #4853.
22. NSW Legislative Assembly, Votes and Proceedings 1859, ordered printed Nov 30, 1860.
23. IMK, SC – 1860 – Appendix to Kelly evidence.
24. IMK, SC – 1860 – Appendix to Kelly evidence.
25. IMK, SC – 1860 – Q546.
26. *Maitland Mercury*, December 10, 1859.
27. Sir Alfred Stephen, SC – 1860 – Q51-61.
28. Joseph Andrews, SC – 1862 – Appendix p82.

20: The Disputed Lease

1. This section comes from Tim Leane in two sources, SC – 1863 – Q297-452 and SC – 1863 – Appendix A, p4.
2. Another confirmation that while Begbie nominally owned Waterview in 1859, he had not taken possession of it, and Kelly/Leane were still using it.
3. Tim Leane, SC – 1863 – Appendix A, p4.
4. SC – 1863 – Q445.
5. SC – 1863 – Appendix A, p4.
6. SC – 1863 – Appendix A, p4.
7. William McLean, SC – 1863 – Appendix A, p5.
8. *Land Records*, Old system, Book 65, No. 206 – copy not original.
9. William McLean, SC – 1863 – Appendix A, p5.
10. Joseph Andrews, SC – 1863 – Appendix A, p7.
11. Robert Abbott, SC –1863 – Q14.
12. Joseph Andrews, SC – 1863 – Appendix A, p7.
13. Joseph Andrews, SC – 1863 – Appendix A, p5-6.
14. Reuben Richards, SC – 1863 – Appendix A, p2.
15. Robert Abbott, SC – 1863 – Q40.

16. *Land Records*, Old system, Book 65, No. 206.

21: The Smear

1. Political Reports, *Empire* and *Sydney Morning Herald*, February 4, 1860.
2. NSW Legislative Assembly, Votes and Proceedings: Votes #55, February 3, 1860.
3. Select Committee – 1860. This chapter is based entirely on this document. Unlike Parliament itself, the Select Committee recorded all questions and answers. This enabled Members to read the record and make an informed decision before casting a vote on the matter.
4. SC – 1860 – Q69-71.
5. Sir Alfred Stephen, SC – 1860 – Q72.
6. SC – 1860 – Q120-122.
7. *Sydney Morning Herald*, February 13, 1860.
8. *Sydney Morning Herald*, February 15, 1860.
9. SC – 1860 – Q159-160.
10. IMK, SC – 1863 – Q1003.
11. SC – 1860 – Q189.
12. SC – 1860 – Q212-220.
13. SC – 1860 – Q239.
14. SC – 1860 – Q321-322, Q337-338, Q367, Q348.
15. SC – 1860 – Q377-378.
16. SC – 1860 – Q380.
17. SC – 1860 – Q387.
18. SC – 1860 – Q525-542.
19. SC – 1860 – Q706.
20. *Sydney Morning Herald*, March 2, 1860.
21. SC – 1860 – Q734-736.
22. George Rowley, SC – 1860 – Q768-770.
23. There is no other source for this story.
24. SC – 1860 – Q755, Q762-766.
25. SC – 1860 – Q833-836, Q881-883.
26. SC – 1860 – Q927-929.

27. SC – 1860 – Q967.
28. SC – 1860 – Q977-979, Q984-986, Q1006-1009, Q1026.
29. SC – 1860 – Q1051-1052.
30. Robert Blake, SC – 1860 – Q1068.
31. Justice Dickinson, SC – 1862 – Appendix, p19.
32. IMK, SC – 1862 – Q1908.

22: A Worried Man

1. Joseph Andrews, SC – 1862 – Appendix, p82.
2. *NSW State Records*, 2/8995, Skerrett Insolvency #4853.
3. Joseph Andrews, SC – 1862 – Appendix, p82.
4. Edward Cory, *NSW State Records*, 2/8995, Skerrett Insolvency #4853.
5. Tim Leane, SC – 1863 – Q406-408.
6. David Baxter, SC – 1863 – Appendix, p4.
7. David Baxter, SC – 1863 – Appendix A, p4, and Court Report, *Sydney Morning Herald*, May 31, 1860.

23 Slander

1. Justice Dickinson's Notes, SC – 1863 – Appendix, p1. All quotes in this section are taken from Dickinson's notes.
2. Justice Dickinson's Notes do not *explicitly* state this, but Richards' statements that Binkin accompanied him to Ganget, and he was alone with Kelly between 12 and 4 can only be reconciled with Binkin's departure.
3. Justice Dickinson's Notes, SC – 1863 – Appendix, p3.
4. Tim Leane, SC – 1863 – Q406-407.
5. This was a receipt for two-years rent on the first paddock Richards rented 1858-59. Kelly claimed never to have received this rent, and that this receipt was a forgery.
6. This appears to be when Kelly had hopes of getting Ann Richards to testify for her.
7. Court Report, *Sydney Morning Herald*, June 7, 1860.
8. Court Report, *Empire*, June 6, 1860.
9. Justice Dickinson's Notes, SC – 1863 – Appendix, p7.
10. Court Report, *Empire*, June 7, 1860, gives a full account of the addresses to the jury by Darvall and Manning.
11. Flett's evidence on Kelly's misspelling of "Reuben" was not reported in the newspaper or in the Judge's Notes of the trial. There is only reference to it in Manning's summing up.
12. Laurence Spyer, SC – 1862 – Q1646, footnote, and Henry Selby, SC – 1862 – Q1844-1855.
13. Robert Abbott, SC – 1863 – Q143-149.
14. Robert Abbott, SC – 1863 – Q142.
15. Mark Spence, SC – 1863 – Q275.
16. Thomas New, Letter to his mother dated May 13, 1860, *New Thomas and Thomas W. New Papers*, Mitchell Library. New commented that the Fletts were "not at all stuck up".
17. Robert Abbott, SC – 1863 – Q76.

24: What is a Forgery?

1. William Mullen, SC – 1862 – Q1542-1608.
2. William Mullen, SC – 1862 – Q1560.
3. William Mullen, SC – 1862 – Q1573.
4. William Mullen, SC – 1862 – Q1564-1567.
5. Nicholas Binkin, SC – 1863 – Q934-992.
6. Nicholas Binkin, SC – 1863 – Q938.
7. Nicholas Binkin, SC – 1863 – Q943.
8. Nicholas Binkin, SC – 1863 – Q956.
9. Court Report, *Maitland Mercury*, April 11, 1857.
10. Patrick Connolly, SC – 1863 – Appendix, p10.
11. John Paton, SC – 1863 – Appendix,

Notes

p10.
12. Henry Selby, SC – 1862 – Q1854.
13. Henry Selby, SC – 1862 – Q1867.
14. John Smithers, SC – 1862 – Q1633.
15. Mark Spence, SC – 1863 – Q243.
16. The quotes are from Justice Dickinson's Notes, SC – 1863 – Appendix, p7, but he does not make it clear that Flett is being tested. That comes from Darvall's summary as reported by *Empire*, June 7, 1860.
17. Kelly stated it was definitely not her signature.
18. SC – 1860 – Q1012-1020.
19. Justice Dickinson's Notes, SC – 1863 – Appendix, p7.
20. John Ryan Brenan, SC – 1862 – Q643.

25: Back in the Valley
1. Ann Andrews, SC – 1862 – Appendix, p84.
2. James Skerrett, SC – 1860 – Q1122-1129.
3. Tim Leane, SC – 1863 – Q331-343.
4. *Maitland Mercury*, June 14, 1860. The letter was signed 'R R' but it was certainly not Reuben Richards.
5. The Attorney General wrote to Magistrate Day in another case (detailed in Chap 26) refusing to give him advice.
6. Maria Cooper, SC – 1862 – Separate Appendix E.
7. IMK, SC – 1862 – Q2017.
8. IMK, SC – 1862 – Q2024. Kelly named the man as Mr. Pass.
9. IMK, SC – 1862 – Q2012.
10. Therese Archinal, *The Andrews on the Manning*, p100-103.

26: The Rich Insolvent
1. Joseph *Andrews Insolvency*, *NSW State Records*, 2/9008, Insolvency #5013.
2. *Land Records*, Old system, Book 92, No. 230.
3. Robert Sempill, SC – 1862 – Q1808.

4. Robert Sempill, Affidavit 19/10/1861, *Andrews Insolvency*.
5. Robert Sempill, Affidavit 19/10/1861, *Andrews Insolvency*.
6. Joseph Andrews, Affidavit 13/12/1861, *Andrews Insolvency*.
7. Robert Sempill, Letter 21/7/1860, *Andrews Insolvency*.
8. Robert Sempill, Letter 23/7/1860, *Andrews Insolvency*.
9. Arthur Kingsmill, Letter 28/7/1860, *Andrews Insolvency*.
10. Arthur Kingsmill, Letter 28/7/1860, *Andrews Insolvency*.
11. Arthur Kingsmill, Letter 26/2/1861, *Andrews Insolvency*.
12. Robert Sempill, Letter 2/8/1860, *Andrews Insolvency*.
13. Robert Sempill, Affidavit 7/11/1861, *Andrews Insolvency*.
14. Reuben Richards – Inventory, 13/8/1860, *Andrews Insolvency*.
15. Reuben Richards – Inventory, 13/8/1860, *Andrews Insolvency*. Richards' atrocious spelling was obvious in these papers. For example, the "map" of Mount George was written at "mat".
16. Arthur Kingsmill, Affidavit unsigned, *Andrews Insolvency*.
17. Arthur Kingsmill, Affidavit 26/2/1861, *Andrews Insolvency*.
18. Arthur Kingsmill, Affidavit 28/8/1861, *Andrews Insolvency*.
19. Robert Sempill, Affidavit Nov 7, 1861, *Andrews Insolvency*.
20. There are no other details of this case as records have not survive from the Wingham Bench
21. Joseph Andrews, Affidavit Dec 13, 1861, *Andrews Insolvency*.
22. Robert Sempill, Affidavit Nov 7, 1861, *Andrews Insolvency*.
23. William Andrews, Letter undated, *Andrews Insolvency*.
24. Court Depositions, Oct 10, 1860,

Andrews Insolvency.
25. Court Report, *Maitland Mercury*, Oct 30, 1860.
26. Court Report, *Maitland Mercury*, Oct 30, 1860.
27. Court Report, *Maitland Mercury*, Nov 5, 1861.
28. Letter by Ann Andrews, undated, *Andrews Insolvency.* "Nowandoc" was spelled as "Nowandock".
29. Letter (unsigned) by Joseph Andrews, undated, *Andrews Insolvency.*
30. William McLean, Letter, *Empire*, January 15, 1861.
31. Searle's Account, *Andrews Insolvency.*
32. Malcolm Shaw, Affidavit Nov 15, 1861, *Andrews Insolvency.*
33. Ann Andrews, Deposition Feb 6, 1861, *Andrews Insolvency.*

27: Confession
1. Ryan Brenan, SC – 1862 – Q658-670.
2. Ryan Brenan, SC – 1862 – Q699.
3. William Turner, SC – 1862 – Appendix, p23-24.
4. Ryan Brenan, SC – 1862 – Q698.
5. Ryan Brenan, SC – 1862 – Q682-684, Q699.
6. Samuel Turner, SC – 1863 – Appendix A, p25.
7. Joseph Andrews, SC – 1863 – Appendix A, p26-27.
8. John Hargrave, SC – 1862 – Appendix C, p38.
9. Ryan Brenan, SC – 1862 – Q695.
10. Ryan Brenan, SC – 1862 – Q697.
11. Pamphlet dated June 28, 1862, printed by IMK.

28: The Trust of the Trustees
1. Alfred Begbie, *NSW State Records*, 2/9017, Begbie Insolvency #5158.
2. Theodor Muller, *Neunzehn Jahre am Australien.*
3. Joseph Andrews, SC – 1862 – Q1301.
4. Alfred Begbie, Affidavit Aug 18, 1860 and Waldemaar Cooper, Affidavit Aug 16, 1860, *Andrews Insolvency.*
5. Alfred Begbie, Deposition Dec 6, 1860, Begbie Insolvency.
6. Maria Cooper, SC – 1862 – Separate Appendix E.
7. Tim Leane, SC – 1863 – Q319, Q372, Q386.
8. Manning River Report, *Empire*, Nov 12, 1860.
9. *NSW State Records*, 2/9017, Begbie Insolvency #5158.
10. Maria Cooper, SC – 1862 – Separate Appendix E.
11. *NSW State Records*, 2/8995, Skerrett Insolvency #4853.
12. IMK, SC – 1862 – Q2089, Q1967-1983.
13. William Cape, SC – 1862 – Q2108-2116.

29: Assault and Battery
1. IMK, SC – 1863 – Q1066-1079.
2. IMK, SC – 1863 – Q1083-1086.
3. IMK, Court Deposition, *NSW State Records*, 9/6423, Richards, 1860.
4. Robert Abbott, SC – 1863 – Q38-43, and Court Report, *Empire*, Nov 30, 1860.
5. Robert Abbott, SC – 1863 – Q32 and Court Report, *Sydney Morning Herald*, Nov 30, 1860.
6. Court Deposition, *NSW State Records*, 9/6423, Richards, 1860.
7. SC – 1863 – Appendix A, p20-27, and Court Reports, Nov 24, 1860, *Empire* and *Sydney Morning Herald.*
8. Andrew Mort, Court Deposition, *NSW State Records*, 9/6423, Richards, 1860.
9. Court Reports, Dec 5, 1860, *Sydney Morning Herald* and *Empire.*
10. Court Report, *Sydney Morning*

Notes

Herald, Jan 3, 1861.

30: Judgement
1. Insolvency Reports, Maitland Mercury, Nov 8, 1860 and Nov 15, 1860.
2. Joseph Andrews, Affidavit Jan 4, 1861, *Andrews Insolvency*.
3. Receipt, Dec 8, 1860, *Andrews Insolvency*.
4. Robert Andrews, Affidavit Dec 13, 1860, *Andrews Insolvency*.
5. Robert Andrews, Affidavit Dec 13, 1860, *Andrews Insolvency*.
6. Insolvency Report, Maitland Mercury, Dec 18, 1860.
7. Letter to Editor, *Empire*, Dec 28, 1860.
8. Letter to Editor, *Empire*, Dec 29, 1860.
9. Letter to Editor, *Empire*, Jan 15, 1861.
10. Letter to Editor, *Empire*, Jan 15, 1861.
11. Court Report, *Empire*, Jan 5, 1861.
12. Alexander Gray, Affidavit Jan 31, 1861, *Andrews Insolvency*.
13. William McLean, Letter to Editor, *Empire*, Jan 15, 1861.
14. Court Judgement, *Sydney Morning Herald*, Feb 15, 1862.
15. MacFarland Report Sep 18, 1861, *Andrews Insolvency*.
16. Editorial, *Empire*, Feb 6, 1861.
17. *Maitland Mercury*, Feb 5, 1861.
18. Manning River Report, *Maitland Ensign*, July 20, 1861. The report contained no other details. The same report also noted that Paddy Connolly had once again been committed for cattle stealing, but a trial does not seem to have eventuated.
19. Court Report, *Maitland Mercury*, Aug 13, 1861, the main source for the trial.
20. Court Report, *Maitland Mercury*, Aug 13, 1861.
21. Court Report, *Maitland Ensign*, Aug 14, 1861.
22. Court Report, *Maitland Mercury*, Oct 29, 1861.
23. Insolvency Report, Maitland Mercury, Sep 21, 1861 and MacFarland Report, Sep 18, 1861, *Andrews Insolvency*.
24. Robert Sempill, Affidavit Oct 19, 1861, *Andrews Insolvency*.
25. Robert Sempill, SC – 1862 – Q1691.
26. Sempill's October 19 affidavit made no mention of the letters.
27. Robert Sempill, Affidavit Nov 7, 1861, *Andrews Insolvency*.
28. Joseph Andrews, Affidavit Dec 6, 1861, *Andrews Insolvency*.
29. Joseph Andrews, Affidavit Dec 13, 1861, *Andrews Insolvency*.
30. Court Judgement, *Sydney Morning Herald*, Feb 15, 1862.

31: Petitions
1. Election Report, *Empire*, Dec 20, 1860.
2. Election Report, *Maitland Mercury*, Jan 1, 1861.
3. NSW Legislative Assembly, Votes and Proceedings 1861-62, p335.
4. NSW Legislative Assembly, Votes and Proceedings 1861-62, p377.
5. Pamphlet dated June 28, 1862, printed by IMK. Therese Archinal found this pamphlet inside a book from the library of Joseph Andrews, while researching her book on the Andrews family.
6. From "former members" at website www.parliament.nsw.gov.au Dec 2003.
7. From "former members" at website www.parliament.nsw.gov.au Dec 2003.
8. Attached to Report of Isabella Mary Kelly Select Committee, NSW Legislative Assembly, Votes and Proceedings 1862, Votes #119.
9. NSW Legislative Assembly, Votes and Proceedings 1862, Votes #69.

32: The Select Committee

1. SC – 1862 – Q147-148.
2. SC – 1862 – Q278-282.
3. SC – 1862 – Q305-314.
4. 1862 Select Committee Minutes, Oct 22, 1862.
5. SC – 1862 – Q392.
6. Reuben Richards Insolvency, 1864, *NSW State Records*, 2/9122, Insolvency #6763.
7. SC – 1862 – Q555-564.
8. SC – 1862 – Q565-572.
9. SC – 1862 – Q589-599.
10. SC – 1862 – Q600.
11. Political Report, *Sydney Morning Herald*, Oct 24, 1862.
12. SC – 1862 – Q687.
13. Stated in the Report issued by the Select Committee. NSW Legislative Assembly, Votes and Proceedings 1862, Votes #119.
14. SC – 1862 – Q997.
15. SC – 1862 – Q1010.
16. SC – 1862 – Q1016.
17. SC – 1862 – Q1031-1033.
18. SC – 1862 – Q1072-1089.
19. SC – 1862 – Q1138-1146.
20. SC – 1862 – Q1254-1256.
21. SC – 1862 – Q1284-1285.
22. *Magnificent Manning and Municipality of Wingham*, G. S. Hill, p20 and Robert Broomfield, p52.
23. SC – 1862 – Q1302.
24. SC – 1862 – Q1493-1495.
25. SC – 1862 – Q1508-1510.
26. SC – 1862 – Q1517.
27. SC – 1862 – Q1597-1599.
28. SC – 1862 – Q1606-1608.
29. SC – 1862 – Q1877.
30. Court Reports of both *Empire* and *Sydney Morning Herald* of November 29, 1862 and December 1, 1862.
31. Court Reports of both *Empire* and *Sydney Morning Herald* of December 6, 1862.
32. SC – 1862 – Q1917.
33. SC – 1862 – Q1905.
34. SC – 1862 – Q2058-2079.
35. SC – 1862 – Q2084-2087.
36. SC – 1862 – Q2107.
37. Many of the members of this Committee were also on a number of other committees, which were also trying to complete their business.
38. The third opinion stated in the Report was badly worded. It could be interpreted as meaning Sir Alfred Stephen *deliberately* misled the jury, and nowhere in the evidence was this ever suggested. A more likely rendition of this sentence should have included the phrase: "was calculated *by the Committee* to mislead the jury"

33: Question 843

1. Editorial, *Empire*, Jan 20, 1863.
2. NSW Votes & Proceedings, 1863, Votes 4 p27, Votes 5 p33, Votes 6 p36.
3. Political Report, *Sydney Morning Herald*, July 2, 1863.
4. Mr. Arnold, who did not attend any meetings of the 1862 Select Committee, was also included in the list of Committee members. His chairmanship of the 1860 Select Committee may have been the reason for this, allowing him to attend if required.
5. NSW Legislative Assembly, *Votes and Proceedings*: Votes #6, July 1, 1863.
6. From "former members" at website www.parliament.nsw.gov.au Dec 2003.
7. SC – 1863 – Q153-154.
8. SC – 1863 – Q 107-113.
9. SC – 1863 – Q 132-137.
10. William Allen, Political Report, *Sydney Morning Herald*, Dec 9, 1863.
11. William Allen, Political Report, *Empire*, Dec 9, 1863.
12. Robert Abbott, SC – 1863 – Q190-202.
13. SC – 1863 – Q240.

14. SC – 1863 – Q529-542.
15. SC – 1863 – Q543.
16. SC – 1863 – Q544-546.
17. John Allan, *The Allan Family*, p8.
18. SC – 1863 – Q564-565.
19. SC – 1863 – Q587-588.
20. SC – 1863 – Q655-665.
21. SC – 1863 – Q665-667.
22. SC – 1863 – Q750-755, 830-831.
23. *Land Records*, Old system, Book 81, No. 637.
24. The conveyancing document also includes the sale of fifty-three acres to Reuben Richards, despite the fact this had been negated before 1859, giving more support to Kelly's claim that she knew nothing of the sale of Mount George.
25. *Land Records*, Old system, Book 92, No. 230. The mortgage included a 31-acre block of land at Harrington and a 14-acre block at Tinonee, but would account for less than 10% of the mortgage value.
26. SC – 1863 – Q756-759, 834-836, 841.
27. SC – 1863 – Q843.
28. SC – 1863 – Q844.
29. SC – 1863 – Q854-857.
30. SC – 1863 – Q922-925.
31. Binkin may have been located using the Judge's Notes to the Richards/Andrews trial, handed in by Robert Abbott. These record Richards using the name Binkin as his witness for the lease, and Dew's evidence he was a tobacconist.
32. SC – 1863 – Q956.
33. SC – 1863 – Q992.
34. This is almost certainly Robert Searle, at whose place Skerrett stayed when released from prison in 1859. The transcripts are made from oral statements while the interview is in progress, and considering the different accents, it is not surprising these kinds of mistakes were made e.g. Tinoona for Tinonee (pronounced Tin-o-nee).
35. SC – 1863 – Q-1009-1023.
36. SC – 1863 – Q1034.
37. SC – 1863 – Q1041-1043.
38. SC – 1863 – Q698, 703-705.
39. SC – 1863 – Q706, 710.
40. SC – 1863 – Q1064-1079.
41. SC – 1863 – Q1115-1120.

34: A Final Decision

1. Political Report, *Maitland Mercury*, Oct 22, 1863.
2. Political Report, *Empire*, Dec 9, 1863.
3. The parliamentary debate derives from both Political Reports of Sydney Morning Herald and *Empire* for Dec 9, 1863.
4. Political Report, *Sydney Morning Herald*, Dec 9, 1863.
5. Political Report, *Empire*, Dec 9, 1863.
6. Political Report, *Empire*, Dec 9, 1863.
7. Editorial, *Empire*, Dec 12, 1863.
8. John Allan, *The Allan Family*, p7. This appears in a copy of the original manuscript in Newcastle Public Library, but was edited out of the printed book by Fitzpatrick.
9. Printed with the 1863 Select Committee Report in *Votes and Proceedings*.
10. Maria Cooper, SC – 1862 – Separate Appendix E. p9.
11. Advertisement, *Maitland Mercury*, July 2, 1864 and repeated on July 7.
12. *Maitland Mercury*, Mar 17, 1998, p11. Benjamin Cook bought the horses. The branding irons have passed down through the family to the current holders Harry Boyle and son Geoffrey.
13. Kempsey Political Report, *Empire*, Dec 17, 1864.
14. *Australian Dictionary of Biography*, Volume 4, p199-201.
15. Election Reports, *Maitland Mercury*, Dec 31, 1864 and *Empire*, Jan 9, 1865.

16. Election Report, *Empire*, Jan 9, 1865.
17. Political Report, *Empire*, May 6, 1865.
18. Political Report, *Empire*, May 6, 1865.
19. Political Report, *Empire*, May 6, 1865.
20. Political Report, *Sydney Morning Herald*, May 17, 1865.
21. Political Report, *Sydney Morning Herald*, May 17, 1865.

35: Slipping Away
1. *Land Records*, Old system, Book 95, No. 236.
2. *Australian Dictionary of Biography*, Volume 2, p149.
3. Originally named Gary Owen Estate, Brenan's property was renamed Callan Park after its sale. Website www.callan-park.com/history April 2004.
4. IMK Insolvency, *NSW State Records*, 2/9206, Insolvency #7904.
5. IMK Insolvency, *NSW State Records*, 2/9206, Insolvency #7904.
6. Report, *Manning River News*, Oct 5, 1867.
7. Letter published *Wingham Chronicle*, Nov 15, 1918.
8. Robert Cox, *Wingham Chronicle*, June 24, 1932.
9. P. Lowry, Letter to the Editor, *Wingham Chronicle*, May 8, 1936. The address of Lowry was given as Sweetman St., off Hale St., Red Hill, Brisbane.
10. Political Report, *Sydney Morning Herald*, May 17, 1871.
11. Bill Beatty, *A Treasury of Australian Folk Tales and Traditions*, p163.
12. Gordon Dennes, *Wingham Chronicle*, July 15, 1932.
13. Gordon Dennes, *Dungog Chronicle*, Nov 24, 1931.
14. Political Report, *Sydney Morning Herald*, May 17, 1871.
15. Political Report, *Sydney Morning Herald*, May 17, 1871.
16. Political Report, *Manning River News*, May 27, 1871.
17. NSW Birth Deaths and Marriages, #00851, Mary Isabella Kelly.
18. Robert Cox, *Wingham Chronicle*, June 24, 1932.
19. G. S Hill quoted by F. A. Fitzpatrick, Bungay Bungay article, *Wingham Chronicle*, May 19, 1939.
20. IMK, SC – 1863 – Q781.
21. James Holledge, *Australia's Wicked Women*, p110.
22. Kate Kelly drowned on Oct 6, 1898, in the Forbes Lagoon aged thirty-five.

Appendix 1: Completing the lives of some characters
1. Therese Archinal, *The Andrews on the Manning*, p19-28.
2. Obituary, *Wingham Chronicle*, Oct 22, 1902.
3. Obituary, *Dungog Chronicle*, Aug 5, 1930.
4. Manning River Report, *Empire*, Oct 1, 1863. Dew was identified by the clothes he was wearing.
5. Henry Flett Obituary, *Sydney Mail*, December 1, 1877, p921.
6. *Manning River News*, Jan 1, 1870.
7. John Paton, Deposition, SC – 1863 – Appendix C.
8. *NSW State Records*, Mitchells Island School Admin File, 5/16872.2.
9. Richards Insolvency, *NSW State Records*, 2/9122, Insolvency #6763.
10. Richards Insolvency, *NSW State Records*, 2/9471, Insolvency #11237.
11. *Manning River News*, Mar 16, 1904, reports that Reuben Richards, J. P., met with an accident. This is most likely Reuben Richards Senior.
12. Robert Sempill, SC – 1862 – Q1808.

Notes

13. NSW Votes & Proceedings, 1863, Vol. 3, p777.
14. NSW BDM, Death Certificate #1410/1893, Charles Blake Skerrett.
15. Skerrett Insolvency, *NSW State Records*, 2/9142, Insolvency #7039.

Bibliography

John Allan, *The Allan Family*, Wingham Chronicle, 1928.
Therese Archinal, *The Andrews on the Manning*, Taree, 2004
Bill Beatty, *A Treasury of Australian Folk Tales and Traditions*, Ure Smith, Sydney, 1960.
W. K. Birrell, *The Manning Valley, Landscape and Settlement 1824 – 1900*, Jacaranda Press, 1987
W. F. Connors, *Pioneering Days Around Taree*, Taree, 1985
Warren Cross, *Legal Administration of the Manning Valley, An Historical Analysis 1828-1900*, Manning Valley Historical Society Journal, Number 11, September 2000.
F. A. Fitzpatrick (Editor), *Magnificent Manning and Municipality of Wingham*, Wingham, 1925.
F. A. Fitzpatrick (Editor), *Peeps Into The Past, Pioneering Days on the Manning*, Cumberland Argus, Parramatta, 1914.
Rod & Wendy Gow (Transcribers), *Journal of Proceedings of William Wilmet Board, The Diary of a Pioneer, 1843-1855*, Taree, 1996.
Frank Hawkins, *Brigalow, Brushbox & 'Black Boys', A Folk History of the Mount George Area*, 1999, Maitland.

James Holledge, *Australia's Wicked Women*, Horwitz Publications, Sydney, 1963.

William Joy and Tom Prior, *The Bushrangers*, Shakespeare Head Press, Sydney, 1963.

Cathy Keppie, *The Story of Isabella Mary Kelly*, Manning Valley Historical Society Journal, Number 4, May 1998.

Manning Valley Historical Society, *Down To the Sea in Ships, A History of Sea and Watercraft built on the Manning*, Taree, 2002

Manning Wallamba Family History Society, *Pre 1860 Pioneer Register*, Imprint Copy Control, Taree, 2001

Ian McDonell, *The Days of Wynter*, Edition 2, 1989

Ian McDonell and John Ramsland, *Road, Punt and Rail – Taree as a Pioneering Township, 1830 to 1913*, Article in the *Royal Australian Historical Society Journal*, March 1990, Vol. 75, Part 4.

Port Macquarie Historical Society, *Port Macquarie The Windingsheet*, Editors Gwendoline Griffin and Ronald Howell, Uptin Print, Port Macquarie, 1996.

John Ramsland, *The Struggle Against Isolation, A History of the Manning Valley*, Library of Australian History, 1987.

John Ramsland, *Custodians of the Soil, A History of Aboriginal-European Relationships in the Manning Valley*, Greater Taree City Council, 2001.

Order your copy of:
The Trials of Isabella Mary Kelly

by Maurie Garland
ISBN 1920785 69 8   RRP   AU$25.95   Qty .....

                    Postage within Aust.   AU$8.00   .....

                    TOTAL* $_____
                    * All prices include GST

Name: _____

Address: _____

_____

_____

Phone: _____

Email Address: _____

Method of Payment:

❏ Money Order ❏ Cheque ❏ Bankcard ❏ MasterCard ❏ Visa

Cardholders Name: _____

Credit Card Number: _____

Signature:_____ Expiry Date: _____

Allow 21 days for delivery.

Payment to:
  Better Bookshop (ABN 14 067 257 390)
  PO Box 12544
  A'Beckett Street, Melbourne, 8006
  Victoria, Australia
  Fax: +61 3 9671 4730
  Email: betterbookshop@brolgapublishing.com.au

BE PUBLISHED
Great News for Authors

COLLABORATIVE PUBLISHING through a successful Australian publisher.

A writing career begins with a first published book.

Brolga provides a wide ranging service to assist authors to bring their work to a marketable, professionally-produced book. The service can start with how to prepare your manuscript, or how to research the book trade. Additionally, Brolga Publishing provides:

- Editorial appraisal
- Cover design
- Typesetting
- Trade distribution

Enquiries to:

Brolga Publishing Pty Ltd
PO Box 12544, A'Beckett Street
Melbourne, 8006, Victoria, Australia

Fax: (03) 9671 4730
Email: markzocchi@brolgapublishing.com.au
ABN: 46 063 962 443